# Microsoft® Works 4.5 *for* WINDOWS®

## Tutorial & Applications

*William R. Pasewark, Sr., Ph.D.*

Professor Emeritus, Texas Tech University

Works Management Consultant


*William R. Pasewark, Jr., Ph.D., C.P.A.*

University of Houston

SOUTH-WESTERN EDUCATIONAL PUBLISHING

Team Leader: Steve Holland
Managing Editor: Carol Volz
Project Manager: Dave Lafferty
Consulting Editor: Custom Editorial Productions, Inc.
Marketing Manager: Steve Wright
Production: Custom Editorial Productions, Inc.

ISBN: 0-538-72158-8

Library of Congress Catalog Card Number: 95-47943

2 3 4 5 6 7 8 9 10 PR 03 02 01 00 99

Printed in the United States of America

International Thomson Publishing

South-Western Educational Publishing is a division of International Thomson Publishing, Inc. The ITP trademark is used under license.

Microsoft® is a registered trademark of Microsoft Corporation.

# PREFACE

● ● ● ● ● ● ● ● ● ● ● ● ● ● ● ● ● ● ●

## *To the Student*

**C**omputers affect our daily lives. They schedule television programs and advertisements; operate cash registers; print newspapers, books, and documents; keep records of athletic events; control telephone communications; monitor automobile engine performance; and generate course schedules and grade reports for schools.

You may already have a working knowledge of computers, or you may have little or no computer experience at all. In either case, *Microsoft Works 4.0 for Windows 95: Tutorial and Applications* will help you further develop your level of computer competency.

### Microsoft Works 4.0 for Windows— An Integrated Software Package

Microsoft Works 4.0 for Windows 95 is an *integrated* software package, which means that it combines four popular computer programs: word processing, database, spreadsheet, and communications. These can be used for many applications such as writing letters or research papers (the Works Word Processor), making lists of names and addresses (the Works Database), recording income and expenses (the Works Spreadsheet), and exchanging information (Works Communications). You can easily combine documents and information from the various applications.

Integrated software is commonly used in academic, business, career, and personal settings to help you complete routine tasks more quickly and accurately, thus improving your efficiency and productivity.

### Microsoft Works 4.0 for Windows 95: Tutorial and Applications—Learn and Apply

The authors planned this book to provide a realistic, complete, and successful learning experience for you. Objectives listed at the beginning of each chapter give you an overview of the chapter. Short segments of text explain new information and tell why it is important. Then, activities with numbered steps guide you through the computer operation. These activities give you a chance to practice the concepts you have just learned. The book includes many illustrations and activities to simplify complex concepts and operations. A summary, true/false and completion questions, and applications at the end of each chapter help you review the chapters.

Within *Microsoft Works 4.0 for Windows 95: Tutorial and Applications*, the authors share with you their enthusiasm about how powerful a tool a computer can be in your life.

## Student's Guide for Using this Book

Reading this guide before starting work in this book will help you to learn faster and easier.

The following terminology and procedures are used in this book:

■ *Text* means words, numbers, and symbols that are printed.

■ *Keying* (also called keyboarding) means entering *text* (also called data) into a computer. The terms *keying* and *typing* are sometimes used interchangeably.

■ After computer concepts are explained in the text, you will practice the concepts in a hands-on activity that will involve using the keyboard and the mouse.

The different type styles used in this book have special meanings:

■ Individual keys that you will press are in bold type:

**Esc, Ctrl, Tab.**

■ Text you will key into the computer is in bold type:

Key **Grade** as the field name.

■ Filenames are italicized in upper and lower case letters:

Open *Activity 14-1* from the template disk.

■ Words in this book that you will also see on the screen are in italics:

Click in the box beside *Personal Information* and click **OK.**

■ Key terms (words defined in the text and listed in the glossary) are in bold and italics:

*TaskWizards* are programs within Works that automate certain common Works tasks, such as creating address lists and form letters.

# To the Teacher

In today's world, understanding computer concepts and knowing how to apply computer skills are essential for every student. Students enter computer courses with widely varying levels of skill and knowledge. Some may already know several software packages; others may not have been exposed to computers at all.

*Microsoft Works 4.0 for Windows 95: Tutorial and Applications* is designed for new and experienced learners as they develop computer competency using an integrated computer software package. The tutorial can be structured for courses of study from 30 to 90 class meetings in length, making it easily adaptable to a variety of curriculum patterns.

## System Requirements

Microsoft Works 4.0 for Windows 95 has the following computer requirements:

- Microsoft Windows 95 operating system or Microsoft Windows NT Workstation version 3.51 or later.

- 386DX or higher processor (486 recommended).

- 6 MB of memory for Windows 95 (8 MB recommended); 12 MB of memory for Windows NT Workstation.

- 3.5" high- or low-density disk drive

- 5 MB of free space on hard disk to install; 20 MB for complete installation

- VGA or higher-resolution video adapter (Super VGA-256 color recommended)

- To print, any Windows-compatible printer

- Mouse or other pointing device

- To communicate, a 2400 or higher baud modem (9600 baud modem recommended)

## Microsoft Works—An Integrated Software Package

Microsoft Works 4.0 for Windows 95 is an integrated software package. Contained within this single comprehensive program are four programs:

- The Works Word Processor, with graphics capability

- The Works Spreadsheet, with charting capability

- The Works Database, with reporting capability

- The Works Communication program

These programs, also called tools, can be used independently or in any combination. For example, you can easily integrate a chart from the spreadsheet tool into a letter from the word processor tool, or attach a list from the database to a memo created in the word processor and send it all electronically to another location.

Integrated computer software packages increase efficiency and productivity, and are becoming common in the workplace. Exposure to this type of software package is a definite advantage to students in their academic, personal, and career lives.

Students who learn any Microsoft Works program will benefit from the enormous amount of transfer of learning that will occur when they use any other Microsoft product, such as Word, Excel, Access, PowerPoint, Microsoft Office for Windows, and Microsoft Office for Windows 95.

## Teaching and Learning Aids

This instructional package is designed to simplify instruction and to enhance learning with the following learning and teaching aids:

### TEXTBOOK—THE TUTORIAL

- *Learning objectives* listed at the beginning of each chapter give students an overview of the chapter.

- *Step-by-step instructions* for specific operations allow students to progress independently. When the same operations are repeated, instructions are "faded;" that is, fewer specific instructions are included, challenging the student gradually to perform the operations without prompting.

- *Computer activities* immediately follow the presentation of new concepts and instructions. The activities give students the opportunity to apply what they have just learned.

- *Integration* and *simulation* chapters teach students how to merge the word processing, spreadsheet, and database tools.

- *Illustrations,* including numerous screen captures, explain complex concepts and serve as reference points when students complete activities.

- *Chapter summaries* provide quick reviews for each chapter, entrenching the main points in the student's mind.

- *True/False and completion questions* and *computer reinforcement applications* follow each chapter to gauge students' understanding of the chapter's information and operations. The applications offer minimal instruction so students must apply concepts previously introduced.

- *Appendices* list the Works TaskWizards and the proofreader's marks students will need to know for completing the simulation chapter.

- The *glossary* is a list of common computer terms and definitions.

- A *comprehensive index* supplies quick and easy accessibility to specific parts of the tutorial.

## THE TEACHER'S MANUAL

The comprehensive teacher's manual includes a variety of aids for planning the course of study, presenting information, and managing the classroom. All are designed to ensure a successful and enjoyable teaching experience. The manual includes the following features:

- Guidelines for *scheduling students* with varying abilities.

- *General teaching suggestions* include strategies for effective instruction with a minimum of stress.

- *Specific teaching suggestions* are presented for each chapter.

- *Reproducible* chapter and unit tests with answers.

- An *Application Progress Record* can be reproduced for each student, and a *Grading Scale for Documents,* which is a guide for evaluating students' work.

## THE TEMPLATE DISK

The template disk contains pre-keyed text and selected graphics for activities and applications and may be copied for students. This disk allows students to use more class time learning computer operations rather than keying large amounts of text into the computer.

## THE SOLUTIONS DISK

The solutions disk contains solutions to selected activities and all applications so that you can verify formatting and students' disks.

## STUDENTS' REPRODUCIBLE EXERCISES

This 48-page, 8½" × 11" unbound packet contains duplicates of the true/false questions, completion questions, and reinforcement applications at the end of each chapter in the student's book.

# The Authors' Commitment

In writing *Microsoft Works 4.0 for Windows 95: Tutorial and Applications*, the authors dedicated themselves to creating a complete and appealing instructional package to make teaching and learning an interesting, successful, and rewarding experience for both teachers and students. The authors assembled in one resource all the materials and aids a teacher needs to create a learning experience in which students can successfully master skills that will serve them in their academic and career endeavors, as well as in their personal lives.

# Acknowledgments

The authors thank Stephen Collings, Laura Melton, Joseph Powell, and Dawna Walls for their dedicated and effective contributions to this publication. The authors also wish to thank the many professional South-Western sales representatives who make educationally sound presentations to teachers about our books. The authors appreciate very much their valuable function as "bridges" between the authors and the teachers.

# Books by the Authors

## Transfer of Learning

Screens, commands, and operations for Microsoft Works programs are similar to other Microsoft products such as Word, Excel, Access, PowerPoint, and Microsoft Office for Windows 95. Students who learn any version of Microsoft Works will benefit from the *transfer of learning* that occurs when they use other Microsoft programs. Instructions for the Microsoft Works books authored by the Pasewarks are also similar — and even identical — to instructions in the other Microsoft application books authored by them. Students who learned Works 3.0 by using *Microsoft Works 3.0 for Windows* in a beginning computer course will learn the upgrade rapidly and easily from this book, *Microsoft Works 4.0 for Windows 95* — and they will find other books, such as *Microsoft Office for Windows 95,* just as easy to follow.

The Microsoft Windows books listed here are available exclusively from South-Western Educational Publications. Titles for Macintosh and DOS versions of Microsoft applications are also available, as well as for ClarisWorks, and Express Publisher, PFS: First Publisher, and Publish It! desktop publishing software.

## Windows 3.0, 3.1, and 3.11

### TUTORIAL AND APPLICATIONS SERIES
*Microsoft Works for Windows 2.0: Tutorial and Applications* (for high school)
*Microsoft Works for Windows 2.0: A Practical Approach* (for college)
*Microsoft Works for Windows 3.0: Tutorial and Applications*

### QUICK COURSE SERIES
*Microsoft Works for Windows 3.0: Quick Course*

### APPLICATIONS FOR REINFORCEMENT SERIES
*Microsoft Works 2.0/3.0 for Windows: Applications for Reinforcement*

## Windows 95

### TUTORIAL AND APPLICATIONS SERIES
*Microsoft Works 4.0 for Windows 95: Tutorial and Applications*
*Microsoft Office 7.0 for Windows 95: Tutorial and Applications*

### QUICK COURSE SERIES
*Microsoft Works 4.0 for Windows 95: Quick Course*
*Microsoft Office for Windows 95: Quick Course*

### APPLICATIONS FOR REINFORCEMENT SERIES
*Microsoft Works 4.0 for Windows 95: Applications for Reinforcement*

# Table of Contents

## UNIT 4

# DATABASES

UNIT 5

# TASKWIZARDS AND COMMUNICATIONS

# INTRODUCTION

# MICROSOFT WINDOWS 95 BASICS

## CHAPTER 1

## OBJECTIVES
### When you complete this chapter, you will be able to:

1. Understand the background and advantages of a graphical user interface.

2. Start Microsoft Windows 95.

3. Perform common mouse operations.

4. Move, resize, scroll through, maximize, minimize, and close windows.

5. Use menus.

6. Use Windows 95 Help.

# *Introduction to Windows 95*

**W**hen the IBM® PC was introduced in 1981, it was not nearly as powerful as today's computers. The operating system, known as DOS (Disk Operating System), could process a limited number of commands that the user had to key. A simple operation such as copying a file required the user to know the DOS command COPY, to know where the file to be copied was located, and to be able to tell the computer where it should be copied to. This process usually meant accurately keying letters, numbers, and symbols and carefully checking to be sure the file wasn't going somewhere it shouldn't.

As computer **hardware,** the physical components of a computer, became more advanced, computer **software,** the lists of instructions that computers follow to perform specific tasks, progressed too. IBM PCs and PC compatibles still relied on the DOS operating system to interpret commands from the user, and users still had to key these commands on a keyboard. But computer programs became easier to use as programmers built in better ways for the user to interact with the computer.

In 1985, the Microsoft Corporation introduced the first version of Windows, a new way for PC users to communicate with their computers. Windows is a *graphical user interface (GUI)*. This means that the user actually interacts with the computer by means of graphics, or pictures. Instead of having to use the keyboard to enter commands, a user can use a mouse to point at pictures or words that tell the computer to do specific tasks. In earlier versions of Windows, DOS was still running in the background. But Windows 95 replaces the previous combination of DOS and Windows with one new operating system.

You can see how a GUI (pronounced "gooey") would be much easier to use. Instead of having to memorize the DOS instructions for opening an application, you can simply point at a pictorial representation of the application and Windows 95 will launch it for you.

Also, all programs designed for Windows 95—and for earlier versions of Windows that will work in Windows 95—have similar features: files are opened, saved, and printed in the same way; many commands are the same from program to program; even the screen looks the same from program to program. After you have learned one Windows 95 program, you can easily learn others.

If you have never used Windows 95, this chapter will teach you what you need to know to feel comfortable using Microsoft Works 4.0 for Windows 95.

# *Starting Windows 95*

**I**f Windows 95 is already installed, it should start automatically when you turn on the computer. If your computer is on a network, you may need to follow a few other steps, which your instructor can help you with.

**ACTIVITY**

## Starting Windows 95

● ● ● ● ● ● ● ● ● ● ● ● ● ● ● ● ● ● ● ● ● ● ● ● ● ● ● ● ● ● ● ● ● ● ● ● ● ● ● ● ● ●

In this activity, you will start your computer and Windows 95. This activity assumes that Windows 95 is already installed on your hard disk.

1. Turn on the computer.

2. After a few moments, Microsoft Windows 95 will appear.

When Windows 95 starts up, the first window you see is the desktop. The *desktop* is the space where your work takes place. It has icons that allow you to access and work with programs and files. With Windows 95 you can customize and organize your desktop by creating files, folders, and shortcuts. Later, you will explore the desktop. First, you need to make friends with a mouse.

# Partners with a Mouse

Graphical user interfaces such as Microsoft Windows 95 speed the work of the user by teaming the user with a mouse. A *mouse* is a device that rolls on a flat surface and has one or more buttons on it (see Figure 1-1). (You may use a *trackball,* which is an alternative form of a mouse. It has an embedded ball for your fingers and palm to rotate.) The mouse allows you to communicate with the computer by pointing to and manipulating graphics and text on the screen. The *pointer,* which appears as an arrow on the screen, indicates the position of the mouse.

The four most common mouse operations are point, click, double-click, and drag. These operations are outlined in Table 1-1. Once these operations *click* in your mind, you will see the *point* of using a mouse, and your computer will never again be a *drag* to use.

**FIGURE 1-1**
A mouse makes user interface easier by providing a way to point to and manipulate graphics and text on the screen.

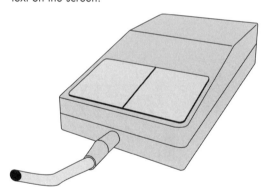

**TABLE 1-1**
Common Mouse Operations

| OPERATION | DEFINITION |
| --- | --- |
| Point | Moving the mouse pointer to a specific item on the screen |
| Click | Pressing the mouse button and quickly releasing it while pointing to an item on the screen (the term "click" comes from the noise you hear when you press and release the button) |
| Double-click | Clicking the mouse button twice, quickly, while keeping the mouse still |
| Drag | Pointing to a location on the screen, pressing and holding the mouse button, and moving the pointer while the button is pressed; releasing the button ends the drag operation |

## The Desktop

Figure 1-2 illustrates a typical desktop screen. Your screen may vary slightly from the figure. For example, there may be shortcut icons displayed. The main features of the desktop screen are labeled on the figure and discussed below:

■ The *Start* button brings up menus which give you a variety of options such as starting a program, finding help, or shutting down the computer.

■ The *taskbar,* located at the bottom of the screen, tells you the name of all the open programs. Figure 1-2 shows that Microsoft Works is open.

■ *My Computer* is a program that helps you organize and manage your files.

■ The *Recycle Bin* is a place to get rid of files or folders that are no longer needed.

■ Other *icons,* or small pictures, which represent programs waiting to be opened.

**FIGURE 1-2**
The desktop is organized to help you work productively.

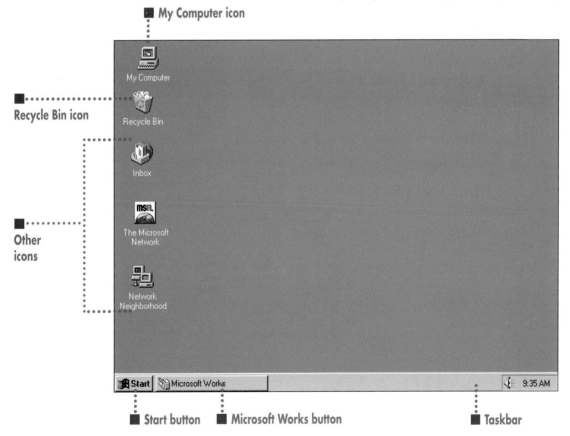

# Using the Mouse to Explore the Desktop

In this activity, you will practice basic mouse operations while you explore the Windows 95 desktop screen.

1. Move the mouse around on your desk (or mouse pad) and watch the pointer move on the screen. Do not press the mouse buttons yet.

2. Point to the **Start** button.

3. Click the left mouse button. A menu of choices appears above the Start button as shown in Figure 1-3.

4. Point to **Programs** without clicking. Another menu appears.

5. Point to **Accessories** without clicking. Another menu appears.

6. Click on **Calculator.** The calculator appears. The title bar at the top tells you that *Calculator* is the name of the open window.

7. Move the calculator by clicking on the title bar and holding down the left mouse button. While continuing to hold down the

**FIGURE 1-3**
Clicking the Start button brings up a menu of choices.

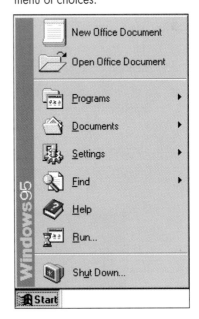

left mouse button, drag the calculator to the bottom of the screen. Release the mouse button.

8. Close the calculator by clicking the **Close** button (the X) on the right side of the title bar.

# *Using Windows*

**W**hether a window is a program window or a document window, you can change its shape, size, and location.

## Moving and Resizing Windows

Sometimes you will have several windows on the screen at the same time. To work more effectively, you may need to move or change the size of a window.

**ACTIVITY**

# *1-3*  Moving and Resizing Windows

In this activity, you will move and resize a window.

1. Open the Control Panel by clicking **Start, Settings, Control Panel.**

2. In the last activity, you used the mouse to drag the calculator to a new location. Use the same procedure to drag the Control Panel window to the top and center of your screen.

3. Point anywhere on the border at the bottom of the Control Panel window. The pointer will turn into a vertical two-headed arrow.

4. While the pointer is a two-headed arrow, drag the bottom border of the window down to enlarge the window.

5. Point to the border on the right side of the Control Panel window. The pointer will turn into a horizontal two-headed arrow.

6. While the pointer is a two-headed arrow, drag the border of the window to the right to enlarge the window.

7. It is possible to resize two sides of a window at the same time. Point to the lower right corner of the window border. The pointer becomes a two-headed arrow pointing diagonally.

8. Drag the border into the window from the lower right corner to resize both edges at the same time until scroll bars appear on the window's borders (see Figure 1-4).

**FIGURE 1-4**
Scroll bars appear when there is more to be displayed than the window can show.

As you can see from the activity you just completed, the pointer is not always the same arrow. The shape of the pointer is an indication of what the computer is doing. For example, sometimes the pointer will turn into an hourglass to indicate that the computer is temporarily busy. When the hourglass pointer appears, wait for the pointer to change back to an arrow, which should not take long depending on the speed and memory capabilities of your computer.

## Scroll Bars

A *scroll bar* appears on the edges of windows any time there is more to be displayed than a window can show at its current size. A scroll bar can appear along the bottom edge and/or along the right side of a window. Scroll bars appeared in the last step of the previous activity because the window was too small to show all the icons at once.

Scroll bars are a convenient way to move quickly to another part of the window's contents. On the scroll bar is a sliding box called the **scroll box.** The scroll box indicates your position within the window's contents. When the scroll box reaches the bottom of the scroll bar, you have reached the end of the window's contents. Scroll arrows are located at the ends of the scroll bar. Clicking on a scroll arrow moves the window in that direction over the contents of the window.

ACTIVITY

*1-4* **Scrolling**

In this activity, you will practice using the scroll bar, scroll box, and scroll arrows. This activity assumes that the Control Panel window is open on the screen.

1. If the Control Panel window does not have scroll bars on its edges, resize the window until both scroll bars appear (see Figure 1-4).

2. Click the scroll arrow that points to the right. The contents of the window shift to the left.

3. Press and hold the mouse button on the same scroll arrow. The contents of the window scroll quickly across the window. Notice that

the scroll box moves to the extreme right of the scroll bar.

4. You can also scroll by dragging the scroll box. Drag the scroll box on the horizontal (left-to-right) scroll bar from the extreme right to the extreme left.

5. Drag the scroll box on the horizontal scroll bar to the middle of the scroll bar.

6. Drag the scroll box on the vertical (up-and-down) scroll bar to the middle of the scroll bar.

7. The final way to scroll is to click on the scroll bar. Click the horizontal scroll bar to the right of the scroll box. The contents scroll left.

8. Click the horizontal scroll bar to the left of the scroll box. The contents scroll right.

9. Scroll the Control Panel window until the horizontal scroll box is at the extreme left of the scroll bar.

10. Scroll the Control Panel window until the vertical scroll box is at the top of the scroll bar.

11. Resize the Control Panel until the scroll bars disappear.

## Other Window Controls

Three other important window controls, located on the right side of the title bar, are the *maximize button,* the *minimize button,* and the ***Close button*** (see Figure 1-5). The maximize button enlarges a window to full size. The minimize button shrinks a window to a button on the taskbar. The button on the taskbar is labeled and you can click it any time to make the window reappear. The Close button is used to close a window.

**FIGURE 1-5**
The maximize button, minimize button, and Close button provide efficient window handling.

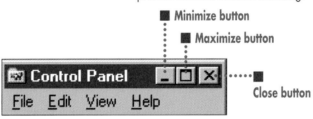

**ACTIVITY**

## 1-5 Maximizing Windows

In this activity, you will use the maximize button to enlarge a window.

1. The Control Panel window should still be the size you left it in the previous activity.

2. Click the **maximize** button.

When a window is maximized, the maximize button is replaced by the restore button (see Figure 1-6). The *restore button* returns the window to the size it was before the maximize button was clicked.

**FIGURE 1-6**
The restore button returns a maximized window to its regular size.

■ Restore
button

ACTIVITY

## Restoring, Minimizing, and Closing Windows

In this activity, you will restore the window that was maximized in the last activity, minimize the window, and then close the window.

1. Click the **restore** button on the Control Panel window (see Figure 1-6).

2. Click the **minimize** button on the Control Panel window. The window is reduced to a button on the taskbar.

3. Click the **Control Panel** button on the taskbar to open the window again.

4. Click the **Close** button to close the window.

# Menus

To find out what a restaurant has to offer, you look at the menu. You can also look at a *menu* on the computer's screen to find out what a computer program has to offer. Menus in computer programs show what your options are and let you choose one of the options. Menus can be accessed from the *menu bar* (see Figure 1-7), which contains the names of the program's menus. Menus can also be accessed from the Start button on the desktop.

Most restaurants give you only one menu from which to choose. Computers often give you several menus at one time. Each menu's name is in the menu bar. First you choose a menu, then an item from that menu.

**FIGURE 1-7**
Menus can be accessed from the menu bar at
the top of the screen.

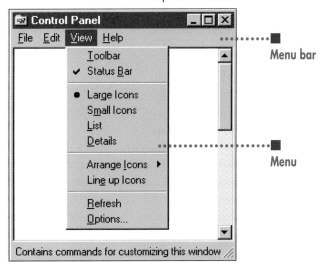

Menu bar

Menu

## Using Menus

In this activity, you will practice using menus.

1. Open the Notepad by clicking **Start, Programs, Accessories, Notepad.**

2. Click **Edit** on the menu bar. The Edit menu appears.

3. Click **Time/Date** to display the current time and date.

4. Click **File** on the menu bar. The File menu appears (see Figure 1-8).

5. Click **Exit.** A save prompt dialog box appears.

6. Click **No.** The Notepad window disappears and you return to the Windows 95 desktop.

**FIGURE 1-8**
The File menu offers an alternative way to
exit a program.

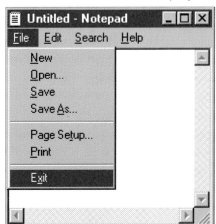

# *The Help Menu*

**T**his chapter has covered only a few of the many features of Windows 95. For additional information, Windows 95 has an easy-to-use help system.

## Windows 95 Help

Use the Windows 95 Help as a quick reference when you are unsure about a function. Windows 95 Help is accessed through the Help menu, which is available from the Start button and in the menu bars of most Windows programs. In the Windows 95 Help program, you can choose either to see the table of contents, as shown in Figure 1-9, or to search the help system using the Index or Find command. If you need assistance using the Windows 95 Help program, choose How To, Use Help from the Contents tab.

**FIGURE 1-9**
The Help program is a convenient source of information about Windows 95.

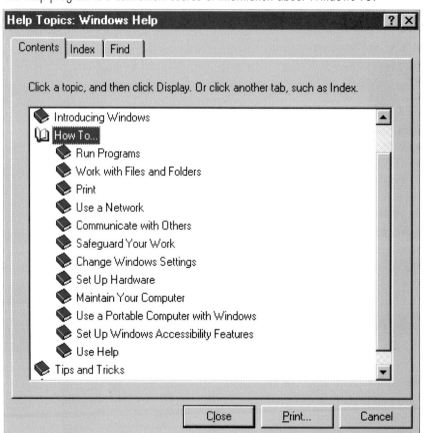

## ACTIVITY

# 1-8  Using Help

• • • • • • • • • • • • • • • • • • • • • • • • • • • • • • • •

In this activity, you will practice getting help on specific topics.

1. Open Help by clicking **Start, Help.**

2. Click the **Contents** tab if it is not already selected.

3. Double-click on **How To, Use Help.**

4. Double-click **Finding a topic in Help.**

5. Read the Help window; then, click **Help Topics.**

6. Click the Index tab.

7. Key **Close button;** then, click **Display.**

8. Click **Quitting a Program;** then, click **Display.**

9. Read the Help window; then, close the Help program by following the instructions you read in the Help window.

# Now, On to Good Works

**N**ow that you have learned the basics of Windows 95, you will get to know Microsoft Works 4.0 for Windows 95 in the next chapter.

# Summary

■ Microsoft Works is a graphical user interface (GUI) for IBM and compatible computers. A graphical user interface makes it easier to use a computer. The desktop organizes your work and the Start button brings up menus which give you a variety of options.

■ In Windows 95, almost everything on the screen is in a window. These windows can be moved, resized, opened, and closed. If all the contents of a window cannot be displayed in the window's current size, scroll bars appear to allow you to move to the part of the window you want to view. Windows can be maximized to fill the screen or minimized to a button on the taskbar.

■ Menus are an important part of Windows 95. Menus allow you to choose commands to perform different actions. Menus are accessed from the Start button on the desktop or from a program's menu bar near the top of the window.

■ The Windows 95 Help program provides additional information about the many features of Windows 95. You can access the Help program from the Start button or from the menu bar within Windows programs.

• • • • • • • • • • • • • •

# REVIEW ACTIVITIES

## TRUE/FALSE

**Circle T or F to show whether the statement is true or false.**

**(T)** **F**    1. Windows 95 replaces the previous version of Windows and DOS with one operating system.

**T** **(F)**    2. With a graphical user interface, you can only enter commands with the keyboard.

**(T)** **F**    3. When Microsoft Windows 95 starts, the desktop appears.

**(T)** **F**    4. A mouse makes a graphical user interface easier to use.

**T** **(F)**    5. Sliding describes the action of holding a mouse button while moving the mouse on a flat surface.

**T** **(F)**    6. The taskbar indicates the position of the mouse.

**T** **(F)**    7. Scroll bars appear when all items in the window are visible.

**(T)** **F**    8. To maximize a window, click the restore button.

**(T)** **F**    9. Menus can be accessed from the menu bar.

**(T)** **F**    10. The Help menu is available from the Start button.

## COMPLETION

**Write the correct answer in the space provided.**

1. Name one factor that makes graphical user interfaces easier to use than nongraphical user interfaces, such as DOS.

   *You use a mouse for graphical user interfaces*

2. Describe the drag mouse operation.

   *Pointing to a location on the screen, press & hold mouse button down and move the pointer*

3. What button do you click to have the option of starting a program, finding help, or shutting down the computer?

   *Start button*

4. What is the purpose of the Recycle Bin?

_to store folders & files_
_no longer needed_

5. What does it mean when the mouse pointer becomes an hourglass?

_Computer is temporarily busy_

6. How do you move a window?

_use mouse and drag when two headed arrow_
_appears on borders_

7. What does the scroll box indicate?

_there is more to be displayed than the_
_window can show_

8. Where is the Close button located?

_upper right hand side (X)_

9. What does the minimize button do?

_Window is reduced to a_
_button on the taskbar_

10. What does a menu bar contain?

_commands to perform different actions_

# WORKS BASICS

## OBJECTIVES
### When you complete this chapter, you will be able to:

1. Explain the concept of an integrated software package.

2. Start Works from Windows 95.

3. View the Introduction to Works.

4. Use files and directories.

5. Exit Works.

# *Introduction to Works*

**M**icrosoft Works for Windows 95 is an integrated software package. An *integrated software package* is a program that combines several computer tools into one program. Works consists of a word processor tool, a spreadsheet tool, a database tool, and a communications tool. The word processor tool enables you to create documents such as letters and reports. The spreadsheet tool works with numbers to prepare items such as budgets or to determine loan payments. The database tool organizes information such as addresses or inventory items. The communications tool allows you to communicate with other computers. Because Works is an integrated program, the tools can be used together. For example, numbers from a spreadsheet can be included in a letter created in the word processor.

# *Starting Works*

**W**orks is started from the desktop screen in Windows 95. To start Works in Activity 2-1, click the Start button. Then, click Programs, the Microsoft Works 4.0 folder/window icon, and Microsoft Works 4.0.

## ACTIVITY

# 2-1

## Starting Works

In this activity, you will start Works. This activity assumes that Windows 95 is already running on your computer.

1. Click the **Start** button to open the Start menu.

2. Click **Programs** to open the Programs menu.

3. Click the **Microsoft Works 4.0** folder/window icon to open the Microsoft Works 4.0 menu.

4. Click **Microsoft Works 4.0.** Works starts. The Works Task Launcher dialog box appears (see Figure 2-1).

The Works Task Launcher has three tabs to help you get started. The TaskWizards tab creates a document for you. The Existing Documents tab allows you to open a document you have already created. The Works Tools tab opens a new word processor, spreadsheet, database, or communications document.

**FIGURE 2-1**
With the Works Task Launcher, you can choose between three methods of starting a document.

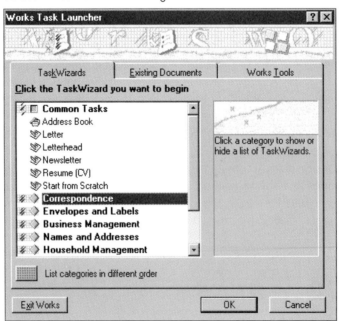

# Viewing the Introduction to Works

**W**orks includes an introduction that describes how you can use the Works tools to increase productivity. In the next activity, you will view the Introduction to Works to get an overview of Works for Windows 95.

## ACTIVITY

### Viewing the Introduction to Works

In this activity, you will view the Introduction to Works.

1. Click **Cancel** to close the Works Task Launcher.

2. Choose **Introduction to Works** from the **Help** menu. The opening screen appears, as in Figure 2-2.

3. Read the screen; then, click the **right arrow** button at the bottom of the screen.

4. Continue clicking the **right arrow** button and reading.

5. Click **Done** when you reach the last screen.

**FIGURE 2-2**
The Introduction to Works will give you an overview of the key features of Microsoft Works 4.0 for Windows 95.

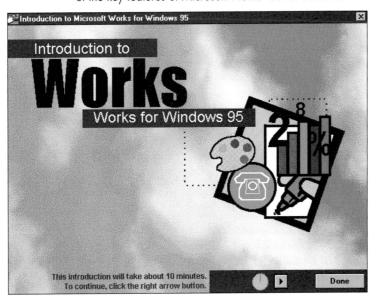

# Working with Files

In all of the Works tools, you *open, save,* and *close* files in the same way. Opening a file means loading a file from a disk onto your screen. Saving is done two ways. The Save command saves a file on a disk using the current name. The Save As command saves a file on a disk using a new name. The Save As command can also be used to save a file in a new location. Closing a file removes it from the screen.

To work with files, you also need to know about filenames, directories, subdirectories, and paths.

## Filenames

Unlike programs designed for the early versions of Windows and DOS, you are not limited to eight characters with which to name your files. A filename may contain up to 255 characters and may include spaces. Rarely, however, will you need to use this many characters to name a file. Name a file with a descriptive name that will remind you of what the file contains. The authors of this book have chosen names that are descriptive and easy to use. Follow their examples in naming your files, whether for this course or outside of this course. The filename can include most characters found on the keyboard with the exception of those shown in Table 2-1.

**TABLE 2-1**
Characters That Cannot Be Used in Filenames

| CHARACTER | CHARACTER NAME | CHARACTER | CHARACTER NAME |
|-----------|----------------|-----------|----------------|
| * | asterisk | < | less than sign |
| \ | backslash | . | period |
| [] | brackets | ? | question mark |
| : | colon | " | quotation mark |
| , | comma | ; | semicolon |
| = | equal sign | / | slash |
| > | greater than sign | \| | vertical bar |

## Directories and Subdirectories

Because computer disks have such a large capacity, it is not unusual for a floppy disk to contain dozens of files or for a hard disk to contain hundreds or thousands of files. To organize files, a disk can be divided into directories and subdirectories. A *directory* groups files that have something in common. For example, your hard disk has a directory that holds the program files necessary to run Works. You can also create directories for your documents. A *subdirectory* is a directory within a directory. For example, you could create a directory to group all of the files you are working on in computer class. Within that directory, you could have several subdirectories that group files for each tool or each chapter.

When you open a file, you must tell Works where the file is. When you save a file, you must tell Works where you want to save the file. You specify the location of a file by giving Works a **path** (also called a **pathname**). The path consists of the disk drive letter and the directory. For example, if the file you want to open is on a disk in the A drive, in a directory named Letters, the path is *A:\Letters*.

To indicate a subdirectory in a path, you just extend the path with another backslash and the name of the subdirectory. For example, within the Letters directory you can have a subdirectory for each of the people to whom you frequently write letters. If within the Letters directory there is a Gabriel subdirectory, the path to the files in the Gabriel subdirectory is *A:\Letters\Gabriel*.

The colon appears in a path to separate the drive letter from the rest of the path. The backslash is used to separate directories, subdirectories, and files in a path. Many times you will see a specific filename at the end of a path. For example, *C:\Reports\Finance\May* specifies the location of a file named May, on drive C, in the Reports directory, in the Finance subdirectory.

When you choose Open from the File menu, the Open dialog box appears (see Figure 2-3). The Open dialog box enables you to open a file from any available disk and directory. The Look in box, near the top of the dialog box, is where you select the disk drive that contains the file you want to open. Below that is a list that shows you what directories are on the disk using pictures of folders. A folder is an appropriate way to show a directory or subdirectory graphically because, like a folder, a directory groups files that have something in common.

**FIGURE 2-3**

The Open dialog box can open a file from any available disk and directory.

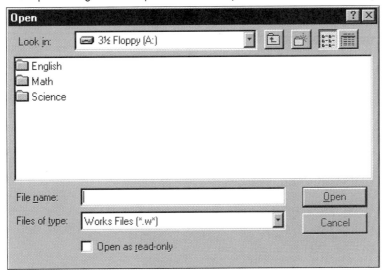

# ACTIVITY

## 2-3 Changing Disk Drives and Directories

• • • • • • • • • • • • • • • • • • • • • • • • • • • • • • • • • • • • • • • • • •

In this activity, you will practice navigating through directories on a disk.

1. Click the **Existing Documents** tab.

2. Click the **Open a document not listed here** button. The Open dialog box appears.

3. Insert your template disk into drive A.

4. Click on the **down arrow** at the right of the Look in box to display the available disk drives.

5. Click **3 1/2 Floppy (A:).** The Letters directory appears as a folder, as shown in Figure 2-4.

6. Double-click the **Letters** folder. The subdirectories within the Letters directory will appear (see Figure 2-5).

7. Double-click the **Gabriel** folder. The names of the files in the Gabriel subdirectory are displayed.

**FIGURE 2-4**
Directories are shown as folder icons.

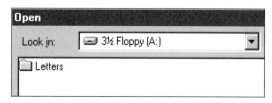

**FIGURE 2-5**
Within the Letters directory are several subdirectories.

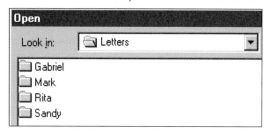

8. Click on **Ski trip.**

9. Click **Open** to open the file.

10. Leave the file open for the next activity.

You can see how directories can help organize and identify documents. In the same subdirectory as the letter to Gabriel is a spreadsheet for comparing ski trip options. In the next activity, you will open the spreadsheet that goes with the letter. Notice that Works remembers the subdirectory where you are currently working. Therefore, opening the second file in the Gabriel subdirectory is quick and easy.

## ACTIVITY

## Opening a File from the Current Directory

In this activity, you will open the spreadsheet that is mentioned in the ski trip letter to Gabriel.

1. Choose **Open** from the **File** menu. The Gabriel folder is still open in the Open dialog box.

2. Click on **Ski cost** in the list of files.

3. Click **Open** to open the spreadsheet.

4. Choose **Close** from the **File** menu. *Ski cost* closes.

5. Choose **Close** from the **File** menu. Do not save changes. *Ski trip* closes. The Works Task Launcher appears.

6. Click the **Existing Documents** tab if it is not already selected.

### Shortcut for Loading Recently Used Files

In the Existing Documents tab of the Works Task Launcher is a list of recently used files. The top file in the list is the most recently opened document. To open one of the recently used files, highlight the file you wish to open and click OK. If the file is on a floppy disk, you must be sure that the correct disk is in the drive.

The bottom of the File menu shows the filenames of the four most recently opened documents. The filename with the number 1 beside it is the most recently opened document. When a new file is opened, each filename moves down to make room for the new number 1 file. To load one of the files, you simply choose it as if it were a menu selection. If the document you are looking for is not in the File menu, use Open to load it from the disk.

# *Ending Your Works Session*

**T**he File menu provides the option to exit Works. You may also exit Works from the Works Task Launcher using the Exit Works button. Exiting Works takes you back to the Windows 95 desktop. Always remove your data or template disks before turning off the computer.

# 2-5 Exiting Works

• • • • • • • • • • • • • • • • • • • • • • • • • • • • • • •

In this activity, you will exit Works and return to the Windows 95 desktop.

1. Notice the <u>E</u>xit Works button in the bottom left corner of the Works Task Launcher. This button provides one option for exiting Works.

2. Click **Cancel** to close the Works Task Launcher.

3. Pull down the **File** menu. Notice the files listed at the bottom of the menu. These are the four most recently used files mentioned in the previous section.

4. Choose **E<u>x</u>it Works.** Works will close and the desktop will appear on the screen.

## If You Do Not Finish Before the End of Class

If you need to exit Works while working on an activity or application, save your work on your data disk and exit Works. When you resume work, open the document from your data disk and continue.

# *Summary*

- Microsoft Works is an integrated software package. Works consists of a word processor tool, a spreadsheet tool, a database tool, and a communications tool. The documents of an integrated software package can be used together.

- Works is started from the desktop by clicking the Start button, Programs, the Microsoft Works 4.0 folder, and Microsoft Works 4.0. The Introduction to Works is started by choosing it from the Help menu in the Works program.

- No matter which tool you are using, files are opened, saved, and closed the same way. Filenames may contain up to 255 characters and may include spaces. Files can be saved on a disk in groups, called directories. The location of a file is specified using a path. Recently used files can be opened quickly by choosing the filename from the bottom of the File menu. To exit Works, choose Exit Works from the File menu, or choose the Exit Works button from the Works Task Launcher.

• • • • • • • • • • • • • •

# REVIEW ACTIVITIES

## TRUE/FALSE

**Circle T or F to show whether the statement is true or false.**

**T** F 1. An integrated software package is a computer program that combines common tools into one program.

T **F** 2. Works is started from the File menu. *Microsoft Works 4.5*

× **T** F 3. The Works Task Launcher appears when Works is started.

**T** F 4. The Introduction to Works can be started from the Help menu.

**T** F 5. In all Works tools, you open, save, and close files in the same way.

T **F** 6. A filename can contain a maximum of eight characters.

T **F** 7. A path is a group of files with something in common.

**T** F 8. Directories are represented graphically as folders.

T **F** 9. The bottom of the Open menu shows the filenames of the four most recently opened documents.

T **F** 10. Exiting Works takes you back to the Works Task Launcher.

## COMPLETION

**Write the correct answer in the space provided.**

1. List the four primary tools that make up Works.

    *WORD PROCESSOR, Spreadsheet, data base, & communications*

2. How do you start Works? *double click Michoft Works on Desktop*

    *FROM DESKTOP by clicking STARI BUTTON PROGRAMS, the Microsoft Works 40 folder and Microsoft Works 40.*

3. List the three tabs in the Works Task Launcher.

    *TASKWIZARDS EXISTING Documents & Works Tools*

4. What is the difference between the Save and Save As commands?

    *SAVE AS COMMAND SAVES a file on a disk using a SAME NEW NAME    SAVE COMMAND SAVES a file on a disk using different NAME*

5. What does closing a file do?

_removes it from the screen_

6. What is a subdirectory?

_directory within a directory_     _folder within a folder were files go_

7. What separates directories, subdirectories, and files in a path?

_backslash_

8. What does the Open dialog box enable you to do?

_open a file from any available disk and directory_

9. Which tab of the Works Task Launcher lists recently used files?

_Existing Documents_

10. Which menu provides the option to exit Works?

_File provides the option to exit works_

# WORD PROCESSING

# WORD PROCESSING BASICS

## CHAPTER 3

## OBJECTIVES

**When you complete this chapter, you will be able to:**

1. Understand basic concepts of word processing.
2. Start the word processor.
3. Understand the parts of the word processor screen.
4. Key text into the word processor.
5. Save and open a document.
6. Move the insertion point.
7. Edit text.
8. Preview and print a document.

## *What Is Word Processing?*

**W**ord processing is the use of computer software to enter and edit text. Using word processing software, such as the word processor in Works, you can create and edit documents easily. Words keyed on a word processor are stored in the computer's memory or on a disk. You don't print the text on paper until after you have edited your document on the screen.

## *Starting the Word Processor*

**A**s you have already learned, you start Works from the Windows 95 Start menu by clicking on the Programs menu. Then, find the Microsoft Works 4.0

folder and click on the Microsoft Works 4.0 icon. If you need a reminder about Windows 95, review Chapter 1. When the Task Launcher appears, you can click on the Works Tools tab and then click on the Word Processor tool. Works will open a new document screen.

**A C T I V I T Y**

# 3-1 Starting Works and Creating a New Word Processing Document

In this activity, you will start Works and create a new word processing document.

1. With Windows 95 running, click the **Start** button and then click on **Programs.** A menu of programs will appear. Click on **Microsoft Works 4.0.** Another list appears.

2. Click on **Microsoft Works 4.0.** The Works Task Launcher appears.

3. Click the **Works Tools** tab. The Works Tools window appears as shown in Figure 3-1.

4. Click the **Word Processor** button. A new word processor document appears with

**FIGURE 3-1**
The Works Tools tab lets you open your choice of the Works tools.

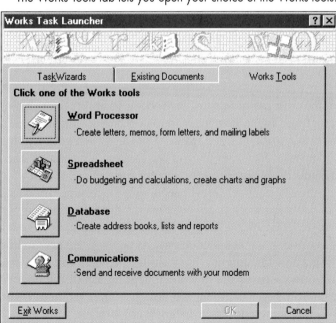

*Unsaved Document 1* in the title bar, as shown in Figure 3-2.

5. Choose **Ruler** from the **View** menu to show the ruler on the screen.

6. Leave the document window on the screen for the next activity.

**FIGURE 3-2**
The first new word processing document opened is automatically named *Unsaved Document 1* until you save it with another name. *Page layout*

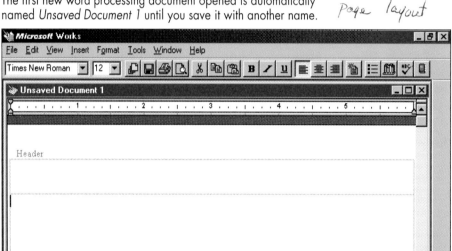

One of the most useful features of Works is its ability to open more than one document at a time. While you are working on one document, you can create a new document and work on it for awhile. You can switch back and forth as often as you like. Suppose, for example, you are creating a resume in one document. While the resume document is on the screen, you can create a new document in which to key the cover letter you will send with the resume. If you want to send two different cover letters, you can even open a third document in which to key the second cover letter. All the tools in Works allow you to open new documents while you are working on other documents, as you will see later in this book.

Opening a new document is very simple. You choose New from the File menu, and Works displays the new document on top of the document that is already open. The new document window becomes the active window. The title bar of the active window is a different color or intensity than the title bar of the inactive window. It is easy to move back and forth between documents: Just click on the title bar of the document you want to work on, and it will become the active window and come to the front of the screen. You can also choose a document you want to become active in the Window menu. You can enter text only in an active window.

## ACTIVITY

# 3-2  Creating a New File While Works Is Running

In this activity, you will create a new word processing document from within the word processor and switch between documents.

1. Choose **New** from the **File** menu. The Works Task Launcher appears.

2. Click the **Word Processor** button. Another word processing window appears on top of *Unsaved Document 1* with *Unsaved Document 2* in the title bar. Notice that the title bar of *Unsaved Document 2* is a different color than the title bar of *Unsaved Document 1*. This means it is the active window. Although you chose to create a new word processor file using the Word Processing tool, you could also have chosen to open a new database or spreadsheet file. You can access any Works tool from any other tool.

3. Click on the *Unsaved Document 1* title bar and notice that it becomes the active

window. *Unsaved Document 2* disappears from the screen because it is now behind *Unsaved Document 1*.

4. To bring *Unsaved Document 2* to the front again, click the **Window** menu. At the bottom of the menu, you will see your two documents listed, with a check mark beside *1 Unsaved Document 1*. Click on **2 Unsaved Document 2.** The menu will close and *Unsaved Document 2* will once again be the active window.

5. Choose **Close** from the **File** menu. The *Unsaved Document 2* window closes and the *Unsaved Document 1* window remains on the screen.

6. Leave the *Unsaved Document 1* window on the screen for the next activity.

# Word Processor Windows

If you look closely at your screen, you will see that you really have two windows on the screen: the Microsoft Works window and the window containing

*Unsaved Document 1.* The window containing Microsoft Works is called the application window. No matter which tool you choose to use in Works, you will always see this window on your screen. The *Unsaved Document 1* window is called the document window. This is the window where you will actually do your work. In the word processor, the first document window that appears on your screen is called *Unsaved Document 1.* In the spreadsheet, the first document window is called *Unsaved Spreadsheet 1.* In the database, the first document window is called *Unsaved Database1*, and in the communications tool, the first document window is called *Unsaved Communication 1.* All these document windows share some features that will make your work easier, as shown in Figure 3-3.

*Application windows document windows can only saved document with a name*

**FIGURE 3-3**
The document window is located within the application window.

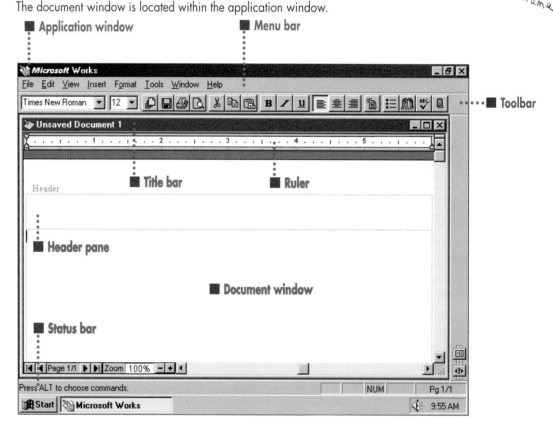

## Identifying Parts of the Screen

In Chapter 2, you learned the names of some of the parts of the screen. As you look at your screen, you will see the features you learned plus some additional features that appear only in the word processor and only in Page Layout view. A *title bar* is at the top of every window. It contains the name of the program. The *menu bar* is the horizontal bar at the top of the application window that contains menu titles from which you can choose a variety of word processing commands. The *toolbar,* located directly below the menu bar, contains common word processing commands you can use by simply clicking the correct button. Using the *ruler,* located directly below the title bar, you can quickly change indentions, tabs, and margins. The *header pane* is at the top of each new document in Page Layout view. At the bottom of the application window is a one-line *status bar.* The message in the status bar gives you directions on how to access menus and summarizes the actions of commands that you choose.

The toolbar uses icons to remind you of the function of each of the buttons. If you do not know the function of a toolbar button, move the mouse pointer to the button, but do not click. The name of the function will appear below the button.

## ACTIVITY

# 3-3 Exploring the Toolbar

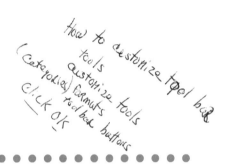

In this activity, you will move the pointer over the buttons in the toolbar to become acquainted with their functions.

1. Move the pointer to the Task Launcher button on the left end of the toolbar (the button with the three sheets of colored paper on it). Do not click. When the pointer is resting on the button, the name of the button will appear below it.

2. Move the pointer to the right, resting the pointer on each button, until you have read the names of each of the buttons.

3. Click the **Task Launcher** button on the toolbar. The Task Launcher appears, just as

it would if you had chosen New from the File menu.

4. Click the **Word Processor** button in the Task Launcher. Another word processing window appears. The new window's title is *Unsaved Document 3* because it is the third word processing window you have opened since starting Works.

5. Choose **Close** from the **File** menu. The *Unsaved Document 3* window closes.

6. Leave the *Unsaved Document 1* window on the screen for the next activity.

## Changing Views

Works has two ways to look at text on the screen. Page Layout view, which is the default view, is shown on your screen now. Page Layout view shows how your document will look when it is printed. It shows all formatting and the header pane at the top of the page and the footer pane at the bottom.

Normal view does not display a page the way it will look when printed. It shows some formatting and shows the header and footer at the top of the first page only. In addition, some text may not wrap exactly like it will when printed. You can change the view at any time from the View menu.

ACTIVITY

## 3-4   Changing Views

•  •  •  •  •  •  •  •  •  •  •  •  •  •  •  •  •  •  •  •  •  •  •  •  •  •  •  •  •  •  •  •  •

In this activity, you will change views.

1.  Choose **Normal** from the **View** menu. The view is changed to normal. Scroll to the top of the page and notice the *H* and *F.* This is where headers are displayed in Normal view.

2.  Choose **Page Layout** from the **View** menu. Scroll up and down to notice the header pane at the top of the page and the footer pane at the bottom of the page.

3.  Switch back to Normal view.

## Changing the Size of the Windows

When you open a new document window, it does not fill all of the space available in the application window. As you learned in Chapter 1, you can maximize the windows to take advantage of the entire screen. Figure 3-4 will remind you where to find the maximize and minimize buttons.

**FIGURE 3-4**
The maximize button changes the size of a window while the minimize button reduces a window to an icon.

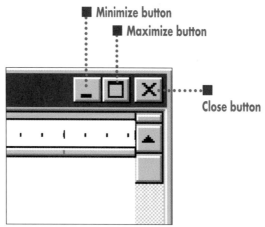

■ Minimize button
■ Maximize button
Close button

# ACTIVITY

## Maximizing Windows

• • • • • • • • • • • • • • • • • • • • • • • • • • • • • • • • • • •

In this activity, you will maximize the document window. The application window should already be maximized. If it is not, click the application window's maximize button before beginning step 1.

1. Click the document window's **maximize** button. The document window expands to fill the application window. The windows

appear as in Figure 3-5. Notice that the document window's title bar has disappeared, and the application window's title bar now reads *Microsoft Works - Unsaved Document 1* to let you know what document you are in.

2. Leave *Unsaved Document 1* on the screen for the next activity.

**FIGURE 3-5**

The document window and application window appear maximized.

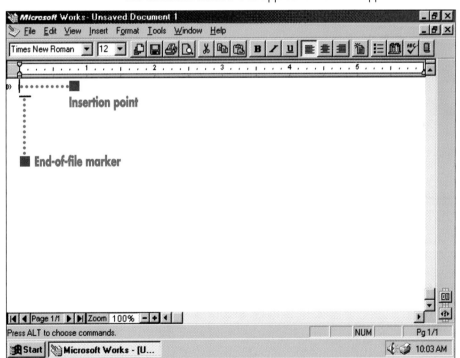

# *Entering Text*

**L**ook again at Figure 3-5 or at your screen. The vertical blinking line in the document window is called the ***insertion point.*** The insertion point marks your place in the text and shows where the next character you key will appear. The horizontal line is called the ***end-of-file marker.*** It moves down as you enter a new line of text and marks the end of the document. The insertion point cannot be moved below the end-of-file marker.

When you begin to enter text, you will notice that the insertion point moves to the right in front of each letter you key. As you reach the right side of the window, the insertion point automatically moves to the next line. This feature is called ***wordwrap.*** It is one feature that sets word processors apart from typewriters, on which you must manually return each time you wish to type a new line.

No one is perfect. You will make typographical errors while keying text. If you make a mistake while keying the paragraph in Activity 3-6, press the Backspace key to delete characters to the left of the insertion point and then continue keying the paragraph.

**ACTIVITY**

**3-6** **Entering Text**

• • • • • • • • • • • • • • • • • • • • • • • • • • • • • • • • • • • • • • • • • •

In this activity, you will key a paragraph of text.

1. Key the following text. As you key, watch what happens to the words as you reach the

end of a line. Your screen should resemble Figure 3-6 when you have finished.

> In 1961, NASA launched the first chimpanzee into space. This chimp, named Ham, traveled a total distance of 422 miles at a top speed of 1,200 miles per hour. Ham helped pioneer safe space travel during the infancy of the United States Space Program.

**2.** The text you entered wrapped at the end of each line to start a new line. Your insertion point is now to the right of the last character, and the end-of-file marker appears directly below the text, as in Figure 3-6.

Press **Enter** to move the insertion point down one line.

**3.** Leave the *Unsaved Document 1* window on the screen for the next activity.

**FIGURE 3-6**
Letters appear to the left of the insertion point as you key.

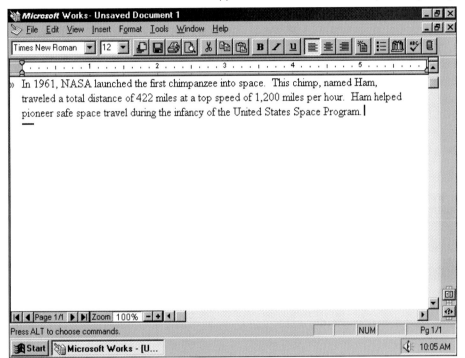

# *Saving Your Work*

**S**aving is one of the most important features of any computer program. You can store files you have created on a floppy disk or on the computer's hard drive. It is a good idea to get in the habit of saving often. An electrical failure can cause you to lose a document you have not yet saved, and if that document was long and tedious, you are really out of luck!

All Windows 95 applications give you two ways to save a file: with the Save and Save As commands. The first time you save a file, you will not have to choose between these two commands. When you select Save or Save As from the File menu, Works will automatically present you with the Save As dialog box. In this dialog box, you can key the name you wish to give your file and choose where you want Works to save it. Works will then store the file in that location with the name you have supplied and return you to your document.

The next time you want to save your document, you again choose Save. This time, you will not see a dialog box, and Works will save the current document by overwriting the previous version of it. You won't see the saving process on the screen, but the status bar tells you that Works is saving your file to disk.

If you wish to give your existing file a different name or save it to a new location, you can choose Save As from the File menu. Once again, you will see the Save As dialog box. Enter the new name or destination for the file, and Works will store a new copy of the file according to your directions.

Beside the Save command in the File menu are two letters connected by a plus sign. These letters are called a *key combination.* A key combination always contains a plus sign, which indicates that you are to press two keys at the same time. To use a key combination, hold down the first key while you press the second. Key combinations are often used as shortcuts for commands. In this case, Ctrl+S is a shortcut for the Save command. Pressing Ctrl+S will save your file just as if you had selected the Save command. As you use menus in Works, be alert to the key combinations that offer you keyboard shortcuts for commands. When your hands are already on the keyboard, a key combination can be a better shortcut than a toolbar button.

### ACTIVITY

# 3-7  Saving a Document

● ● ● ● ● ● ● ● ● ● ● ● ● ● ● ● ● ● ● ● ● ● ● ● ● ● ● ● ● ● ● ● ● ●

In this activity, you will save the document you created in the previous activity under a specific name. You will also key an additional paragraph and save it in the same file.

1. Choose **Save As** from the **File** menu. The Save As dialog box appears, as shown in Figure 3-7.

2. In the **File name** box, key **orbit** as the filename of the document.

3. Place your data disk in drive A. In the **Save in** box, choose your floppy disk drive, which is usually identified as *3 1/2 Floppy (A:).*

4. Click **Save.** Works saves the document and returns you to your document.

5. Press **Enter** to create a blank line.

6. Key the paragraph that appears in the following box.

```
The Soviet Union was the first country to send a female
into orbit. Her name was Valentina Tereshkova. Sally Ride
was the first American woman to travel in space. Ride's job
on the mission was to help recover a stranded satellite.
```

*Copy a disk*

**FIGURE 3-7**
The Save As dialog box allows you to save a document
with a specific name or in a specific drive or directory.

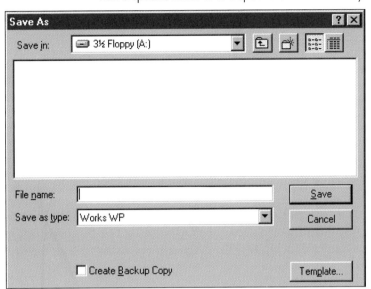

7. Click the **Save** button on the toolbar as a shortcut to the Save command. The file is saved under the name *orbit* and includes the additional text you entered (see Figure 3-8).

8. Now select the **File** menu again and look at the **Save** command. Notice that at the right side of the menu are the letters *Ctrl+S*.

**FIGURE 3-8**
The additional text is saved with the original text.

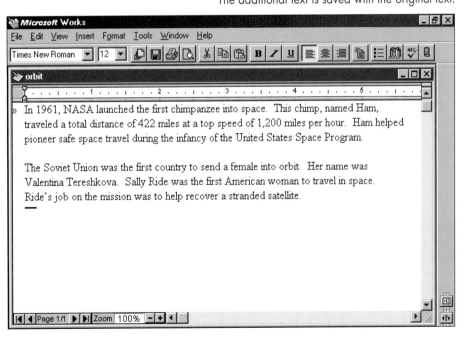

**9.** Choose **Close** from the **File** menu. *Orbit* closes and the Works Task Launcher appears.

**10.** Leave the Works Task Launcher on your screen for the next activity.

# Opening a Saved Document

**S**ometimes you may be unable to finish an entire document at one time. If you have to quit a document before you are finished with it, you can save it according to the instructions in the previous section. Then, when you are ready to work on the document again, you simply open the document and continue working.

You can open a recently used file through the Works Task Launcher or the Open dialog box. You can access the Open dialog box by choosing Open from the File menu or clicking *Open a document not listed here* in the Works Task Launcher.

## Opening an Existing File

In this activity, you will open the file you created in the previous activity using a method for opening recently used files that you learned in Chapter 2. The Task Launcher should be on your screen.

**1.** Click the **Existing Documents** tab.

**2.** Highlight *orbit* in the list of recently used files.

**3.** Click **OK.** The file appears in the document window.

**4.** Leave the document on the screen for the next activity.

# Moving the Insertion Point

**W**orks offers two different methods of moving the insertion point: the mouse and keyboard commands. For short documents, you may find it faster to move the insertion point using the mouse. As you move the mouse pointer through the document window, it assumes the shape of an **I-beam.** To move the insertion point, place the I-beam where you want the insertion point to be and then click the left mouse button. The blinking insertion point will appear.

If you are working with a long document, you may find it tedious to use the mouse pointer to move the insertion point. Scrolling through a document of several pages using the mouse can take a long time. In this case, it will be faster to use the keyboard to move your insertion point. Table 3-1 shows the keys you can press to move your insertion point both short and long distances.

**TABLE 3-1**
Keyboard Shortcuts for Moving the Insertion Point

| PRESS | TO MOVE THE INSERTION POINT |
|---|---|
| Right arrow | Right one character |
| Left arrow | Left one character |
| Down arrow | To the next line |
| Up arrow | To the previous line |
| End | To the end of a line |
| Home | To the beginning of a line |
| Page Down | To the next screen |
| Page Up | To the previous screen |
| Ctrl+Right arrow | To the next word |
| Ctrl+Left arrow | To the previous word |
| Ctrl+End | To the end of the document |
| Ctrl+Home | To the beginning of the document |

**ACTIVITY**

# 3-9  Moving the Insertion Point

In this activity, you will move the insertion point by using the mouse and the keyboard. *Orbit* should be open, and the insertion point should be blinking in the upper left corner.

1. Move the mouse pointer to the end of the first line in the first paragraph. Click once. The insertion point moves to the end of the line.

**2.** Press **Ctrl+End** to move the insertion point to the end of the document.

**3.** Move the mouse pointer to the left of the first word in the document. With the I-beam showing, click once. (If the mouse pointer's arrowhead is present, you may highlight the entire line by mistake.)

**4.** Press **Ctrl+Right arrow** four times to move to the word *launched* in the first line.

**5.** Leave the document on the screen for the next activity.

# Editing Text

**W**hen you use a word processor, you can edit your document on the screen and print the final copy after you are completely satisfied with it. In this section, you will learn the most basic forms of editing your document: inserting, selecting, and deleting text and moving and copying blocks of text.

## Inserting Text

You already know one way to insert text: move the insertion point to the place you want the text and begin keying. You can also use the Overtype option to insert text. *Overtype* does just what its name says. It replaces the characters on the screen with new characters as you enter them. You turn Overtype on and off by pressing the Insert key, which, on most keyboards, is located in the group of six keys above the arrow keys. The Overtype option can also be turned on through the Options command in the Tools menu. Be careful not to replace more characters than you intend to when using Overtype. Overtype allows you to type over not only characters but also spaces between words.

ACTIVITY

 **Inserting Text**

● ● ● ● ● ● ● ● ● ● ● ● ● ● ● ● ● ● ● ● ● ● ● ● ● ● ● ● ● ● ● ● ● ● ● ● ●

In this activity, you will insert text in a document. *Orbit* should be on your screen.

**1.** Move the insertion point to one space after the word *female* in the first line of the second

paragraph. Key **astronaut.** Remember to leave one space before and after *astronaut*.

**2.** Move the insertion point before the word *orbit* in the first line of the second paragraph.

Press **Insert** to toggle the Overtype option on. The letters *OVR* should appear in the bottom right corner of your screen.

3. Key **space.** The word *orbit* disappears.

4. Press **Insert** to toggle off the Overtype option.

5. Press **Ctrl+S** to choose Save from the File menu. Remember, pressing Ctrl+S, clicking the Save button, and choosing Save from the File menu all have the same effect. The file is saved and includes the changes you made.

6. Leave the document on the screen for the next activity.

## Selecting Text

*Selecting* means highlighting a block of text. The block can be as small as one word or as large as an entire document. Once you have selected a block of text, you can edit the entire block at once. This speeds operations such as large deletions and changes to line spacing.

A C T I V I T Y

 **Selecting Text**

In this activity, you will select text using the mouse. *Orbit* should be on your screen.

1. Move the mouse pointer to before the first word in the first paragraph.

2. Press the left mouse button and drag the mouse pointer to the end of the last word of the first sentence.

3. Release the mouse button. The first sentence of the first paragraph should appear highlighted. Click to remove the highlighting.

4. Move the mouse pointer before the first word of the second paragraph. Drag the mouse pointer down until the paragraph appears highlighted. Release the mouse button. Click to remove the highlighting.

5. Leave the document on the screen for the next activity.

## Deleting Text

No matter how good a typist you are, you will make typographical errors while keying text. One of the first editing skills you must master, therefore, is how to delete text. Works gives you two different ways to delete characters. You can use either the *Backspace key* or the *Delete key.* Pressing the Backspace key deletes the character to the left of the insertion point; pressing the

Delete key removes the character to the right of the insertion point. If you hold down either of these keys, it will continue to remove characters until you release the key. This is an easy way to remove a whole line of text.

# Using the Backspace and Delete Keys

In this activity, you will delete text with the Backspace and Delete keys. *Orbit* should be on your screen.

1. Place the insertion point before the word *on* in the phrase *on the mission* in the last line of the second paragraph.

2. Hold down the **Delete** key until the words *on the mission* disappear. Remember to leave a blank space between the remaining words.

3. Place the insertion point after the word

*stranded* in the last line of the second paragraph.

4. Hold down the **Backspace** key until the word *stranded* disappears. Again, leave one blank space between the remaining words. Your document should appear similar to Figure 3-9.

5. Save the document.

6. Leave the document on the screen for the next activity.

**FIGURE 3-9**
The Delete and Backspace keys are useful for deleting phrases.

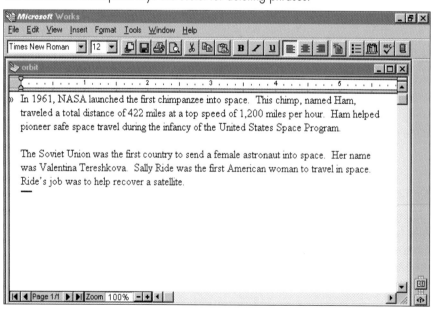

## Using the Clipboard to Move and Copy Text

At some point when you are editing a document, you will probably wish you had put a certain paragraph last or a specific sentence first. A word processor gives you a lot of control over the organization of your document. If you do not like where a paragraph is, a couple of simple steps can move it to a better location. If you need to repeat a sentence, you can copy it to other locations using only a few keystrokes.

The Works feature that makes these moving and copying operations so easy is the Clipboard. The *Clipboard* is a temporary storage place in memory. You send text to the Clipboard by using either the Copy command or the Cut command. Then, you can retrieve that text by using the Paste command. You can paste the Clipboard text as many times as you want. The Clipboard will store the text you send to it until you send another block of copy or until you clear the Clipboard. The Clipboard does not provide long-term storage; saving a file does. When you turn off the computer, the text in the Clipboard is lost.

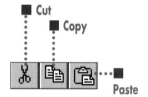

### MOVING TEXT

When you want to move text from one location to another, use the Cut and Paste commands. The Cut command places selected text on the Clipboard. The Paste command recalls the text from the Clipboard and pastes it at the location of the insertion point in the word processing document. If this seems like the kind of editing you used to do with scissors, you're right. This operation is often referred to simply as *cutting and pasting*. But it is far easier to do it on the screen than with paper, scissors, and glue.

### ACTIVITY

## Moving Text with Cut and Paste

In this activity, you will cut text from a document and paste it to a different location within the document. *Orbit* should be on your screen.

1. Beginning with the first word of the first paragraph, drag the mouse to highlight the entire paragraph.

2. Choose **Cut** from the **Edit** menu. The para-graph you selected disappears from the screen. It has been placed on the Clipboard.

3. If the insertion point is blinking above the remaining paragraph, press **Delete** to delete the extra space above the paragraph.

4. Place the insertion point after the period following the last word of the last sentence in

the paragraph, *satellite*. Press **Enter** twice to create a blank line.

**5.** Choose **Paste** from the **Edit** menu. The paragraph reappears, as shown in Figure 3-10.

**6.** Save the document.

**7.** Leave the document on the screen for the next activity.

**FIGURE 3-10**
The Cut and Paste commands allow you to move entire paragraphs from one place to another in a document.

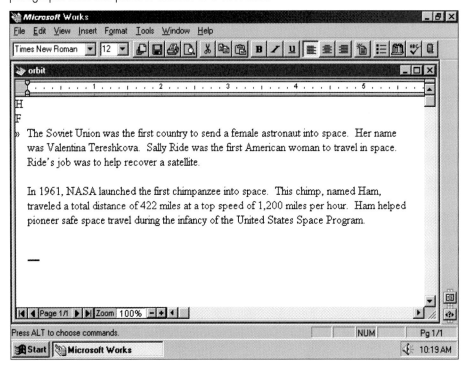

## COPYING TEXT

The Copy command is similar to the Cut command. When you choose the Copy command, however, a copy of your highlighted text is placed on the Clipboard while the original text remains on the screen. You use the Paste command, as before, to retrieve the copied text from the Clipboard.

# ACTIVITY 3-14
## Copying Text with Copy and Paste

In this activity, you will copy text from a document and paste it in a different location within the document. *Orbit* should be on your screen.

1. Using the mouse, highlight the paragraph that begins with *The Soviet Union*.

2. Choose **Copy** from the **Edit** menu. A copy of the text you selected is placed on the Clipboard. Notice that the highlighted text remains on the screen.

3. Place the insertion point after the period following the last sentence of the second paragraph. Press **Enter** twice.

4. Click the **Paste** button on the toolbar. A copy of the paragraph reappears. The original text remains at the top of the document, as shown in Figure 3-11.

5. Save the document.

6. Leave the document on the screen for the next activity.

**FIGURE 3-11**

The first paragraph has been copied and pasted below the second paragraph.

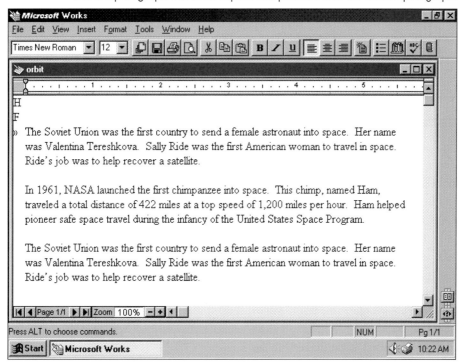

## Another Way to Copy and Move Text: Drag and Drop

When copying and moving text a short distance, you can use a quick method called *drag and drop*. To use the drag and drop method to move text, highlight the text you want to copy or move and move the mouse pointer into the highlighted text. The pointer will change to an arrow with the word *DRAG* below it. Using the mouse, drag the text to the location where you want to move or copy the text. As you begin dragging, the word below the mouse pointer will change to *MOVE*. When the pointer reaches the location where you want the text to appear, release the mouse button.

To use the drag and drop method to copy text, perform the same steps as when moving text using the drag and drop method. While dragging, hold down the Ctrl key. The word *COPY* will appear below the pointer. When you release the mouse button, the text is placed at the pointer location while the originally highlighted text remains unchanged.

## ACTIVITY

# 3-15 Using the Drag and Drop Method to Move and Copy Text

In this activity, you will use the drag and drop method to move a paragraph. *Orbit* should be on your screen.

1. Highlight the first paragraph of the document, and the blank line below the paragraph.

2. Position the pointer over the highlighted text. The pointer will appear as an arrow with the word *DRAG* below it.

3. Using the mouse, drag the pointer to the bottom of the document. As the pointer is dragged, the word *MOVE* will appear below the pointer. Release the mouse button. The paragraph is moved to the bottom of the document.

4. Double-click the word *chimpanzee* in the first sentence of the document to highlight it.

5. Position the pointer over the highlighted text.

6. While holding down the **Ctrl** key, drag the pointer between the words *a* and *satellite* at the end of the document. As you drag, the word *COPY* will appear below the pointer. When the mouse button is released, the word *chimpanzee* will be copied to the new pointer location. Release the Ctrl key after the mouse button. Otherwise you will not copy the selected text, only move it.

7. Highlight and delete the entire last paragraph. If necessary, adjust the spacing around the remaining paragraphs.

8. Save the document and leave it open for the next activity.

# Previewing Your Document

The Print Preview command enables you to look at a document as it will appear when printed. The command allows you to zoom in and out to help find mistakes before you print your document. Zoom In enlarges the document while Zoom Out reduces the size of the document in Print Preview.

**ACTIVITY**

## 3-16 Previewing Your Document

In this activity, you will preview the document you have created. *Orbit* should be on your screen.

1. Click the **Print Preview** button on the toolbar. The document you created appears with the entire page visible, as in Figure 3-12.

2. Click the **Zoom In** button. The document enlarges.

3. Click the **Zoom In** button again. The document enlarges to an even greater size.

**FIGURE 3-12**
Print Preview allows you to look at a document before you print it.

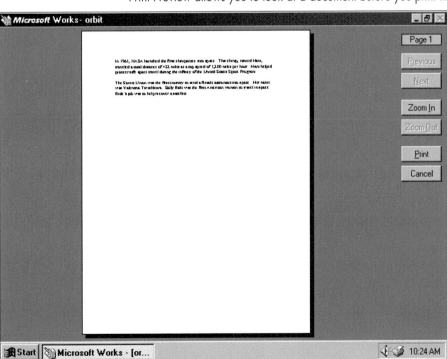

**4.** Point to the right scroll arrow. Click several times to view the entire document.

**5.** Click **Zoom Out** twice to view the document again with the entire page visible.

**6.** Click the **Cancel** button. The document window reappears.

**7.** Leave the document on the screen for the next activity.

# *Printing Your Document*

**T**he Print command enables you to print your document on paper. After you choose the Print command, the Print dialog box, shown in Figure 3-13, will appear showing the printing options. The Works default is set to print an entire document. You can, however, print multiple copies of a document or print specific pages. For example, if you wanted to print pages 5, 6, and 7 in a ten-page document, you would choose Pages, key 5 in the from box, key 7 in the to box, and click OK. The Print button is located on the toolbar and provides a shortcut to printing a document from the File menu.

**N O T E :**  *Clicking the Print button on the toolbar or in Print Preview skips the Print dialog box and begins printing immediately using the current settings.*

**FIGURE 3-13**
The Print dialog box appears after you choose Print from the File menu.

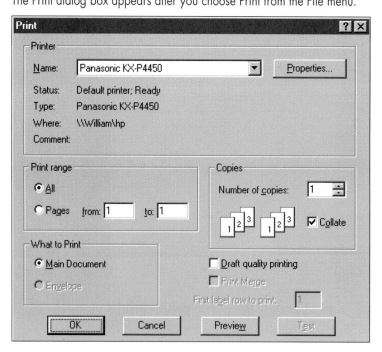

# ACTIVITY

## 3-17 Printing Your Document

In this activity, you will print the document you have created. *Orbit* should be on your screen.

1. Choose **Print** from the **File** menu. If a First-time Help dialog box appears, click **OK.** The Print dialog box appears.

2. Click **OK.** A message appears showing the status of the printing document. In a few moments, the document should start printing. Wait for the page to print.

3. Choose **Close** from the **File** menu.

# Summary

- Word processing is the use of computer software that manipulates text. Text can be edited without rekeying the entire document.

- The application window and the document window can be maximized and minimized to take full advantage of the screen. The menu bar, the toolbar, the ruler, and the status bar are features of the word processor that make working with a document easier.

- Words keyed on the word processor will appear after the insertion point. The end-of-file marker marks the end of the document. Wordwrap moves text nearing the end of a line to the next line and eliminates the need to press Enter at the end of every line.

- Works has two ways to look at text on the screen. Page Layout view shows how your document will look when it is printed. Normal view does not display a page the way it will print. Formatting, headers, footers, and wordwrap are not shown exactly like they will be when printed.

- Documents can be saved under a designated name with the Save As command and updated with the Save command. Files can be opened after being saved.

- Editing text with Works is a much easier process than pencil-and-paper editing. The insertion point may be moved in the document window with the mouse or the keyboard. Features such as delete, insert, cut, copy, and paste speed editing.

- The Print Preview command shows the finished document as it will appear when printed. The Print command produces a hard copy of your document on a printer.

• • • • • • • • • • • • •

# REVIEW ACTIVITIES

## TRUE/FALSE

**Circle T or F to show whether the statement is true or false.**

**T** F     1. Word processing involves the use of a computer program to enter and edit text.

**T** F     2. The New command is accessed through the File menu.

T **F**     3. The toolbar is located directly above the menu bar.

T **F**     4. The insertion point cannot be moved past the end-of-file marker.

T **F**     5. When entering text in the word processor, you must press Enter at the end of every line.

**T** F     6. You can choose Save or Save As the first time you save a file.

T F     7. The Open command is accessed through the File menu.

T **F**     8. The insertion point can be moved only with the mouse.     *mouse arrow keys*

**T** F     9. Pressing the Insert key turns the Overtype option on or off.

**T** F     10. The Print Preview command may be used to help find mistakes before printing.

## COMPLETION

**Write the correct answer in the space provided.**

1. What is the difference between Page Layout view and Normal view?

   *Page Layout view shows how document will look when printed (Print Preview). Normal view does not display the page the way it will print.*

2. List three parts of the word processor window discussed in this chapter.

   *Microsoft works*     *title bar*     *status bar*
   *Unsaved document 1*     *tool bar*     *menu bar*
   *Unsaved document 2*     *Ruler*

3. What feature allows you to key text without pressing Enter at the end of every line?

   *WORD WRAP*

4. Describe the differences between the two types of Save commands.

   *documents can be saved under a designated name with Save As and updated with the Save command*     *Files can be opened after being saved*

*existing*

*Click file not listed*
*here*

**5.** Describe one way to open an existing file.   *fast launcher*

CLICK EXISTING Documents

Highlight orbit in the list of Recently used files

Click OK

**6.** What does the mouse pointer change to when moved through the document window?

I-beam

**7.** How do you move the insertion point to the end of a document using the keyboard?

Ctrl END

**8.** When using the drag and drop method to copy text, what key must be held down while dragging?

Ctrl

**9.** What is the advantage of using the Print Preview command?

shows the finished document as it will look
when printed                    ZOOM

**10.** Describe the steps in printing a document.

from File menu choose Print

click OK

## application 3-1

**In the blank space, write the letter of the keystroke that matches the insertion point movement.**

_G_ 1. To the next screen

_K_ 2. To the end of the document

_A_ 3. Right one character

_E_ 4. To the end of the line

_C_ 5. To the next line

_D_ 6. To the previous line

_B_ 7. Left one character

_J_ 8. To the previous word

_F_ 9. To the beginning of the line

_L_ 10. To the beginning of the document

_I_ 11. To the next word

_H_ 12. To the previous screen

a. Right arrow

b. Left arrow

c. Down arrow

d. Up arrow

e. End

f. Home

g. Page Down

h. Page Up

i. Ctrl+Right arrow

j. Ctrl+Left arrow

k. Ctrl+End

l. Ctrl+Home

## application 3-2

1. Open *Application 3-2* from your template disk.

2. Insert an *f* in the word *effective* in the first sentence of the document.

3. Delete the word *can* in the second sentence of the document.

4. Delete the comma and the word *meaningless* in the third sentence.

5. Insert the sentence *Use correct punctuation.* before the word *Correct* in item number 3.

6. Remove the template disk and insert your data disk.

7. Choose **Save As** from the **File** menu. Key **writing** in the **File name** box. Change the drive to **a:.** Click **Save.** A message will appear asking you to insert the disk containing *Application 3-2*.

8. Remove your data disk and insert your template disk. Click **Retry.** You'll get a message saying *"Will you be saving to a different floppy disk...."* Click **Yes.**

9. You will be prompted to insert the floppy you want to save the file on. Remove the template disk and insert your data disk. Click **Retry.** The document is saved as *writing* on your data disk.

10. Switch to Print Preview.

11. Preview the document. Zoom in to check your corrections.

12. Print the finished document.

13. Close the document. At the *"Save changes to writing?"* prompt, click **No.**

# application 3-3

1. Open *Application 3-3* from your template disk.

2. Key the words **student housing** before the word *orientation* in the last sentence of the first paragraph.

3. Insert an **m** in the word *roommate* in the first sentence of the second paragraph.

4. Delete the room number *607* in the third paragraph and key **425**.

5. Delete the words *junior and senior* students in the third paragraph and key **entering freshman**.

6. Use drag and drop to move the fourth paragraph and place it after the period following the word *studying* in the last sentence of the second paragraph. Add space before the sentence as necessary. Delete any extra blank lines that remain between the paragraphs.

7. Remove the template disk and insert your data disk.

8. Choose **Save As** from the **File** menu. Key **housing** in the **File name** box. Change the drive to **a:**. Click **Save.** A message will appear asking you to insert the disk containing *Application 3-2.*

9. Remove your data disk and insert your template disk. Click **Retry.** You'll get a message saying *"Will you be saving to a different floppy disk...."* Click **Yes.**

10. You will be prompted to insert the floppy you want to save the file on. Remove the template disk and insert your data disk. Click **Retry.** The document is saved as *housing* on your data disk.

11. Preview the document. Zoom in to check your revisions. Print the finished document. Close the document.

# STRENGTHENING WORD PROCESSING SKILLS

CHAPTER

4

## OBJECTIVES
### When you complete this chapter, you will be able to:

1. Use the Undo command.

2. Change margins in a document.

3. Understand and choose fonts.

4. Change indents, alignment, and spacing in a document.

5. Set and use tabs.

6. Insert page breaks.

7. Use the Spelling Checker and Thesaurus.

## *Undo*

**W**hen editing a document, you will sometimes delete text accidentally or change your mind about a deletion immediately after you press the Delete key. This is when the Undo command is useful. The *Undo* command will reverse a previous command to delete text or change the format of text. It will also reverse commands you will learn about later, such as the Spelling Checker, the Thesaurus, and the Replace command. The Undo command, however, will reverse only the most recent change. The Undo command can be accessed from the Edit menu or by pressing Ctrl+Z.

# *Margins*

**A** *margin* is the amount of space between the edge of a page and the printed or written text in a document. If you do not specify the amount of space to use as margins, Works will set the space to a standard setting, called the default margins. You might, however, want to change the default margins to suit a particular type of document. For example, a document to be placed in a three-ring spiral notebook might require more white space on the left edge and, therefore, a wider left margin.

The margins of a document are changed from the Page Setup dialog box, shown in Figure 4-1. Notice how the lower part of the Page Setup dialog box is divided into three sections. Each section has a tab that you click to access the section. You can change settings in more than one section before clicking OK.

**FIGURE 4-1**
The Page Setup dialog box contains the document's default margins.

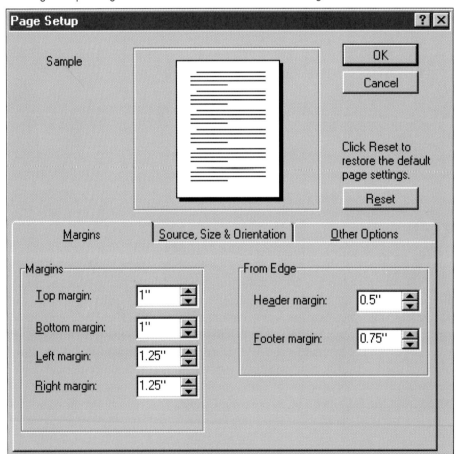

## ACTIVITY 4-1

### Adjusting a Document's Margins

In this activity, you will change a document's margins.

1. Start Works if it is not already running on your computer.

2. Open *Activity 4-1* from your template disk.

3. Use **Print Preview** to observe the existing margins. Click **Cancel** to return to your document.

4. Choose **Page Setup** from the **File** menu. The Page Setup dialog box appears.

5. If the Margins section is not showing, click the tab labeled **Margins.**

6. The insertion point appears in the Top margin box. Key **1.25**. As new values are entered, the sample document in the dialog box will reflect the changes. Press **Tab.**

7. In the Bottom margin box, key **1.25**.

8. Press **Tab** to move to Left margin box. Key **1.5**.

9. Click **OK.** The top and bottom margins are now set at 1.25 inches. The right margin is set at 1.25 inches, and the left margin is set at 1.5 inches. Use Print Preview to view the changes that you have made.

10. Remove the template disk and insert your data disk.

11. Choose **Save As** from the **File** menu. Key **mountain** in the **File name** box. Change the drive to **a:.** Click **Save.** A message will appear asking you to insert the disk containing *Activity 4-1.*

12. Remove your data disk and insert your template disk. Click **Retry.** You'll get a message saying *"Will you be saving to a different floppy disk...."* Click **Yes.**

13. You will be prompted to insert the floppy you want to save the file on. Remove the template disk and insert your data disk. Click **Retry.** The document is saved as *mountain* on your data disk.

14. Leave the document open for the next activity.

# Fonts

The term *font* refers to the shape of the characters belonging to a particular family of type. A font is also called a *typeface.* Just as clothing comes in different designs, fonts have different designs. Like clothing, type can be dressy or casual.

## Choosing a Font

When you are creating a document, you should consider what kind of impression you want to make. Do you want your document to look dressy or formal? Or do you want it to look casual or informal? The fonts shown in Figure 4-2 would result in four very different-looking documents.

**FIGURE 4-2**
Fonts can give text very different appearances.

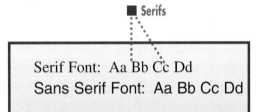

This font is called Arial.
**This font is called Impact.**
This font is called Brush Script.
This font is called Times New Roman.

If you look closely at the first line in Figure 4-3, you can see small lines at the ends of the characters. These lines are called *serifs.* If a font has these serifs, it is called a *serif font.* If a font does not have serifs, it is called a *sans serif font.* Serif fonts are generally considered to be "dressier" than sans serif fonts, and are often used for the text portion of a document. Sans serif fonts are often used for titles, headings, and page numbers.

**FIGURE 4-3**
Examples of serif and sans serif fonts.

■ Serifs

Serif Font:  Aa Bb Cc Dd
Sans Serif Font:  Aa Bb Cc Dd

## Changing the Font

You can use the Font Name box located on the toolbar to change the font. In the Font Name box, Works shows you what each font looks like. To change text to in a different font, select the text and choose a font from the Font Name box. You might want to change the

■ Font Name

font of the title of a document, for example, to set it apart from the body of the document. To do this, you would select the title and choose a font from the Font Name box. If the text has not yet been entered, choose a font from the Font Name box before you key the text.

## ACTIVITY

# 4-2 Changing the Font

• • • • • • • • • • • • • • • • • • • • • • • • • • • • • •

In this activity, you will change the font of the text in a document.

1. Choose **Select All** from the **Edit** menu. The entire document becomes highlighted.

2. Click the arrow to the right of the **Font Name** box. A list of fonts appears.

3. Choose **Times New Roman.** You may have to use the scroll bar to locate this font. If Times New Roman is not available, choose another serif font that looks similar to the text used in this book. The document will appear in the chosen font.

4. Click anywhere in the document to remove

the highlight, then highlight the title of the document, *MOUNTAINS.*

5. Choose a sans serif font, such as GillSans or Arial, from the Font Name box in the toolbar. The title appears in the selected font, as shown in Figure 4-4. Click the mouse button to remove the highlight.

6. Save the document. Leave the file open for the next activity.

**FIGURE 4-4**
The title appears in a font different from the other text.

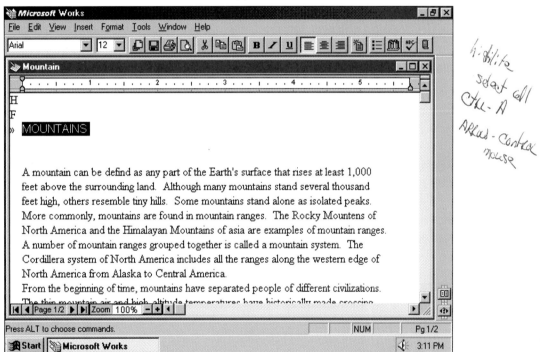

## Style

Changing fonts is one way to alter the appearance of your text. Another way to emphasize text is to change the style of the font. *Type style* refers to certain standard changes in the appearance of a font. Common styles are boldface, italic, and underline. These styles can be applied to change the appearance of any font.

When you begin keying a document in the word processor, you are using a normal style. This is the style you will most likely use for the body of your document. However, you will probably want to use other styles for particular features in your document. For example, you may want to emphasize your title by

**FIGURE 4-5**
Fonts can appear in different styles, such as the
default normal, boldface, italic, and underline.

*script*
*Sub script*
*strike thru*

> This is Times New Roman normal.
> **This is Times New Roman bold.**
> *This is Times New Roman italic.*
> <u>This is Times New Roman underlined.</u>

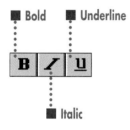

applying a boldface style to it. Titles of books and magazines
should appear in italic style. Headings will show up more
clearly if you boldface them. Figure 4-5 illustrates these different type styles.

Works allows you to change type style using the toolbar.
Clicking the Bold, Italic, or Underline buttons will apply the
style to, or remove the style from, the selected text. The type
styles can be used individually or can be combined. Table 4-1
shows keyboard shortcuts that can be used as an alternative to
the toolbar.

**TABLE 4-1**
Keyboard Shortcuts for Choosing Type Style

| TYPE STYLE | PRESS |
|------------|-------|
| Bold | Ctrl+B |
| Italic | Ctrl+I |
| Underline | Ctrl+U |
| Normal | Ctrl+Spacebar |

**ACTIVITY**

## Changing the Type Style

• • • • • • • • • • • • • • • • • • • • • • • • • • • • • • • • • • • • • •

In this activity, you will change the type style.
*Mountain* should be on your screen.

**1.** Highlight the title of the document.

2. Click the **Bold** button on the toolbar. The title becomes bold.

3. Highlight the word *mountain* in the first sentence of the first paragraph. Click the **Italic** button on the toolbar. The word *mountain* appears in italics.

4. Click the **Bold** button on the toolbar. The word appears in italics and boldface.

5. Click the **Bold** button again to remove the boldface style. The word appears in italics only. Remove the highlight by clicking in the document. Your document should appear similar to Figure 4-6.

6. Highlight the second paragraph, which begins *From the beginning of time....*

7. Press **Ctrl+U** to underline the text. Press **Ctrl+I** to make the paragraph appear in italics, also. Press **Ctrl+B** to apply boldface to the paragraph.

8. Press **Ctrl+Spacebar** to quickly return the paragraph to normal style. Remove the highlight.

9. Save the document. Leave the file open for the next activity.

**FIGURE 4-6**
Type styles improve the appearance and functionality of a document.

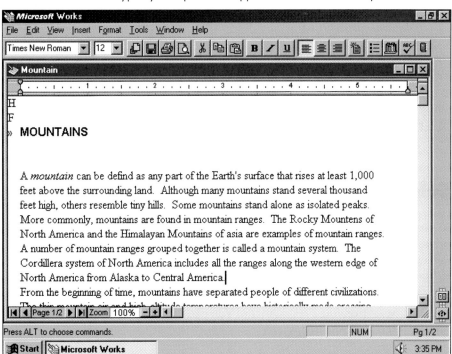

## Size

*Type size* is determined by measuring the height of characters in units called points. There are 72 points in an inch. A common type size is 12 point. Figure 4-7 illustrates the Arial font in 10, 14, and 18 point. You can change type size by using the Font Size box on the toolbar.

**FIGURE 4-7**
Different sizes can be selected within the same font.

This is Arial 10 point.
This is Arial 14 point.
This is Arial 18 point.

**A C T I V I T Y**

# 4-4 Changing the Type Size

In this activity, you will change the type size. *Mountain* should be on your screen.

**1.** Highlight the title, *MOUNTAINS*. Do not highlight the blank line after it.

**2.** Click the arrow to the right of the **Font Size** box. A list of font sizes appears.

**3.** Choose **14** point. The title appears in 14 point size. Remove the highlight.

**4.** Save the document. Leave the file open for the next activity.

## Color

Works allows you to change text on your screen to colors. Colors are fun to use and can add interesting effects to your documents. If you have a color printer, you can even print your document as it appears on your screen. If you have a printer with black ink or toner only, the document will print in black and shades of gray.

To change the color of text on your screen, highlight the text and choose Font and Style from the Format menu. You can choose the color you want in the Format Font and Style dialog box.

**ACTIVITY**

## Changing the Color of Text

In this activity, you will change the color of text. *Mountain* should be on your screen.

1. Highlight the title.

2. Choose **Font and Style** from the **Format** menu. The Format Font and Style dialog box appears.

3. Click the arrow under **Color.** A list of colors appears. Scroll down and choose Red. Notice the characters in the Sample box are red.

4. Click **OK.** Remove the highlight. The title appears in red.

5. Highlight the title.

6. Choose **Font and Style** from the **Format** menu.

7. Choose **Auto** as the color. Click **OK.** Remove the highlight. The title changes back to black.

8. Save the file. Leave it open for use in the next activity.

### The Format Font and Style Dialog Box

Choosing Font and Style from the Format menu accesses the Format Font and Style dialog box. The Font and Style dialog box allows you to set font, style, and size from a dialog box, rather than from the toolbar. A sample text box shows how text will look with the chosen font, size, color, style, and position.

# *Indenting*

**A**n *indent* is the space you place between text and a document's margin. You can indent text from either the left or the right margin, or from both margins. Indents can be used to make text more readable or to set off some parts of the text from the rest of it. For example, it is common to indent the first line of a paragraph to make the text easier to read.

You can indent text by using the indent markers on the ruler, shown in Figure 4-8. The first-line indent marker is located above the left-indent marker at the left edge of the ruler, and the right-indent marker is at the right side of the ruler. To indent text, you simply drag one of these markers to the desired point on the ruler.

**FIGURE 4-8**
The indent markers are located on the ruler.

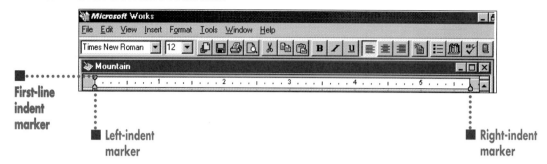

**First-line indent marker**

**Left-indent marker**

**Right-indent marker**

## First-Line Indents

Changing the first-line indent gives you many different ways to vary the look of your text. Using the first-line indent marker along with the left-indent marker lets you automatically indent paragraphs as you enter your text or create hanging indents in which the first full line of text is followed by indented lines. This feature is useful for bibliographies and lists.

Because the first-line indent and the left indent are often used together, they sometimes move at the same time. If you drag the first-line indent marker to the right, for example, the left-indent marker will not move. But when you drag the left-indent marker, the first-line indent marker will also move. You must use care when pointing at these markers to be sure you drag the one you want.

*highlite paragraph marks*
*Control C copy*
*Control V Paste*
*Paste special*

**A C T I V I T Y**

## Changing First-Line Indents

In this activity, you will change the first-line indents of paragraphs. *Mountain* should now be on the screen.

1. Place the insertion point anywhere in the first paragraph.

2. Drag the left-indent marker to the right. If a First-time Help dialog box appears, click OK. Refer to Figure 4-8 to be sure you drag

the correct marker. Notice that the first-line indent marker moves with the left-indent marker. Release the mouse button at the 1/2-inch mark on the ruler.

3. Now, drag the first-line indent marker to the left. (Be sure to position the pointer over the correct marker.) Release the mouse button at the 0-inch mark on the ruler (where you started). The first line of

text begins at the 0-inch mark and the remaining lines are indented 1/2 inch. This is called a *hanging indent.*

4. Drag the first-line indent marker to the right and release the mouse button at the 1-inch mark on the ruler. You have created a *paragraph indent.* Any text you key when you have a paragraph indent set will automatically indent the first line.

5. Drag the left-indent mark to the left. Release the mouse button at the 0-inch mark on the ruler. Notice that the first-line indent marker also moves, so your paragraph is still indented. The first line is indented 1/2 inch and the remaining lines are against the left margin.

6. Drag the first-line indent mark to the left. Release the mouse button at the 0-inch mark on the ruler. All lines are at the 0-inch mark.

7. Highlight all text except the title and the table at the end.

8. Drag the first-line indent marker to the right. Release the mouse button at the 1/2-inch mark on the ruler. The six paragraphs appear with a first-line indent of 1/2 inch. Remove the highlight.

9. Press **Ctrl+Home** to return to the beginning of the document.

10. Save the document. Leave the file open for the next activity.

## Indenting from Both Margins

As discussed above, you can indent from either the left or right margin, or both. Indenting from both margins is useful for setting off paragraphs from the main body of the text. This is commonly done for long quotations or for setting lines of poetry or equations.

**ACTIVITY**

### 4-7 Indenting from Both Margins

In this activity, you will indent a paragraph from both margins. *Mountain* should be on your screen.

1. Place the insertion point anywhere in the fifth paragraph, which begins with *An orangy.*

2. Drag the first-line indent marker to the left. Release the mouse button at the 0-inch mark on the ruler.

3. Drag the left-indent marker to the right. Release the mouse button at the 1-inch mark on the ruler.

*highlight text just part of it.*
*click mouse*
*Shift key page down*
*down arrow key*

**4.** Drag the right-indent marker to the left. Release the mouse button at the 5-inch mark. Refer back to Figure 4-8 if necessary to locate the right-indent marker.

**5.** Save the document. Leave the file open for the next activity.

SAVE
CTRL-S

# *Alignment*

**A**lignment determines how text is aligned at the margins. Left-aligned text lines up at the left edge of the page and has a ragged right edge. Left-aligned text is easy to read because your eye has a smooth edge of text to return to after reading a line. Centered text is aligned in the middle of a page. Centering is useful for positioning headings and titles.

Right-aligned text lines up at the right edge of the page and has a ragged left edge. Right-aligned text is often used to align small amounts of text, such as a page number or a date.

Justified text lines up on both sides of a page. Works inserts extra space between words in justified text to form smooth edges. This gives it the appearance of a newspaper column. Figure 4-9 illustrates the different types of alignment.

**FIGURE 4-9**
Text can be aligned left, centered, right, or justified.

> This text is left aligned.
>
> This text is centered.
>
> This text is right aligned.
>
> This text is justified because text at both the left and right margins is aligned. This text is justified because text at both the left and right margins is aligned.

You can align text by clicking the buttons on the toolbar or by choosing the Paragraph command from the Format menu.

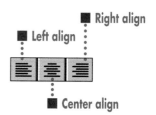

Left align
Right align
Center align

# ACTIVITY
# 4-8 Aligning Text

● ● ● ● ● ● ● ● ● ● ● ● ● ● ● ● ● ● ● ● ● ● ● ● ● ● ● ● ● ● ● ● ● ●

In this activity, you will align text in a document. *Mountain* should be on your screen.

1.  Press **Ctrl+Home** to move the insertion point to the beginning of the document.

2.  Highlight the title of the document.

3.  Click the **Center Align** button on the toolbar. The title is centered.

4.  Place the insertion point anywhere in the first paragraph. Click the **Right Align** button on the toolbar. The paragraph appears right aligned.

5.  Choose **Paragraph** from the **Format** menu. The Format Paragraph dialog box

appears. At the top of the dialog box, click the **Indents and Alignment** tab. The dialog box should look similar to Figure 4-10.

6.  Choose **Justified** in the box under Alignment. Click **OK.** The paragraph appears justified.

7.  Choose **Paragraph** from the **Format** menu. Choose **Left** in the box under Alignment. This is an alternative to using the Left Align button on the toolbar.

8.  Click **OK.** The paragraph appears left aligned.

9.  Save the document. Leave the file open for the next activity.

**FIGURE 4-10**
The Indents and Alignment section of the Format Paragraph dialog box allows you to set the alignment of a paragraph.

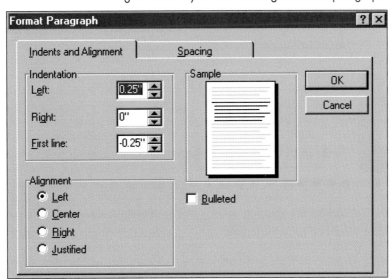

# Spacing

**S**pacing refers to the distance between lines of text or paragraphs. You can single-space text or add any amount of space between lines of text. If you wish, Works will also insert space between paragraphs.

By default, Works single-spaces text; there is no extra space between lines of text. Single-spaced text is commonly used in business letters. You might also use single-spaced text in newsletter articles and for parts of long documents, such as footnotes, bibliographies, or long quotations.

To make text more readable, you can choose to add space between lines of text. Double-spaced text has a full blank line between each line of text. Usually, reports and term papers are double-spaced. Speeches are often typed using triple-spaced text, with two full blank lines between lines of text so that a speaker can easily keep his or her place in the speech while looking back and forth between the notes and the audience.

Works offers two ways to change the line spacing of your document. You can use the keyboard shortcuts in Table 4-2, or you can use the Format Paragraph dialog box to add any amount of line space you want.

Another way to increase the readability of a page of text is to add spaces between the paragraphs. Works lets you add space before or after a paragraph, and you can decide how much space to add in each place. To add space around paragraphs, you must use the Format Paragraph dialog box.

**TABLE 4-2**
Spacing Keyboard Shortcuts

| LINE SPACING | SHORTCUT |
| --- | --- |
| Single | Ctrl+1 |
| One-and-a-half | Ctrl+5 |
| Double | Ctrl+2 |

## ACTIVITY

### Adjusting the Spacing

In this activity, you will adjust the spacing in a document. *Mountain* should be on your screen.

1. Highlight everything from the first word in the first paragraph to the end of the document.

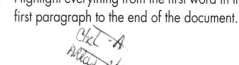

**2.** Press **Ctrl+2.** The text in the document becomes double-spaced.

**3.** Place the insertion point anywhere in the fifth paragraph, which begins *An orangy.* Press **Ctrl+1.** The paragraph becomes single-spaced.

**4.** Place the insertion point anywhere in the fourth paragraph.

**5.** Choose **Paragraph** from the **Format** menu. The Format Paragraph dialog box appears.

**6.** Click the **Spacing** tab. The Spacing section appears, as in Figure 4-11.

**7.** Double-click in the **After** box. The contents become highlighted.

**8.** Key **1**. Click **OK.** Works places a blank line after the fourth paragraph.

**9.** Save the document. Leave the file open for the next activity.

**FIGURE 4-11**
The Spacing section of the Format Paragraph dialog box allows you to set spacing.

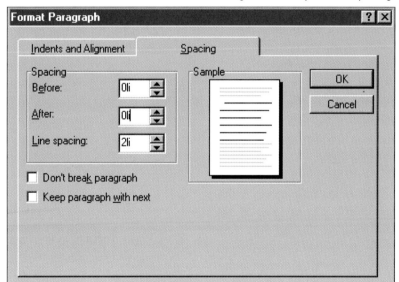

# *Tabs*

*Tabs* mark the place the insertion point will stop when the Tab key is pressed. Tabs are useful for creating tables or aligning numbered items. Default tab stops in Works are set every half inch. Text can be aligned, however, with decimal, left-aligned, right-aligned, or centered tabs, as shown in Figure 4-12. Notice that different tab symbols appear over the different types of tab settings.

**FIGURE 4-12**

Use tabs to align columns in a table or list.

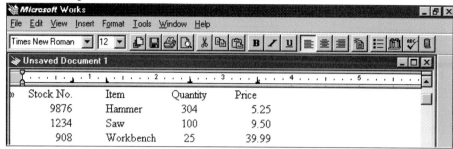

**ACTIVITY**

# 4-10 Setting Tabs

In this activity, you will set different tab stops. *Mountain* should be on your screen.

1.  Place the insertion point after the period following *27,923 ft.* in the table. Press **Enter.** Notice the tab markers on the ruler. These markers indicate that the tabs in the table have already been preset. You will now key the last entry in the table.

2.  Press **Tab.** The insertion point moves to the decimal tab stop at 0.8 inches. Key **5**. Remember to key a period after the *5*.

3.  Press **Tab.** The insertion point moves to the left-aligned tab stop at 1.2 inches. Key **Makalu 1**.

4.  Press **Tab.** Again, the insertion point moves to a left-aligned tab stop at 2.4 inches. Key **Nepal/China**.

5.  Press **Tab.** The insertion point moves to the right-aligned tab stop at 4.2 inches. Key **27,824 ft.** Remember to key a period after *ft.*

6.  Now you will insert your own tab stops to create column headings for the table. Place the insertion point after the period following the word *world* at the end of the sixth paragraph.

7.  Press **Enter.**

8.  Choose **Tabs** from the **Format** menu. The Format Tabs dialog box appears, as in Figure 4-13. The Tabs dialog box allows you to specify exactly where you want each column head to begin.

9.  Insert tab stops following these steps:
    a.  In the box under Tab stop position, key **1.2**. Click **Set.** Works inserts a left-aligned tab stop on the ruler.

**FIGURE 4-13**

The Tabs dialog box allows you to specify exactly where you want your tab stops.

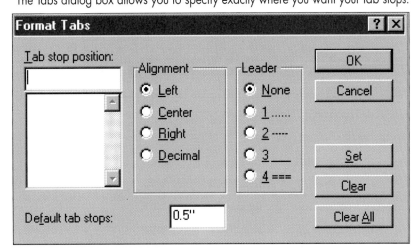

**b.** Key **2.9**. Choose **Center** in the Alignment box. Click **Set.** Works inserts a centered tab stop on the ruler.

**c.** Key **4.2.** Choose **Right** in the Alignment box. Click **Set.** Works inserts a right-aligned tab stop on the ruler. Click **OK.**

**10.** Create the column headings following these steps:

**a.** Press **Tab.** Click the **Underline** button on the toolbar. Key **Mountain**. Click the **Underline** button to discontinue using the underline style font. Remember that selecting an option that is already on will turn off that option. If you do not turn off Underline, the underline will trail across the screen to the next tab.

**b.** Press **Tab.** Click the **Underline** button on the toolbar. Key **Location**. Click the **Underline** button again.

**c.** Press **Tab.** Click the **Underline** button on the toolbar. Key **Height**. Click the **Underline** button to turn off Underline.

**11.** You will notice that the column headings are not centered over the columns. Works allows you to drag tab markers to fine-tune the alignment of text. Drag the left-aligned tab marker to the right until the *Mountain* column heading appears centered over the column.

**12.** Drag the centered tab stop to fine-tune the alignment of the *Location* column heading.

**13.** Drag the insertion point to the left until the *Height* column heading appears centered over the column. The table should now include an added entry and underlined column headings centered above the columns, as in Figure 4-14.

**14.** Save the document. Leave the file open for the next activity.

**FIGURE 4-14**
Works allows you to fine-tune alignment by dragging tabs.

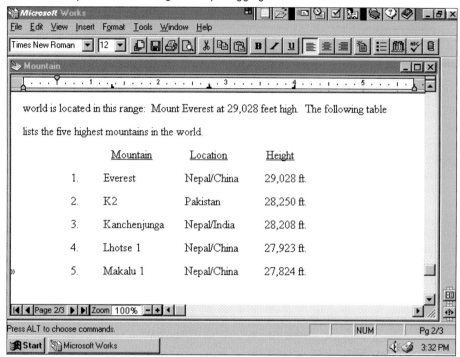

# *Page Breaks*

*>> page marker begin of next page*

**W**hen a document has more text than will fit on one page, Works must select a place in the document to end one page and begin the next. The place where one page ends and another begins is called a ***page break.*** Works automatically inserts page breaks where they are necessary. You may also insert a page break manually. You would want to insert a page break manually when an automatic page break separates a heading from the text that follows it. To insert a page break manually, select Page Break from the Insert menu or press Ctrl+Enter.

An automatic page break is indicated by a small symbol at the left side of the screen, }}. This symbol points to the first line of the next page. A page break that is inserted manually is indicated with a dotted line across the screen.

# ACTIVITY

## 4-11 Inserting Page Breaks

In this activity, you will insert a page break. *Mountain* should be on your screen.

1.  Place the insertion point after the period following the last word in the sixth paragraph of the document.

2.  Choose **Page Break** from the **Insert** menu. The dotted line indicates that a page break has been inserted, as shown in Figure 4-15. The table is now on page 3 of the document.

3.  Save the document. Leave the file open for the next activity.

**FIGURE 4-15**

A dotted line across the screen indicates that a page break has been inserted manually.

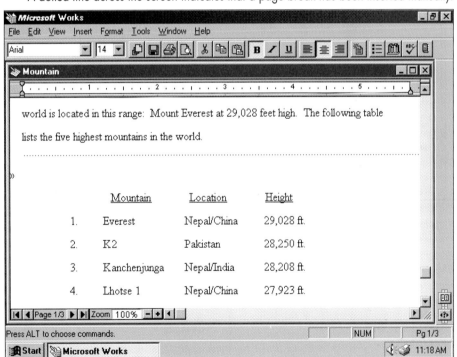

# Using the Spelling Checker

**W**orks contains a dictionary of more than 100,000 words to check the spelling of words in your document. You can check an entire document or portions of the document by using the Spelling button on the toolbar or by choosing the Spelling command in the Tools menu.

The Spelling dialog box shown in Figure 4-16 contains options that allow you to check the spelling of words, ignore words, change misspelled words, or add words to your own custom dictionary. Table 4-3 explains each of the available options. The dictionary checks spelling only. It will not find grammatical errors.

**FIGURE 4-16**
The Spelling dialog box contains several options for checking the spelling of a document.

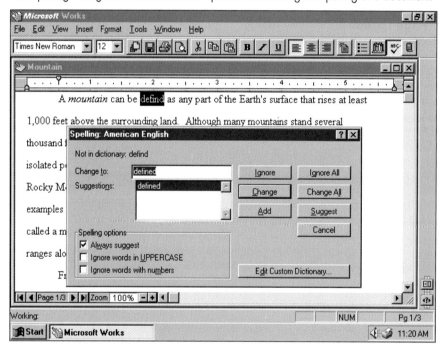

**TABLE 4-3**
Spelling Dialog Box Options

| OPERATION | ACTION |
| --- | --- |
| Ignore | Ignores only the highlighted word |
| Ignore All | Ignores all instances of the same word |
| Change | Changes only the highlighted word |
| Change All | Changes all instances of the same word |
| Add | Adds the highlighted word to the custom dictionary |
| Suggest | Displays a list of proposed spellings |

# ACTIVITY

# 4-12 Checking a Document's Spelling

In this activity, you will check your document for spelling errors. *Mountain* should be on your screen.

1. Press **Ctrl+Home** to move the insertion point to the beginning of the document.

2. Press the **Spelling Checker** button on the toolbar.

3. The word *defind* is highlighted in the text and the Spelling dialog box appears. (If it covers up the misspelled word, you can drag the dialog box to a more convenient place on your screen.) Note that the misspelled word also appears in the Change to box. The word *defined* is suggested. Click **Change.** Works replaces the misspelled word and continues checking.

4. The word *Mountens* is highlighted. The word *Mountains* is suggested. Click **Change.** Works replaces the misspelled word and continues checking.

5. The word *asia* is highlighted and the Spelling

dialog box notes that this is an irregular capitalization error. Click **Change.** Works replaces the error and continues checking.

6. Several proper names and technical words will appear that are not in the Spelling Checker dictionary. They are all spelled correctly. Click **Ignore All** after each one until the next spelling error appears.

7. The word *worldd* is highlighted. Click **Change.** Works replaces the error and continues checking.

8. Press **Ignore All** to ignore each of the remaining proper names.

9. A message will appear indicating that Works has finished checking for spelling errors. Click **OK.** The insertion point returns to the beginning of the document.

10. Save the document. Leave the file open for the next activity.

# *Using the Thesaurus*

The 200,000-word Works *Thesaurus* is a useful feature for finding a synonym, or a word with a similar meaning, for a word in your document. The Thesaurus command is in the Tools menu.

• • • • • • • • • • • • • • • • • • • • • • • • • • • • • • • •

In this activity, you will find a synonym using the Works Thesaurus. *Mountain* should be on your screen.

1. Place the insertion point on the word *tiny* in the second sentence of the first paragraph.

2. Choose **Thesaurus** from the **Tools** menu. The Thesaurus dialog box appears, as in Figure 4-17. The box under Meanings contains a list of the meanings of *tiny*. The box under Replace with synonym contains a list of synonyms for *tiny*.

3. Choose **small** in the **Replace with synonym** box.

4. Click **Replace.** Works replaces the word *tiny* with *small*.

5. Save the document.

6. Click the **Print** button on the toolbar to print the entire document.

7. Close the file.

**FIGURE 4-17**
The Thesaurus dialog box contains a list of meanings and synonyms for a selected word or phrase.

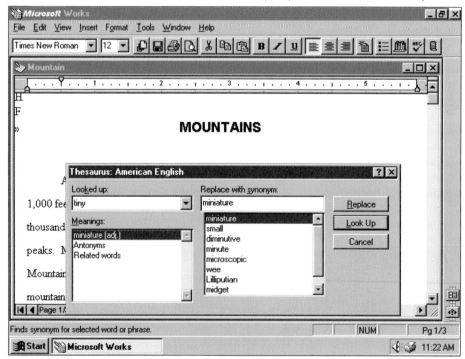

# *Summary*

■ The Undo command is useful for restoring the most recent formatting and editing changes. Although Works provides default margins for a page, margins can be changed to suit a particular type of document you are creating.

■ The term *font* refers to the shape of the characters belonging to a particular family of type. Fonts can be chosen by using the toolbar or the Font and Style command in the Format menu. Fonts can appear in a number of sizes and standard type styles, such as bold, italic, or underline. You can change the color of text in the Format Font and Style dialog box.

■ Indenting the first line or the left and right sides of a paragraph can alter the paragraph's appearance. Indents can be changed by moving the indent markers on the ruler or by using the Paragraph command in the Format menu. Text can be centered, aligned right, aligned left, or justified. Line spacing can be adjusted to leave no space, one space, or a specified amount of space between lines of text. Paragraph spacing can be adjusted to change space between paragraphs of text. Tabs are useful for creating tables and aligning numbered items. A manual page break can be inserted to control where Works breaks the text into pages.

■ Works contains a dictionary of more than 100,000 words. The Spelling command corrects capitalization and spelling errors. The Spelling command, however, will not correct grammatical errors. The Works Thesaurus is a useful synonym finder for a variety of words.

● ● ● ● ● ● ● ● ● ● ● ● ● ●

# REVIEW ACTIVITIES

## TRUE/FALSE

**Circle T or F to show whether the statement is true or false.**

(T)  F     **1.** The Undo command can correct only the most recent change you have made to your document.

(T)  F     **2.** The Page Setup dialog box is accessed through the File menu.

T  (F)     **3.** The style and size of a document's fonts can be changed only by using the toolbar.  *Font*  *toolbar*

(T)  F     **4.** An indent in which the first line of text begins at the left margin and the remaining lines are indented is called a hanging indent.

T  (F)     **5.** Justified text is ragged on the right margin.

T  (F)     **6.** By default, Works double-spaces text.  *SINGLE space*  *Right left tabs*

(T)  F     **7.** The Tabs dialog box contains four options for aligning tabs.

T  (F)     **8.** A page break can be inserted by pressing Ctrl+Insert on the keyboard.

T  (F)     **9.** The Spelling command is useful for checking grammatical errors involving word usage.  *use WORD to correct grammatical error*

*Tools* T  (F)     **10.** The Thesaurus command is found on the Insert menu.

## COMPLETION

**Write the correct answer in the space provided.**

**1.** Through which menu is the Undo command accessed?

     *EDIT*

**2.** What term describes the space between the edge of a page and the printed or written text in a document?

     *margin*

**3.** What are the small lines at the ends of some characters called?

     *Serif*  *SANS serif*

**4.** What are the units of measurement that determine type size?

     *Points*

5. Name four ways that text can be aligned.

   *left, right centered*
   *justified*

6. What key is pressed to move the insertion point to the next tab stop?

   *TAB key*

7. If no tab stops are set, where does Works place default tab stops?

   *every half inch*

8. Through which menu is the Page Break command accessed?

   *INSERT*

9. What is the purpose of the Change button in the Spelling dialog box?

   *corrects spelling so you can change a work that may fit better*

10. What type of word is the Thesaurus useful for finding?

    *SYNONYN*

*application 4-1*

**Refer to Figure 4-18 and match the letter of the toolbar or ruler part with the name of the item given below.**

_C_ 1. Italic button

_I_ 2. Underline button

_D_ 3. Center Align button

_F_ 4. Right-indent marker

_A_ 5. Font Name box

_G_ 6. Right Align button

_J_ 7. Bold button

_K_ 8. Left-indent marker

_B_ 9. Font Size box

_H_ 10. Left Align button

_E_ 11. Spelling Checker button

_L_ 12. First-line indent marker

**FIGURE 4-18**
The toolbar and the ruler

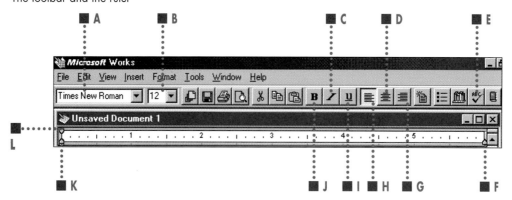

# application  4 - 2

**In this application, you will change the font and font size in a document.**

1. Open *Application 4-2* from your template disk.

2. Select the uppercase and lowercase characters.

3. Change the font to the first font in the Font box.

4. Set the font to 24 point (or largest size available if largest size is smaller than 24) in the Font Size box.

5. Look closely at the font to determine if it is a serif or sans serif font. Record the name of the font and whether it is serif or sans serif on a sheet of paper.

6. Repeat for each font available in the Font box.

7. Close the document. Do not save the document.

# application  4 - 3

**In this application, you will format a document from your template disk.**

1. Open *Application 4-3* from your template disk.

2. Change the font of the document to Times New Roman. If Times New Roman is not available on your computer, choose another serif font.

3. Change the left and right margins to 1.5 inches.

4. Center the title of the document: *Briarcliff High School Update.* Change the size of the font to 16 point. Use italic and boldface styles for the title.

5. Change the color of the title to Blue.

6. Place the insertion point below the title after the words *Briarcliff High School.* Set a centered tab at 3 inches and a right-aligned tab at 5.5 inches.

7. On the same line as the words *Briarcliff High School,* key **Volume 4, No. 7** at the 3-inch tab stop. Key **April 10, 19--** at the 5.5-inch tab stop.

8. Boldface each paragraph heading.

9. Left-justify the first paragraph.

10. Check the spelling of the document.

11. Save the finished document on your data disk as *update*.

12. Preview and print the document.

# application 4-4

**In this application, you will format a document from your template disk.**

1. Open *Application 4-4* from the template disk.

2. Highlight the title of the document.

3. Change the font to Arial 14 point. Boldface and center the title.

4. For the first two paragraphs, create paragraph indents (first-line indents) of .5 inches.

5. Indent the quotation (and the person's name who said the quote) that begins *"Someday..."* .5 inches on the left and right margins.

6. Right align the name of the person who said the quote, *--William....*

7. Create paragraph indents of .5 inches for the next two paragraphs.

8. Indent the quotation (and the person's name who said it) that begins, *"I would be..."* .5 inches on the left and right margins.

9. Right align the name of the person who said the quote.

10. Create hanging indents of .5 inches for the remaining two paragraphs.

11. Double-space the entire document.

12. Single-space the two quotations. (Include the name of the person who said it.)

13. Change the top margin to 1.5 inches, the bottom margin to 1.25 inches, and the left and right margins to 1.5 inches.

14. Insert a manual page break before the paragraph that starts, *There are a number....*

15. Use the Thesaurus to find a synonym for the word *humans* in the first sentence.

16. Save the document as *space* on your data disk.

17. Print and close the document.

# CREATING PROFESSIONAL-LOOKING DOCUMENTS

## CHAPTER 5

## OBJECTIVES

**When you complete this chapter, you will be able to:**

1. Use columns.

2. Add graphics to a document using Draw and insert clip art.

3. Scale and wrap text around graphics.

4. Add borders and shading to paragraphs and add borders to pages.

5. Create and use templates.

# Using Columns

Sometimes a document can be more effective if the text is in multiple columns. A newsletter is an example of a document that often has two or more columns. Columns are easy to create in Works. The entire document, except for the headers and footers, will be made into columns. All you have to do is specify the number of columns you want and how much space you want between the columns. You can also specify whether you want a line separating the columns. Columns are created using the Columns dialog box, shown in Figure 5-1.

The columns will not appear side by side in Normal view mode. To see the columns side by side, switch to Page Layout view. When columns are defined, you will be prompted to change to Page Layout view.

**FIGURE 5-1**
The Columns dialog box allows you to specify
how many columns you want in your document.

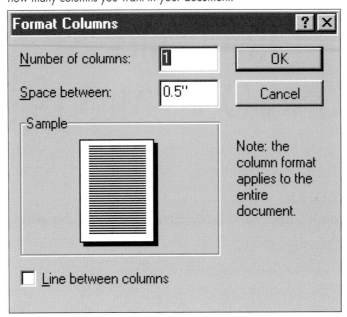

# 5-1 Creating Columns in a Document

In this activity, you will create two columns in a document.

1. Open *Activity 5-1* from your template disk.

2. Use Print Preview to view the document. Click **Cancel** to return to your document.

3. Choose **Columns** from the **Format** menu. The Format Columns dialog box appears.

4. Key **2** in the **Number of columns** box. Make sure the **Line between columns** option is checked. Click **OK.** A message

will appear asking if you would like to switch to Page Layout view.

5. Click **Yes.** The document is shown in two columns.

6. If the *E* is at the bottom of the left column, place the insertion point in front of it and press **Enter** enough times to force the *E* heading to the second column.

7. Save the document on your data disk as *columns*. Print and close the document.

# *Drawing Graphics Using Microsoft Draw*

**T**he word processor allows you to enhance documents by adding graphics. *Graphics* are pictures that help illustrate the meaning of the text, make the page more attractive, or make the page more functional. Works includes a drawing program, Microsoft Draw, to enable you to add drawings to your documents.

Figure 5-2 shows a document created with Works. The letter takes a professional appearance with the addition of a letterhead that includes wrapped gifts created in Draw.

**FIGURE 5-2**

The gift graphics created in Draw are a great addition to this letterhead.

*Festive Gift Wrap Service*
9025 Holiday Drive
Tucson, Arizona 87077
405-555-Wrap

June 30, 19--

Mr. Alan Wordarski
P.O. Box 56
Tucson, AZ 87520

Dear Mr. Wodarski:

We are pleased to announce the expansion of our store on Holiday Drive. At our newly decrorated facility, you'll still receive the same quality customer service you expect. And, we're pleased to bring you new products and services that we think will help you relax and enjoy the many special occasions and events in your busy life. These new products and services include the following:

- Party Planning Coordinator
- Party Supplies by Parties Etc.
- Greeting Cards by New Dimension
- Balloon Bouquets
- Gift Baskets

We have enjoyed serving you in the past, and we look forward to serving you in the future. Please don't hesitate to call if you have any questions regarding our products and services.

Sincerely,

Bob and Barbara Bennigan
Owners

## Starting Draw

Before you start Draw, you need to place the insertion point at the location where you want the finished graphic to appear. This is because you will actually leave the word processor document window, create the graphic in the Draw window, and then return to the word processor window. The graphic you create will automatically appear at the insertion point location. For example, if you want the graphic to appear at the top of the document, move the insertion point to the left of the first character in the document. If you want the graphic inserted between two paragraphs, place the insertion point on a blank line between them. When you are ready to create your graphic, choose Drawing from the Insert menu.

## Starting Draw

In this activity, you will create a new document, position the insertion point, and start Draw.

1. Create a new word processor document.

2. Key **This is above the drawing.** (Key the period.)

3. Press **Enter** twice.

4. Key **This is below the drawing.** (Key the period.)

5. Position the insertion point on the blank line between the two lines of text.

6. Choose **Drawing** from the **Insert** menu. A Microsoft Drawing window similar to that shown in Figure 5-3 appears. On your screen, the Draw window may appear in a different size or position than in Figure 5-3.

7. Leave the Draw window open for the next activity.

**FIGURE 5-3**

The Draw window appears in front of your document.

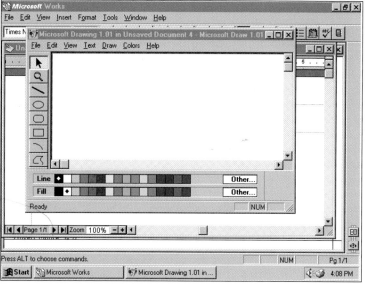

## The Draw Window

Figure 5-4 illustrates the parts of the Draw window. The Toolbox holds tools for drawing lines, rectangles, circles, and more (see Table 5-1). At the bottom of the window is a color palette that you can use to add color to the shapes you draw. Across the top of the window are menus that provide other options. You'll explore these options further in the activities in this chapter.

**FIGURE 5-4**

The Draw window provides the tools for drawing graphics.

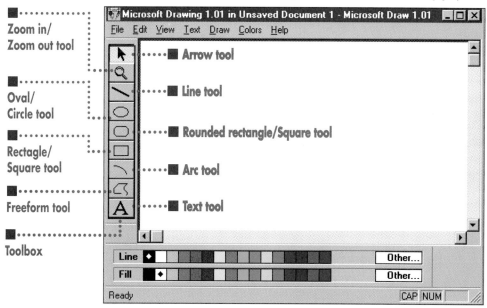

**TABLE 5-1**
Summary of the Drawing Tools That Appear in the Toolbox

| TOOL NAME | FUNCTION |
|---|---|
| Arrow tool | Lets you select and manipulate objects. To use, click on the arrow. The insertion point will assume the pointer shape. |
| Zoom In/Zoom Out tool | Changes the magnification of a drawing. To use, click on the magnifying glass and drag it to the area of your drawing you want to enlarge. Clicking while holding the Shift key will reverse the magnification. |
| Line tool | Draws straight lines. To use, position the pointer where you want the line to begin, then click and hold the mouse button and drag to where you want the line to end. |
| Oval/Circle tool | Draws ovals and circles. To use, click and hold the mouse button, then drag to draw the oval or circle. To force the object to be a perfect circle, hold down the Shift key as you drag. |
| Rounded Rectangle/ Square tool | Draws rectangles and squares with rounded corners. To use, click and hold the mouse button, then drag to draw. To force the object to be a perfect square with rounded corners, hold down the Shift key as you drag. |
| Rectangle/Square tool | Draws rectangles and squares. To use, click and hold the mouse button, then drag to draw. To force the object to be a perfect square, hold down the Shift key as you drag. |
| Arc tool | Draws arcs. To use, click and hold the mouse button, then drag to draw. |
| Freeform tool | Draws polygons and freehand objects. To draw straight sections, click at each endpoint or vertex. To draw free hand, drag. You can mix straight sections and freehand drawing in the same object. |
| Text tool | Allows you to include text with your drawing. |

## ACTIVITY

## 5-3 Drawing a Graphic

• • • • • • • • • • • • • • • • • • • • • • • • • • • • • • •

In this activity, you will create a simple drawing.

1. Click the **Rectangle/Square** tool.

2. Move the pointer to the work area.

3. Press and hold the mouse button and drag to draw a rectangle about 1 inch tall and

2 inches wide. Release the mouse button when you're satisfied with your rectangle.

4. Click the **Oval/Circle** tool.

5. Move the pointer to the left of the rectangle you just drew.

6. Draw a circle with a diameter of about 1 inch.

7. Leave the Draw window open for the next activity.

## Selecting an Object

When you first drew the objects in Activity 5-3, you probably noticed the little squares that appeared at the edges of the graphic when you released the mouse button. These small squares are called *handles.* They indicate that the object is selected and allow you to manipulate the selected object. As soon as you choose another tool, the selection handles around an object disappear. Before you can copy, move, delete, or otherwise manipulate an object, you will have to select it.

To select an object, you use the Arrow tool. When you choose the Arrow tool, the insertion point becomes an arrow pointer. Click on the object you want to select. The selection handles appear around the object, and you can now manipulate the object.

To deselect an object, click on another object or anywhere in the drawing window.

## Resizing an Object

Handles do more than indicate that an object is selected. They also allow you to resize an object. Often during the process of creating a drawing, you will realize that the line, rectangle, or circle you just drew isn't quite the right size. Resizing is easy. You simply select the object to make the handles appear, and then drag the handles inward or outward to make the object smaller or larger.

ACTIVITY

 **Selecting, Resizing, and Moving Objects**

• • • • • • • • • • • • • • • • • • • • • • • • • • • • • • • • • •

In this activity, you will select and resize the objects you drew in Activity 5-3.

1. Click the **Arrow** tool and select the rectangle.

2. Drag the upper right handle of the rectangle

to enlarge it until it measures about 2 inches tall and 3 inches wide.

3. Select the circle. Now you will move the circle into the rectangle. Place the Arrow pointer anywhere inside the circle, hold down the mouse button, and drag the circle

to its new position. When you release the mouse button, the selection handles will reappear.

4. By dragging the circle's handles, resize it

until it becomes an oval that fits snugly inside the rectangle.

5. Leave the Draw window open for the next activity.

## Returning to the Word Processor

When you are satisfied with your graphic, exit Draw and return to the word processor. Works will ask you if you want to update your word processor file. If you say yes, your graphic will appear at the insertion point in your document.

ACTIVITY

## Returning to the Word Processor

In this activity, you will exit Draw and return to the word processor.

1. In the Draw window, choose **Exit and Return** from the **File** menu. A dialog box appears asking if you want to save changes to your document.

2. Click **Yes.** The Draw window closes. Your document should look similar to Figure 5-5.

**FIGURE 5-5**
When you exit Draw, the graphic is inserted in your document.

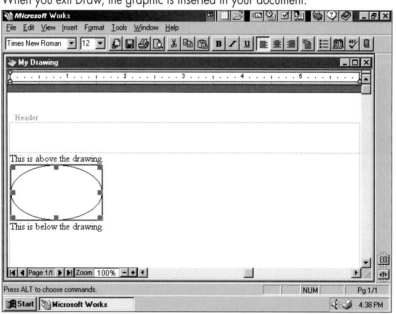

**3.** Save the file on your data disk as *My Drawing.*

**4.** Print and close the document.

# *Working in Draw*

**D**raw provides many features for working with drawings. In this section, you will learn about some of the more important features.

## Selecting More Than One Object

Sometimes you will want to select more than one object. Works gives you two ways to select more than one object. The first is called *shift-clicking.* The second method is to draw a selection box around a group of objects.

### SHIFT-CLICKING

To shift-click, hold down the Shift key and click each of the objects you want to select. Use shift-clicking when you need to select objects that are not close to each other or when the objects you need to select are near other objects you do not want to select. If you select an object by accident, click it again to deselect it.

### DRAWING A SELECTION BOX

Using the Arrow tool, you can drag a selection box around a group of objects. Objects included in the selection box will be selected. Use a selection box when all of the objects you want selected are near each other and can be surrounded with a box. Be sure your selection box is large enough to enclose all the selection handles of the various objects. If you miss a handle, that item will not be selected.

### COMBINING METHODS

You can also combine these two methods. First, use the selection box, then shift-click to include objects that the selection box may have missed.

## Grouping Objects

As your drawing becomes more complex, you will find it necessary to "glue" objects together into groups. Grouping objects allows you to work with more than one object as though they were one object. To group objects, select the objects you want to group and choose Group from the Draw menu. Objects can be ungrouped using the Ungroup command.

## Grid Snap

One of the most difficult parts of drawing with a computer drawing program is aligning and sizing objects. To help with this problem, Draw provides an invisible grid on your screen. Objects automatically align to the nearest grid line. This feature is called *grid snap.* This makes it easy, for example, to draw three lines that are an equal distance apart. You can place each line one grid distance from the next. The result is perfectly spaced lines.

There will be times, however, when you will want to place an object more precisely. For example, when you are drawing the details on your graphic, grid snap may not allow you to place two objects as close together as you would like. To allow for more precise alignment, the program provides a way to turn off grid snap. The Draw menu has a command called Snap to Grid. Choosing the Snap to Grid command will toggle grid snap on or off. If the command has a check mark by it when you pull down the menu, grid snap is on.

## Layering

In Draw, each object you create can be changed, moved, or deleted at any time. This is an advantage of drawing on a computer rather than on paper. The computer will allow you to lift your mistakes right off the screen and try again. The objects you create with Draw are laid on top of each other. When you create an object, it is placed on top of other objects that already have been drawn. Sometimes you will need to rearrange the order in which objects are layered. Draw provides two commands for doing this: Send to Back and Bring to Front. Both commands are in the Edit menu. The Send to Back command moves the selected object or objects to the bottom layer. The Bring to Front command moves the selected object or objects to the top layer.

## Cutting, Copying, Pasting, and Deleting Objects

Objects can be cut, copied, and pasted like text. The Cut and Copy commands place a copy of the selected image on the Clipboard. Pasting an object from the Clipboard places the object in the Draw window. You can then move it into position.

You can easily delete an object by selecting it and pressing the Delete key.

## Exploring Draw on Your Own

Other features are available when you are creating your own drawings. You may want to experiment with the menu commands not presented in this chapter. Use the Help menu if you need some additional instruction.

# *Inserting Clip Art*

You may sometimes want to use art from another source rather than drawing it yourself. Graphics that are already drawn and available for use in documents are called *clip art.* Clip art libraries offer artwork of common objects that can speed up and possibly improve the quality of your work. Figure 5-6 illustrates how clip art adds flair to an immunizations poster. To insert clip art, choose ClipArt from the Insert menu. The Microsoft ClipArt Gallery 2.0 will appear with many different clip art images. You can even add clip art from other sources to the ClipArt Gallery. To insert an image from the Gallery, simply click on the one you want and choose Insert. The image will appear on your screen at the location of your insertion point.

**FIGURE 5-6**
Clip art adds a professional look to this poster.

# FREE Immunizations
# for Children under 2

## Saturday, September 7
## 10 a.m. to 4 p.m.

**Children's Health Services**
**195 Elk Crossing**

Although the graphics you import are already created, you can alter the way they appear on the page. When you resize a graphic, the length and width may not maintain the same proportions. To change the size of, or *scale* of, a graphic so that its proportions are correct, you can choose Picture from the Format menu. The Format Picture dialog box appears where you can key in an exact size or percentages of length and width scale.

# ACTIVITY
## 5-6 Inserting and Scaling Clip Art

In this activity, you will insert a piece of clip art from the Works program.

1. Open *Activity 5-6* from your template disk. The document opens in Page Layout view.

2. Scroll down to the last paragraph of the document. Place the insertion point before the first word in the last paragraph.

3. Choose **Clip**A**rt** from the **Insert** menu. The Microsoft ClipArt Gallery 2.0 appears.

If you've not used the clip art before, follow the instructions given in the two dialog boxes that appear and load the clip art.

4. Under Categories, click **Academic.**

5. Click the picture of the red books, as shown in Figure 5-7. At the bottom of the window beside *Description* is the word *Books.* Your screen may show more clip art than in Figure 5-7.

**FIGURE 5-7**
Microsoft ClipArt Gallery 2.0 allows you to easily insert a clip art picture.

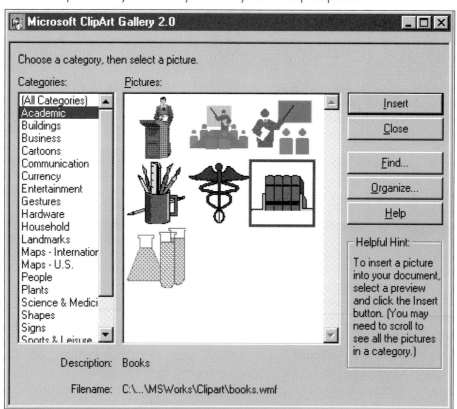

6. Click **Insert.**

7. Scale the size of the clip art by choosing **Pictu̲re** from the **Forma̲t** menu. The Format Picture dialog box appears.

8. Click the **Size** tab. In the Scaling box (NOT the Size box) beside Width, key **105**.

9. Key **105** beside Height in the Scaling box. Click one time in the Size, Height entry. In the Size box, make sure the measurements there are approximately 1.65″ beside Width and .95″ beside Height. If your measurements are different, key these height and width measurements in the Size box. The 105 percentage you keyed in the Scaling box may change.

10. Click **OK.** The size of the clip art should be about the same as that shown in Figure 5-8.

11. Save the document on your data disk as *BHS Update.*

12. Leave the document open for the next activity.

**FIGURE 5-8**
Scaling clip art allows you to keep the original proportions.

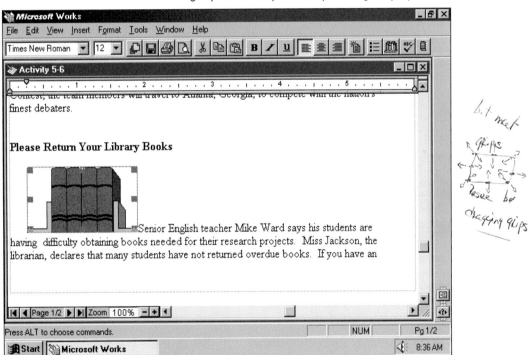

# *Wrapping Text Around Graphics*

In the activities up to this point, you inserted a graphic into the text and scaled it. As text is added or deleted, the graphic moves with the text. You can, however, place a graphic at a position on the page and have the text wrap around the graphic.

To make text wrap around a graphic, select the graphic and choose Format Picture from the Format menu. The Format Picture dialog box has a Text Wrap section (see Figure 5-9) that allows you to specify that the graphic be given an absolute position.

**FIGURE 5-9**
The Text Wrap section of the Format Picture dialog box allows you to specify whether your graphic will be inserted in a position in the text or placed at an absolute position on the page.

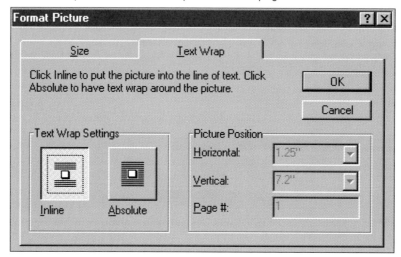

## Wrapping Text Around Graphics

In this activity, you will make text wrap around the clip art you inserted in the previous activity.

1. Click on the graphic of the book. Selection handles appear around the graphic.

2. Choose **Text Wrap** from the **Format** menu. The Format Picture dialog box appears.

3. Click the **Absolute** button in the Text Wrap

Settings box. Click **OK.** The text wraps around the graphic.

4. Drag the graphic down and to the left until your screen appears similar to Figure 5-10.

5. Use Print Preview to view the page as it will print.

6. Save the document. Leave the document open for the next activity.

**FIGURE 5-10**
Dragging the graphic causes the text to realign itself around the new position.

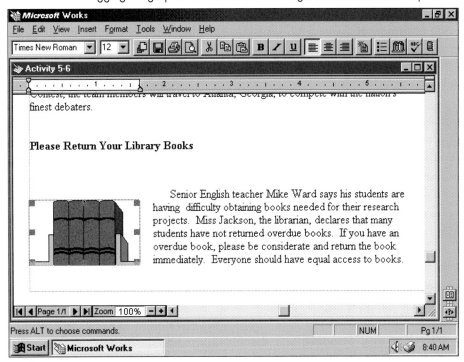

# *Adding Borders and Shading*

**B**orders and shading add interest and emphasis to text. However, be sure to use them sparingly and wisely. Too many borders or shades on a page can make it look cluttered and hard to read.

## Adding Borders to Paragraphs

Borders are single, double, or thick lines around a paragraph that are used to emphasize the text. You can even choose a color for your border in the Borders and Shading dialog box. For example, you might want to place a blue thick-lined border around the title of a document. You can place a border on any side of a paragraph, or you can completely surround the paragraph with a box.

## Adding Shading to Paragraphs

You can also add shading—grays or colors—to paragraphs or lines of text. Simply highlight the text you want to shade and access the Borders and Shading dialog box. From here, you can choose the pattern you want and the foreground and background colors.

## Adding Borders to Pages

Just as you can add borders to paragraphs, you can add borders to entire pages. In the Borders and Shading dialog box, you can choose the line style and color of border that you want. You can even place the border at any distance from the edge of the page, such as 1 inch.

## Adding Borders and Shading

In this activity, you will add borders to paragraphs and pages and add shading to text. *BHS Update* should be on your screen.

1. Place the insertion point in the title of the document, *Briarcliff High School Update*.

2. Choose **Borders and Shading** from the **Format** menu. The Borders and Shading dialog box appears, as shown in Figure 5-11.

3. Choose **Outline** in the Border box. Click the thin double-line style (at the top of the second column) in the Line style box.

4. In the Color box, choose **Red.** Click **OK.** A red double-lined border is placed around the title of the document, as shown in Figure 5-12.

**FIGURE 5-11**
The Borders and Shading dialog box allows you to change the style of the borders.

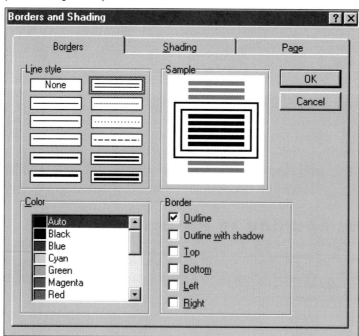

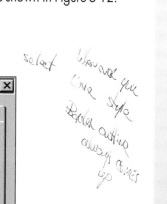

**FIGURE 5-12**
Borders are useful when you want to emphasize text.

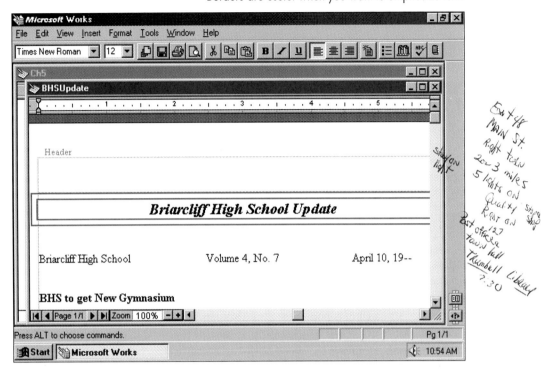

5. Highlight the line of text below the title, which contains the volume number and date.

6. Choose **Borders and Shading** from the **Format** menu. The Borders and Shading dialog box appears.

7. Click the **Shading** tab. In the Shading box, click the fourth pattern from the top. At the bottom of the Shading box under *Description, 25%* will appear.

8. In the Foreground color box, choose **Blue.** In the Background color box, choose **White.** Click **OK.** The line now contains a blue 25% pattern (called a screen) shade.

9. Choose **Borders and Shading** from the **Format** menu. The Borders and Shading dialog box appears.

10. Click the **Page** tab. In the Line style box, click the thick line style at the bottom of the first column.

11. In the Color box, choose **Blue.**

12. In the Distance from page edge box beside Left/right, click the down arrow until **0.5"** appears in the box. Beside Top/bottom, click the down arrow until **0.5"** appears in the box.

13. Click **OK.** A blue border appears around the page.

14. Scroll back to the bottom of the document and check the text around the graphic. Adding the borders caused a slight shift in the text that may change the way the text wraps around the graphic. Adjust the graphic's position if necessary.

**15.** Print the document. Remember that unless you have access to a color printer, your borders and shades will print in black or gray.

**16.** Save and close the document.

# *Using Templates*

**S**uppose you are a traveling sales representative and you must file a report each week that summarizes your sales and the new contacts you have made. Parts of this report will be the same each week, such as the document's format and the headings within the report. It would be tedious to recreate the document each week. Works solves this problem by allowing you to create a template for documents that you use frequently. A template is like a blank form that you can fill in with new information each time you open it. A report template would save all formatting, font choices, and text that does not change, allowing you to fill in only the new information each week. Templates are not limited to the word processor. Spreadsheets and databases also can be saved as templates.

Do not confuse the Works templates with the template disk that you use with this book. Both use the word template because they both involve taking an unfinished document and completing it.

## Creating a Template

Creating your own template is easy. Any document you have can be made into a template. The Save As dialog box includes a Template button. Click the button and you will be prompted to enter a name for the template. The template will be available in the TaskWizards section of the Task Launcher under User Defined Templates.

**ACTIVITY**

# *5-9* Creating a Letterhead Template

In this activity, you will create a letterhead template.

**1.** Create a new word processor document.

**2.** Choose **ClipArt** from the **Insert** menu. The Microsoft ClipArt Gallery appears.

**3.** Under Categories, scroll down and click **Plants.**

**4.** Click on the picture of the red tulips and click **Insert.**

5. Click the **Center Align** button on the toolbar to center the graphic.

6. Select the graphic and choose **Pictu̲re** from the **F̲ormat** menu. The Format Picture dialog box appears.

7. Key **33** in the **Scaling Width** box. Key **34** in the **Scaling Height** box. Click one time in the **Size, Height** box. Make sure the Height is 1.17″ and the Width is 1.36″. If your measurements are different, key these measurements in the Size, Height and Width entries. Click **OK.** The graphic is scaled down so that it will be the appropriate size for use in a letterhead.

8. Using whatever fonts are available to you, create a letterhead like the one illustrated in Figure 5-13.

**FIGURE 5-13**
A letterhead makes a useful template.

**9.** When you finish creating the letterhead, choose **Save As** from the **File** menu.

**10.** Click the **Template** button. The Save As Template dialog box appears, as shown in Figure 5-14.

**11.** Key **Flower Letterhead XXX** (replace XXX with your initials) as the template name. Click **OK.**

**12.** Close the document on the screen. Do not save the changes.

**FIGURE 5-14**
The Save As Template dialog box allows you to add a template to the User Defined Templates in the Task Launcher.

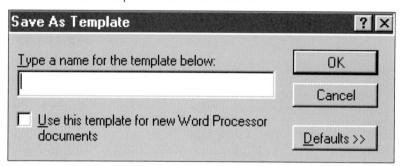

You can use the template you created as many times as needed. In the next activity, you will create a new document using the letterhead template and save the document.

# ACTIVITY
# 5-10  Using the Letterhead Template

In this activity, you will use the letterhead template you created in the previous activity.

**1.** The Task Launcher should be on your screen.

**2.** Click the **TaskWizards** tab.

**3.** Scroll down and click on **User Defined Templates.**

**4.** Double-click on *Flower Letterhead XXX.* The letterhead appears on the screen.

**5.** Key the letter in Figure 5-15.

**6.** Save the document on your data disk as *Flower Letter.*

**7.** Print and close the document.

**FIGURE 5-15**
Using a template, you can create a professional-looking letter in a short time.

**Beautiful Flowers Unlimited**
101 Green Street
San Antonio, Texas 78227
Phone: 210-555-1234  Fax: 210-555-1255

October 13, 19--


Mrs. Julie Reveiz
1971 Industrial way
Miami, FL 33100

Dear Mrs. Reveiz:

Thank you for your request for information regarding tulip bulbs. Tulips are beautiful
flowers available in many different colors, as you will see in the enclosed brochure. I feel
confident our tulips will look wonderful in your garden.

If you have any questions, please contact me at the number on this letterhead.

Sincerely,



Bob Lightfoot

BL

Enclosures

# Summary

- Documents can be created with multiple columns. The entire document, except for the headers and footers, will be made into columns.

- Graphics can enhance documents by illustrating text or making the page more attractive or functional. Microsoft Draw is a program that adds graphics to word processor documents. Graphics can be created in Draw or imported from an existing file. Graphics are added to a document by positioning the insertion point, starting Draw, drawing the graphic, and returning to the word processor. Or, you can insert clip art using the ClipArt Gallery.

- Graphics created in Draw are made up of one or more objects. Draw provides a Toolbox of tools, such as lines, rectangles, ovals, and more, for drawing objects. The menus in Draw provide many options for working with graphic objects. Graphics can be placed in an absolute position on the page so that the text can wrap around the graphic.

- You can add borders to paragraphs to emphasize a title or important paragraph. Borders can appear on any side of a paragraph or can surround the entire paragraph. You can also add colored and/or patterned shading to any line of text or to one or more paragraphs. In addition, you can add a border around the entire page of a document.

- Templates allow you to save the format, font choices, and text of commonly produced documents. The templates can be opened from the Task Launcher.

• • • • • • • • • • • • •

# REVIEW ACTIVITIES

## TRUE/FALSE

**Circle T or F to show whether the statement is true or false.**

T  F  1. Columns only appear in Page Layout view and Print Preview.

(T)  F  2. The Arrow tool allows you to select and manipulate objects.

T  (F)  3. Selection boxes are small squares that appear around a selected object.

(T)  F  4. Grid snap causes objects to align to the nearest object.

(T)  F  5. Draw creates objects in layers.

(T)  F  6. To get text to wrap around a graphic, the graphic is given an absolute position on a page.

T  (F)  7. The Borders and Shading command is in the Tools menu.

(T)  F  8. Templates are opened from the Task Launcher.

T  (F)  9. Templates can only be created for the word processor.

(T)  F  10. You can use a template as many times as needed.

## COMPLETION

**Write the correct answer in the space provided.**

1. Give an example of a document that often has two or more columns.

_Newsletter_

2. What are the steps involved in inserting a graphic you create in a word processor document?

_Position the insertion point, start draw, draw the graphic, and return to word processor_   _ok can you clip art kse_

3. What command makes several objects work together as one?

_Draw_

4. How can you force the Rectangle/Square tool to draw a perfect square?

_Hold down shift key and drag_

5. Explain how you would resize a rectangle.

_select object to make the handles appear and drag handles inwards or outwards_

6. What is the difference between resizing and scaling a graphic?

_SCALING a graphic proportions are correct_ _Resize graphic_ _may not maintain_ _proportions_

7. If a graphic is not placed in an absolute position, what happens when text above the graphic is added or deleted?

_It will not wrap_

8. Name a reason for using paragraph borders.

_to emphasize the text_

9. What three operations can you do in the Borders and Shading dialog box?

_Line style, color of border distance from edge of page_

10. Give one example of when a template could be used.

_letterhead_

*application  5 - 1*

**Refer to Figure 5-16 and write the letter of the Toolbox part next to the correct name of the item given below.**

FIGURE 5-16

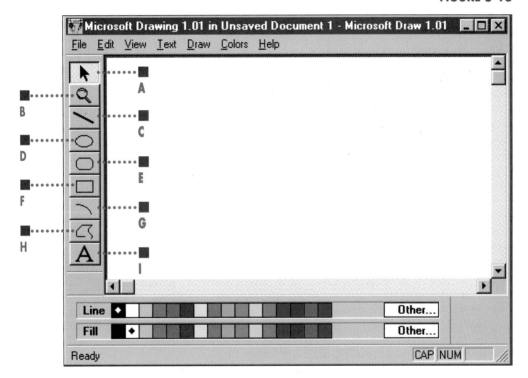

*G* **1.** Arc tool

*B* **2.** Zoom In/Zoom Out tool

*I* **3.** Text tool

*A* **4.** Arrow tool

*H* **5.** Freeform tool

*E* **6.** Rectangle/Square tool

*C* **7.** Line tool

*D* **8.** Oval/Circle tool

*F* **9.** Rounded Rectangle/Square tool

## *application 5-2*

1. Create a new word processing document.

2. Change the left and right margins to 2 inches.

3. Create a packing list like the one in Figure 5-17. Use borders to create the line and the box.

FIGURE 5-17

# Packing List

This package contains the following:

Q44DX Computer
VGA Monitor
Extended Keyboard
Mouse
Power Cord
Getting Started Guide
System User's Guide
4 Diskettes
Registration Card

> Note: If one or more items is missing from this package, contact your dealer immediately.

4. Save the document as *Packing*. Print the document.

5. Save the document as a template named *Packing List*.

6. Close the document.

7. Create a new document using Packing List as a template.

8. Replace the items on the template list with the following:

   **Quad-Speed CD ROM**

   **Multimedia Upgrade Kit**

   **2 4MB SIMMs**

   **14.4K Send/Receive Fax Modem**

   **100-PK 3-1/2" High Density Diskettes**

9. Save the document as *New List*.

10. Print and close.

1. Open *Application 5-3* from the template disk.

2. Format the document into three columns with lines between the columns.

3. Place the insertion point after the *d* in the word *toward* in the first column, second paragraph.

4. Insert the clip art picture with the Description *PC Presentation* from the *People* category in the Microsoft ClipArt Gallery 2.0.

5. Scale the clip art to 130% (width and height) and wrap text around the graphic using the absolute setting. Make sure the Size of the graphic is 2.03" in Width and 2.31" in Height.

6. Drag the clip art to the bottom of the first column so that it rests on the dotted margin line.

7. Place the insertion point before the *T* in the word *To* in the third column after the quotation.

8. Insert the clip art picture of the Earth (the one that shows the United States) from the Maps—International category.

9. Scale the picture to 33% (width and height) and wrap text around it using the absolute setting. Make sure the size of the graphic is 1.32" in Width and 1.33" in Height.

10. Preview the document.

11. Highlight and shade the title using a 25% pattern, blue foreground color, and white background color.

12. Create a green page border using the double-line style with the thick upper line and the thin lower line.

13. Save the document as *Space Story*.

14. Print and close.

# ADVANCED WORD PROCESSING OPERATIONS

CHAPTER

6

## OBJECTIVES
### When you complete this chapter, you will be able to:

1. Open and save a document as text.

2. Work with multiple documents.

3. Use the Paste Special command to format text.

4. Work with multi-page documents.

5. Find specific data and replace it with other data.

6. Insert special characters, headers, footers, and footnotes.

7. View hidden formatting characters.

8. Print documents in portrait and landscape orientation.

# *Opening Text Files*

**S**uppose you and a classmate are working together on a project that requires you both to use a word processing program. You intend to use Works, but your friend has another word processing application. Will you be able to use her files?

The answer is yes. The Works word processor can open documents created by other applications in a form called a ***text file.*** A text file is a document that does not contain any of the codes that control fonts, font size, and type style. Works uses a file format called ***ASCII*** when opening a file created by another type of word processor. ASCII is an acronym for American Standard Code for Information Interchange. The ASCII format was developed to provide a standard for communication between different types of programs. Text files are commonly saved with the extension .TXT to indicate they contain only ASCII characters.

When a document is opened in Works as text, it will not contain any of the formatting codes inserted in the original document, such as codes to control font choice, font size, margins, and so on. This is because these codes are not ASCII characters. After you open a text file, you can insert these codes yourself to format the document.

To open a document as text, choose Open from the File menu. If the document has a .TXT filename extension, choose Text in the Files of type box. If the file you want to open doesn't have a .TXT extension, then select the document in the File name box. After you click OK, Works will open the document. You can then edit it the same way you would edit any other word processing document.

You can save a document as text by choosing Save As from the File menu. Choose Text in the Save as type box. A message will appear asking if you want to save the document without formatting. Click OK. Works saves the document. Remember that you will lose all codes that control formatting, such as fonts, font sizes, and margins, when you save a document as text.

*With caut* FILES OF TYPE *.W*

*[*, *] all type that are listed*

# ACTIVITY

# 6-1 Opening a Text Document

In this activity, you will open a text document. Works should be running and the Works window should be maximized.

1. Choose **Open** from the **File** menu. The Open dialog box appears.

2. Choose **a:** from the **Look in** box.

3. Click the Files of type box arrow. A list of file types appears.

4. Choose **Text (*.txt)** as the file type. The filename *Activity 6-1* appears in the file box.

5. Choose *Activity 6-1.* Click **Open.** The Open File As dialog box appears, as shown in Figure 6-1.

6. Click the **Word Processor** button. The file

appears in the document window.

7. Leave the document open for the next activity.

**FIGURE 6-1**
You can open a text file in the word processor, spreadsheet, or database by clicking the appropriate button in the Open File As dialog box.

# *Working with More Than One Document*

**R**emember, Works allows you to have more than one document open at a time. This is useful when you want to move or copy text between two documents. You can have as many as eight files open at one time.

In Chapter 3, you were introduced to the two ways to switch between documents. You will remember that the quickest way is to click in the window or on the title bar of the document you want to become active. The other way to switch is to use the Window menu. At the bottom of the Window menu are the names of the documents that are currently open. Choosing one of these documents from the Window menu will make that document active and bring it to the front.

## ACTIVITY

 **6-2**  **Switching between Documents**

In this activity, you will review opening an additional document and switching between documents.

1. Choose **Open** from the **File** menu. The Open dialog box appears.

2. Choose *Activity 6-2.* Click **Open.** The *Activity 6-2* document appears in front of the *Activity 6-1* document, as shown in Figure 6-2. You can see that *Activity 6-2* is the active document because the title bar is darkened and it appears in front of the *Activity 6-1* document.

3. Click the title bar of the *Activity 6-1* document. The window is brought to the front and becomes the active window.

4. Choose **2** **Activity 6-2** from the **Window** menu. The document again moves to the front and becomes active.

5. Leave the documents open for the next activity.

**FIGURE 6-2**

In Works, two to eight documents can be open at the same time.

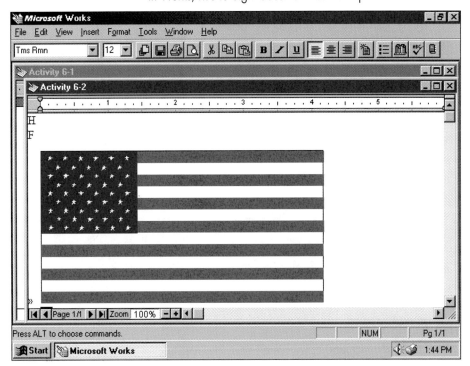

## Arranging Windows

When you have more than one document open on your screen, it can become tedious to switch among them. Some operations, such as moving or copying text between documents, would be easier if you could rearrange the document windows on your screen.

One way to arrange windows on your screen is to resize and move the windows manually. Any window that is not maximized can be resized and moved. As you learned in Chapter 1, you can use the mouse to drag the entire window to a new location. Dragging an edge or corner of a window resizes it.

But you don't have to arrange your windows manually. Most Windows programs, including Works, provide two ways to automatically arrange windows on the screen: cascading and tiling.

### CASCADE

The Cascade command in the Window menu overlaps the windows and arranges them so that the titles are visible, as shown in Figure 6-3. An active cascaded window will appear in front of the other windows and will have a darkened title bar. Up to six windows can be cascaded on the screen with their titles visible.

**FIGURE 6-3**

The Cascade command overlaps document windows.

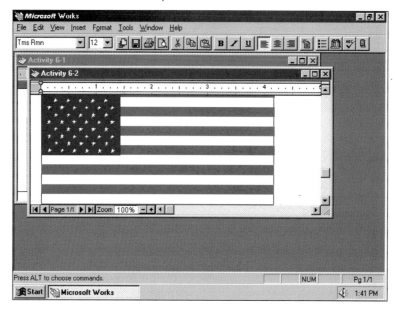

## TILE

The Tile command in the Window menu arranges windows so that they do not overlap each other. The Tile command will place windows side by side as shown in Figure 6-4. An active tiled window will appear with a darkened title bar. If more than three windows are opened, the Tile command will stack them. Up to eight windows can be tiled on the screen at one time.

**FIGURE 6-4**

The Tile command places windows side by side.

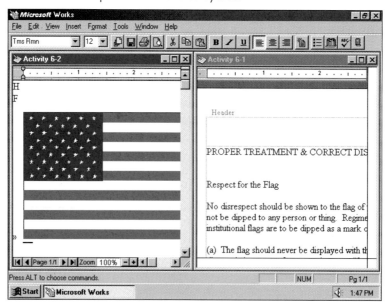

ACTIVITY

# 6-3 Arranging Windows with Cascade and Tile

In this activity, you will arrange windows using the Cascade and Tile commands. *Activity 6-1* and *Activity 6-2* should be on your screen. *Activity 6-2* should be the active window.

1. Choose **Cascade** from the **Window** menu. The windows are resized and cascaded, as in Figure 6-3.

2. Choose **Tile** from the **Window** menu. The windows are placed side by side, as in Figure 6-4.

3. Leave the documents open for the next activity.

## Copying and Moving Text between Documents

Just as you can copy or move text within a document, you can copy or move data from one document to another. For example, you might copy a paragraph from one document to another, or you might move a whole section from one report to another. It is easiest to transfer text between two documents while the documents are tiled or cascaded.

ACTIVITY

# 6-4 Copying and Moving Text between Documents

In this activity, you will copy and move text between two documents. *Activity 6-1* and *Activity 6-2* should be tiled on your screen.

1. Click anywhere in *Activity 6-1* to make it the active window.

2. Choose **Select All** from the **Edit** menu. The text in the document is highlighted.

3. Click the **Copy** button on the toolbar. The text is placed on the Clipboard.

4. Click anywhere in the *Activity 6-2* window. *Activity 6-2* becomes the active window.

5. Press the **Right arrow** key to move the insertion point to the right side of the flag. Press **Enter** three times to create two blank lines.

**6.** Click the **Paste** button on the toolbar. The text you copied from *Activity 6-1* is placed in *Activity 6-2*.

**7.** Click anywhere in the *Activity 6-1* window.

**8.** Choose **Close** from the **File** menu. *Activity 6-1* closes, leaving *Activity 6-2* on the screen.

**9.** Click the **maximize** button to maximize the *Activity 6-2* window.

**10.** Highlight the flag graphic and the title of the document.

**11.** Click the **Center Align** button. The flag and the title of the document are centered.

**12.** Save the document to your data disk as *U.S. Flag*. Leave the document open for the next activity.

# *Copying Format and Style*

 ften you will spend time formatting a paragraph with indents or tabs and then find that you need the same format in another part of the document. The Paste Special command allows you to copy the format or style of a block of text, rather than the text itself. The command can be used to quickly apply a complicated format or style to text.

**ACTIVITY**

## *6-5* Copying Format and Style

In this activity, you will copy the format and style of text.

**1.** Change the style of the title and the first heading, *Respect for the Flag*, to boldface.

**2.** With *Respect for the Flag* still highlighted, choose **Copy** from the **Edit** menu.

**3.** Highlight the second heading, *Time and Occasions for Display*. Choose **Paste Special**

from the **Edit** menu. The Paste Special dialog box appears, as shown in Figure 6-5.

**FIGURE 6-5**
The Paste Special dialog box allows you to choose whether to copy character style or paragraph format.

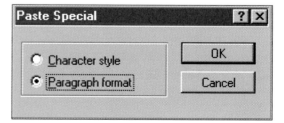

4. Choose **Character Style** and click **OK.** The boldface style that was copied from the first heading is applied.

5. Highlight the paragraph near the top of the document that begins *(a) The flag.*

6. Choose **Paragraph** from the **Format** menu. In the Indents and Alignment section, key **0.25** in the Left indent box and **-0.25** in the 1st Line Indent box. Choose **OK.** The paragraph now has a hanging indent.

7. With the paragraph still highlighted, click the **Copy** button on the toolbar.

8. Highlight all of the paragraphs from the paragraph that begins *(b) The flag should never touch* to the paragraph that begins *(k) The flag.*

9. Choose **Paste Special** from the **Edit** menu. The Paste Special dialog box appears.

10. Paragraph Format is chosen by default, so click **OK.** The paragraphs each become formatted with the hanging indent, as shown in Figure 6-6.

**FIGURE 6-6**

The Paste Special command is used to copy the style or format of text, rather than the text itself.

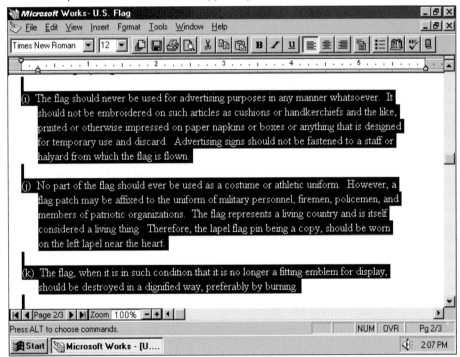

11. Highlight all of the paragraphs below the *Time and Occasions for Display* heading.

12. Choose **Paste Special** from the **Edit** menu. The Paste Special dialog box appears. Click **OK.**

13. Save the document. Leave the document open for the next activity.

# Working with Multi-page Documents

**W**hen a document is only one page long, it isn't hard to edit or format the text. These tasks become more challenging in multi-page documents because you cannot see the whole document on your screen at once. Works provides several tools that will help you get around in a long document and control how the pages of your document display on the screen.

## Splitting Windows

Works lets you view two parts of your document at once by using the Split command from the Window menu. Suppose you want to edit text and accompanying footnotes at the same time. By splitting your document, you can see both parts of the document. Each area of the document, called a *pane,* contains separate scroll bars to allow you to move through that part of the document.

ACTIVITY

## 6-6 Splitting Windows

• • • • • • • • • • • • • • • • • • • • • • • • • • • • • • • • • • • •

In this activity, you will split the document window. *U.S. Flag* should be on your screen.

1. Press **Ctrl+Home** to return to the beginning of the document.

2. Choose **Split** from the **Window** menu. A horizontal bar appears with the mouse pointer as a positioning marker.

3. Position the bar so that the document window is divided into two equal parts.

4. Click the mouse button. The document window is split into two separate panes, each with independent scroll bars and rulers, as shown in Figure 6-7.

5. Press the down scroll arrow in the bottom pane of the split window. Notice that the document scrolls downward while the flag in the upper pane remains stationary.

6. Place the mouse pointer on the horizontal bar until the pointer again turns into a positioning marker. Double-click on the split bar. The upper pane disappears.

7. Leave the file open for the next activity.

**FIGURE 6-7**
The Split command divides the document window into two
panes, each with an independent set of scroll bars and rulers.

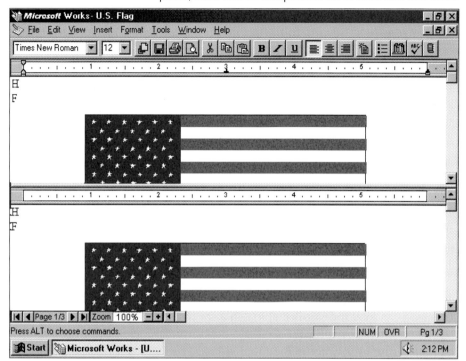

## The Go To Command

One of the quickest ways to move through a document is to use the Go To command. Go To allows you to skip to a specific page in a document. To skip to a page, choose Go To from the Edit menu. Then key the page number you want to move to in the Go To box. Click OK. Works will move the insertion point to the page number you specified.

## The Paginate Now Command

Works automatically breaks long documents into pages by inserting page breaks. This process is called *pagination.* To keep from interrupting your work, Works paginates as you enter and edit text. Because Works is spending only part of its time paginating, it may need a few moments to repaginate your document completely. There may be times, however, when you need to see the result of pagination before you can continue your work. You can have Works stop everything it is doing and devote all its time to repaginating your document by choosing Paginate Now from the Tools menu, or by pressing F9.

## Paragraph Breaks

Sometimes you may not want page breaks to split a paragraph or separate a paragraph from text after the paragraph. For example, you would not want a table to be split across two pages or a paragraph heading to be separated from the text following it. The Spacing section of the Format Paragraph dialog box allows you to control how paragraphs break during pagination. If the *Don't break paragraph* option is checked, the paragraph will not be split by an automatic page break. If the *Keep paragraph with next* option is checked, the current paragraph and the one following it will appear on the same page. To use these options, place the insertion point in the paragraph you want to affect and choose Paragraph from the Format menu. You may have to click the Spacing tab to access the Spacing section of the Format Paragraph dialog box.

# Find

Using the Find command, you can quickly search a document for every occurrence of a specific word or phrase. The Find command moves the insertion point from its present position to the next occurrence of the word or phrase for which you are searching.

Find can locate whole or partial words. For example, Works can find the word *all* or any word with all in it, such as *fall, horizontally,* or *alloy.* The Find command can look for words that match a specific capitalization. For example, if you wanted to search for the word *page* in lowercase letters, you would click the Match case option in the Find dialog box. Works would find *page,* but not *Page* or *PAGE.*

It is also possible to search for words using a question mark along with a word in the Find or Replace dialog box. Each question mark, called a **wildcard,** represents a single character in the same position in a word. See Table 6-1 for an example.

**TABLE 6-1**
Using Wildcards in the Word Processor

| TO FIND AND REPLACE | KEY |
| --- | --- |
| Both Caleb and Kaleb | ?aleb |
| Any five-letter word beginning with *a* and ending with *n* | a???n |
| June and July | Ju?? |

## ACTIVITY

# 6-7

### Searching for Text

• • • • • • • • • • • • • • • • • • • • • • • • • • • • • • • • • • • • •

In this activity, you will use the Find command to find text in a document. *U.S. Flag* should still be on your screen.

1. Place the insertion point before the *P* in the word *PROPER* at the beginning of the document.

2. Choose **Find** from the **Edit** menu. The Find dialog box appears as shown in Figure 6-8.

3. In the Find what box, key **weather**. Click on **Find Next.** (Due to the presence of the clip art, you may get a message that says: "This action cannot be completed because the 'Microsoft Works' program is busy..."

Click **Cancel** and Works will continue with the task.) The insertion point moves to the word *weather.*

4. Click **Find Next** again. The next occurrence of weather is highlighted.

5. Click **Find Next** again. The search reaches the end of the document without finding another occurrence of weather. Click **No** to remove the message and click **Cancel** to close the Find dialog box.

6. Leave the document open for the next activity.

**FIGURE 6-8**

The Find dialog box is used to find a specific word or phrase in a document.

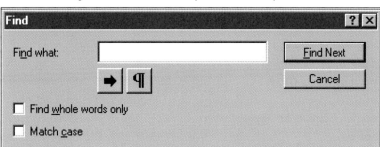

# *Replace*

**T**he Replace command is an extended version of the Find command. Replace has all the features of Find. In addition, however, the Replace dialog box, shown in Figure 6-9, allows you to replace a word or phrase with another word or phrase that you specify. The replacements can be done individually, or all occurrences can be replaced at once.

**FIGURE 6-9**
The Replace dialog box contains different options to find and replace words.

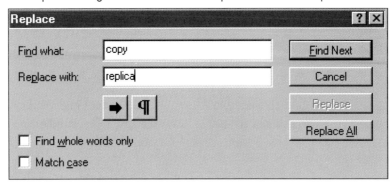

# ACTIVITY 6-8 Replacing Text

● ● ● ● ● ● ● ● ● ● ● ● ● ● ● ● ● ● ● ● ● ● ● ● ● ● ● ● ● ● ● ● ● ●

In this activity, you will use the Replace command to find and replace text. *U.S. Flag* should still be on your screen.

**1.** Place the insertion point before the *P* in *PROPER* at the beginning of the document.

**2.** Choose **Replace** from the **Edit** menu. The Replace dialog box appears.

**3.** In the Find what box, key **copy**.

**4.** Place the insertion point in the Replace with box. Key **replica**.

**5.** Click **Replace All.** (You may get a message that says: "This action cannot be completed because the 'Microsoft Works' program is busy..." Because Works has already gone through all the text, click **Cancel.**) The status line indicates the number of times (1) that Works replaced the word *copy*. Click **Close** to close the Replace dialog box.

**6.** Save the document. Leave the document open for the next activity.

# Special Characters

**W**orks has a number of special characters that can help you format your document. You can insert some of these characters using the Special

Character command and choose others from the Insert menu. For example, you can insert characters that control hyphenation and that automatically print the time or the date. Special characters are particularly useful in headers and footers, as you will see in the next section.

FIGURE 6-10
The Insert Special Character dialog box contains several special character choices you can add to a document.

To insert a special character, move the insertion point to the place you want the character to appear. Choose Special Character from the Insert menu. In the Insert Special Character dialog box, shown in Figure 6-10, choose the desired special character and click Insert. Some of the special character commands, such as Date and Time, are listed in the Insert menu. To insert these, place your insertion point where you want the character inserted, then choose its command from the Insert menu. Table 6-2 lists the special characters you can add to a document.

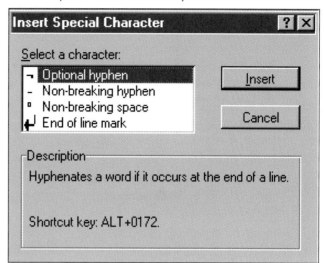

**FIGURE 6-10**
The Insert Special Character dialog box contains several special character choices you can add to a document.

**TABLE 6-2**
Special Characters

| CHARACTER | MEANING |
|---|---|
| End-of-line mark | Starts a new line but not a new paragraph |
| Optional hyphen | Hyphenates a word if it is at the end of a line |
| Non-breaking hyphen | Prevents a hyphenated word from breaking at the end of a line |
| Non-breaking space | Prevents related words, such as first and last names, from breaking at the end of a line |
| Page Number | Inserts the current page number in a document and is displayed as *page* on the screen |
| Document Name | Inserts the filename in a document and is displayed as *filename* on the screen |
| Date and Time | The Insert Date and Time dialog box lists several forms of dates and times you can insert into your document including the current date and time. |

# Headers and Footers

**H**eaders and footers can be inserted by keying text in the Header pane or Footers pane in Page Layout view or by keying text beside the H or F at the beginning of a document in Normal view. A *header* is text that is printed at the top of each page; a *footer* is text that is printed at the bottom of each page, as shown in Figure 6-11.

**FIGURE 6-11**
Headers contain text that is printed at the top of a page, whereas a footer is printed at the bottom of a page.

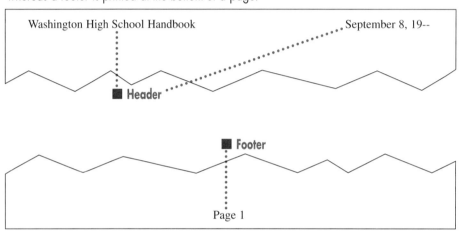

Washington High School Handbook                                        September 8, 19--

■ Header

■ Footer

Page 1

Headers and footers may contain more than one line of text. To start a new line, place the insertion point after the last character in the first header or footer line and press Enter.

In Normal view, you can go to the beginning of the document where the H and F are by choosing Header or Footer from the View menu.

## ACTIVITY 6-9 Working with Headers and Footers

In this activity, you will add headers and footers to a document. *U.S. Flag* should be on your screen.

Your screen should look like Figure 6-12. If a First-time Help menu appears, click **OK**.

**1.** Choose **Header** from the **View** menu.

**2.** Key **Your Name.** Left align your name.

**FIGURE 6-12**

Headers and footers can be inserted by keying text after the header and footer marks.

Header mark

Footer mark

3. Press **Tab** two times. Choose **Page Number** from the **Insert** menu. The symbol *page* is inserted into the document indicating that the page number will appear when the document is printed.

4. Choose **Page Setup** from the **File** menu. The Page Setup dialog box appears, as shown in Figure 6-13. Click the **Other Options** tab if it isn't showing already. Click the box next to the *No header on first page* option. Click **OK.** Usually headers and footers are omitted on the first page of a document.

5. Place the insertion point after the paragraph footer mark, *F*.

6. Press **Tab** once to move the insertion point to the centered tab stop.

7. Key **U.S. Code TITLE 36**.

8. Choose **Page Setup** from the **File** menu. Click the **Other Options** tab. Click the box next to the *No footer on first page* option.

9. Click **OK.**

10. Highlight the header and footer lines. Change the header and footer to a sans serif font. Change the font size to 8 point. If your computer cannot accommodate this size, change the headers and footers to a size smaller than the default font. Use Print Preview or Page Layout view to see your changes.

11. Save the document. Leave the document open for the next activity.

**FIGURE 6-13**
You can specify not to print the header on the first page of a document.

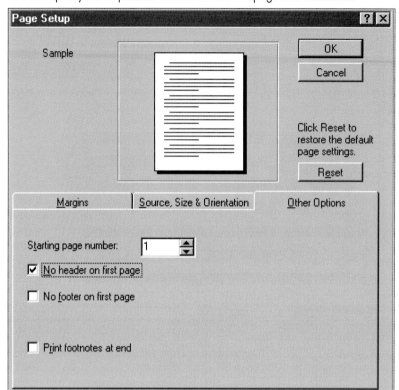

# *Footnotes*

**A** *footnote* is used to document quotations, figures, summaries, or other text that you do not want to include in the body of your document. Footnotes can be edited, deleted, moved, or copied like other text. After you create a footnote, a number or the special mark (symbol) you specified in the Footnote dialog box will appear in the document and the corresponding footnotes will appear printed at the end of the document.

# ACTIVITY

## 6-10 Working with Footnotes

In this activity, you will add footnotes to your document. *U.S. Flag* should be on your screen.

1. Place the insertion point after the period following the word *honor* in the first paragraph of the document.

2. Choose **Footnote** from the **Insert** menu. The Insert Footnote dialog box appears, as shown in Figure 6-14. The Numbered option appears highlighted in the Footnote style box. This indicates that your footnotes will be numbered.

**FIGURE 6-14**
You can represent footnotes in the text with numbers or symbols.

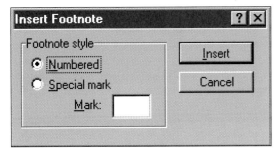

3. Click **Insert.** The Footnote pane appears at the bottom of the document window with the insertion point blinking after the number *1*, as in Figure 6-15.

4. Key **Section 176. Respect for the Flag.** (Key the period.)

5. Scroll down in the document window until the heading *Time and Occasions for Display* appears. Place the insertion point after the word *Display* in the heading.

6. Choose **Footnote** from the **Insert** menu. After the Footnote dialog box appears, click **Insert.**

7. The insertion point appears blinking after the number *2* in the Footnote pane. Key **Section 174. Time and Occasions for Display.** (Key the period.)

8. Choose **Footnotes** from the **View** menu to hide the Footnote pane.

9. Use Print Preview to view the footnotes you added. They appear at the end of the document. Return to the document window.

10. Save the document. Leave the file open for the next activity.

**FIGURE 6-15**

Footnotes can be edited, deleted, moved, or copied in the Footnote pane.

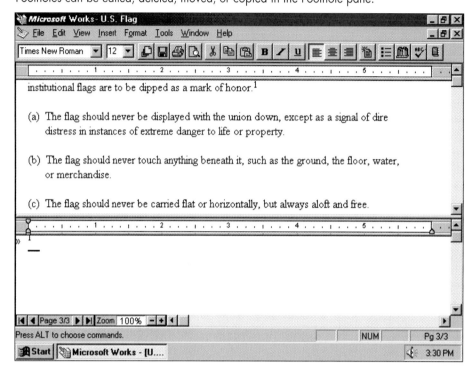

You can make footnotes appear at the bottom of each page rather than at the end of the document. In the Other Options section of the Page Setup dialog box is an option to specify whether footnotes print at the end of the document or at the bottom of each page.

# View All Characters

The All Characters command is used to view hidden formatting characters. These are characters that are hidden, such as paragraph returns or end-of-line marks. Being able to see these hidden characters can help you edit your text.

## ACTIVITY

# 6-11 Viewing Hidden Characters

In this activity, you will view hidden characters in a document. *U.S. Flag* should be on your screen.

1. Choose **All Characters** from the **View** menu. Works makes the paragraph returns and spacebar characters visible, as shown in Figure 6-16.

2. Scroll through the document to observe the different characters.

3. Again, choose **All Characters** from the **View** menu. The characters are hidden.

4. Save and print the document.

5. Close the document.

**FIGURE 6-16**
Choosing the All Characters command from the View menu makes hidden formatting characters appear.

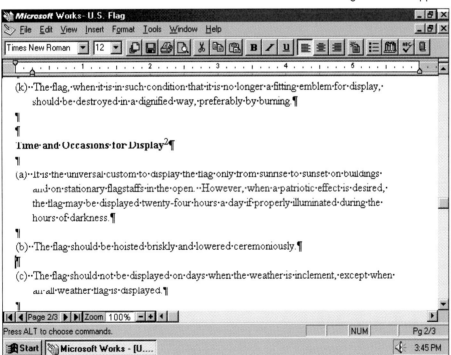

# Printing in Portrait and Landscape Orientation

**D**ocuments printed in portrait orientation, as seen in Figure 6-17, are longer than they are wide. The default in Works is set to print pages in portrait orientation. In contrast, documents printed in landscape orientation, as seen in Figure 6-18, are wider than they are long. Most documents are printed in portrait orientation. Some documents, however, such as documents with graphics or numerical information, look better when printed in landscape orientation.

**FIGURE 6-17**
Document pages printed in portrait orientation are longer than they are wide.

**Mountain Cabin
Open House**

This beautiful mountain cabin features three bedrooms, two bathrooms, a wood-burning fireplace, and a hot tub. Located five miles south of Pine Bluff, Colorado, on Old Elm Road, this cabin is just 20 miles from Slippery Slope Ski Resort.

Come see for yourself on November 19!
R.S.V.P. (845) 555-0097

FIGURE 6-18
Document pages printed in landscape orientation are wider than they are long.

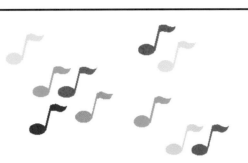

**The Choir and Drama Students Present:**

*Nicholas Ermal's*

*The Harmonious Jangle of Sound*

**Friday, October 25
Saturday, October 26
8:00 p.m.
G.H. Snyder Auditorium**

ACTIVITY

## Printing in Portrait and Landscape Orientation

In this activity, you will change the orientation of a document.

1. Open *Activity 6-12* from your template disk. Use Print Preview to view the document before you make any changes and return to your document.

2. Choose **Page Setup** from the **File** menu. The Page Setup dialog box appears.

3. Switch to the **Source, Size & Orientation** tab of the dialog box.

4. Choose the **Landscape** option. Click **OK.**

5. Choose **Print** from the **File** menu. The Print dialog box appears.

6. Click the **Properties** button. A printer dialog box appears. Click the **Paper** tab if it is not already selected.

**7.** If the dialog box that appears has an option for landscape orientation, choose it. Click **OK.**

**8.** Use Print Preview to view the changes you have made and return to your document.

**9.** Save the document to your data disk as *Landscape.*

**10.** Print and close the document.

# *Word Count*

After you have completed a document, you may want to know how many words it contains. The Word Count command can count words in your document quickly. The insertion point can be located anywhere in the document when you use Word Count. You can count the words in a specific section of text by first highlighting the text and then using Word Count. To use Word Count, choose Word Count from the Tools menu. A message will appear with the number of words in the document. Click OK.

# *Summary*

- A text file does not contain any codes, such as those used to control fonts, margins, and paragraph formatting. Working with multiple documents is made easier by the Cascade and Tile commands. These commands allow you to position windows on the screen.

- Character style and paragraph format can be duplicated with the Paste Special command. Multi-page documents are sometimes difficult to edit. The Split command, the Go To command, and the Paginate Now command allow you to work with multi-page documents more effectively.

- Headers and footers can be inserted by keying text in the Header pane or Footer pane in Page Layout view or by keying text beside the H or F at the beginning of a document in Normal view.

- The Find and Replace commands let you quickly search a document for a specific word. Works allows you to add headers, footers, special characters, and footnotes to a document. The All Characters command reveals hidden characters.

- In portrait orientation, a printed page is longer than it is wide. In landscape orientation, a printed page is wider than it is long. The Word Count command will count the words in a document.

● ● ● ● ● ● ● ● ● ● ● ● ● ●

# REVIEW ACTIVITIES

## TRUE/FALSE

**Circle T or F to show whether the statement is true or false.**

T (F) 1. A text file contains codes that control fonts, margins, and paragraph formatting.

(T) F 2. The Cascade command overlaps open document windows.

(T) F 3. The Paste Special command allows you to copy the format or style of text, rather than the text itself.

(T) F 4. You can split a document into two panes by using the Split command.

T (F) 5. The Paginate Now command counts the words in the document. *word count*

(T) F 6. The Find command will find and replace a word.

(T) F 7. Headers and footers can appear on every page of a document.

T (F) 8. You can use only numbers for footnotes.

(T) F 9. The All Characters command is used to view hidden formatting characters.

T (F) 10. The default in Works is set to print pages in landscape orientation.

## COMPLETION

**Write the correct answer in the space provided.**

1. What type of filename extension is normally attached to the end of a text file?

   _.TXT to indicate they contain only ASCII characters_

2. What command places open document windows side by side?

   _Tile from windows_

3. To copy the indents or tabs from one paragraph to another, which option must be chosen in the Paste Special dialog box?

   _Paragraph format_

4. What command can quickly move the insertion point to a specific page?

   _____

5. What character is used as a wildcard in the Find or Replace dialog boxes?

   _quest mark ?_

6. List two examples of special characters that you can insert into text.

_headers, footers_
_foot notes_

7. What is the purpose of a footnote?

_quotations, figures, summaries or other text that you don't want in the body._

8. What dialog box allows you to choose whether footnotes appear at the bottom of each page or at the end of the document?

_Insert_

9. In which menu is the All Characters command?

_View_

10. What is the difference between landscape orientation and portrait orientation?

_landscape - is wider than it is longer_
_portrait - is longer than it is wider_

# REINFORCEMENT APPLICATIONS

## application 6-1

**In the blank space on the left, write the letter from the right column that matches the special character and its meaning.**

*C* 1. End-of-line mark

*F* 2. Optional hyphen

*B* 3. Non-breaking hyphen

*G* 4. Non-breaking space

*D* 5. Page number

*E* 6. Date and Time

*A* 7. Document Name

a. Inserts the filename in a document and is displayed as *filename* on the screen

b. Prevents a hyphenated word from breaking at the end of a line

c. Starts a new line but not a new paragraph

d. Inserts the current page number in a document and is displayed as *page* on the screen

e. Inserts your choice of several forms of dates and times

f. Hyphenates a word if it is at the end of a line

g. Prevents related words, such as first and last names, from breaking at the end of a line

## application 6-2

1. Open *Mountain* from your data disk.

2. Find the word *frequently* in the document and replace it with *usually*.

3. Add a header with your name left-aligned and insert the page number at a right-aligned tab at 5.5 inches. The header should not print on the first page.

4. Insert the long form of the date (for example: May 7, 1999) centered in a footer. The footer should not print on the first page.

5. Change the font of the headers and footers to Arial 10 point.

6. Save the document as *Headers and Footers*. Print and close the document.

# application 6-3

1. Open *Application 6-3a* from the template disk.

2. Open the text file *Application 6-3b* from the template disk. (*Hint:* Don't forget to indicate the type of file in the open dialog box.)

3. Cascade the windows.

4. Tile the windows.

5. Select all the text in *Application 6-3b* and copy it.

6. Place the insertion point after the date in *Application 6-3a* and insert a page break.

7. With the insertion point at the beginning of the second page, paste the text from *Application 6-3b*.

8. Close *Application 6-3b* and maximize the window of *Application 6-3a*.

9. Boldface and center the title at the beginning of the document, not on the cover sheet.

10. Boldface the *Introduction* and *Dietary Guidelines for Americans* headings.

11. Highlight the first paragraph and create a first-line indent of .25 inches.

12. Copy and paste this paragraph format to all the other paragraphs (not the headings).

13. Place the insertion point after the word *practices* in the second paragraph at the end of the first sentence.

14. Insert a numbered footnote. Key **U.S. Department of Agriculture and U.S. Department of Health and Human Services, "Nutrition and Your Health: Dietary Guidelines for Americans," Home and Garden Bulletin No. 232, 3d edition, 1990, p. 3**.

15. Place the insertion point after the next sentence, which is a quotation.

16. Insert a numbered footnote. Key **"Dietary Guidelines for Americans: No-nonsense Advice for Healthy Eating," FDA Consumer, November 1985, p. 11**.

17. Place the insertion point after the word *moderation* in the last line of the list.

18. Insert a numbered footnote. Key **"Nutrition and Your Health," p. 4**. Print the footnotes at the end of the document.

19. Choose **F̲ootnotes** from the **V̲iew** menu.

20. Preview the document. Save it as *American Diet*. Print and close.

# UNIT 3

# SPREADSHEETS

# SPREADSHEET BASICS

CHAPTER

7

## OBJECTIVES

**When you complete this chapter, you will be able to:**

1. Define the term spreadsheet.

2. Identify the parts of the spreadsheet.

3. Move the highlight in the spreadsheet.

4. Select cells and enter data in the spreadsheet.

5. Change column width and edit cells.

6. Change the appearance of a cell.

7. Save and print a spreadsheet.

# *What Is a Spreadsheet?*

**A** *spreadsheet* is a grid of rows and columns containing numbers, text, and formulas. The purpose of a spreadsheet is to solve problems that involve numbers. Before computers, spreadsheets were created with pencils on ruled paper. Calculators were used to solve complicated mathematical operations (see Figure 7-1). Computer spreadsheets also contain rows and columns, but they perform calculations much faster and more accurately than spreadsheets created with pencil, paper, and calculator.

Spreadsheets are used in many ways. For example, a spreadsheet can be used to calculate a grade in a class, prepare a budget for the next few months, or determine payments to be made on a loan. The primary advantage of the spreadsheet is the ability to complete complex and repetitious calculations accurately, quickly, and easily. For example, you might use a spreadsheet to calculate your grade in a class. Your instructor may use a spreadsheet to calculate grades for the entire class.

**FIGURE 7-1**
Computer spreadsheets automate calculations and are replacing
spreadsheets prepared with paper, pencil, and calculator.

Besides calculating rapidly and accurately, spreadsheets are flexible. Making changes to an existing spreadsheet is usually as easy as pointing and clicking with the mouse. Suppose, for example, you have prepared a budget on a spreadsheet and have overestimated the amount of money you will need to spend on books. You may change a single entry in your spreadsheet and watch the entire spreadsheet recalculate the new budgeted amount. You can imagine the work this change would require if you were calculating the budget with pencil and paper.

# *Parts of a Spreadsheet*

**Y**ou can open a new spreadsheet by starting Works and clicking the Spreadsheet button under the Works Tools tab of the Works Task Launcher. When the spreadsheet appears on the screen, you will see some of the basic features that you learned in the word processor: the title bar, the menu bar, and the toolbar. However, other parts of the spreadsheet, such as the Formula Bar and the grid of cells created by columns and rows, do not appear in the word processor. Figure 7-2 shows the parts of the spreadsheet.

*Columns* appear vertically and are identified by letters at the top of the spreadsheet window. *Rows* appear horizontally and are identified by numbers on the left side of the spreadsheet window. A *cell* is the intersection of a row and column and is identified by a *cell reference*, the column letter and row number (for example, C4, A1, B2).

The *Formula Bar* appears directly below the toolbar in the spreadsheet. On the far left side of the Formula Bar is the cell reference box that identifies the *active cell.* The active cell is the cell ready for data entry. On the grid of

**FIGURE 7-2**
Some parts of the spreadsheet are similar to the word processor screen.
The spreadsheet, however, has additional parts used with numerical data.

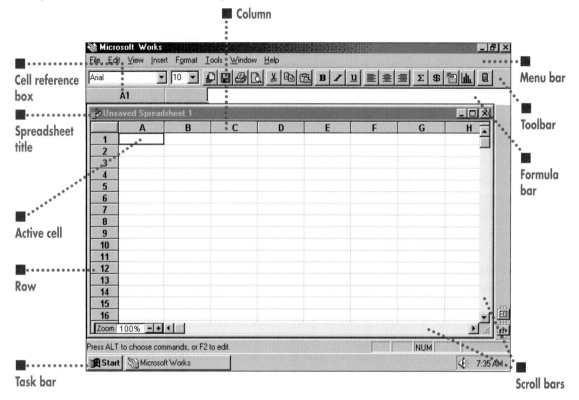

cells, the active cell is surrounded by a dark border. Your screen currently shows a border around the active cell (A1) on the spreadsheet, and the reference of the cell should appear in the cell reference box on the Formula Bar.

In the word processor, the point at which a character is keyed is indicated by the cursor. In the spreadsheet the entry point is indicated by a ***highlight.*** You may change the active cell by moving the highlight from one cell to another.

# *Opening an Existing Spreadsheet*

**W**hen you choose Spreadsheet, Works automatically opens a new spreadsheet, temporarily titled Unsaved Spreadsheet 1, such as the one that currently appears on the screen. Open an existing spreadsheet by using the File menu.

# ACTIVITY 7-1

## Opening an Existing Spreadsheet

● ● ● ● ● ● ● ● ● ● ● ● ● ● ● ● ● ● ● ● ● ● ● ● ● ● ● ● ● ● ● ● ● ● ● ● ● ● ●

In this activity, you will open an existing spread-sheet file.

1.  If you have not already done so, open Works.

2.  The Works Task Launcher should be on your screen. Click the **Existing Documents** tab, then click the **Open a document not listed here** button. The Open dialog box will appear.

3.  In the **Look in** selection box, click the down arrow to show your computer's drives.

4.  Click the drive containing your template disk in the Drives list. The files on the disk will appear in the File Name list.

5.  Double-click the filename **Activity 7-1** in the File Name list. The spreadsheet will appear on the screen.

6.  Maximize the document window. Your screen should appear similar to Figure 7-3.

7.  Leave *Activity 7-1* on the screen for the next activity.

**FIGURE 7-3**

The spreadsheet is ideal for solving numerical problems, such as preparing a summer budget.

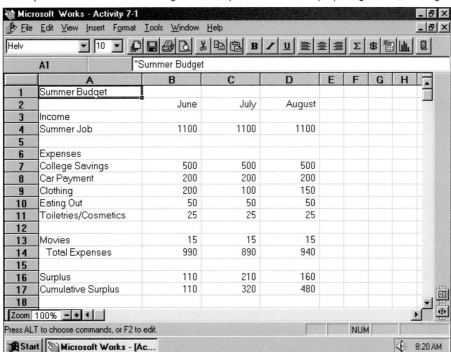

# Moving the Highlight in a Spreadsheet

**W**hen working with a large spreadsheet, you may not be able to view the entire spreadsheet on the screen. You can scroll throughout the spreadsheet using the mouse by dragging the scroll box in the scroll bar to the desired position. You can also move the highlight to different parts of the spreadsheet using direction keys or the Go To command in the Edit menu or by pressing the F5 key on your keyboard.

**NOTE:** *When an arrow key is held down, the movement of the highlight will repeat and move quickly.*

## Using Keys to Move the Highlight

You can move the highlight by pressing certain keys or key combinations. Table 7-1 illustrates the use of these keys. You will see that many of these keys and key combinations are familiar to you from the word processor.

**TABLE 7-1**
You may move the highlight in the spreadsheet by pressing direction keys.

### HIGHLIGHT MOVEMENT

| TO MOVE | PRESS |
|---|---|
| Left one column | Left arrow |
| Right one column | Right arrow |
| Up one row | Up arrow |
| Down one row | Down arrow |
| To the first cell of a row | Home |
| To the last cell of a row containing data | End |
| To Cell A1 | Ctrl+Home |
| To the last row or column containing data | Ctrl+End |
| Up one window | Page Up |
| Down one window | Page Down |
| Left one window | Ctrl+Page Up |
| Right one window | Ctrl+Page Down |

## Using the Go To Command to Move in the Spreadsheet

You may want to move the highlight to a cell that does not appear on the screen. The fastest way to move to the cell is by using the Go To command in the Edit menu and then designating the cell reference of the cell in which you want the highlight to appear. The F5 key may be used as a shortcut to access the Go To command.

ACTIVITY

## Moving the Highlight in the Spreadsheet

In this activity, you will move the highlight in a spreadsheet. *Activity 7-1* should be on your screen.

1. Move to the last cell in the spreadsheet by pressing **Ctrl+End.** The highlight will move to the lower right side of the spreadsheet.

2. Move to the first cell of the row by pressing **Home.** The highlight will appear in a cell containing the words *Cumulative Surplus.*

3. Move up one cell by pressing the **Up arrow** key. The highlight will appear in a cell containing the word *Surplus.*

4. Move to Cell B4 by using the Go To command:
   a. Press **F5.** The Go To dialog box will appear.
   b. Key **B4**.
   c. Click **OK.** The highlight should move to Cell B4.

5. Leave *Activity 7-1* on the screen for the next activity.

# *Selecting a Group of Cells*

In later chapters, you will perform operations on more than one cell at a time. A selected group of cells is referred to as a ***range.*** In a range, all cells touch each other and form a rectangle. The range is identified by the cell in the upper left corner and the cell in the lower right corner, separated by a colon (for example, A3:C5). To select a range of cells, place the highlight in one corner of the range of cells and drag the highlight to the cell in the opposite corner. As you drag the highlight, the range of selected cells will become shaded (except for the cell you originally selected), as in Figure 7-4.

**FIGURE 7-4**

A range is selected by dragging the highlight from one corner of a range to the opposite corner.

| | A | B | C | D | E | F | G | H |
|---|---|---|---|---|---|---|---|---|
| 1 | Summer Budget | | | | | | | |
| 2 | | June | July | August | | | | |
| 3 | Income | | | | | | | |
| 4 | Summer Job | 1100 | 1100 | 1100 | | | | |
| 5 | | | | | | | | |
| 6 | Expenses | | | | | | | |
| 7 | College Savings | 500 | 500 | 500 | | | | |
| 8 | Car Payment | 200 | 200 | 200 | | | | |
| 9 | Clothing | 200 | 100 | 150 | | | | |
| 10 | Eating Out | 50 | 50 | 50 | | | | |
| 11 | Toiletries/Cosmetics | 25 | 25 | 25 | | | | |
| 12 | | | | | | | | |
| 13 | Movies | 15 | 15 | 15 | | | | |
| 14 | Total Expenses | 990 | 890 | 940 | | | | |
| 15 | | | | | | | | |
| 16 | Surplus | 110 | 210 | 160 | | | | |
| 17 | Cumulative Surplus | 110 | 320 | 480 | | | | |
| 18 | | | | | | | | |

Microsoft Works - Activity 7-1 — File Edit View Insert Format Tools Window Help — Helv — 10 — B2:D11 — June — Zoom 100% — Press ALT to choose commands, or F2 to edit. — NUM — Start — Microsoft Works - [Ac... — 8:44 AM

**ACTIVITY**

# 7-3

## Selecting a Range of Cells

• • • • • • • • • • • • • • • • • • • • • • • • • • • • • • • • • •

In this activity, you will practice selecting ranges of cells. *Activity 7-1* should be on your screen.

1. Select the range B4:D4:
   a. Move the pointer to Cell B4.
   b. Hold down the mouse button and drag to the right until D4 is highlighted.
   c. Release the mouse button. B4:D4 will appear in the cell reference box on the left side of the Formula Bar.

2. Select the range B2:D17:

   a. Move the pointer to Cell B2.
   b. Hold down the mouse button and drag down and to the right until D17 is highlighted.
   c. Release the mouse button. B2:D17 will appear in the cell reference box on the Formula Bar.

3. Leave *Activity 7-1* on the screen for the next activity.

# Enting Data into a Cell

**S**preadsheet cells may contain data in the form of text, numbers, or formulas. Text consists of alphabetical characters and is usually in the form of headings, labels, or explanatory notes. In the Formula Bar, textual data is preceded by a quotation mark, which indicates that the data in the cell will not be used in calculations performed by the spreadsheet. Numbers can be in the form of values, dates, or times. Formulas are equations that calculate a value stored in a cell. (Formulas will be discussed in Chapter 9.)

Data is entered by keying the data and then either clicking the Enter button or pressing the Enter key. If you choose not to enter data, you may simply click the Cancel button in the Formula Bar (indicated by an X) and the keyed data will be deleted. If you make a mistake, the Undo command is available in the Edit menu to reverse your most recent change.

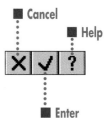

**ACTIVITY**

## Entering Text and Numbers in Cells

In this activity, you will enter text and numbers into cells of a spreadsheet. *Activity 7-1* should appear on your screen. Notice that Row 12 does not contain data. Suppose you would like to change the budget to include expenses of $25 a month for compact discs.

1. Move the highlight to Cell A12 and key **Compact Discs**. As you key, the letters will appear both in the cell and in the Formula Bar.

2. Click the **Enter** button (indicated by a check mark) in the Formula Bar or press the **Enter** key. Notice that the words in the Formula Bar are preceded by a quotation mark

to indicate that they are textual data that will not be used in calculations.

3. Move to Cell B12 and key **25**. Before entering the data by clicking the Enter button, notice that the total expenses for June are 990.

4. Click the **Enter** button. The amount of total expenses for June changes from 990 to 1015. You can now appreciate the value of the spreadsheet in making quick calculations when data in the budget problem changes. Also, notice the data, 25, is not preceded by a quotation mark. This is because the data is numerical and may be used in calculations in the spreadsheet.

**5.** Enter **25** into Cells C12 and D12. Notice how the spreadsheet recalculates the amounts each time you make a change. Your screen should appear similar to Figure 7-5.

**6.** Leave *Activity 7-1* on the screen for the next activity.

**FIGURE 7-5**
Both text and numbers may be entered into spreadsheet cells.

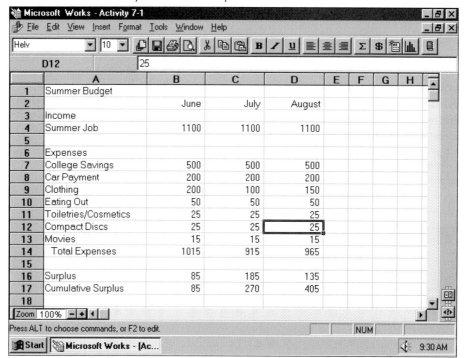

# *Changing Cell Width and Height*

**S**ometimes the data you key will not fit in the column. When numerical data is wider than the column, Works will respond by displaying a series of number signs (######) in the cell. This problem is easily remedied by placing the mouse pointer on the boundary of the right edge of the column heading. The pointer will then change into two arrows with the word *ADJUST* under it. To widen the column, drag to the right until the column is the desired size.

ADJUST

You can also change the height of a row by dragging the bottom edge of the row heading. Right now you may see no reason to change the height of a row; however, when you add more data into a single cell, you may need to make the cell taller.

**A C T I V I T Y**

# 7-5

## Widening a Column

In this activity, you will change the width of a column on a spreadsheet. *Activity 7-1* should appear on your screen.

**1.** Key **September** into Cell E2 and press **Enter.** (If a First-time Help dialog box appears, click **OK.**) Because the entry is too large for the column, a series of number signs (#) will appear in the cell.

**2.** Place the mouse pointer to the right of the heading for Column E. The pointer should turn into a double-headed arrow.

**3.** Drag the double-headed arrow to the right and release. The word *September* should appear in Cell E2. If it does not, you may need to drag the double-headed arrow farther. You may notice that, although the data is text, it is not preceded by a quotation mark ("). Because September is a name of a month, and can be used in some calculations, it is treated as numerical data.

**4.** Leave *Activity 7-1* on the screen for the next activity.

## Best Fit

Suppose you have a column full of data of varying widths. You want the column to be wide enough to display the longest entry, but no wider than necessary. The Column Width dialog box (shown in Figure 7-6) has an option called Best Fit that will select the width that will give you the best fit. The Best Fit option can also be used to adjust row height using the Row Height dialog box.

To use the Best Fit option, select the column or row to adjust. If adjusting a column, choose Column Width from the Format menu. If adjusting a row, choose Row Height from the Format menu. Choose the Best Fit option and click OK.

**FIGURE 7-6**
The Best Fit option in the Column Width dialog box automatically selects the width that gives the best fit for your data.

| Column Width | ? X |
|---|---|
| Column width: [12] | OK |
| Standard | Best Fit | Cancel |

## Text Wrap

Text that is too long for a cell will spill over into the next cell, if the next cell is empty. If the next cell is not empty, the text that does not fit into the cell will not display. You can choose to have text wrap within a cell in the same way text wraps within a word processor document. The row height will be automatically adjusted to show all of the lines of text. To turn on the text wrap option, choose Alignment from the Format menu. The Wrap Text check box is in the Alignment dialog box.

# ACTIVITY

## 7-6  Best Fit and Text Wrap

In this activity, you will use the Wrap Text option and adjust column widths using Best Fit. *Activity 7-1* should be on your screen.

**1.** Move the highlight to Cell A1.

**2.** Key **Personal Budget for the Summer**. Press **Enter.** The text spills into the next cell.

**3.** Choose **Alignment** from the **Format** menu.

**4.** Choose the **Wrap text** option. Click **OK.** The text wraps in the cell and automatically adjusts the cell height.

**5.** Choose **Column Width** from the **Format** menu. The Column Width dialog box appears.

**6.** Click **Best Fit.** The column widens to allow the long title to fit without wrapping.

**7.** Manually adjust the width of column A to the width of the data in Cell A11. Your screen should appear similar to Figure 7-7.

**8.** Leave *Activity 7-1* on the screen for the next activity.

### FIGURE 7-7
With the Wrap Text option, a cell can contain more than one line of text.

| Microsoft Works - Activity 7-1 | | | | | | | |
|---|---|---|---|---|---|---|---|
| File Edit View Insert Format Tools Window Help | | | | | | | |
| Helv ▼ 10 ▼ | | | | | | | |
| A1 | "Personal Budget for the Summer | | | | | | |

| | A | B | C | D | E | F | G |
|---|---|---|---|---|---|---|---|
| 1 | Personal Budget for the Summer | | | | | | |
| 2 | | June | July | August | September | | |
| 3 | Income | | | | | | |
| 4 | Summer Job | 1100 | 1100 | 1100 | | | |
| 5 | | | | | | | |
| 6 | Expenses | | | | | | |
| 7 | College Savings | 500 | 500 | 500 | | | |
| 8 | Car Payment | 200 | 200 | 200 | | | |
| 9 | Clothing | 200 | 100 | 150 | | | |
| 10 | Eating Out | 50 | 50 | 50 | | | |
| 11 | Toiletries/Cosmetics | 25 | 25 | 25 | | | |
| 12 | Compact Discs | 25 | 25 | 25 | | | |
| 13 | Movies | 15 | 15 | 15 | | | |
| 14 | Total Expenses | 1015 | 915 | 965 | | | |
| 15 | | | | | | | |
| 16 | Surplus | 85 | 185 | 135 | | | |
| 17 | Cumulative Surplus | 85 | 270 | 405 | | | |

Zoom 100%

Press ALT to choose commands, or F2 to edit.  NUM

Start  Microsoft Works - [Ac...  11:23 AM

# Changing Data in a Cell

**A**s you work with the spreadsheet, you may change your mind about data or make a mistake. If so, you may edit, replace, or clear existing data in cells of the spreadsheet.

## Editing Data

Editing is performed when only minor changes to cell data are necessary. Data in a cell may be edited in the Formula Bar by using the Edit key, or F2 on your keyboard. To edit data in a cell, select the cell by placing the highlight in the cell and pressing F2. A cursor similar to the one in the word processor will appear in the Formula Bar. You may use the cursor to change the data shown in the Formula Bar. Press Enter to reenter the data.

You may prefer to use the mouse to edit a cell. First, click the cell you want to edit; then click in the Formula Bar at the place you want to change the data. After you have made the changes you need, click the Enter button.

## Replacing Data

Cell contents are usually replaced when you must make significant changes to cell data. To replace cell contents, select the cell, key the new data, and enter the data by clicking the Enter button or by pressing the Enter key.

## Clearing Data

Clearing a cell will empty the cell of all its contents. To clear an active cell, you may either press the Delete key or choose the Clear command in the Edit menu.

## ACTIVITY

**7-7**

### Changing Data in a Cell

In this activity, you will change data in a cell by editing, replacing, and clearing. *Activity 7-1* should be on your screen. Make the following changes to cells in the spreadsheet:

1. Cell A16 contains the word *Surplus*. Edit the cell so that it will contain the words *Cash*

*Surplus:*

a. Move the highlight to **A16.**

b. Press **F2.** A cursor should appear in the Formula Bar.

c. Move the cursor between the quotation mark and the *S* by pressing the Left arrow key.

**d.** Key **Cash** and a space.

**e.** Press **Enter.** The edited contents should appear in the cell.

**2.** Cell A3 now contains the word *Income*. Replace this word with the word *Revenue*:

**a.** Move the highlight to **A3.**

**b.** Key **Revenue**.

**c.** Click the **Enter** button on the Formula Bar.

**3.** In the previous activity, you entered the word *September* into E3. Suppose you change your mind and now want to delete that entry:

**a.** Move the highlight to **E2.**

**b.** Press the **Delete** key. The contents should be cleared from the cell. Your screen should appear similar to Figure 7-8.

**4.** Leave *Activity 7-1* on the screen for the next activity.

### FIGURE 7-8
Changes may be made to a cell in a spreadsheet by editing or replacing data.

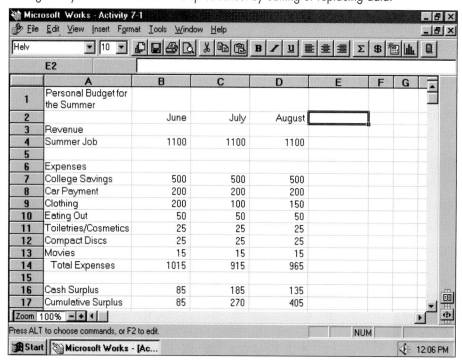

# *Changing Cell Appearances*

**Y**ou can change the appearance of a cell's contents to make them easier to read. In this section, you will learn to alter the appearance of cell contents by changing the font, font size, style, alignment, format, and borders. Examples of alternative appearances are shown in Figure 7-9.

Most of the changes use the toolbar, shown in Figure 7-10, which provides shortcuts to many spreadsheet commands.

**FIGURE 7-9**

The appearance of cell contents may be changed in style, alignment, and format.

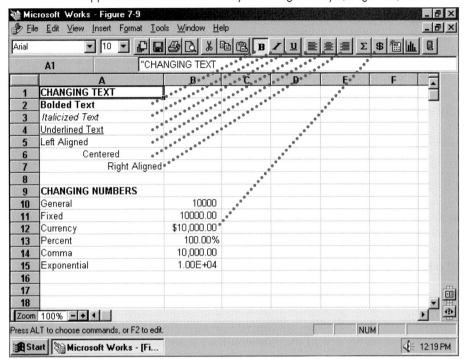

**FIGURE 7-10**

Spreadsheet cells can be formatted quickly using the toolbar.

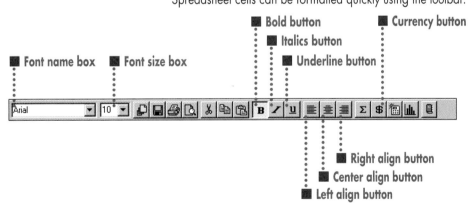

## Fonts and Font Sizes

The font and font size may significantly affect the readability of the spreadsheet if you decide to print it. The number and types of fonts available are determined by the printer you are using. You can choose different fonts for different parts of a spreadsheet. For example, you may want your numbers displayed in a 12-point serif font, and the spreadsheet's title in an 18-point sans serif font.

Changing fonts in a spreadsheet is similar to changing fonts in the word processor. Highlight the cells you want the change to affect and choose the font and size you desire. You can use the toolbar or the Format menu.

## Style

Bolding, italicizing, or underlining can add emphasis to the contents of a cell. Highlight the cell or cells you want to change and click the appropriate style button in the toolbar. To return the contents of the cell to a normal style, simply click the button again.

In addition to the styles available on the toolbar, you can add shading to cells to add emphasis. Choose the Shading command in the Format menu. Choose a pattern and color from the dialog box.

## Cell Alignment

You may align the contents of a cell or cells in three ways: against the left margin of the cell, in the center of the cell, or against the right margin of the cell. Works will automatically align all text entries (those preceded by a quotation mark when viewed in the Formula Bar) with the left side of the cell. All numbers are aligned on the right side of the cell unless a different alignment is specified. To change the alignment of the cell, place the highlight in the cell and click the alignment button you prefer. To access alignment options not present on the toolbar, choose Alignment from the Format menu.

## Formats

Several cell formats are available for the spreadsheet. The default format is called *general format,* which accommodates both text and numerical data. However, you can use several other formats (see Table 7-2). You may format a cell by highlighting the cell or range and choosing Number from the Format menu.

**TABLE 7-2**
Cells of a spreadsheet may be formatted in several ways.

## CELL FORMATS

| FORMAT | DISPLAY |
|---|---|
| General | The default format; displays both text and numerical data as keyed |
| Fixed | Displays numerical data with a fixed amount of places to the right of the decimal point |
| Currency | Displays numerical data preceded by a dollar sign |
| Comma | Displays numerical data with commas every third decimal place |
| Percent | Displays numerical data followed by a percent sign |
| Exponential | Displays numerical data in scientific notation |
| Leading Zeros | Displays numerical data with a specified number of decimal places to the left of the decimal point |
| Fraction | Displays numerical data as fractional values |
| True/False | Displays the word True for all nonzero number values and False for zero |
| Time | Displays text and numerical data as times |
| Date | Displays text and numerical data as dates |
| Text | Displays data combining numbers and special characters, such as phone numbers with hyphens, in a way that the data will not be used for calculation |

## Borders

Emphasis may be added to a cell by placing a border around its edges. You may place the border around the entire cell or only on certain sides of the cell.

**ACTIVITY**

# Changing the Appearance of Cells in the Spreadsheet

In this activity, you will change the appearance of the cells in a spreadsheet. *Activity 7-1* should be on your screen. Change the appearance of some of the cells in the spreadsheet by following these steps:

1. Bold the following cells for emphasis:
   a. Move the highlight to **A1.**
   b. Click the **Bold** button on the toolbar. The words in Cell A1 become bold.
   c. Drag the mouse pointer from **B2** and

release in **D2** to define the range B2:D2. The group of cells will become shaded. (B2 will not be shaded.)

 **d.** Click the **Bold** button in the toolbar. All of the month names in the cells should become bold.

 **e.** Bold the following cells using the same procedure: **A3, A6, A14, A16,** and **A17.** If necessary, widen column A to accommodate the data in Cell A17.

**2.** Underline the names of the months to show they are column headings:

 **a.** Select the range **B2:D2.**

 **b.** Click the Underline button on the toolbar.

**3.** Align the names of the months in the centers of the columns:

 **a.** Make sure **B2** through **D2** are still selected.

 **b.** Click the **Center Align** button on the toolbar.

**4.** Format the following cells in currency format by selecting with the highlight and clicking the Currency button on the toolbar: **B4, C4, D4, B17, C17,** and **D17.** **$**

**5.** Format the cell range from B7 through D16 in Comma format:

 **a.** Select the range **B7:D16.**

 **b.** Choose **Number** from the **Format** menu. Choose the **Comma** option in the Number dialog box. Click **OK.** The selected group should change to a comma format with two decimals to the right of the decimal point.

**6.** Italicize the account names:

 **a.** Click **A4.**

 **b.** Click the **Italic** button.

 **c.** Select **A7** through **A13.**

 **d.** Click the **Italic** button.

**7.** Place a border around the spreadsheet title, *Personal Budget for the Summer:*

 **a.** Highlight **A1.**

 **b.** Choose **Border** from the **Format** menu. The Border dialog box will appear.

 **c.** Click the **Outline** box. A line should appear in the box. If any of the other boxes in the Border dialog box contain a line, click the boxes so that the additional lines are removed.

 **d.** Click **OK.** Cell A1 should appear with a border on all sides of the cell. Your screen should appear similar to Figure 7-11.

**8.** Leave *Activity 7-1* on the screen for the next activity.

**FIGURE 7-11**
The appearance of cell contents may be changed
by bolding, underlining, and centering.

| | A | B | C | D | E | F | G |
|---|---|---|---|---|---|---|---|
| 1 | **Personal Budget for the Summer** | | | | | | |
| 2 | | **June** | **July** | **August** | | | |
| 3 | **Revenue** | | | | | | |
| 4 | *Summer Job* | $1,100.00 | $1,100.00 | $1,100.00 | | | |
| 5 | | | | | | | |
| 6 | **Expenses** | | | | | | |
| 7 | *College Savings* | 500.00 | 500.00 | 500.00 | | | |
| 8 | *Car Payment* | 200.00 | 200.00 | 200.00 | | | |
| 9 | *Clothing* | 200.00 | 100.00 | 150.00 | | | |
| 10 | *Eating Out* | 50.00 | 50.00 | 50.00 | | | |
| 11 | *Toiletries/Cosmetics* | 25.00 | 25.00 | 25.00 | | | |
| 12 | *Compact Discs* | 25.00 | 25.00 | 25.00 | | | |
| 13 | *Movies* | 15.00 | 15.00 | 15.00 | | | |
| 14 | **Total Expenses** | 1,015.00 | 915.00 | 965.00 | | | |
| 15 | | | | | | | |
| 16 | **Cash Surplus** | 85.00 | 185.00 | 135.00 | | | |
| 17 | **Cumulative Surplus** | $85.00 | $270.00 | $405.00 | | | |

*(Microsoft Works - Activity 7-1 — cell A1 contains "Personal Budget for the Summer)*

# Saving a Spreadsheet

**Y**ou can save spreadsheets using the same process you learned for word processor documents. The first time you save a spreadsheet, you will see the Save As dialog box asking you to name the spreadsheet. Once a spreadsheet has been saved, the Save command will update the latest version on disk.

## ACTIVITY

### 7-9 Saving a Spreadsheet

In this activity, you will save the file *Activity 7-1* to a new name.

1. Choose **Save As** from the **File** menu. The Save As dialog box will appear.

2. Click the **Save in** box and specify the drive of your data disk.

3. Key **Summer Budget** in the **File name** box. Click **Save.** The document is saved as *Summer Budget* on your data disk. Leave the document open for the next activity.

# Basics of Printing a Spreadsheet

**P**rinting a spreadsheet is similar to printing a word processor document. There are options available to print part of a spreadsheet or to change the way your spreadsheet prints. You will learn more about these options in the next chapter. For now you will print the entire spreadsheet using what you learned in the word processor.

## Printing a Spreadsheet

In this activity, you will print the spreadsheet on your screen.

1. Choose **Print** from the **File** menu. The Print dialog box will appear. This spreadsheet has only one page and you want only one copy, so you will not need to make any changes in the default settings.

2. Click **OK.** The spreadsheet should begin printing.

3. Choose **Close** from the **File** menu. If you are asked to save changes, click **Yes.** The spreadsheet closes.

# *Summary*

■ The purpose of a spreadsheet is to solve problems involving numbers. The primary advantage of the spreadsheet is to complete complex and repetitious calculations quickly and easily.

■ The spreadsheet consists of columns and rows intersecting to form cells. Each cell is identified by a cell reference, which is the letter of the column and number of the row. You may move to different cells of the spreadsheet by using a series of keystrokes or by scrolling with the mouse. Both text and numerical data may be entered into the spreadsheet. Data may be altered by editing, replacing, or deleting.

■ The appearance of cell data may be changed to make the spreadsheet easier to understand. Font and font size may be changed for the entire spreadsheet. Style (bolding, italicizing, and underlining) and alignment (left, center, and right justification) of individual cells may be changed and borders may be added. In addition, the appearance of the cell may be changed to accommodate data in a variety of numerical formats.

● ● ● ● ● ● ● ● ● ● ● ● ● ●

# REVIEW ACTIVITIES

## TRUE/FALSE

**Circle T or F to show whether the statement is true or false.**

T (F) **1.** The primary advantage of the spreadsheet is to summarize text documents.

(T) F **2.** A cell is the intersection of a row and column.

T (F) **3.** The active cell reference will appear in the toolbar.

T (F) **4.** The Go To command saves a file and exits Works.

T (F) **5.** To select a group of cells, click each cell individually until all cells in the range have been selected.

(T) F **6.** The Clear command removes the contents of a cell.

(T) F **7.** The best way to make minor changes to existing data in a cell is to key new data and press the Enter key.

T (F) **8.** To change the cell to exponential format, choose the Number command from the Format menu and choose the Exponential option.

T (F) **9.** Border formats define the portion of the spreadsheet that will be saved when the Save command is selected.

T (F) **10.** Saving a spreadsheet file differs significantly from saving a word processing file.

## COMPLETION

**Write the correct answer in the space provided.**

**1.** What term describes a cell that is ready for data entry?

_____ ACTIVE _____

**2.** How are columns identified in a spreadsheet?

COLUMNS are Vertical r are
identified by a letter at the top

**3.** What indicates that a cell is ready to accept data?

highlight

4. What keys should be pressed to move the highlight to the last cell of the spreadsheet?

*Ctrl + END*

5. When text data appears in the Formula Bar, what punctuation mark precedes the text?

*" Quotation marks*

6. How does Works respond when numerical data is too wide for the column in which it has been entered?

*number marks # # #*

7. What key is pressed to edit data in an active cell?

*F2*

8. What key is pressed to clear data from an active cell?

*Delete*

9. What part of the spreadsheet provides shortcuts for the most frequently used commands?

10. What forms of cell alignment are available in the spreadsheet?

*left, Right and center*

## *a p p l i c a t i o n   7 - 1*

**In the blank space, write the letter of the keystroke that matches the highlight movement.**

**Movement**

F __ **1.** Left one column

G __ **2.** Right one column

I __ **3.** Up one row

K __ **4.** Down one row

D __ **5.** To the first cell of a row

C __ **6.** To the last cell of a row containing data

A __ **7.** To Cell A1

H __ **8.** To the last row or column containing data

B __ **9.** Up one window

L __ **10.** Down one window

E __ **11.** Left one window

J __ **12.** Right one window

**Keystroke**

a.  Ctrl+Home

b.  PageUp

c.  End

d.  Home

e.  Ctrl+Page Up

f.  Left arrow

g.  Right arrow

h.  Ctrl+End

i.  Up arrow

j.  Ctrl+Page Down

k.  Down arrow

l.  Page Down

# application 7-2

**In the blank space, write the letter of the key or mouse procedure that matches the spread-sheet operation. You may use the items in the right column more than once if necessary. For some questions, more than one answer may be correct; however, you are required to identify only one of the correct answers.**

## Spreadsheet Operation

_c_ 1. Open an existing spreadsheet file

___ 2. Move to a specific cell

___ 3. Edit data in a cell

_e_ 4. Widen a spread-sheet column

___ 5. Clear data in a cell

_d_ 6. Change the style of a cell to italics

___ 7. Change the format of a cell to expo-nential

___ 8. Change the align-ment of a cell

___ 9. Add borders to a cell

_c_ 10. Save a spreadsheet file

___ 11. Exit Works

## Key or Mouse Procedure

a. Choose a command in the Format menu

b. Press the Delete key

c. Choose a command in the File menu

d. Click a button on the toolbar

e. Drag a double-headed arrow

f. Press the F5 key

g. Press the F2 key

## application 7-3

As a volunteer for a local environmental awareness group, you have agreed to collect and survey the type of trash discarded on a one-mile stretch of highway in your community. To help with your survey calculations, you have prepared the spreadsheet *Application 7-3* to account for trash items you have collected. Complete the spreadsheet by performing the following steps:

1. Open the file *Application 7-3* from the template disk.

2. Enter the following number of trash items collected for Week 4. The totals for each category should change as you enter the data.

| | |
|---|---|
| Beer Cans | 15 |
| Soda Cans | 5 |
| Fast Food Items | 20 |
| Newspaper Pages | 3 |
| Other Paper Items | 10 |
| Cigarette Butts | 17 |

3. In addition to the items above, you picked up a tennis shoe. Enter a new category in Cell A11 called *Clothing*. Then enter the number **1** in Cell E11.

4. You made a mistake when entering data for Week 3. Edit the cell for cigarette butts to show 18 rather than 16.

5. Save the file as *Litter* to your data disk and leave the file open for the next activity.

## application 7-4

In Application 7-3, you updated a spreadsheet by entering new data. In this application, you will improve the appearance of your spreadsheet so that you may present your results. Complete the following steps in the spreadsheet:

1. Change the appearance of the following cells and cell ranges in the style indicated:
   a. Change Cell A1 to bold.
   b. Change Range A3:F3 to bold.
   c. Change Range B3:F3 to underline.
   d. Change Range A13:F13 to bold.
   e. Change Range F5:F11 to bold.
   f. Change Range B11:F11 to have a border on the bottom.

2. Save the file.

3. Print and close the file.

# STRENGTHENING SPREADSHEET SKILLS

## OBJECTIVES
### When you complete this chapter, you will be able to:

1. Copy data to other cells.

2. Move data to other cells.

3. Insert and delete columns and rows.

4. Freeze headings.

5. Protect parts of a spreadsheet.

6. Use print options when printing a spreadsheet.

# Copying Data

**W**hen creating or enlarging a spreadsheet, you may want to use the same text or numbers in another portion of the spreadsheet. Rather than key the same data over again, the data may be copied. There are several ways to copy data in a spreadsheet. In this chapter, you will learn to copy and paste, use the drag and drop method, fill down, and fill right. These operations can significantly decrease the amount of time you need to prepare a spreadsheet.

**NOTE:** *Although copying data can increase the efficiency of creating a spreadsheet, there is one danger. Data copied into a cell will replace data already in that cell. Check your destination cells for existing data before copying.*

## Copy and Paste
The Copy command duplicates the contents of a cell or cells on the Clipboard so that you can enter the data in another part of the spreadsheet, as seen in Figure 8-1. The Copy command, however, will not affect the data in the original cell(s).

**FIGURE 8-1**

Data in one part of the spreadsheet may be duplicated in another
part of the spreadsheet by using the Copy and Paste commands.

| | A | B | C | D | E | F | G |
|---|---|---|---|---|---|---|---|
| 1 | SEMESTER GRADES | | | | | | |
| 2 | | Grade | Percent | Weight | | | |
| 3 | **English** | | | | | | |
| 4 | Homework | | | 0.00 | | | |
| 5 | Exam 1 | | | 0.00 | | | |
| 6 | Exam 2 | | | 0.00 | | | |
| 7 | Exam 3 | | | 0.00 | | | |
| 8 | Final Exam | | | 0.00 | | | |
| 9 | Semester Grade | | | 0.00 | | | |
| 10 | | | | | | | |
| 11 | Homework | | | 0.00 | | | |
| 12 | Exam 1 | | | 0.00 | | | |
| 13 | Exam 2 | | | 0.00 | | | |
| 14 | Exam 3 | | | 0.00 | | | |
| 15 | Final Exam | | | 0.00 | | | |
| 16 | Semester Grade | | | 0.00 | | | |
| 17 | | | | | | | |
| 18 | | | | | | | |

After placing the highlight in the part of the spreadsheet where the data is
to be copied, use the Paste command to enter the stored data into the cell or
cells. It is not necessary to select the entire range of cells; you need only highlight the upper left corner of the range into which data will be copied.

The data stored on the Clipboard will remain until it is replaced with new
data. If you would like to make multiple copies, you may simply choose the
Paste command once more.

**ACTIVITY**

# Copying and Pasting

In this activity, you will practice copying and
pasting. *Activity 8-1* is a spreadsheet intended
to calculate the semester grade of an English
class. The spreadsheet will be expanded to calculate the grades of history and biology
classes.

1. Open the file *Activity 8-1* from your template disk. The spreadsheet contains
columns for grades and percentages of
homework and examinations.

2. Maximize the document window.

3. Expand the spreadsheet to calculate grades for a history class:
   a. Select range **A4:D9.**
   b. Choose **Copy** from the **Edit** menu.
   c. Highlight **A11.**
   d. Choose **Paste** from the **Edit** menu. The range of cells should be copied from A4:D9 to A11:D16.

4. Key **History** into **A10.**

5. Leave *Activity 8-1* on the screen for the next activity.

**N O T E :**  *You may also copy using buttons on the toolbar rather than choosing commands in the Edit menu.*

## Using the Drag and Drop Method

Like the word processor, the spreadsheet allows you to quickly copy cells using the drag and drop method. First highlight the cells you want to copy. Then, while holding down the Ctrl key, drag the cells to a new location and release the mouse button. What makes the process different from the word processor is that you must drag from the border of the highlighted cells. You will know you are pointing to the correct place when the word *DRAG* appears below the pointer.

**A C T I V I T Y**

## Copying with Drag and Drop

In this activity, you will copy cells using the drag and drop method. *Activity 8-1* should be on your screen.

1. Expand the spreadsheet to calculate grades for a biology class:
   a. Select range **A11:D16.**
   b. Move the pointer to the top edge of Cell A11. When you have the pointer in the correct position, the word *DRAG* will appear below the pointer.
   c. While holding down the **Ctrl** key (notice that the word *COPY* replaces *DRAG*), drag down until the pointer is in Cell A18. Release the mouse button. The data will be copied from A11:D16 to A18:D23.

2. Key **Biology** into Cell A17.

3. Bold the contents of Cells A10 and A17. Compare your screen to Figure 8-2.

4. Leave *Activity 8-1* on the screen for the next activity.

**FIGURE 8-2**

Copying and pasting speeds the process of creating a spreadsheet.

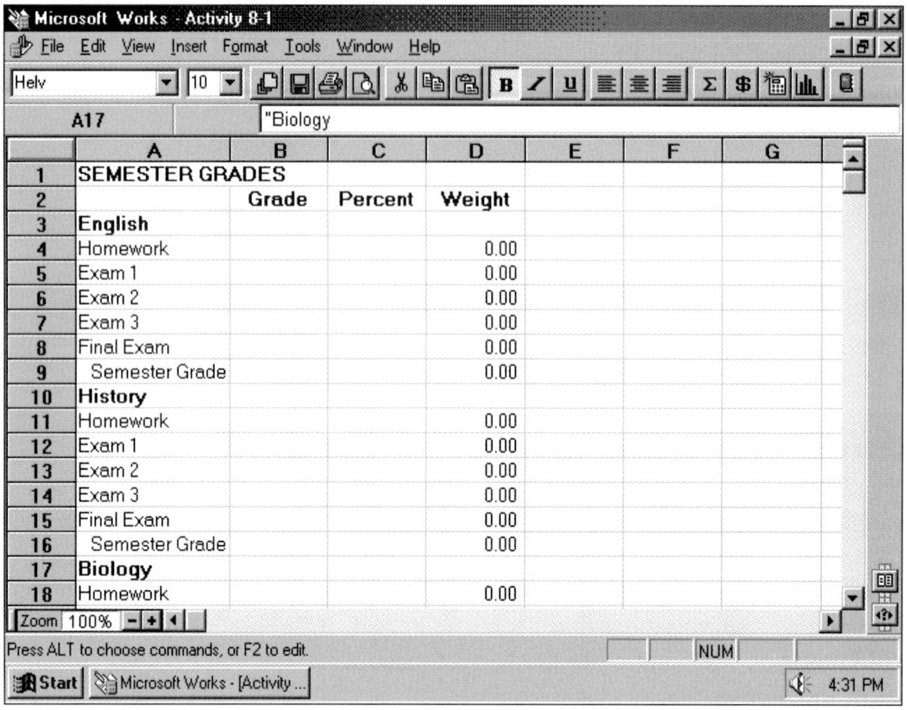

## Fill Down and Fill Right

The Fill Down and Fill Right commands copy data into the cell(s) adjacent to the original. The Fill Down command will copy data into the cell(s) directly below the original cell, as shown in Figure 8-3. The Fill Right command will copy data into the cell(s) to the right of the original cell, as shown in Figure 8-4. Either command will make multiple copies if more than one destination cell is selected. For example, the Fill Down command can copy data into the next several cells below the original cell. The Fill commands are somewhat faster than copying and pasting because filling requires choosing only one command. However, filling can be used only when the destination cells are adjacent to the original cell.

**FIGURE 8-3**

The Fill Down command copies data to adjacent cells below the original cell.

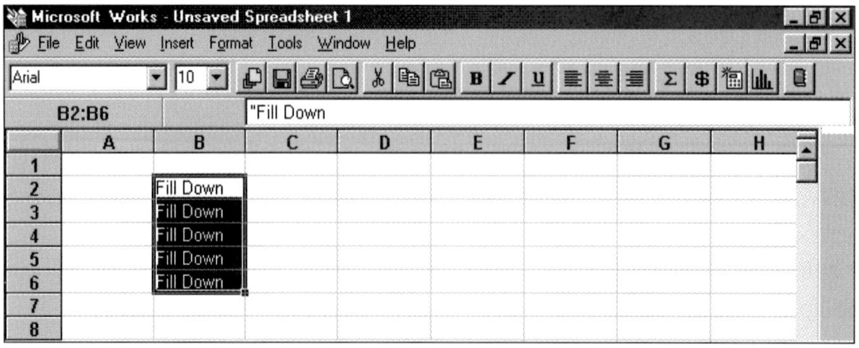

**FIGURE 8-4**

The Fill Right command copies data to adjacent cells to the right of the original cell.

| | A | B | C | D | E | F | G | H |
|---|---|---|---|---|---|---|---|---|
| 1 | | | | | | | | |
| 2 | | Fill Right | Fill Right | Fill Right | Fill Right | Fill Right | | |
| 3 | | | | | | | | |
| 4 | | | | | | | | |
| 5 | | | | | | | | |
| 6 | | | | | | | | |
| 7 | | | | | | | | |
| 8 | | | | | | | | |

Microsoft Works - Unsaved Spreadsheet 1 — File Edit View Insert Format Tools Window Help — Arial — 10 — B2:F2 — "Fill Right

## ACTIVITY

## Using the Fill Down Command

In this activity, you will enter grade and percentage data into a spreadsheet using the Fill Down command. *Activity 8-1* should be on your screen. The following table shows the data for grades earned in classes. Follow the steps below to enter this data in the spreadsheet:

1. Each of the exams in English is 20% of the semester grade. Enter the percent for the exams in English by following these steps:
   **a.** Enter **.2** in Cell C5. (.2 is the decimal equivalent of 20%.)
   **b.** Drag from C5 to C7 to select the range to be filled.
   **c.** Choose **Fill Down** from the **Edit** menu.

The contents of Cell C5, 20.00%, will be copied to Cells C6 and C7.

2. Use the same procedure to enter percentages for the history and biology exams. Enter **.2** in Cell C12 and **.15** in Cell C19.

3. Use the Fill Down command to copy data from C12 to C13:C14 and C19 to C20:C21.

4. Enter the remaining data into the spreadsheet by inserting the percentages for homework and final exams; enter the grades for all items.

| Subject | Grade | Percent |
|---|---|---|
| **English** | | |
| Homework | 87 | 10.00% |
| Exam 1 | 82 | 20.00% |
| Exam 2 | 75 | 20.00% |
| Exam 3 | 78 | 20.00% |
| Final Exam | 81 | 30.00% |

| **Subject** | **Grade** | **Percent** |
|---|---|---|
| **History** | | |
| Homework | 76 | 5.00% |
| Exam 1 | 74 | 20.00% |
| Exam 2 | 80 | 20.00% |
| Exam 3 | 77 | 20.00% |
| Final Exam | 79 | 35.00% |
| **Biology** | | |
| Homework | 89 | 30.00% |
| Exam 1 | 92 | 15.00% |
| Exam 2 | 87 | 15.00% |
| Exam 3 | 95 | 15.00% |
| Final Exam | 93 | 25.00% |

5. After completing the spreadsheet you may notice that the semester grades have been calculated based on the data entered. Compare your screen to Figure 8-5.

6. Leave *Activity 8-1* on your screen for the next activity.

**FIGURE 8-5**
In this spreadsheet, the Fill Down command was used to copy the percentages for the exams from Cell C5 to Cells C6 and C7.

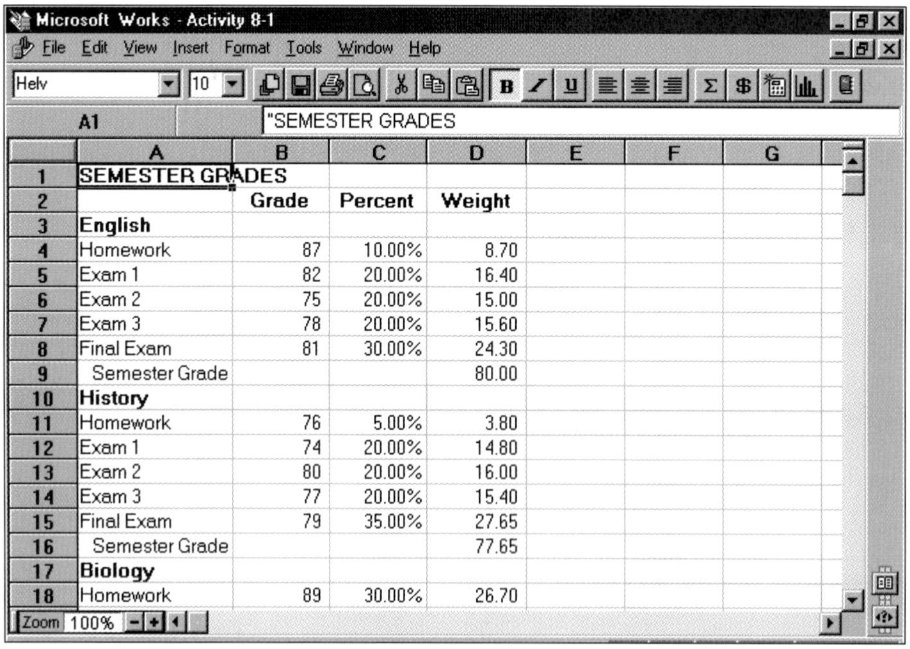


| | A | B | C | D | E | F | G |
|---|---|---|---|---|---|---|---|
| 1 | SEMESTER GRADES | | | | | | |
| 2 | | Grade | Percent | Weight | | | |
| 3 | English | | | | | | |
| 4 | Homework | 87 | 10.00% | 8.70 | | | |
| 5 | Exam 1 | 82 | 20.00% | 16.40 | | | |
| 6 | Exam 2 | 75 | 20.00% | 15.00 | | | |
| 7 | Exam 3 | 78 | 20.00% | 15.60 | | | |
| 8 | Final Exam | 81 | 30.00% | 24.30 | | | |
| 9 | Semester Grade | | | 80.00 | | | |
| 10 | History | | | | | | |
| 11 | Homework | 76 | 5.00% | 3.80 | | | |
| 12 | Exam 1 | 74 | 20.00% | 14.80 | | | |
| 13 | Exam 2 | 80 | 20.00% | 16.00 | | | |
| 14 | Exam 3 | 77 | 20.00% | 15.40 | | | |
| 15 | Final Exam | 79 | 35.00% | 27.65 | | | |
| 16 | Semester Grade | | | 77.65 | | | |
| 17 | Biology | | | | | | |
| 18 | Homework | 89 | 30.00% | 26.70 | | | |

# Moving Data

**D**ata is sometimes moved in the spreadsheet to improve the appearance of the spreadsheet. Moving is referred to in Works as cutting and pasting.

Previously, you learned that the Copy command places data on the Clipboard so that it may be copied into another area of the spreadsheet. The Cut command also places selected data on the Clipboard; however, it will remove data from its original position in the spreadsheet. Because cut data is stored on the Clipboard, you may restore the data at any time by simply choosing the Paste command.

The drag and drop method can be used to move data in the spreadsheet. The procedure is the same as you learned earlier in this chapter, except you do not hold down the Ctrl key. This actually makes the drag and drop method the easiest way to move data in a spreadsheet because you can do it without touching a key or using a menu.

## ACTIVITY

## Moving Data in a Spreadsheet

In this activity, you will move data in a spreadsheet file. *Activity 8-1* should be on your screen. You decide that the spreadsheet may be easier to read if there is a blank row between each class. Perform the following operations to move the data:

1. Move the data for Biology down two rows:
   a. Select range **A17:D23.**
   b. Click the **Cut** button on the toolbar. The data in the range will disappear from the spreadsheet.
   c. Highlight **A19.**
   d. Click the **Paste** button on the toolbar. The data will appear in the range A19:D25.

Cut Button

Paste Button

2. Move the data for History down one row using the drag and drop method:
   a. Select range **A10:D16.**
   b. Move the pointer to the top edge of Cell A10. When you have the pointer in the correct position, the word *DRAG* will appear below the pointer.
   c. Using the mouse, drag down until the pointer is in Cell A11. Release the mouse button. The data will appear in the range A11:D17. Your screen should be similar to Figure 8-6.

3. Leave *Activity 8-1* on the screen for the next activity.

## FIGURE 8-6
The Copy command duplicates data in a spreadsheet;
the Cut command moves data to another part of the spreadsheet.

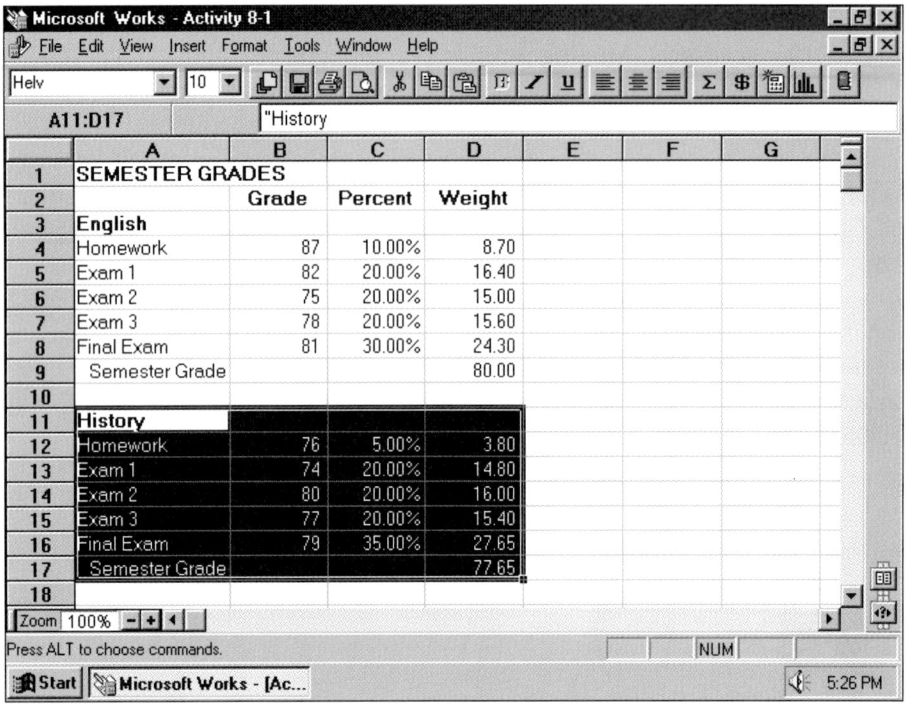

# Inserting and Deleting Rows and Columns

The appearance of the spreadsheet may also be changed by adding and removing rows and columns of the spreadsheet. In fact, in the previous activity, you could have inserted rows between the classes rather than move existing data.

Inserting adds a row above the highlight or a column to the left of the highlight. Deleting removes the row or column in which the highlight appears. The Delete Row or Delete Column command is potentially dangerous because it erases the data contained in the row or column. If you accidentally delete the wrong column or row, the data in the column or row will be erased. The data may be restored only by selecting the Undo command in the Edit menu.

# ACTIVITY

## Inserting and Deleting Rows and Columns

In this activity, you will insert a row and insert and delete a column in the file *Activity 8-1*, which should be on your screen. Perform the following steps:

1. Insert a row near the top of the spreadsheet:
   **a.** Highlight any cell in Row 3.
   **b.** Choose **Insert Row** from the **Insert** menu. Row 3 will be blank. The original Row 3 will be moved to Row 4, and all rows below it will shift down one row.

2. Suppose you want to include a column in the spreadsheet for the date the examination was taken. Insert a column between Columns A and B:
   **a.** Highlight any cell in Column B.
   **b.** Choose **Insert Column** from the **In-**

**sert** menu. A blank column will appear as Column B. The original Column B will be moved to Column C, and all the columns to its right will also shift rightward.
   **c.** Key **Date** in Cell B2.
   **d.** Press **Enter.**

3. Suppose you change your mind about the date column. Delete Column B:
   **a.** Highlight any cell in Column B.
   **b.** Choose **Delete Column** from the **Insert** menu. The date column will disappear, and the columns to its right will now shift back to the left.

4. Leave *Activity 8-1* on the screen for the next activity.

# Freezing Titles

Often a spreadsheet can become so large that it is difficult to view the entire spreadsheet on the screen. As you scroll to lower parts of the spreadsheet column, titles at the top or side of the spreadsheet may disappear from the screen, making it difficult to identify the contents of the column. For example, you may have noticed that the column titles (Grade and Percent) in previous activities scrolled off the screen when you were working in the lower part of the spreadsheet.

Freezing will keep the row or column titles on the screen no matter where you scroll in the spreadsheet. To freeze titles, select the Freeze Titles command in the Format menu. All rows above the highlight and columns to the left of the highlight will be frozen. Frozen titles are indicated by a check mark in the Format menu by the Freeze Titles command. (See Figure 8-7.) To unfreeze a row or column title, choose the Freeze Titles command again; the check mark will disappear and the titles will be unfrozen.

**FIGURE 8-7**
The check mark by the Freeze Titles command indicates that headings in the spreadsheet will remain on the screen no matter where the highlight is moved.

| Format |
|---|
| Number... |
| Alignment... |
| Font and Style... |
| Border... |
| Shading... |
| Protection... |
| AutoFormat... |
| Set Print Area |
| ✔ Freeze Titles |
| Row Height... |
| Column Width... |

## Freezing Titles

In this activity, you will freeze the column headings in a spreadsheet. *Activity 8-1* should be on your screen.

1. Highlight **A3.**

2. Choose **Freeze Titles** from the **Format** menu. The column headings in Rows 1 and 2 are now frozen.

3. Click **Format** again and notice the check mark beside the Freeze Titles command. This indicates titles are now frozen.

4. Scroll to the lower part of the spreadsheet. You will notice that the column headings remain at the top of the screen no matter where you move.

5. Choose **Freeze Titles** from the **Format** menu. The column headings are no longer frozen.

6. Leave *Activity 8-1* on the screen for the next activity.

# *Protecting Cells*

**P**rotecting data in a cell prevents anyone from making changes to the cell inadvertently. In other words, the cell becomes "locked" until someone removes the protection.

To use the Protect Data command, you must first select the cells you want to protect, then choose the Protection command from the Format menu. When the Protection dialog box appears, as shown in Figure 8-8, click the Locked check box. After the Locked option is on, you may protect the cells by choosing the Protect Data check box.

Works locks the entire spreadsheet as a default option. In other words, if you select the Protect Data command in a new spreadsheet, the entire spreadsheet will be protected. Therefore, you need to "unlock" all contents of the spreadsheet before selecting the specific cells you want to lock.

If you attempt to change the data in cells after they have been protected, Works will display a message telling you the cells cannot be changed. If you intend to change the cells, you must first unprotect them.

**FIGURE 8-8**
The Locked check box in the Protection dialog box must be turned on before you can protect data.

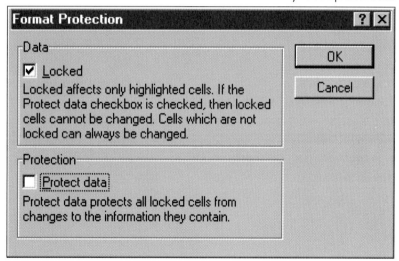

**ACTIVITY**

# 8-7 Protecting Cells

In this activity, you will protect the cells in a portion of the spreadsheet. Suppose you plan to add future classes at the bottom of the spreadsheet and plan to use the original portion of the file *Activity 8-1* as a long-term record of your grades. Because your past grades cannot be changed, you desire to protect the data so that they are not changed by mistake.

1. Unlock all data in the spreadsheet:
   a. Select **A1:D26.**
   b. Choose **Protection** from the **Format** menu. The Protection dialog box will appear with the Locked check box checked.
   c. Click the **Locked** check box until it becomes blank.
   d. Click **OK.**

2. Lock the data to be protected:
   a. Select the range **A4:D26,** which contains the classes for which grades have already been recorded.
   b. Choose **Protection** from the **Format** menu. The Protection dialog box will appear.

   c. Click the **Locked** check box until a check appears.
   d. Click the **Protect data** check box until a check appears.
   e. Click **OK.** The selected range is now protected.

3. Check the protection of the cells (Figure 8-9):
   a. Move the highlight to **B5,** a cell within the protected range.
   b. Key **45**.
   c. Click the **Enter** box. Works should display a message telling you the cell cannot be changed.
   d. Click **OK** to close the message.

4. Turn the protection off:
   a. Choose **Protection** from the **Format** menu.
   b. Click the **Protect data** check box to clear it.
   c. Click **OK.**

5. Leave *Activity 8-1* on the screen for the next activity.

**FIGURE 8-9**
**FIGURE 8-9**
If data is entered into a protected cell, a dialog box stating that
the cell is locked will appear. The dialog box also contains
directions on how to unlock and unprotect a protected cell.

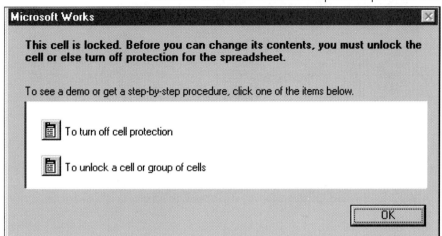

If you desire to enter data into cells currently protected, clear the Protect
Data check box in the Protection dialog box. You may then enter data without
the dialog box appearing. To protect the cells again, choose the Protect Data option once more.

# Using Print Options When Printing a Spreadsheet

In Chapter 7 you printed a spreadsheet using the default settings. There
are, however, commands to help you control the way your spreadsheet prints.

## Setting the Print Area

You may print the entire spreadsheet or a portion of the spreadsheet. The
Set Print Area command tells Works the part of the spreadsheet you want to
print. To designate the area you want to print, select the range and then, in the
Format menu, choose Set Print Area.

## Setting the Margins and Page Size

The Page Setup command in the File menu will produce a dialog box that
allows you to set page margins, set page lengths and widths, designate page
numbers, and determine whether column letters, row numbers, and gridlines
should be printed. The Page Setup dialog box is divided into three sections.
Figure 8-10 shows all three sections of the Page Setup dialog box.

**FIGURE 8-10**
The Page Setup dialog box has three sections for setting
options such as margins, page dimensions, and page numbers.

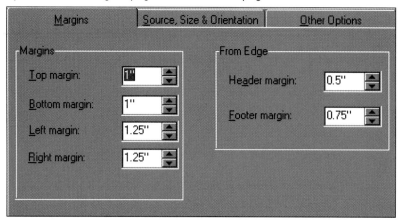

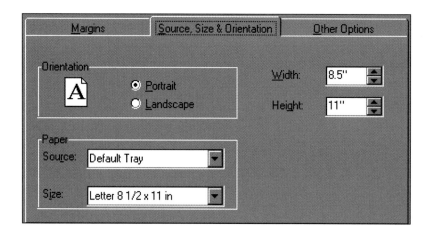

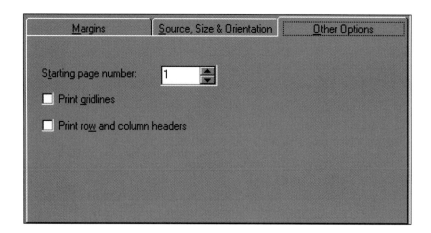

## THE MARGINS SECTION

The Margins section of the dialog box allows you to change the margins of the printed page by entering the desired margin in the appropriate box.

## THE SOURCE, SIZE AND ORIENTATION SECTION

The Source, Size and Orientation section of the dialog box allows you to choose Portrait or Landscape orientation. Landscape orientation can be useful for wide spreadsheets. You may also designate the size of the paper on which you will print.

## THE OTHER OPTIONS SECTION

The Other Options section of the dialog box has three options.

- *Starting page number* designates the page number of the first page of the spreadsheet. To change the number of the first page, click the box and enter a new page number.

- When the *Print gridlines* check box contains a check, Works will print the gridlines appearing between the cells. If the check box is not checked, the gridlines will not be printed.

- When the *Print row and column headers* check box contains a check, Works will print the row number and column letter.

# Previewing a Spreadsheet before Printing

The Print Preview command of the spreadsheet is exactly the same as in the word processor. The Print Preview command shows how your printed pages will appear before you actually print them. To access the Print Preview screen (see Figure 8-11), choose the Print Preview command from the File menu or click the Print Preview button on the toolbar. When you have finished previewing the printed pages, you may either return to the spreadsheet by clicking Cancel or print the spreadsheet by clicking Print.

**FIGURE 8-11**

Use the Print Preview screen to check the spreadsheet before printing.

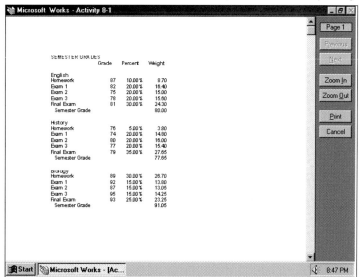

# Using Print Options

• • • • • • • • • • • • • • • • • • • • • • • • • • • • • • • • • • • • • • • • • • •

In this activity, you will print the spreadsheet in file *Activity 8-1.*

**1.** Set the area of the spreadsheet to be printed:
   **a.** Select **A1:D26.**
   **b.** Choose **Set Print Area** from the **Format** menu. A message appears asking you to verify the change in print area. Click **OK.**

**2.** Change the margin of the printed document:
   **a.** Choose **Page Setup** from the **File** menu. The Page Setup dialog box will appear. If the Margins section is not already showing, switch to the Margins section.

   **b.** Change the **Left margin** setting from **1.25"** to **1".**
   **c.** Click **OK.**

**3.** Preview the spreadsheet to be printed:
   **a.** Click the **Print Preview** button on the toolbar.
   **b.** Click the **Zoom In** button twice. A portion of the previewed page will become larger so that it can be examined in more detail.

**4.** Click the **Print** button. The spreadsheet should begin printing.

**5.** Save the file to your data disk as *Semester Grade* and close the file.

# *Summary*

- The data in a spreadsheet can be moved or copied to another location in the spreadsheet by using the Cut, Copy, Paste, Fill Right, and Fill Down commands from the Edit menu. These commands can save time by eliminating the need to rekey large quantities of data. The drag and drop method can also be used to copy and move data in spreadsheets.

- The appearance of the spreadsheet can be changed by inserting or deleting rows and columns. When a spreadsheet becomes large, the column or row titles will disappear from the screen as you scroll to distant parts of the spreadsheet. You may keep the titles on the screen at all times by freezing them.

- The cells of a spreadsheet may be protected from accidental change by choosing the Protection command from the Format menu. The protection can be applied to the entire spreadsheet or to a portion of the spreadsheet. Cells may be unprotected if changes are necessary.

- The Set Print Area command designates the portion of the spreadsheet you want to print. The Page Setup command controls the page size and the margins that will be printed. To view the spreadsheet as it will appear before actually printing it, use the Print Preview command.

• • • • • • • • • • • • • •

# REVIEW ACTIVITIES

## TRUE/FALSE

**Circle T or F to show whether the statement is true or false.**

**T   F**   1. If you copy into cells already containing data, the data will be replaced by the copied data.

**T   F**   2. The Fill Down and Fill Right commands are available only if you plan to copy to cells adjacent to the original cell.

**T   F**   3. The Paste command is used for both copying and moving.

**T   F**   4. Deleting a row or column will erase the data contained in the row or column.

**T   F**   5. The Insert Column command is in the Format menu.

**T   F**   6. When using the Delete Row command, the row above the highlight will be deleted.

**T   F**   7. The Freeze Titles command will freeze rows above and columns to the right of the highlight.

**T   F**   8. A message will appear if you attempt to edit a cell that has been protected.

**T   F**   9. The Page Setup command is used to designate the part of the spreadsheet that will be printed.

**T   F**   10. A spreadsheet may be previewed before printing by clicking the Print Preview button on the toolbar or by choosing the Print Preview command in the File menu.

## COMPLETION

**Write the correct answer in the space provided.**

1. What command is always used in conjunction with the Copy command and the Cut command?

_____

_____

2. Identify the four methods of copying data in the spreadsheet.

_____

_____

3. In what menu are the commands used for copying data located?

_____

_____

4. What are the two commands used to move data to a new location?

_____

_____

5. What should you do if a column or row is deleted by accident?

_____

_____

6. What command keeps the titles of a spreadsheet on the screen no matter where the highlight is moved?

_____

_____

7. The Protection command is contained in which menu?

_____

_____

8. Identify three actions performed in the Page Setup dialog box.

_____

_____

9. What section of the Page Setup dialog box allows you to choose landscape orientation?

_____

_____

10. What does the Print gridlines check box in the Page Setup command do?

_____

_____

# REINFORCEMENT APPLICATIONS

*application 8-1*

**In the blank space, write the letter of the spreadsheet command that will solve the spreadsheet problem.**

## Spreadsheet Problem

___ 1. You are tired of keying repetitive data.

___ 2. A portion of the spreadsheet would be more useful in another area of the spreadsheet.

___ 3. You forgot to key a row of data in the middle of the spreadsheet.

___ 4. You no longer need a certain column in the spreadsheet.

___ 5. Column headings cannot be viewed on the screen when you are working in the lower part of the spreadsheet.

___ 6. You would like to avoid entering data in cells that should not be altered.

___ 7. Your boss would rather not view your spreadsheet on the screen and has requested a copy on paper.

___ 8. You would like to print only a portion of the spreadsheet.

## Spreadsheet Commands

a. Print command or Print button on the toolbar

b. Fill Right, Fill Down, or Copy command

c. Insert Row or Insert Column command

d. Protection command

e. Cut command, Paste command

f. Set Print Area command

g. Delete Row or Delete Column command

h. Freeze Titles command

# *application   8 - 2*

**The file *Application 8-2* is a spreadsheet for the Bates family, which is preparing to purchase furniture for a new home. The spreadsheet is not currently organized by rooms in the house. In addition, the family wants to purchase more than one piece of certain items.**

1. Open *Application 8-2*. Organize the spreadsheet following the format given in the table. The new spreadsheet should have furniture items organized by rooms, with proper headings. Remember to use the Fill Down command to copy repetitive items and the Insert Row command to provide headings. Use the Cut and Paste commands or drag and drop to move some of the data.

2. Print the spreadsheet.

3. Save the spreadsheet to your data disk as *Furniture* and close the file.

**Furniture Purchases**

| Item | Purchase Price |
|------|---------------|
| **Utility Room** | |
| Washer | $340.00 |
| Dryer | $299.00 |
| **Living Room** | |
| Couch | $500.00 |
| Arm Chair | $260.00 |
| End Table | $250.00 |
| End Table | $250.00 |
| **Bedroom** | |
| Bed | $550.00 |
| Dresser | $400.00 |
| Drawers | $250.00 |
| **Dining Room** | |
| Table | $400.00 |
| Dining Chair | $120.00 |
| Dining Chair | $120.00 |
| Dining Chair | $120.00 |
| Dining Chair | $120.00 |

# *a p p l i c a t i o n  8 - 3*

**You are a member of a club that participates in school athletic activities. You have been allocated $1,210 to purchase sports equipment for the club. You decide to prepare a spreadsheet to help you calculate the cost of various purchases. Open the file *Application 8-3* from your template disk and make the following adjustments to the spreadsheet:**

1. Bold and center the column headings appearing in Row 2.

2. Insert a row above Row 3.

3. Freeze the column headings in Row 2. (*Hint:* The highlight should be placed in A3.)

4. Insert a row above Row 8 and key **Bats** into Column A of the new row.

5. Use the Fill Down command to copy the formula in Cell E4 to E5:E11. Do not copy the formula into Cell E12.

6. Format the Cost (D4:D11) and Total (E4:E12) columns for currency.

7. Key the data for Sport and Cost, as given in the table that follows. Use the Fill Down command as needed to copy repetitive data. Widen the columns if necessary.

| Item | Sport | Cost |
| --- | --- | --- |
| Basketballs | Basketball | $28.00 |
| Hoops | Basketball | $40.00 |
| Backboards | Basketball | $115.00 |
| Softballs | Softball | $5.00 |
| Bats | Softball | $30.00 |
| Masks | Softball | $35.00 |
| Volleyballs | Volleyball | $25.00 |
| Nets | Volleyball | $125.00 |

8. The organization has requested you to purchase the items listed below. Any remaining cash should be used to purchase as many basketballs as possible.

| | |
| --- | --- |
| Basketballs | 5 |
| Hoops | 2 |
| Backboards | 2 |
| Softballs | 20 |
| Bats | 5 |
| Masks | 1 |
| Volleyballs | 7 |
| Nets | 1 |

   (*Hint:* Increase the number of basketballs and watch the dollar amount in the total. You should use $1,203.00 and have $7.00 left over.)

9. The costs of these items are not expected to change any time soon. Protect the data in the Cost column (D4:D11) so that the data cannot be accidentally changed. Remember to unlock all the contents of the spreadsheet before locking the portion you want to protect.

10. Print the spreadsheet.

11. Save the spreadsheet to your data disk as *Sports Equipment* and close the file.

# ADVANCED SPREADSHEET OPERATIONS

## OBJECTIVES

**When you complete this chapter, you will be able to:**

1. Use the spreadsheet as a calculator.

2. Enter and edit spreadsheet formulas.

3. Distinguish between relative and absolute cell references.

4. Use the Autosum™ button.

5. Display formulas in the spreadsheet.

6. Perform immediate and delayed calculations.

7. Use function formulas.

# *Using the Spreadsheet as a Calculator*

**A**primary advantage of the spreadsheet is the power of rapid calculation. In fact, the spreadsheet will perform the same functions as a hand or desk calculator.

# 9-1

## Using the Spreadsheet as a Calculator

In this activity, you will observe the computing power of the spreadsheet.

1. Open the file *Activity 9-1* from your template disk. This spreadsheet contains headings for the four primary mathematical functions of addition, subtraction, multiplication, and division.

2. Key **10** in Cell A5 and **24** in Cell C5. The value in Cell E5 should display 34, which is the sum of 10 and 24.

3. Highlight **E5.** Notice that the Formula Bar at the top of the screen displays the formula =A5+C5. The formula indicates that Cell E5 contains the sum of the values in Cells A5 and C5.

4. Key **48** in Cell A14 and **8** in Cell C14. The value in Cell E14 should display 6, which is the result of 48 divided by 8.

5. Highlight **E14.** Notice that the Formula Bar at the top of the screen displays the formula =A14/C14. The formula indicates that Cell E14 contains the result of the value in Cell A14 divided by the value in Cell C14.

6. Experiment by entering numbers into other cells of the spreadsheet. Calculations will take place as soon as you press the Enter key or click the Enter box.

7. Close the file *Activity 9-1* currently on your screen. Do not save the changes.

# *What Are Formulas?*

**S**preadsheets can use numbers entered in certain cells to calculate values in other cells. The equations used to calculate values in a cell are known as *formulas.* Works recognizes the contents of a cell as a formula when an equal sign (=) is the first character in the cell. For example, if the formula =8+6 were entered into Cell B3, the value of 14 would be displayed in the spreadsheet. The Formula Bar displays the formula =8+6, as shown in Figure 9-1.

## Structure of a Formula

A spreadsheet formula is composed of two types of characters: operands and operators. An *operand* is a number or cell reference used in formulas. An *operator* tells Works what to do with the operands. For example, in the formula =B3+5, B3 and 5 are operands. The plus sign (+) is an operator that tells Works

FIGURE 9-1
Works recognizes an entry as a formula when an equal sign is the first character in the cell. In Cell B3, the formula =8+6, displayed in the Formula Bar, produced the value of 14 in the cell.

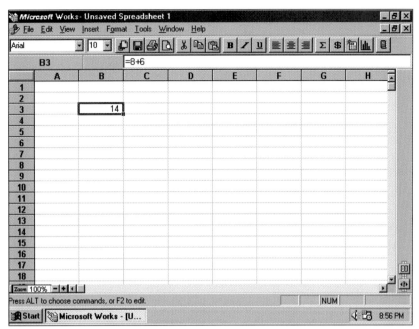

to add the value contained in Cell B3 to the number 5. The operators used in formulas are shown in Table 9-1. You may observe the formulas for the spreadsheet now on your screen by highlighting Cells E5, E8, E11, or E14.

**TABLE 9-1**

Operators tell works what to do with operands.

## FORMULA OPERATORS

| OPERATOR | OPERATION | EXAMPLE | MEANING |
|---|---|---|---|
| + | Addition | B5+C5 | Adds the values in B5 and C5 |
| - | Subtraction | C8-232 | Subtracts 232 from the value in C8 |
| * | Multiplication | D4*D5 | Multiplies the value in D4 by the value in D5 |
| / | Division | E6/4 | Divides the value in E6 by 4 |
| ^ | Exponentiation | B3^3 | Raises the value in B3 to the third power |

## Order of Evaluation

Formulas containing more than one operator are called complex formulas. For example, the formula =C3*C4+5 will perform both multiplication and addition to calculate the value in the cell. The sequence used to calculate the value of a formula is called the *order of evaluation.*

Formulas are evaluated in the following order:

1.  Contents within parentheses are evaluated first. You may use as many pairs of parentheses as you desire. Works will evaluate the innermost set of parentheses first.

2.  Mathematical operators are evaluated in order of priority, as shown in Table 9-2.

3.  Equations are evaluated from left to right if two or more operators have the same order of evaluation. For example, in the formula =20-15-2, 15 would be subtracted from 20; then 2 would be subtracted from the difference (5).

**TABLE 9-2**
The sequence of calculations in a formula is determined by the order of evaluation.

### ORDER OF EVALUATION

| ORDER OF EVALUATION | OPERATOR | SYMBOL |
|---|---|---|
| First | Exponentiation | ^ |
| Second | Positive or negative | + or - |
| Third | Multiplication or division | * or / |
| Fourth | Addition or subtraction | + or - |

# *Editing Formulas*

If you key a formula incorrectly, Works will not let you enter the formula. When you try to enter the formula, an error message will appear. In some cases, Works describes the reason for the error and suggests a correction. In other cases, Works will explain the reason for the error without offering a suggestion. You may accept Works' suggestion, or edit the formula in the same way you edited number and text data in previous chapters.

You may also edit formulas already entered in the spreadsheet. After highlighting the cell, press the Edit key (F2) or click in the Formula Bar and add or delete data as necessary.

Sometimes you might make a mistake entering a formula. For example, you may forget to key a parenthesis or other element of the formula. In such cases, Works will alert you with a dialog box that gives you the option to let Works correct your mistake.

## ACTIVITY

# Entering Formulas into a Spreadsheet

In this activity, you will create formulas that perform calculations using the numbers in spreadsheet file *Activity 9-2*.

1. Open the file *Activity 9-2* from your template disk.

2. Enter the formulas given in the cells. Remember to precede each formula with an equal sign. After you enter a formula, the formula result will appear in the cell. You may check your results by comparing them to the screen shown in Figure 9-2.

| Cell | Formula |
|------|---------|
| C3 | =A3+B3 |
| C4 | =A4-B4 |
| C5 | =A5*B5 |
| C6 | =A6/B6 |

**FIGURE 9-2**
Formulas may be used to determine values in the cells of a spreadsheet.

| | A | B | C | D | E | F | G | H |
|---|---|---|---|---|---|---|---|---|
| 1 | | | | | | | | |
| 2 | | | | | | | | |
| 3 | 141 | 239 | 380 | | | | | |
| 4 | 263 | 509 | -246 | | | | | |
| 5 | 58 | 325 | 18850 | | | | | |
| 6 | 800 | 400 | 2 | | | | | |
| 7 | | | | | | | | |
| 8 | | | | | | | | |
| 9 | | | | | | | | |
| 10 | | | | | | | | |
| 11 | | | | | | | | |
| 12 | | | | | | | | |
| 13 | | | | | | | | |
| 14 | | | | | | | | |
| 15 | | | | | | | | |
| 16 | | | | | | | | |
| 17 | | | | | | | | |
| 18 | | | | | | | | |

C6 | =A6/B6

3. Enter a complex formula in Cell D3 that will add the values in Cells A3 and B3, then multiply the result by 20:
   a. Move the highlight to **D3.**
   b. Key **=(A3+B3)\*20**.
   c. Press **Enter.** The resulting value should be 7600.

4. You can see the importance of the parentheses in the order of evaluation by creating an identical formula without the parentheses:
   a. Move the highlight to **E3.**
   b. Key **=A3+B3\*20**, the same formula as in Cell D3 but without the parentheses.
   c. Press **Enter.** The resulting value in Cell E3 should be 4921. This value differs from the value in Cell D3 because Works multiplied the value in Cell B3 by 20 before adding Cell A3. In Cell D3, the values in Cells A3 and Cell B3 were added together and the sum multiplied by 20.

5. Save the file to your data disk as *Calculation* and leave the file on the screen for the next activity.

# *Relative, Absolute, and Mixed Cell References*

Three types of cell references are used to create formulas: relative, absolute, and mixed. A ***relative cell reference*** adjusts to its new location when copied or moved. For example, in Figure 9-3, if the formula =B2+A3 is copied or moved from Cell B3 to Cell C4, the formula will be changed to =C3+B4. In other words, this particular formula is instructing Works to add the cell directly above to the cell directly to the right. When the formula is copied or moved, the cell references change, but the instructions remain the same.

**FIGURE 9-3**
When Cell B3 is copied to Cell C4, the relative cell reference will change.
When Cell B8 is copied to Cell C9, the absolute cell reference will not change.

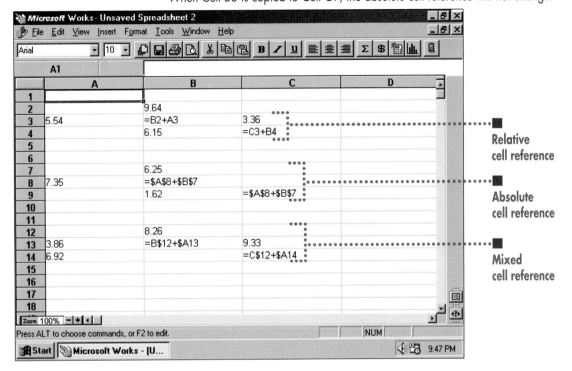

*Absolute cell references* contain row numbers and column letters preceded by a dollar sign ($). They do not adjust to the new cell location when copied or moved. For example, in Figure 9-3, if the formula =$A$8+$B$7 is copied from Cell B8 to Cell C9, the formula will remain the same in the new location.

Cell references containing both relative and absolute references are called *mixed cell references.* When formulas with mixed cell references are copied or moved, the row or column references preceded by a dollar sign will not change; the row or column references not preceded by a dollar sign will adjust relative to the cell to which they are moved. For example, if the formula =B$12+$A13 is copied from Cell B13 to Cell C14, the formula will change to =C$12+$A14.

The use of relative and absolute cell references is important only when you are copying and moving data in a spreadsheet. If you want a moved or copied cell formula to use values in a specific part of the spreadsheet, you should use absolute cell references. If you want a moved or copied cell formula to use values that correspond to the new location of the data, you should use relative cell references.

## Relative and Absolute Cell References

In this activity, you will enter formulas with relative and absolute cell references into the spreadsheet *Calculation,* which should be on your screen.

1. Place the highlight in **D3.** All cell references in the formula =(A3+B3)*20 (shown in the Formula Bar) are relative because neither the row nor the columns are preceded by a dollar sign.

2. Copy the formula in **D3** to **D4.** The value in Cell D4 should be 15440, and the formula in the Formula Bar should be =(A4+B4)*20. The operators in the formula remain the same as the formula in Cell D3. However, because the cell references are relative, the row references in the operands

changed down one row to reflect a change in the location of the formula.

3. Key **=$A$3*($B$3-200)** in Cell D5. The value in Cell D5 should be 5499. The formula in the Formula Bar contains absolute cell references, which are indicated by the dollar signs that precede row and column references.

4. Copy the formula in **D5** to **D6.** The value in Cell D6 should be 5499, the same as in Cell D5. Because the formula in Cell D5 contains absolute cell references, the formula appearing in the Formula Bar should also be exactly the same as the formula for Cell D5.

5. Save and close the file.

# *Creating Formulas Quickly*

**Y**ou have already learned how to create formulas by keying the formula or editing existing formulas. In this section, you will learn ways to create formulas quickly by using the Point and Click method and clicking the Autosum button.

## Point and Click Method

Previously you constructed formulas by keying the entire formula in the cell of the spreadsheet. You may include cell references in a formula more quickly by clicking on the cell you want to reference rather than keying the reference. This is known as the Point and Click method. The Point and Click method is particularly helpful when you have to enter long formulas that contain several cell references.

To enter the formula =A3+B3 in a cell, you would:

1. Highlight the cell that will contain the formula.

2. Press **=.**

3. Click **A3.**

4. Press **+.**

5. Click **B3.**

**ACTIVITY**

## 9-4 Pointing and Clicking to Create Formulas

In this activity, you will create formulas using the Point and Click method. The file *Activity 9-4* is a spreadsheet that records the portions of meat and cheese sold in a sandwich shop during a month. Portions are allocated as in the table given below.

|  | Large | Small |
|---|---|---|
| **Meat** | 6 ounces | 3 ounces |
| **Cheese** | 4 ounces | 2.5 ounces |

Create formulas to calculate the total ounces of meat and cheese sold during the month by completing the following steps:

1. Open the spreadsheet file *Activity 9-4* from your template disk.

2. Enter a formula in D4 to calculate the total ounces of meat sold:
   a. Highlight **D4.**
   b. Key **=(6*.**
   c. Click **B4.**
   d. Key **)+(3*.**
   e. Click **C4.**
   f. Key **).**
   g. Press **Enter.** The amount 1440 will appear in the cell.

3. Use the Fill Down Command to copy the formula in Cell D4 to D5:D7.

4. Enter a formula in Cell D8 to calculate the total ounces of cheese sold:
   a. Highlight **D8.**
   b. Key **=(4*.**
   c. Click **B8.**
   d. Key **)+(2.5*.**
   e. Click **C8.**
   f. Key **).**
   g. Press **Enter.**

5. Use the Fill Down command to copy the formula in Cell D8 to Cell D9.

6. Compare your screen to the one in Figure 9-4.

7. Leave *Activity 9-4* on your screen for the next activity.

## FIGURE 9-4
Spreadsheet formulas may be created quickly using the mouse.

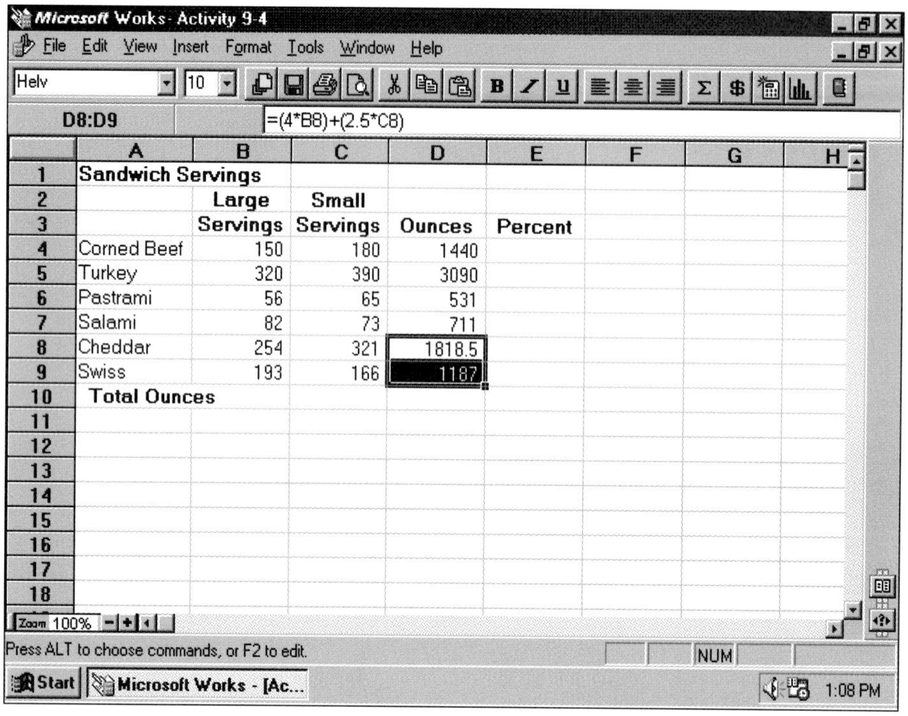

## The Autosum Button

Spreadsheet users frequently need to sum long columns of numbers. Works has a button on the toolbar, the Autosum button, that makes the process of summing a simple operation. The Autosum button has the Greek letter *sigma* ($\Sigma$) on it. When you click the Autosum button, Works scans the spreadsheet to determine the most logical column of numbers to sum in the cell and highlights the range of cells to be summed. This range is displayed in the cell where you want the sum to appear. If you prefer a range other than the one Works selects, choose an alternate range by dragging those cells. When you click the Autosum button a second time, the sum will appear in the cell.

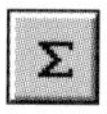

The sum of a range is indicated by a special formula in the Formula Bar called a ***function formula.*** For example, if the sum of the range D5:D17 is entered in a cell, the function formula in the Formula Bar will be =SUM(D5:D17). The SUM function is the most frequent type of function formula. Function formulas will be discussed in detail later in this chapter.

# ACTIVITY

## Creating Formulas Quickly

In this activity, you will perform Autosum operations. *Activity 9-4* should be on your screen. Suppose the manager of a sandwich shop would like to determine the total ounces of meat and cheese sold during the month. The manager also wants to know what percentage each meat and cheese item is of total food items sold.

1. Determine the total ounces of ingredients, both meat and cheese, sold this month by summing D4:D9:
   a. Highlight **D10.**
   b. Click the **Autosum** button. The range D4:D9 should be highlighted. Works has correctly selected the range of cells you would like to sum.
   c. Click the **Autosum** button. The formula =SUM(D4:D9) should appear in the Formula Bar. Cell D10 should display 8777.5, the sum of the numbers in Column D.

2. Format E4:E10 for percent.

3. Determine the percent of total ounces sold for each type of meat and cheese:

   a. Highlight **E4.**
   b. Press **=.**
   c. Click **D4.**
   d. Press **/.**
   e. Key **$D$10**.
   f. Press **Enter.** The cell should display 16.41%. The amount is determined by dividing the value in Cell D4 by the value in Cell D10 (1440 / 8777.5 = 16.41%).

4. Copy the formula in **E4** to **E5:E10** using the Fill Down command. All of the food items should be expressed as a percentage of the total food items. Cell E10 should show 100%.

5. Compare your screen to the one shown in Figure 9-5.

6. Leave *Activity 9-4* on your screen for the next activity.

**FIGURE 9-5**

The Autosum button will add a column of numbers quickly.

| | A | B | C | D | E | F | G | H |
|---|---|---|---|---|---|---|---|---|
| 1 | Sandwich Servings | | | | | | | |
| 2 | | Large | Small | | | | | |
| 3 | | Servings | Servings | Ounces | Percent | | | |
| 4 | Corned Beef | 150 | 180 | 1440 | 16.41% | | | |
| 5 | Turkey | 320 | 390 | 3090 | 35.20% | | | |
| 6 | Pastrami | 56 | 65 | 531 | 6.05% | | | |
| 7 | Salami | 82 | 73 | 711 | 8.10% | | | |
| 8 | Cheddar | 254 | 321 | 1818.5 | 20.72% | | | |
| 9 | Swiss | 193 | 166 | 1187 | 13.52% | | | |
| 10 | Total Ounces | | | 8777.5 | 100.00% | | | |

Cell reference: E4:E10  Formula: =D4/$D$10

# *Formula Helpers*

**T**wo commands, Formulas in the View menu and Options in the Tools menu, can help you to use formulas in the spreadsheet. The Formulas command will replace the values in the cells of the spreadsheet with the formulas that created them. The Use Manual Calculation check box in the Options command of the Tools menu command will prevent spreadsheet formulas from calculating until you press the F9 key.

## Showing Formulas on the Spreadsheet

In previous activities, you were able to view formulas only in the Formula Bar. Cells of the spreadsheet contained the values created by formulas rather than the formulas themselves. When creating a spreadsheet containing many formulas, you may find it easier to organize formulas and detect formula errors when you can view all formulas simultaneously.

Selecting the Formulas command from the View menu will display formulas rather than values in the cells of the spreadsheet. When the Formulas command is selected, a cell that does not contain a formula will display the content entered in the cell. A check mark will appear by the Formulas command in the View menu when the command is turned on. To display values determined by the formulas again, choose the Formulas command once more.

## Delayed Calculations

The calculation of values in the spreadsheet will usually occur as a new value is entered in the spreadsheet, but you can also calculate in the spreadsheet at a specific moment. Delayed calculation can be useful when you are working with a large spreadsheet that will take longer than usual to calculate; or you may want to view the difference in a particular cell after you have made changes throughout the spreadsheet.

To delay calculation, choose the Use Manual Calculation check box in the Options command from the Tools menu. No calculation will occur until you press the F9 key. To return to automatic calculation, click off the Use Manual Calculation check box in the Options command from the Tools menu.

**ACTIVITY**

## Showing Formulas and Delaying Calculation

In this activity, you will view the formulas used to create the spreadsheet in file *Activity 9-4*. You will also delay calculation of changes to the spreadsheet using the Use Manual Calculation option.

1. Choose **Formulas** from the **View** menu.

2. Scroll to the right so that Columns D and E appear on the screen. Each value in the spreadsheet created by a formula has now been replaced by the formula creating the value.

3. Choose **Formulas** from the **View** menu. The values determined by the formulas will reappear on the screen.

4. From the **Tools** menu, choose **Options.**

5. Click the **Data Entry** tab, if it is not already selected.

6. In the Spreadsheet box, click the **Use manual calculation** check box until a check mark appears.

7. Click **OK.**

8. Change the following values in the spreadsheet:
   a. Key **190** in Cell B4.
   b. Key **410** in Cell C5.
   c. Key **96** in Cell B7.

9. Press **F9** while watching the screen. Calculations will be made as you press the key.

10. Save the file to your data disk as *Delicatessen* and close the file.

# Function Formulas

**F**unction formulas are special formulas that do not use operators to calculate a result. They perform complex calculations in specialized areas of mathematics, statistics, logic, trigonometry, accounting, and finance. Function formulas are also used to convert spreadsheet values to dates and times. There are 76 function formulas in Works. In this section, you will learn the more frequently used function formulas.

## Parts of Function Formulas

A function formula contains three components: the equal sign, a function name, and an argument.

- The *equal sign* tells Works a formula will be entered into the cell.

- The *function name* identifies the operation to be performed. A function name is usually two to seven characters long.

- The *argument* is a value, cell reference, range, or text that acts as an operand in a function formula. The argument is enclosed in parentheses after the function name. If a function formula contains more than one argument, the arguments are separated by commas. The range of cells that make up the argument is separated by a colon.

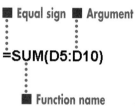

You have already created a function formula in a previous activity by using the Autosum button. When pressed, the Autosum button inserted an equal sign followed by the word *SUM*. The range of cells to be summed was designated within parentheses; for example, =SUM(D5:D10). In this function formula, the word *SUM* is the function name that identifies the operation. The argument is the range of cells that are to be operated upon.

## Mathematical Functions

*Mathematical functions* manipulate quantitative data in the spreadsheet. You have already learned mathematical operations, such as addition, subtraction, multiplication, and division, that do not require function formulas. You have also used the Autosum button to create SUM functions. Two other mathematical functions, the square root and rounding functions, are described in Table 9-3. Notice that two arguments are required to perform the rounding operation.

**TABLE 9-3**
Mathematical functions manipulate quantitative data in the spreadsheet.

## MATHEMATICAL FUNCTIONS

| FUNCTION | OPERATION |
|---|---|
| SQRT(X) | Displays the square root of the value X identified in the argument. For example, =SQRT(C4) will display the square root of the value in Cell C4. |
| ROUND(X, Number of Places) | Displays the rounded value of X to the number of places designated by the second argument. For example, =ROUND(14,23433,2) will display 14.23. If the second argument is a negative number, the first argument will be rounded to the left of the decimal point. |

## ACTIVITY 9-7

## Mathematical Functions

In this activity, you will perform mathematical functions on numbers contained in the file *Activity 9-7*. You may compare your results to the screen shown in Figure 9-6.

1. Open the file *Activity 9-7* from your template disk.

2. Determine the sum of the numbers in Column B using the SUM function:
   a. Highlight **B9.**
   b. Enter **=SUM(B4:B8)**. (The same operation could have been performed using the Autosum button on the toolbar.)

3. Determine the square root of the sum determined in Cell B9 using the SQRT function:
   a. Highlight **B10.**
   b. Enter **=SQRT(B9)**.

4. Round the square root determined in Cell B10 to the tenths place using the ROUND function:
   a. Highlight **B11.**
   b. Enter **=ROUND(B10,2)**.

5. Leave *Activity 9-7* on your screen for the next activity.

## FIGURE 9-6

Mathematical functions perform calculations such as summing, determining square roots, and rounding on spreadsheet data.

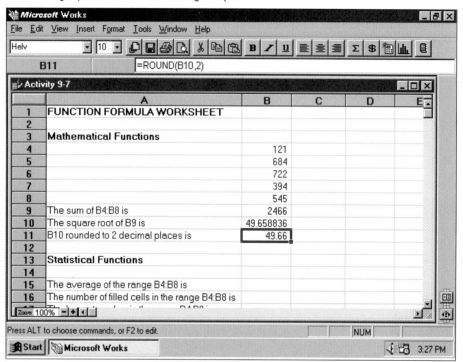

## Statistical Functions

Statistical functions are used to describe large quantities of data. For example, function formulas can be used to determine the average, standard deviation, or variance of a range of data. Statistical functions can also be used to determine the number of values in a range, the largest value in a range, and the smallest value in a range. Table 9-4 shows some of the statistical functions available in Works. Notice that all the statistical functions contain a range for the argument. The range is the body of numbers the statistics will describe.

**TABLE 9-4**

Statistical functions are used to analyze large amounts of numbers.

## STATISTICAL FUNCTIONS

| FUNCTION | OPERATION |
|---|---|
| AVG(Range) | Displays the average of the range identified in the argument. For example, =AVG(E4:E9) will display the average of the numbers contained in the range E4:E9. |
| COUNT(Range) | Displays the number of filled cells in the range identified in the argument. For example, =COUNT(D6:D21) will display 16 if all the cells in the range are filled. |
| MAX(Range) | Displays the largest number contained in the range identified in the argument. |
| MIN(Range) | Displays the smallest number contained in the range identified in the argument. |
| STD(Range) | Displays the standard deviation of the values contained in the range of the argument. |
| VAR(Range) | Displays the variance for the values contained in the range of the argument. |

## ACTIVITY

9-8

## Statistical Functions

• • • • • • • • • • • • • • • • • • • • • • • • • • • • • • • • • • • •

In this activity, you will use function formulas to calculate statistics on a range of values. *Activity 9-7* should be on your screen. You may compare your results to the screen shown in Figure 9-7.

1. Determine the average of the values in the range B4:B8:
   a. Highlight **B15.**
   b. Enter **=AVG(B4:B8)**.

2. Determine the number of filled cells in the range B4:B8:
   a. Highlight **B16.**
   b. Enter **=COUNT(B4:B8)**.

3. Determine the largest number in the range B4:B8:
   a. Highlight **B17.**
   b. Enter **=MAX(B4:B8)**.

4. Determine the smallest number in the range B4:B8:
   a. Highlight **B18.**
   b. Enter **=MIN(B4:B8)**.

**5.** Determine the standard deviation of the range B4:B8:

   **a.** Highlight **B19.**

   **b.** Enter **=STD(B4:B8)**. (Your rounded amount may vary depending on your column width.)

**6.** Determine the variance of the range B4:B8:

**a.** Highlight **B20.**

**b.** Enter **=VAR(B4:B8)**. The value 47962.16 should appear in the cell.

**7.** Leave *Activity 9-7* on the screen for the next activity.

**FIGURE 9-7**
Statistical functions perform various operations, such as finding the average, maximum, minimum, standard deviation, and variance.

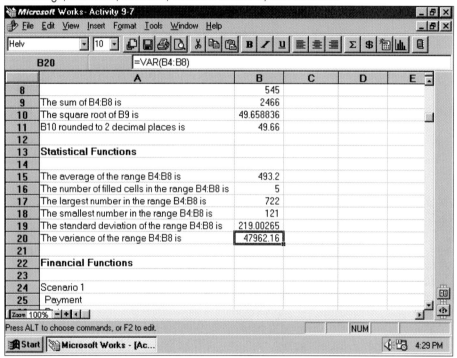

## Financial Functions

Financial functions are used to analyze loans and investments. The primary financial functions are future value, present value, and payment, which are described in Table 9-5.

**TABLE 9-5**

Financial functions are used to analyze loans and investments.

## FINANCIAL FUNCTIONS

| FUNCTION | OPERATION |
|---|---|
| FV(Payment, Rate, Term) | Displays the future value of a series of equal payments (first argument), at a fixed rate (second argument), over a specified period of time (third argument). For example, =FV($100,.08,5) will determine the future value of five $100 payments at the end of five years if you can earn a rate of 8%. |
| PV(Payment,Rate,Term) | Displays the present value of a series of equal payments (first argument), at a fixed rate (second argument), over a specified period of time (third argument). For example, =PV($500,.1,5) will display the present value of five payments of $500 at a 10% rate. |
| PMT(Principal,Rate,Term) | Displays the payment per period needed to repay a loan (first argument), at a specified interest (second argument), for a specified period of time (third argument). For example, =PMT(10000,.01,36) will display the monthly payment needed to repay a $10,000 loan at a 12% annual rate (.01 times 12 months), for three years (36 months divided by 12*). |

\* Rate and term functions should be compatible. In other words, if payments are monthly rather than annual, the annual rate should be divided by 12 to determine the monthly rate.

## ACTIVITY

### 9-9 Financial Functions

● ● ● ● ● ● ● ● ● ● ● ● ● ● ● ● ● ● ● ● ● ● ● ● ● ● ● ● ● ● ● ● ● ● ● ● ●

In this activity, you will calculate answers to three scenarios. Use the lower part of the spreadsheet in the file *Activity 9-7* for your calculations. You may compare your results to the screen shown in Figure 9-8.

**1.** You plan to make six yearly payments of $150 into a savings account that earns 9.5% annually. Use the FV function to determine the value of the account at the end of six years.

## FIGURE 9-8

Financial functions perform various operations, such as finding present and future values.

Microsoft Works - Activity 9-7

| | A | B | C | D | E |
|---|---|---|---|---|---|
| 21 | | | | | |
| 22 | **Financial Functions** | | | | |
| 23 | | | | | |
| 24 | Scenario 1 | | | | |
| 25 | Payment | $150.00 | | | |
| 26 | Rate | 9.50% | | | |
| 27 | Term | 6 | | | |
| 28 | Future Value | $1,142.83 | | | |
| 29 | Scenario 2 | | | | |
| 30 | Payment | $210.00 | | | |
| 31 | Rate | 6.00% | | | |
| 32 | Term | 8 | | | |
| 33 | Present Value | $1,304.06 | | | |
| 34 | Scenario 3 | | | | |
| 35 | Principal | $5,000.00 | | | |
| 36 | Rate | 1.00% | | | |
| 37 | Term | 60 | | | |
| 38 | Payment | $111.22 | | | |

B38 =PMT(B35,B36,B37)

a. Enter **150** in Cell B25.

b. Enter **.095** in Cell B26.

c. Enter **6** in Cell B27.

d. Enter **=FV(B25,B26,B27)** in Cell B28. The savings account will have grown to the amount shown in Cell B28 after six years.

2. You have a choice of receiving $1,200 now or eight annual payments of $210. A typical rate for a savings account in your local bank is 6%. Use the PV function to determine which is the most profitable alternative:

a. Enter **210** in Cell B30.

b. Enter **.06** in Cell B31.

c. Enter **8** in Cell B32.

d. Enter **=PV(B30,B31,B32)** in Cell B33. The best decision is to take the delayed payments because the present value, $1,304.06, is greater than $1,200.

3. You need to borrow $5,000. Your banker has offered you an annual rate of 12% interest for a five-year loan. Use the PMT function to determine what your monthly payments on the loan would be:

a. Enter **5000** in Cell B35.

b. Enter **.01** in Cell B36. [A 1% monthly rate (12% divided by 12 months) is used because the problem requests monthly, rather than annual, payments.]

c. Enter **60** in Cell B37. [A period of 60 months (5 years times 12 months) is used because the problem requests monthly, rather than annual, payments.]

d. Enter **=PMT(B35,B36,B37)** in Cell B38. The value $111.22 will be in the cell. You will have to pay a total of $1,673.20 [($111.22 * 60 months) - $5,000 principal] in interest over the life of the loan.

4. Save the file to your data disk as *Functions* and close the file.

# *Inserting a Function Into a Cell*

**T**here are many more functions available in Works than you have used in this chapter. There are so many that you may need a reminder of what is available or the exact name or usage of a function. The Function command in the Insert menu allows you to browse through all of the available functions to select the one you want. The Insert Function dialog box, shown in Figure 9-9, also provides a brief explanation of any function you choose. The function you choose while in the Insert Function dialog box will be inserted in the current cell.

**FIGURE 9-9**
The Insert Function dialog box allows you to browse through all of the available functions.

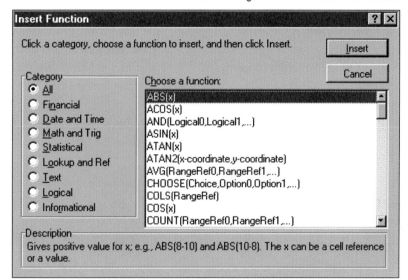

**ACTIVITY**

## 9-10 Using the Insert Function Dialog Box

In this activity, you will insert a function using the Insert Function dialog box.

1. Create a new spreadsheet.

2. Insert today's serial date in Cell A1:
   a. Choose **Function** from the **Insert** menu. The Insert Function dialog box

will appear.
   b. Click the **Date and Time** button.
   c. Click **NOW()** in the **Choose a function** box.
   d. Click the **Insert** button. The function formula =NOW() will appear in Cell A1.
   e. Press **Enter.** A serial date will appear in Cell A1.

3. Format the date:
   a. Choose **Number** from the **Format** menu.
   b. Click the **Date** button.
   c. Choose the fourth option, which displays the month in text form, followed by the date and year in numerical form.
   d. Click **OK.**
   e. Widen Column A to accommodate the date width.

4. Key **NEXT MONTH'S BUDGET** in Cell A2.

5. Key **Spreadsheet Name:** in Cell A16.

6. Repeat the text in Cell A2 in Cell B16 using the following steps:
   a. Highlight **B16.**
   b. Choose **Function** from the **Insert** menu.
   c. Click the **Text** button.

   d. Click **REPEAT** in the **Choose a function** box.
   e. Click the **Insert** button. The function formula =REPEAT(TextValue,Count) will appear. The word TextValue will be shaded.
   f. Key **A2**. The word TextValue will be replaced with Cell A2 in the function formula.
   g. Press **Enter.** A dialog box will appear indicating the formula has an error.
   h. Click **OK.** The word *Count* will appear shaded.
   i. Key **1**.
   j. Press **Enter.** The contents of Cell A2 will be repeated in Cell B16. Compare your screen to Figure 9-10. You may need to widen the columns.

7. Save the screen as *Next Month's Budget* and close the file.

**FIGURE 9-10**
Spreadsheet with function inserted.

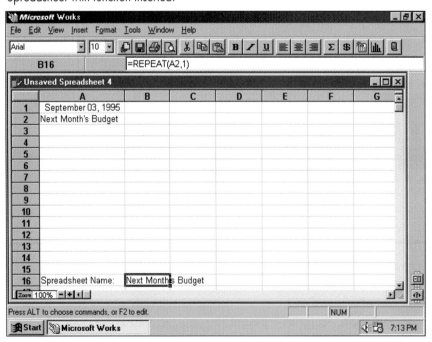

# *Summary*

■ The spreadsheet has the power to perform rapid calculations. Spreadsheet formulas perform calculations on values referenced in other cells of the spreadsheet.

■ Cell references in formulas may be relative or absolute. Relative cell references adjust to a different location when copied or moved. Absolute cell references describe the same cell location in the spreadsheet regardless of where it is copied or moved. Mixed cell references contain both relative and absolute cell references.

■ Formulas may be created quickly by using the Point and Click method. This method inserts cell references by clicking the cell with the mouse rather than keying its column letter and row number.

■ A group of cells may be summed quickly by using the Autosum button on the toolbar. Works will insert the SUM formula function and determine the most likely range to be summed.

■ Function formulas are special formulas that do not require operators. Works has 76 function formulas that may be used to perform mathematical, statistical, financial, and other operations.

● ● ● ● ● ● ● ● ● ● ● ● ● ●

# REVIEW ACTIVITIES

## TRUE/FALSE

**Circle T or F to show whether the statement is true or false.**

**T**   **F**   **1.** A spreadsheet can be used to perform the same functions as a calculator.

**T**   **F**   **2.** An operator is a number or cell reference used in formulas.

**T**   **F**   **3.** In a complex formula, subtraction will be performed before multiplication.

**T**   **F**   **4.** Operations within parentheses will be performed before operations outside parentheses in a formula.

**T**   **F**   **5.** An absolute cell reference will change if the formula is copied or moved.

**T**   **F**   **6.** The Autosum button creates the function formula =SUM in the highlighted cell.

**T**   **F**   **7.** The Formulas command will display formulas rather than values in the spreadsheet.

**T**   **F**   **8.** Manual calculation is performed by pressing the F2 key.

**T**   **F**   **9.** Statistical function formulas are used to analyze loans and investments.

**T**   **F**   **10.** Function formulas do not have operators.

## COMPLETION

**Write the correct answer in the space provided.**

1. Which operator has the highest priority in the order of evaluation in a spreadsheet formula?

   _____

   _____

2. What type of cell reference adjusts to its new location when it is copied or moved?

   _____

   _____

3. What type of cell reference will remain the same when it is copied or moved?

   _____

   _____

4. What technique inserts cell references in a formula by clicking the mouse?

   _____

   _____

5. Which function formula is inserted in a cell by clicking the Autosum button?

_____

_____

6. What toolbar button is used to create a function formula that adds a column of numbers?

_____

_____

7. Which command will display formulas in the spreadsheet?

_____

_____

8. Which command delays calculation until the F9 key is pressed?

_____

_____

9. What is the name of the item enclosed in parentheses in a function formula?

_____

_____

10. What dialog box allows you to browse through spreadsheet functions?

_____

_____

*application 9 - 1*

**Match the letter of the spreadsheet formula to the description of the spreadsheet operation performed by the formula.**

**Spreadsheet Operation**

____ **1.** Adds the values in Cells A3 and A4

____ **2.** Subtracts the value in Cell A4 from the value in Cell A3

____ **3.** Multiplies the value in Cell A3 times 27

____ **4.** Divides the value in Cell A3 by 27

____ **5.** Raises the value in Cell A3 to the 27th power

____ **6.** Divides the value in Cell A3 by 27, then adds the value in Cell A4

____ **7.** Divides the value in Cell A3 by the result of 27 plus the value in Cell A4

____ **8.** Multiplies the value in Cell A3 times 27, then divides the product by the value in Cell A4

____ **9.** Divides 27 by the value in Cell A4, then multiplies the result by the value in Cell A3

____ **10.** Raises the value in Cell A3 to the 27th power, then divides the result by the value in Cell A4

**Spreadsheet Formulas**

a. =A3/(27+A4)

b. =A3^27

c. =A3^27/A4

d. =A3+A4

e. =A3/27

f. =A3/27+A4

g. =(A3*27)/A4

h. =A3-A4

i. =A3*(27/A4)

j. =A3*27

*a p p l i c a t i o n   9 - 2*

**The file *Application 9-2* is a spreadsheet containing several values. Enter formulas in the specified cells that will perform the requested operations. After you enter each formula, write the resulting value in the space provided. When you have completed the application, save the file to your data disk as *Formulas* and close it.**

| Resulting Value | Cell | Operation |
|---|---|---|
| _____ 1. | C3 | Add the values in Cells A3 and B3 |
| _____ 2. | C4 | Subtract the value in Cell B4 from the value in Cell A4 |
| _____ 3. | C5 | Multiply the value in Cell A5 by the value in Cell B5 |
| _____ 4. | C6 | Divide the value in Cell A6 by the value in Cell B6 |
| _____ 5. | B7 | Sum the values in the range B3:B6 |
| _____ 6. | D3 | Add the values in Cells A3 and A4, then multiply the sum by 3 |
| _____ 7. | D4 | Add the values in Cells A3 and A4, then multiply the sum by B3 |
| _____ 8. | D5 | Raise the value in Cell A5 to the 3rd power |
| _____ 9. | D6 | Subtract the value in Cell B6 from the value in Cell A6, then divide by 2 |
| _____10. | D7 | Divide the value in Cell A6 by 2, then subtract the value in Cell B6 |

*a p p l i c a t i o n   9 - 3*

**Your organization, the Entrepreneurs Club, has decided to have a holiday sale in which bags of oranges and grapefruit and tins of fruitcake and hard candy will be sold at a profit. You have been asked to create a spreadsheet that will calculate the bills of individuals who purchase holiday gifts from your organization. Because your organization is not a nonprofit organization, you will be required to charge a sales tax of 4% on each sale. The file *Application 9-3* is a spreadsheet lacking the formulas required to calculate the bills. Complete the spreadsheet following these steps:**

1. Open the file *Application 9-3*.

2. Enter formulas in Cells D7, D8, D9, and D10 to calculate the cost of each food item when quantities are entered in Column C.

3. Enter a formula in Cell D11 to sum the totals in D7:D10.

4. Enter a formula in Cell D12 to calculate a sales tax equal to 4% of the subtotal in Cell D11.

5. Enter a formula in Cell D13 to add the subtotal and sales tax.

6. Change the spreadsheet for manual calculation.

7. Format D7:D13 for currency.

8. Save the file to your data disk as *Food Cost*. The saved data applies to all customers. The spreadsheet is now ready to accept data unique to the individual customer.

9. Suppose a customer purchases three bags of oranges, four bags of grapefruit, two fruitcakes, and one tin of hard candy. Enter the quantities in Column C and press **F9** to calculate.

10. Check the calculations made by the formulas by hand to make sure that you have entered the formulas correctly. If any of the formulas are incorrect, edit them and recalculate the spreadsheet.

11. When you are confident that the spreadsheet is calculating as you intended, print the customer's bill.

12. Close the file without saving the most recent changes.

# application 9-4

**Write the appropriate function formula to perform each of the described operations. You may refer to Tables 9-3 through 9-5 to help you prepare the function formulas.**

_____ 1. Determine the smallest value in A4:A90

_____ 2. Determine the standard deviation of the values in K6:K35

_____ 3. Determine the average of the values in B9:B45

_____ 4. Determine the yearly payments on a $5,000 loan at 8% for 10 years

_____ 5. Determine the value of a savings account at the end of 5 years after making $400 yearly payments; the account earns 8%

_____ 6. Round the value in Cell C3 to the tenths place

_____ 7. Determine the present value of a pension plan that will pay you 20 yearly payments of $4,000; the current rate of return is 7.5%

_____ 8. Determine the square root of 225

_____ 9. Determine the variance of the values in F9:F35

_____ 10. Add all the values in D4:D19

_____ 11. Determine how many cells in H7:H21 are filled with data

_____ 12. Determine the largest value in E45:E92

# application 9-5

**The file _Application 9-5_ contains a spreadsheet of student grades for one examination. Calculate statistics on these grades by following these steps:**

1. Open the file _Application 9-5_ from your template disk.

2. Determine the number of students taking the examination by entering a function formula in Cell B26.

3. Determine the average exam grade by entering a function formula in Cell B27.

4. Determine the highest exam grade by entering a function formula in Cell B28.

5. Determine the lowest exam grade by entering a function formula in Cell B29.

6. Determine the standard deviation of the exam grades by entering a function formula in Cell B30.

7. Save the file to your data disk as _Grades Statistics_ and print it. Close the file.

# application 9-6

Generic National Bank makes a profit by taking money deposited by customers and lending it to others at a higher rate. In order to encourage depositing and borrowing, you have helped the bank develop a spreadsheet that will inform depositors about the future value of their investments. Another portion of the spreadsheet informs borrowers of the yearly payments they must make on their loans. The incomplete spreadsheet is in file *Application 9-6*. Complete the spreadsheet by following these steps:

1. Enter a function formula in Cell B11 that will inform borrowers of the yearly payment. Assume that the loan principal will be entered in Cell B5, the lending rate will be entered in Cell B7, and the term of the loan will be entered in Cell B9. (ERR, indicating an error, will appear in the cell because no data is in the argument cell references yet.)

2. A potential borrower inquires about the payments on a $5,500 loan for four years. The current lending rate is 11%. Determine the yearly payment on the loan.

3. Print the portion of the spreadsheet that pertains to the loan (A1:B12) so that it may be given to the potential borrower.

4. Enter a function formula in Cell B24 informing depositors of the future value of periodic payments. Assume the yearly payments will be entered in Cell B18, the term of the payments will be entered in Cell B20, and the interest rate will be entered in Cell B22. ($0.00 will appear because no data is in the argument cell references yet.)

5. A potential depositor is starting a college fund for her son. She inquires about the value of yearly deposits of $450 at the end of 15 years. The current interest rate is 7.5%. Determine the future value of the deposits.

6. Print the portion of the spreadsheet that applies to the deposits (A14:B25) so that it may be given to the potential depositor.

7. Save the file to your data disk as *Bank* and close it.

# SPREADSHEET CHARTS

CHAPTER

## 10

**OBJECTIVES**

**When you complete this chapter, you will be able to:**

1. Identify the purpose of charting spreadsheet data.

2. Identify the types of spreadsheet charts.

3. Create a chart.

4. Save a chart.

5. Print a chart.

# *What Is a Spreadsheet Chart?*

**A** *chart* is a graphical representation of data contained in a spreadsheet. Charts make the data of a spreadsheet easier to understand. For example, the spreadsheet in Figure 10-1 shows the populations of four major American cities for three years. You may be able to detect the changes in the populations by carefully examining the spreadsheet. However, the increases and decreases in the populations of each city are more easily recognized when the contents of the spreadsheet are illustrated in a chart, such as the one shown in Figure 10-2.

## FIGURE 10-1
Spreadsheets contain numerical data but do not illustrate relationships among data.

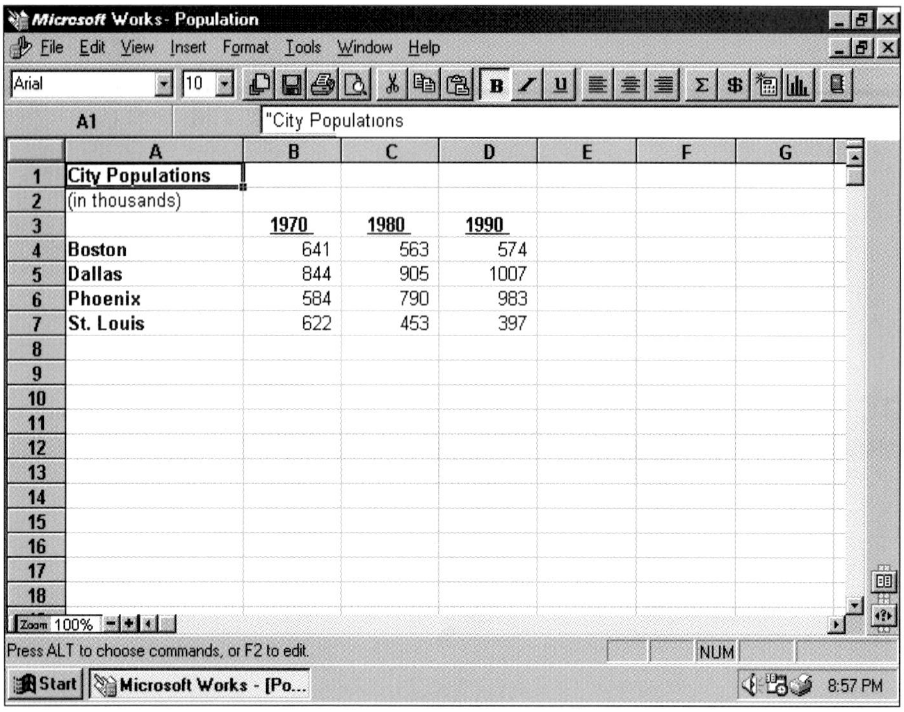

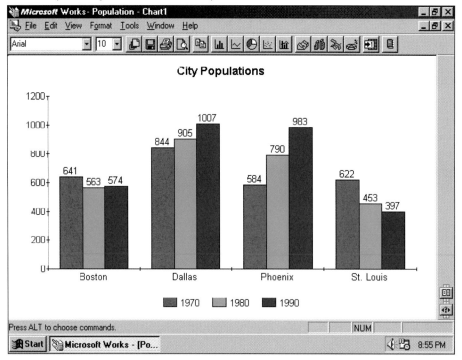

## FIGURE 10-2
Spreadsheet charts are ideal for illustrating the relationships among data contained in a spreadsheet.

# Types of Spreadsheet Charts

In this chapter, you will create four of the most commonly used spreadsheet charts: bar charts, line charts, pie charts, and scatter charts. Each of these types of charts is illustrated in Figure 10-3.

**FIGURE 10-3**

Several types of charts are available in Works. Four of the most commonly used charts are the bar, line, pie, and scatter charts.

Bar chart

Line chart

Pie chart

Scatter chart

## Bar Chart

A *bar chart* uses rectangles of varying heights to illustrate values in a spreadsheet. For example, the bar chart in Figure 10-2 has one vertical bar to show the population of a city for each year. A bar chart is well suited for showing relationships among categories of data. The chart shows how the population of one city compares to populations of other cities.

## Line Chart

A *line chart* is similar to the bar chart except bars are replaced by points connected by a line. The line chart is ideal for illustrating trends of data over time. For example, Figure 10-4, a line chart printed in landscape orientation, shows the growth of the U.S. federal debt from 1980 to 1992. The vertical axis represents the level of the deficit, and the horizontal axis shows years in chronological order, from 1980 to 1992, representing the passage of time. The line chart makes it easy to see how the federal deficit has grown over time.

**FIGURE 10-4**

A line chart is ideal for illustrating trends of data over time.

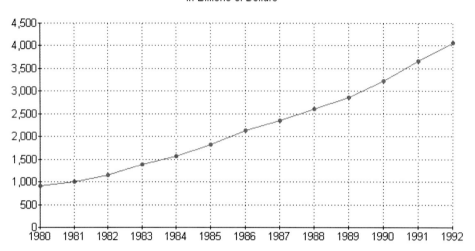

# Pie Chart

*Pie charts* show the relationship of a part to a whole. Each part is presented as a "slice" of the pie. For example, a teacher could create a pie chart of the distribution of grades in a class, as shown in Figure 10-5. Each slice represents the portion of grades given for each letter grade.

**FIGURE 10-5**

Each "slice" of a pie chart represents part of a whole.

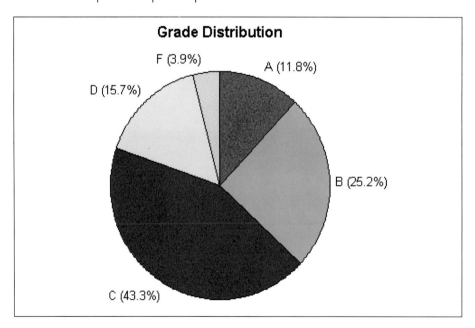

## Scatter Chart

*Scatter charts,* sometimes called XY charts, show the relationship between two categories of data. One category is represented on the vertical (Y) axis, and the other category is represented on the horizontal (X) axis. The result is a "cloud" of data points that may or may not have a recognizable shape. It is not practical to connect the data points with a line because points on a scatter chart usually do not relate to each other, as they do in a line chart. For example, the scatter chart in Figure 10-6 shows a data point for each of 12 individuals based on their height and weight. In most cases, a tall person tends to be heavier than a short person. However, because some people are tall and skinny, whereas others are short and stocky, the relationship between height and weight cannot be represented by a line.

**FIGURE 10-6**

Scatter charts show the relationship between two categories of data, such as height and weight.

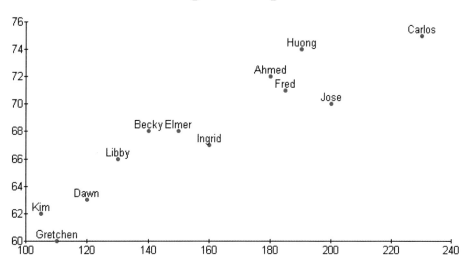

# *Creating a Chart from the Spreadsheet*

To create a chart, begin with a spreadsheet containing data you want to display in a chart. Then highlight the data you want to include in the chart. Choose Create New Chart from the Tools menu, or click the New Chart button on the toolbar. A dialog box appears allowing you to choose what type of chart you want. You can alter the chart to fit your specific requirements.

# 10-1 Creating a Spreadsheet Chart

In this activity, you will create a bar chart illustrating the contents of a spreadsheet. The file *Activity 10-1* is a spreadsheet containing the median income of heads of households according to the educational level they have achieved. The words *High School* have been abbreviated as *HS* and the word *College* as *C*.

1. Open the file *Activity 10-1* from the template disk. Column A contains educational levels and Column B contains the median incomes of those with that level of education.

2. Select the range **A5:B10.** The highlighted items are the data to be included in the chart that you will create.

3. Choose **Create New Chart** from the **Tools** menu. The New Chart dialog box

will appear. In the right side of the dialog box will be a small version of the chart that will be created, as shown in Figure 10-7. The word *Bar* appears in the Chart type portion of the dialog box. The bar chart is the default.

4. Click **OK.** The bar chart you selected will appear on screen.

5. Save the file to your data disk as *Education.* Both the spreadsheet and the chart will be saved.

6. Leave *Education* on the screen for the next activity.

**FIGURE 10-7**
The New Chart dialog box allows you to choose the type of chart you want.

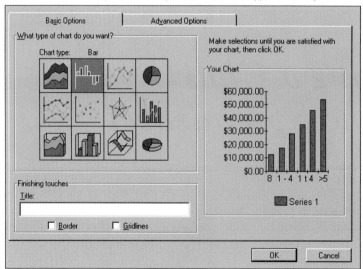

The chart illustrates the value of education in attaining higher income. Notice that the bars get higher on the right side of the chart, indicating that those who stay in school will be rewarded with higher incomes.

You may also notice a slight change in the menus appearing at the top of the screen. Your screen is now showing the chart window. This window is used to create, refine, and print charts prepared from spreadsheet data.

# Switching between Chart and Spreadsheet Windows

A chart is closely related to the spreadsheet from which it is created. For example, if you change the data in a spreadsheet, these changes will automatically be made in the chart created from the spreadsheet.

The initial name of the chart is also related to the spreadsheet from which it is created. Works will name the chart the same name as the spreadsheet, followed by Chart1. If additional charts are created from the spreadsheet, they will become Chart2, Chart3, and so on.

To return to the spreadsheet from which a chart was created, choose the spreadsheet from the Window menu. To access the chart again, select the chart name from the Window menu.

ACTIVITY

## Switching to and from the Chart

In this activity, you will edit *Education - Chart1* by switching to the spreadsheet and editing a cell in the spreadsheet.

1. Choose **Education** from the **Window** menu. The spreadsheet will appear.

2. Edit the contents of Cell A5 from 8 yrs. or less to **<8 yrs.**

3. Choose **Education - Chart1** from the **Window** menu. The chart window will appear. The name under the first bar will be changed to <8 yrs.

4. Leave *Education - Chart1* on the screen for the next activity.

# Inserting Chart Titles

**C**hart titles and headings make the chart easier to understand. Chart titles are centered at the top of the chart. Vertical, or Y-axis, titles appear along the left side of the chart; and horizontal, or X-axis, titles appear along the bottom of the chart.

ACTIVITY

## 10-3 Inserting Chart Titles

In this activity, you will insert headings in the chart *Education - Chart1* by following these steps:

1. Choose **Titles** from the **Edit** menu. The Titles dialog box will appear.

2. Enter **YOUR EDUCATION PAYS** in the Chart Title box.

3. Enter **Incomes For Six Education Levels** in the Subtitle box. (Remember, you may use the Tab key to move to the next box.)

4. Enter **Educational Level** in the Horizontal (X) Axis box.

5. Enter **Median Income** in the Vertical (Y) Axis box.

6. Click **OK.** The titles will appear in the chart.

7. Because there is only one series of data in this chart you may remove the series labels.
   a. Choose **Legend/Series Labels** from the **Edit** menu.
   b. Click the **Auto series check** box until the check mark disappears.
   c. Click **OK.** The series label will disappear from the chart.

8. Compare your screen to the one shown in Figure 10-8.

9. Leave *Education - Chart1* on the screen for the next activity.

**FIGURE 10-8**

Chart titles may be inserted at the top of the chart and along the X- and Y-axes of the chart.

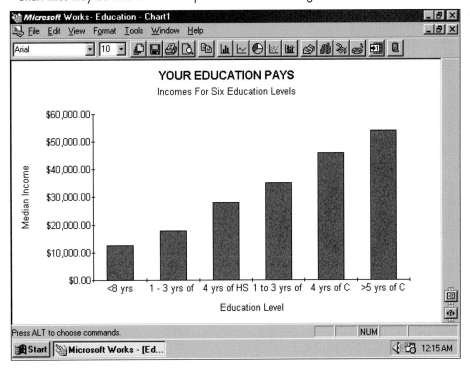

# Naming a Chart

**N**aming a chart is particularly useful after you have prepared several charts from one spreadsheet. These charts may become difficult to distinguish by their chart number and would be easier to recognize with more descriptive names. Change the name of the chart by choosing the Rename command from the Tools menu of the chart window.

**A C T I V I T Y**

 **Naming a Chart**

In this activity, you will rename the chart from Chart1 to Bar Chart by following these steps:

1. Choose **Rename Chart** from the **Tools** menu. The Rename Chart dialog box appears.

2. Key **Bar Chart** in the **Type a name below** text box.

3. Click the **Rename** button. The name in the Select a chart list box will change from *Chart1* to *Bar Chart.*

4. Click **OK.** You may confirm the name change by looking at the chart's title bar, or clicking the Window menu. The new name should appear in the menu.

5. Leave *Education - Bar Chart* on the screen for the next activity.

# Saving a Chart

A spreadsheet chart is considered part of a spreadsheet. When you save the spreadsheet, you will also save the charts you have created from the spreadsheet. Save the spreadsheet and its associated charts by choosing Save from the File menu. The File menu may be accessed from either the spreadsheet window or the chart window.

## 10-5 Saving a Chart

● ● ● ● ● ● ● ● ● ● ● ● ● ● ● ● ● ● ● ● ● ● ● ● ● ● ● ● ● ● ● ● ● ● ●

In this activity, you will save the chart and the spreadsheet it was created from.

1. Choose **Save** from the **File** menu. You will be returned to the chart window.

2. Leave *Education - Bar Chart* on the screen for the next activity.

# Changing the Type of Chart

After you have created a chart, you may change it to a different type by clicking one of the chart buttons that appear on the toolbar of the chart window (see Figure 10-9).

**FIGURE 10-9**
Select the chart type in the toolbar of the chart window.

■ 3-D Area Chart button

■ 3-D Bar Chart button

■ 3-D Line Chart button

■ 3-D Pie Chart button

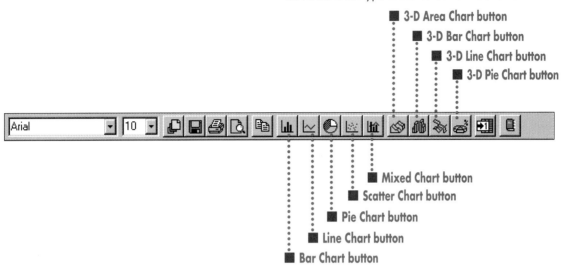

■ Mixed Chart button

■ Scatter Chart button

■ Pie Chart button

■ Line Chart button

■ Bar Chart button

After you click the type of chart in the toolbar, Works will offer several variations of the chart. For example, when the Bar Chart button is clicked, and the Variations tab is clicked, the dialog box shown in Figure 10-10 will appear.

**FIGURE 10-10**
The Bar dialog box displays various bar charts available in Works.

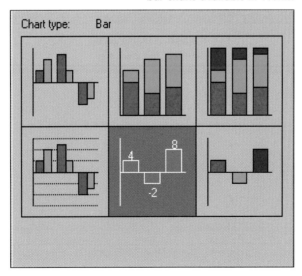

# 10-6 Changing the Type of Chart

In this activity, you will practice changing the type of a chart. The chart *Education - Bar Chart* should be on your screen.

1. Create a bar chart with gridlines by following these steps:
   a. Click the **Bar Chart** button on the toolbar. The Chart Type dialog box will appear.
   b. Click the **Variations** tab. A dialog box will appear.
   c. Click the chart with gridlines in the lower left corner of the Chart type box.
   d. Click **OK.** A bar chart with gridlines will

appear on your screen.

2. Create a line chart with gridlines by following these steps:
   a. Click the **Line Chart** button in the toolbar. The Chart Type dialog box will appear.
   b. Click the **Variations** tab.
   c. Click the fifth option in the Chart type box, which shows an example of a line chart with gridlines.
   d. Click **OK.** A line chart with gridlines similar to that in Figure 10-11 will appear on your screen.

**FIGURE 10-11**
Works will first create a basic line chart in the chart window.

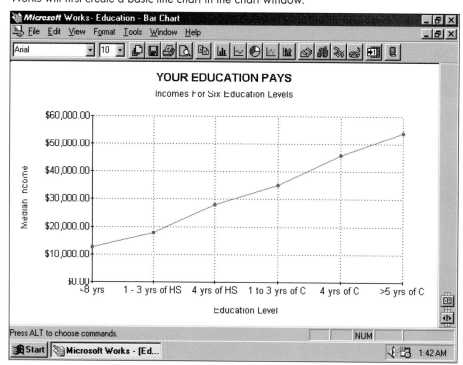

3. In the next activity, you will print this chart. Name and save the chart as a new chart by following these steps:
   a. Choose **Rename Chart** from the **Tools** menu.
   b. Key **Line Chart** in the **Type a name below** text box.

c. Click the **Rename** button.
d. Click **OK.**
e. Choose **Save** from the **File** menu.

4. Leave *Education - Line Chart* on the screen for the next activity.

# *Printing Charts*

**C**harts are printed in the same way word processing documents and spreadsheets are printed. The toolbar of the charts window has a Print and a Print Preview button that will print or preview the chart you plan to print.

### A C T I V I T Y

## Printing a Spreadsheet Chart

● ● ● ● ● ● ● ● ● ● ● ● ● ● ● ● ● ● ● ● ● ● ● ● ● ● ● ● ● ● ● ●

In this activity, you will print *Education - Line Chart*, which should be on your screen.

1. Click the **Print Preview** button. The chart, as it will be printed, will appear.

2. Click the **Print** button.

3. Click **OK.** Printing will begin.

4. After printing is complete, save and close the chart and spreadsheet files.

# *Creating Other Types of Charts*

**Y**ou have already created a bar chart and a line chart. In the remainder of this chapter, you will learn to create a pie chart and a scatter chart.

## Pie Charts

A pie chart differs from a bar or line chart because it uses only one set of data. For example, in the bar chart you created, you compared the level of education to median incomes. Pie charts compare items within one group to other items within the same group. For example, of a total group of pet owners, it may be determined how many (or what percent) own dogs, cats, or fish. When you prepared a bar chart or a line chart, you selected two columns of data. To create a pie chart, you will select only one column of numerical data before choosing the Create New Chart command.

ACTIVITY

# 10-8 Creating a Pie Chart

● ● ● ● ● ● ● ● ● ● ● ● ● ● ● ● ● ● ● ● ● ● ● ● ● ● ● ● ● ● ● ● ● ●

In this activity, you will create a pie chart of the sources of energy production in the United States during 1989.

1. Open the file *Activity 10-8*.

2. Create a pie chart by following these steps:
   a. Select the range **A6:B11.**
   b. Click the **New Chart** button on the toolbar. The New Chart dialog box will appear.
   c. Choose **Pie** from the **What type of chart do you want?** box.
   d. Click **OK.**
   e. Click the **Pie Chart** button on the toolbar.
   f. Click the **Variations** tab.
   g. Choose the chart in the lower right corner of the Chart type box.
   h. Click **OK.**

3. Title the pie chart by following these steps:
   a. Choose **Titles** from the **Edit** menu.
   b. Key **ENERGY PRODUCTION IN THE U.S.** in the Chart Title box.
   c. Key **For the Year 1989** in the Subtitle box.
   d. Click **OK.**

4. Name the chart file by following these steps:
   a. Choose **Rename Chart** from the **Tools** menu.
   b. Key **Production** in the **Type a name below** text box.
   c. Click **Rename.**
   d. Click **OK.**

5. Compare your screen to the one shown in Figure 10-12. Save the file to your data disk as *Energy* and close the file.

**FIGURE 10-12**

Pie charts can express parts as a percentage of a whole.

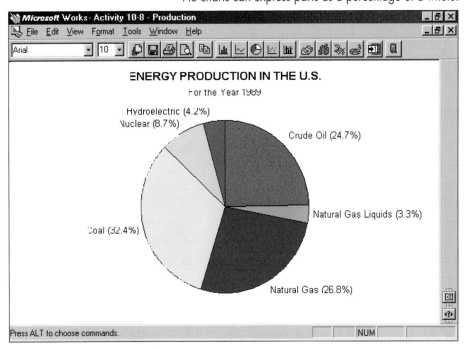

## Scatter Charts

Scatter charts are sometimes referred to as XY charts because they place data points between an X- and Y-axis. Scatter charts are usually more difficult to prepare because Works has difficulty identifying which data should be used as a scale on each axis of the chart. To overcome this, you should designate the X- and Y-axis scales in the Series command in the Edit menu of the chart window.

**ACTIVITY**

## Creating a Scatter Chart

In this activity, you will create a scatter chart. The file *Activity 10-9* is a spreadsheet containing the height and weight of 12 people.

1. Open the file *Activity 10-9*.

2. Prepare a scatter chart in which a data point appears at the intersection of a person's weight on the vertical (Y) axis and

height on the horizontal (X) axis:

a. Select the range **A4:C15**.

b. Click the **New Chart** button on the toolbar. The New Chart dialog box appears. Click **X-Y (Scatter)** in the **What type of chart do you want?** box. Click **OK**. You will be returned to the Chart window.

The vertical (Y) axis scale appears to show the weights of the individuals; however, the horizontal (X) axis scale is not recognizable. Works has not created a logical chart. This chart must be changed to make the horizontal scale recognizable.

3. Refine the chart to include the correct scale on the horizontal axis:
   a. Choose **Series** from the **Edit** menu. The range A4:A15, which contains the people's names, appears in the Category (X) Series box. Because the names cannot produce a numerical scale, the graphed data does not make sense. The contents of the Category (X) Series box should be changed to include the height data.
   b. Key **C4:C15** in the Category (X) Series box.
   c. The Value (Y) Series boxes designate sets of data points appearing on the scatter chart. This chart should include only one set of data points. Delete the contents of the Value (Y) Series 2nd box.
   d. Click **OK.** Data points will appear on the scatter chart, and the horizontal axis will show a scale for the heights.

4. Place labels on the data points of the scatter chart:
   a. Choose **Data Labels** from the **Edit** menu.

b. Key **A4:A15** in the Value (Y) Series 1st box. This will designate the names of the people as the data labels.
c. Click **OK.** The names will appear on each of the data points.

5. Delete the series label:
   a. Choose **Legend/Series Labels** command in the **Edit** menu.
   b. Click the **Auto series labels** check box until the check mark disappears.
   c. Click **OK.**

6. Place titles in the chart:
   a. Choose **Titles** from the **Edit** menu.
   b. Key **HEIGHT AND WEIGHT** in the Title box.
   c. Key **Twelve Person Survey** in the Subtitle box.
   d. Key **Height in Inches** in the Horizontal (X) Axis box.
   e. Key **Weight in Pounds** in the Vertical (Y) Axis box.
   f. Click **OK.** The titles will appear in the chart. Your screen should appear similar to the screen in Figure 10-13.

7. Print the chart in landscape orientation.

8. Save the file to your data disk as *Survey* and close the file.

**FIGURE 10-13**

Scatter charts can show labeled points between two axes.

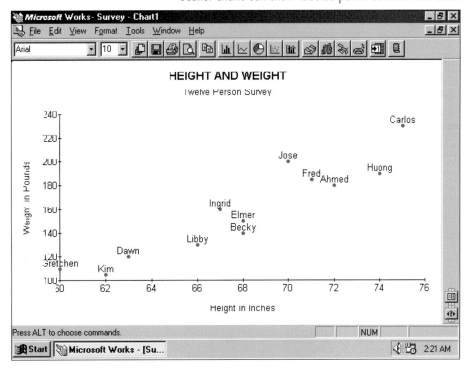

## 3-D Charts

Works allows you to make three-dimensional charts. Three-dimensional charts present data in a more attractive way. Area, Bar, Line, and Pie charts are available in three-dimensional formats.

ACTIVITY

### Creating a 3-D Chart

In this activity, you will create a three-dimensional chart.

1. Open *Energy* from your data disk.

2. Choose **Chart** from the **View** menu. The View Charts dialog box appears.

3. Click **OK.** The pie chart you created in Activity 10-8 appears.

4. Click the 3-D Pie Chart in the toolbar.

5. Click the **Variations** tab. The 3-D Pie dialog box appears.

**6.** Click the chart in the lower right corner of the Chart type box.

**7.** Click **OK.** The pie chart becomes three-dimensional, as shown in Figure 10-14.

**8.** Print the chart in landscape orientation.

**9.** Save the spreadsheet as *Energy 3D* and close the file.

**FIGURE 10-14**
Area, Bar, Line, and Pie charts are available in 3-D.

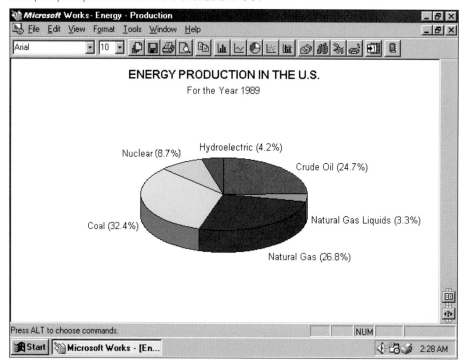

# *Summary*

■ A chart is a graphical representation of spreadsheet data. You can create several types of spreadsheet charts, including bar charts, line charts, pie charts, and scatter charts. A maximum of eight charts may be created from one spreadsheet.

■ Works will automatically suggest a bar chart when the Create New Chart command is chosen. If you prefer a different type of chart, you may select it from the New Chart dialog box or by clicking chart buttons of the toolbar of the chart window.

■ A chart created from a spreadsheet is considered part of that spreadsheet. When you save the spreadsheet, you will also save the charts you have created from the spreadsheet. You may save the spreadsheet and its associated charts by choosing Save from the File menu in either the spreadsheet window or the chart window.

■ Area, Bar, Line, and Pie charts can be created as 3-D charts. 3-D charts present data in a more attractive way.

● ● ● ● ● ● ● ● ● ● ● ● ●

# REVIEW ACTIVITIES

## TRUE/FALSE

**Circle T or F to show whether the statement is true or false.**

T    F      **1.** Charts are a graphical representation of spreadsheet data.

T    F      **2.** Bar charts are the best way to represent data groups that are part of a whole.

T    F      **3.** Line charts are well suited for representing trends over a period of time.

T    F      **4.** A scatter chart produces a "cloud" of data points not connected by lines.

T    F      **5.** A bar chart represents values in the spreadsheet by varying heights of rectangles.

T    F      **6.** Works automatically creates a line chart when the Create New Chart command is chosen.

T    F      **7.** When the spreadsheet data changes, charts created from the spreadsheet will also change.

T    F      **8.** All chart types can be created in 3-D.

T    F      **9.** The charts of a spreadsheet file are erased when the spreadsheet file is closed.

T    F      **10.** A chart may be printed from the chart window.

## COMPLETION

**Write the correct answer in the space provided.**

**1.** What type of chart represents values in a spreadsheet by points connected by a line?

_____

_____

**2.** What type of chart uses rectangles to represent values in a spreadsheet?

_____

_____

**3.** What type of chart is represented by a circle divided into portions?

_____

_____

4. Which toolbar button may be used to create a chart for the spreadsheet?

_____

_____

5. What command is chosen to title a chart?

_____

_____

6. Unless you rename a chart, what will Works name the first chart prepared from a spreadsheet?

_____

_____

7. Which menu contains the Rename Chart command?

_____

_____

8. While in the Chart window, how may you change the type of chart displayed?

_____

_____

9. What characteristics may be added to a bar chart to help in identifying the spreadsheet value a bar represents?

_____

_____

10. What toolbar button in the chart window allows you to see a printed chart before it is printed?

_____

_____

# REINFORCEMENT APPLICATIONS

## application 10-1

**The file *Application 10-1* contains the populations of the world's largest cities. Create a bar chart indicating larger populations with a higher bar.**

1. Open *Application 10-1*.

2. Create a bar chart from the data in A5:B11.

3. Title the bar chart **Population of World's Largest Cities**.

4. Subtitle the chart **In Millions**.

5. Title the vertical axis **Population**.

6. Print the chart.

7. Save the file to your data disk as *Cities* and close the file.

## application 10-2

**You have been running each morning to stay in shape. Over the past ten weeks you have recorded running times along a specified route and entered times in the file *Application 10-2*. Create a line chart indicating the trend in running times over the ten-week period.**

1. Open *Application 10-2*.

2. Create a line chart for the data contained in A4:B12.

3. Title the line chart **Ten-Week Workout Program**.

4. Title the vertical axis **Time in Minutes**.

5. Print the chart.

6. Save the file to your data disk as *Workout* and close the file.

# application 10-3

The file *Application 10-3* contains the number of McDonald's hamburger restaurants in different regions of the world. Create a pie chart in which each slice represents a region in Column A of the spreadsheet.

1. Open Application 10-3.

2. Create a pie chart for the data contained in A4:B8.

3. Title the pie chart **McDonald's Restaurants**.

4. Subtitle the chart **Worldwide Locations**.

5. Print the chart.

6. Save the file to your data disk as *McDonald's* and close the file.

# application 10-4

The file *Application 10-4* contains the study time and examination scores for several students. The instructor for the course is attempting to determine if there is a relationship between study time and examination score. Create a scatter chart of the data in the spreadsheet to indicate the relationship between study time and examination scores. Then label the data points in the scatter chart with the names of the students.

1. Open *Application 10-4*.

2. Create a scatter chart for the data in A4:C21 by accessing the chart window and selecting Option 1 in the XY (Scatter) dialog box.

3. Refine the scatter chart by defining the following in the Series boxes:
   a. The Value (Y) Series 1st should be B4:B21.
   b. The Category (X) Series should be C4:C21.
   c. The Value (Y) Series 2nd should not contain a range.

4. Add data labels to the chart by entering A4:A21 in the Data Labels Value (Y) Series 1st box.

5. Title the scatter chart **Comparison of Exam Grades to Study Time**.

6. Title the horizontal axis **Examination Grades**.

7. Title the vertical axis **Hours of Study**.

8. Print the chart.

9. Save the spreadsheet to your data disk as *Study Hours* and close the file.

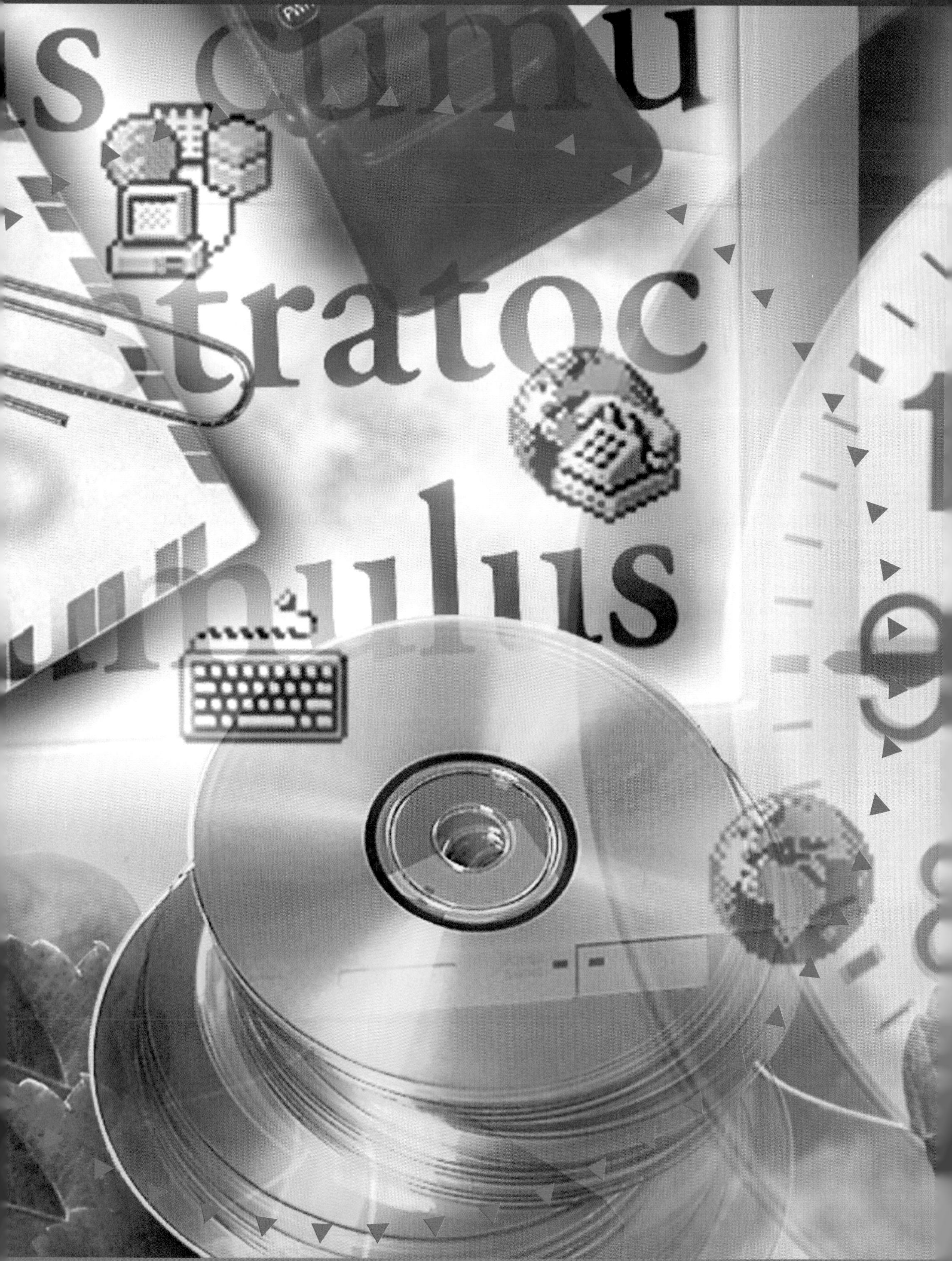

UNIT 4

# DATABASES

# DATABASE BASICS

## OBJECTIVES
### When you complete this chapter, you will be able to:

1. Define a database.

2. Identify the parts of a database.

3. Switch between List and Form views.

4. Move the highlight in a database.

5. Add and delete records in a database.

6. Print, save, and close a database.

7. Design fields.

8. Hide fields and records.

# *What Is a Database?*

**A** *database* is an automated electronic filing system that stores and retrieves information. A database is similar to a filing cabinet that contains folders of information. However, compared to a traditional paper filing system, the database has the following advantages:

1. Records can be retrieved quickly. You can find the information you need by pressing keys rather than searching through folders in a file cabinet.

2. Records can be manipulated easily. Using simple commands, you can sort the records in a number of ways, find a particular record, or select a group of records that meet certain criteria.

3. Records can be stored efficiently. Databases can store large amounts of data on a disk at a low cost. Filing cabinets of folders can require large amounts of space and can be expensive. See Figure 11-1.

**FIGURE 11-1**
Records can be stored efficiently in an electronic database on a disk.

As you will see in a moment, a database looks quite similar to a spreadsheet. Both have columns and rows, a Formula Bar where information is entered, and so on. But, databases and spreadsheets differ in the ways that they are used. A spreadsheet is used primarily for analysis of numerical data. In Chapter 9, for example, you used a spreadsheet to calculate interest on a loan. By contrast, a database is used primarily to store and retrieve records. For example, you will create a database in this chapter to store addresses and telephone numbers.

Databases are typically larger than spreadsheets because they are used for long-term storage of data. The database that keeps track of a club's membership, for example, expands as the names and addresses of new members are added. In a spreadsheet, you usually alter the existing information rather than add more data.

# Starting Works and Opening an Existing Database

In this activity, you will open an existing database file.

1. Start **Microsoft Works 4.0.** The Works Task Launcher appears.

2. Click the **Existing Documents** tab.

3. Click on **Open a document not listed here.** The Open dialog box will appear.

4. Click on the down arrow at the right of the **Look in** box. The list of drives will appear.

5. In the list of drives, click on the drive containing your template disk. The files on the disk will appear in the large window.

6. Click the filename *Activity 11-1* in the list of files in the large window. The filename will appear in the **File name** box.

7. Click **Open.** The database will appear on the screen. If Help is displayed and blocking your full screen, maximize the database window by clicking on the **Shrink Help** icon at the lower right edge of the screen. Your screen should appear similar to Figure 11-2.

8. Leave the file *Activity 11-1* on the screen for the next activity.

**FIGURE 11-2**
The primary parts of the database are the entry, record, and field.

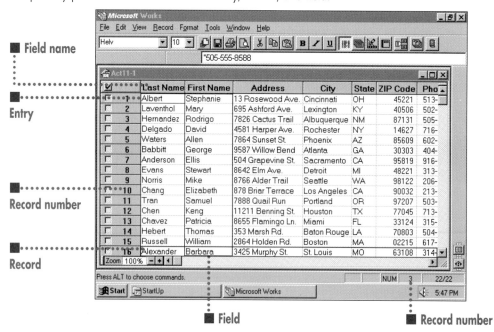

# Parts of a Database

**Y**ou will notice that many parts of the database screen look familiar. Like the word processor and the spreadsheet screens, the database screen shows a title bar, menu bar, scroll bars, status line, and toolbar. The database screen also shows a Formula Bar like the one you used in the spreadsheet section.

Several features will be new to you, however, because they appear only in the database. These features are labeled in Figure 11-2 and are discussed in the next three paragraphs.

Figure 11-2 shows a directory of names, addresses, and phone numbers. The data is arranged so that each kind of information is grouped together. For example, all the last names are in one column and all the first names are in another. These categories of information are called *fields.* This database has seven fields of common information—such as last names, addresses, or ZIP codes. The *field name* at the top of the column helps you to remember what kind of information will be stored in the column.

Each piece of information entered into a field is called an *entry.* In the database shown in Figure 11-2, for example, each name in the Last Name field is an entry.

One complete set of field entries is called a *record.* Each record has a *record number* displayed on the left side of the screen that identifies the sequence of the record in the database. In Figure 11-2, Record 1 consists of the last name, first name, address, city, state, ZIP code, and phone number for Stephanie Albert.

# Viewing a Database

**A**s you become more familiar with databases, you will realize that they can become very large, too large for you to view all records at once. Fortunately, Works allows several options for displaying the data you need on screen.

## List and Form View

A database may be displayed on screen in List view or Form view. The database now on your screen is in *List view,* which is similar in appearance to a spreadsheet. List view is most appropriate when you want to display several records at once. *Form view,* on the other hand, displays one record at a time. It is most appropriate for entering or editing a specific record. List view and Form view are shown in Figures 11-3 and 11-4, respectively.

**FIGURE 11-3**

A database may be displayed in List view, as shown here.

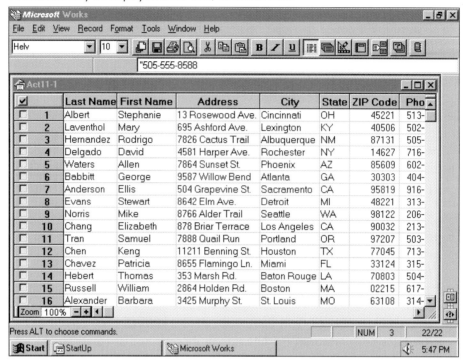

**FIGURE 11-4**

A database may be displayed in Form view, as shown here.

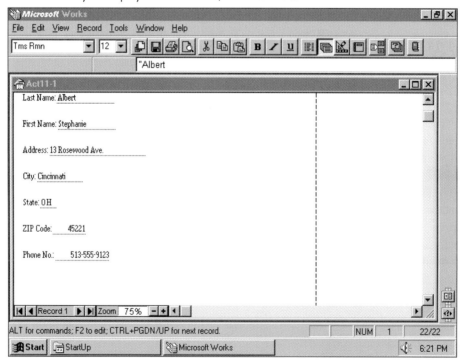

You may switch between List and Form views in three ways:

1. By choosing the Form or List command from the View menu.

2. By pressing the F9 key. Depressing this key only works in List view; from Form view you must use one of the other two methods.

3. By clicking the Form View or List View button on the toolbar.

■ List view button

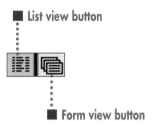

■ Form view button

## ACTIVITY 11-2

## Switching between List and Form View

In this activity, you will switch between List and Form views in the database. The file *Activity 11-1* should be on your screen in List view. Switch between views by following these steps:

1. Press **F9.** The database will appear in Form view.

2. Choose **List** from the **View** menu. The database will return to List view.

3. Click the **Form View** button on the toolbar.

4. Click the **List View** button on the toolbar.

5. Leave the file *Activity 11-1* on the screen for the next activity.

## Splitting the Screen

If a database is very large, you may want to view several parts of it on the screen at the same time by *splitting* the screen. Sections of a split window are called *panes.* By creating panes in the window, you may view as many as four parts of the database at once. For example, the database in Figure 11-5 has been split horizontally to display the records at the top and bottom of the database. The database in Figure 11-6 has been split into four panes. The split screen shows the Phone No. field next to the names, even though it was originally at the extreme right side of the screen.

**FIGURE 11-5**
Splitting the screen horizontally enables you to view
the top and bottom of a database simultaneously.

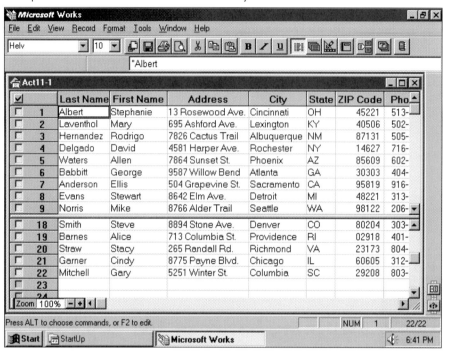

**FIGURE 11-6**
Splitting the screen vertically enables you to view the
left and right sides of a database simultaneously.

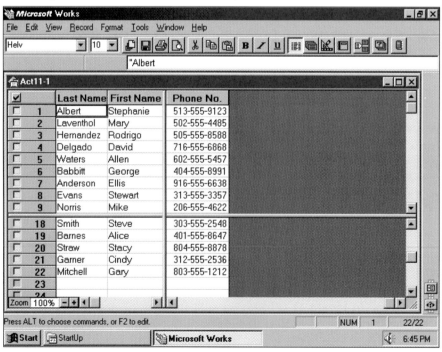

A split box appears on the left side of the horizontal scroll bar and at the top of the vertical scroll bar (see Figure 11-7). As you point to the split box, the mouse pointer will turn into two arrows with the word *ADJUST* below them. To split the screen, drag from the split box to the point where the screen is to be split (or you may split the screen in half simply by double-clicking the split box). After you have split the screens, you may scroll within each of the panes by clicking in the pane and dragging the scroll box.

**FIGURE 11-7**

A database screen is split by dragging from the split boxes.

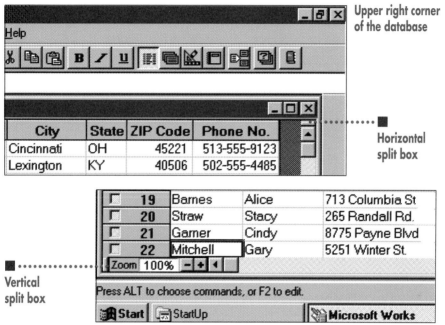

Upper right corner of the database

Horizontal split box

Vertical split box

Lower left corner of the database

**A C T I V I T Y**

*11-3* **Splitting a Database Screen**

In this activity, you will split the screen into four panes. The file *Activity 11-1* should be on your screen in List view.

1. Double-click the horizontal split box in the upper right part of the screen. The screen should split horizontally.

2. Drag from the vertical split box to the right edge of the First Name field. Your screen should appear similar to the screen in Figure 11-8.

3. Click anywhere in the lower right pane of the window.

## FIGURE 11-8
Splitting the screen allows you to view several parts of the database at the same time.

4. Slide the scroll box in the horizontal scroll bar all the way to the right so that the Phone No. field is next to the First Name field on the other side of the split bar. Your screen should look similar to Figure 11-6 on page 250.

5. Return the screen to a single pane by double-clicking the lines that split the window.

6. Slide the scroll box in the horizontal scroll bar all the way to the left and slide the scroll box in the vertical scroll bar to the top.

7. Leave the file *Activity 11-1* on the screen for the next activity.

**NOTE:** *You may also split a spreadsheet in the same way you split the database.*

## Using the Zoom Feature

If a database is large or a record is lengthy, you may want to shrink the database on the screen to view more of the information at once. Or, you may want to enlarge the information in a database or record to see it more clearly. These tasks may be accomplished by using the Zoom icons shown adjacent to the navigation buttons in Figure 11-9 on page 254. Using the icons, which are available in both Form and List view, the database can be reduced to 50 percent or enlarged to 400 percent of the normal (100 percent) screen size. To reduce the size of the database or record on screen and see more information displayed, click the minus icon; to increase the size of the database or record on screen and see less (but larger) information displayed, click the plus icon. You may also enlarge or reduce a database or record by choosing Zoom from the View menu and keying any number from 33 to 1000 in the Custom box or choosing one of the set magnifications listed.

# Moving the Highlight in a Database

In either Form view or List view, the easiest way to move the highlight is by simply clicking that area with the mouse. You can also move the highlight using key commands. Keystroke commands to move the highlight are different in List view and Form view.

## Moving the Highlight in Form View

In Form view, you may scroll within the form of a single record. You will need to scroll only when the record exceeds the size of the screen. Table 11-1 shows the keystrokes for moving the highlight in Form view if you prefer not to use the mouse.

**TABLE 11-1**
Keystrokes move the highlight within a record in Form View.

### FORM VIEW

| TO MOVE | PRESS |
| --- | --- |
| Up one line | Up arrow |
| Down one line | Down arrow |
| Up one window | Page Up |
| Down one window | Page Down |
| To the next field | Tab |
| To the previous field | Shift+Tab |
| To the first field | Home |
| To the last field | End |

The *navigation buttons,* shown in Figure 11-9, allow you to move to other records in the database. The buttons are located in the left part of the status line and are useful for moving to the first, previous, next, or last record in the database. You can also move from record to record using the key combinations shown in Table 11-2.

FIGURE 11-9
Navigation buttons move the highlight from record to record while in Form view.

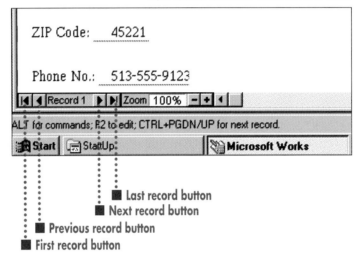

Last record button
Next record button
Previous record button
First record button

**TABLE 11-2**
Keystrokes may be used to move the highlight to other records in Form view.

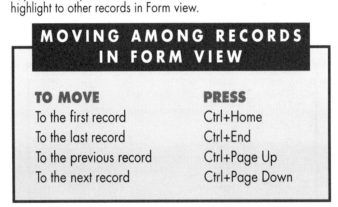

## MOVING AMONG RECORDS IN FORM VIEW

| TO MOVE | PRESS |
| --- | --- |
| To the first record | Ctrl+Home |
| To the last record | Ctrl+End |
| To the previous record | Ctrl+Page Up |
| To the next record | Ctrl+Page Down |

## Moving the Highlight in List View

Moving the highlight in List view is similar to moving it in the spreadsheet. Of course, you may scroll throughout the database using the mouse to drag the scroll bars as you learned in Chapter 1.

You can also move the highlight by pressing certain keys or key combinations. Table 11-3 shows how to move the highlight with keystrokes while in List view.

**TABLE 11-3**
Moving the highlight in List view is similar
to moving the highlight in the spreadsheet.

## LIST VIEW

| TO MOVE | PRESS |
| --- | --- |
| Left one field | Left arrow |
| Right one field | Right arrow |
| Up one record | Up arrow |
| Down one record | Down arrow |
| To the first field of a record | Home |
| To the last field of a record | End |
| To the first field of the first record | Ctrl+Home |
| To the last field of the last record | Ctrl+End |
| Up one window | Page Up |
| Down one window | Page Down |
| Left one window | Ctrl+Page Up |
| Right to last window | Ctrl+Page Down |

## Using the Go To Command to Move in the Database

In the spreadsheet, the Go To command is used to move the highlight to a specific cell by indicating the cell reference (for example, B13). Because cell references are not available in the database, the Go To command asks for a field name instead. After you select the Go To command from the Edit menu, each field in the database will be displayed in the Go To dialog box. When you double-click the field name, Works will place the highlight in that field. The Go To command is available in both Form and List view.

ACTIVITY

# Moving the Highlight in the Database

In this activity, you will move the highlight in a database. Your screen should show the database *Activity 11-1* in List view.

1. Press **Ctrl+Home** to move the highlight to the first entry in the database. The highlight will appear in an entry with the name *Albert*.

2. Press **Ctrl+End** to move to the last record in the database. The highlight will move to the lower right side of the database. The highlight will appear in an entry with the telephone number *803-555-1212*.

3. Press **Home** to move to the first entry of the last record in the database. The highlight should appear in an entry with the name *Mitchell*.

4. Press the **Up arrow** key to move the highlight up one record. The highlight will appear in an entry containing the name *Garner*.

5. Move to the ZIP Code field by using the Go To command:
   **a.** Choose **Go To** from the **Edit** menu.

**b.** Double-click **ZIP Code** in the **Select a field** box. The highlight will appear in an entry containing *60605* in the ZIP Code field.

6. Press **F9** to switch to Form view.

7. Click the **First Record** navigation button to move to the first record in the database. The highlight will appear in an entry containing *45221*.

8. Press **Shift+Tab** to move to the previous field. The highlight will appear in an entry containing *OH*.

9. Press **Ctrl+Page Down** to move to the next record.

10. Click the **Last Record** navigation button to move to the last record in the database. In Form view, the last record will be blank and ready to receive new data.

11. Leave this blank record on the screen for the next activity.

# Adding and Deleting Records in the Database

Once a database has been created, it is simple to add new records to it or to delete records that you no longer need. New records may be entered in either Form or List view. Because Form view displays one record at a time, single records are usually entered in Form view.

Records that are no longer useful may be deleted from the database. To delete a record in Form view, display the record to be deleted on the screen and select the Delete Record command from the Record menu. To delete a record in List view, select the entire record and choose Delete Record from the Record menu.

The Undo command is available to reverse changes made to a database, including deleting records.

## ACTIVITY

## 11-5 Adding and Deleting Records

In this activity, you will add a new record to the database *Activity 11-1.* Your screen should contain a blank record in Form view.

1. Click the line beside the **Last Name** field. The entry will be highlighted.

2. Key **Chester**.

3. Press **Tab.** The highlight will move to the right of the colon beside the First Name field.

4. Key **Tom**.

5. Continue to tab to the next fields and enter the following data:

| | |
|---|---|
| Address: | **3584 Daisy St.** |
| City: | **Washington** |
| State: | **DC** |
| ZIP Code: | **20549** |
| Phone No: | **202-555-8789** |

6. Press **Enter.**

7. Click the **First Record** navigation button. The record for Stephanie Albert of Cincinnati will appear.

8. Choose **Delete Record** from the **Record** menu. The record for Stephanie Albert will disappear and the record for Mary Laventhol of Lexington will appear in place of the deleted record.

**9.** Switch to List view by clicking the **List view** button on the toolbar.

**10.** Select the record for Keng Chen of Houston by clicking Record Number **11.** Selecting the record number highlights the entire record.

**11.** Choose **Delete Record** from the **Record** menu. The record will be deleted from the database.

**12.** Choose **Undo Delete Record** from the **Edit** menu. The record reappears. Your screen should appear similar to Figure 11-10.

**13.** Leave the file *Activity 11-1* on the screen for the next activity.

**FIGURE 11-10**
It is simple to add and delete records in the Works database.

# *Printing Part of a Database*

Large databases are not usually printed. You can probably imagine how many pages it would take to print a database with thousands of records. Instead, large databases are usually summarized and printed in reports. You will learn about reporting in Chapter 14. However, you may want to print a small database or an individual record in a database—instead of creating a report.

## Printing a Small Database from List View

Small databases may be printed as they appear in List view. In other words, rows of records will be printed in the order that they appear on screen. To print a database from List view, choose the Print command from the File menu or click the Print button on the toolbar. If you desire, you can preview the printed database by choosing the Print Preview command from the File menu or by clicking the Print Preview button on the toolbar. If you desire to adjust margins or page characteristics, you can do so by choosing the Page Setup command from the File menu.

**NOTE:** *Printing by clicking the Print button on the toolbar causes printing to begin immediately.*

## Printing Records from Form View

You may also print records as they appear in Form view. Records will be printed, one per page, with fields in the same position as they appear on the screen. To print individual records from Form view, you must first click the *Current record only* option in the *What to Print* box in the Print dialog box, which is shown in Figure 11-11. Otherwise, Works will print a page for every record in the database (quite a printing task if your database contains many records!).

**NOTE:** *When printing from Form View, do not use the Print button from the toolbar unless you want a page printed for every record in the database.*

**FIGURE 11-11**
To print an individual record, click Current record only in the What to Print box in the Print dialog box.

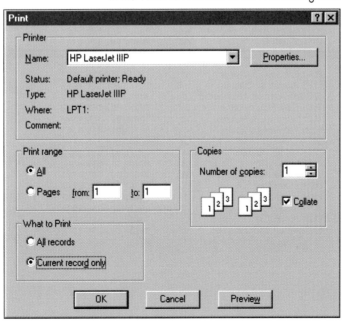

## Printing a Database

In this activity you will print the database *Activity 11-1* from List view and print an individual record from Form view. Your screen should show the database *Activity 11-1* in List view.

1. Choose **Print Preview** from the **File** menu. The database will appear on screen as it would be printed.

2. Click **Print.** The Print dialog box will appear.

3. Click **OK.** The database will print.

4. Select the record for Rodrigo Hernandez (Record Number 2).

5. Press **F9** to switch to Form view.

6. Choose **Print** from the **File** menu.

7. Click the **Current record only** option in the What to Print box in the Print dialog box.

8. Click **OK.** The record will print. Your printed pages should appear similar to the printed pages shown in Figure 11-12.

9. Leave the database *Activity 11-1* on the screen for the next activity.

**FIGURE 11-12**
You may print the entire database as it appears in List view or individual records as they appear in Form view.

| | | | | | |
|---|---|---|---|---|---|
| Laventhol | Mary | 695 Ashford Ave. | Lexington | KY | 40506 502-555-4485 |
| Hernandez | Rodrigo | 7826 Cactus Trail | Albuquerque | NM | 87131 505-555-8588 |
| Delgado | David | 4581 Harper Ave. | Rochester | NY | 14627 716-555-6868 |
| Waters | Allen | 7864 Sunset St. | Phoenix | AZ | 85609 602-555-5457 |
| Babbitt | George | 9587 Willow Bend | Atlanta | GA | 30303 404-555-8991 |
| Anderson | Ellis | 504 Grapevine St. | Sacramento | CA | 95819 916-555-6638 |
| Evans | Stewart | 8642 Elm Ave. | Detroit | MI | 48221 313-555-3357 |
| Norris | Mike | 8766 Alder Trail | Seattle | WA | 98122 206-555-4622 |
| Chang | Elizabeth | 878 Briar Terrace | Los Angeles | CA | 90032 213-555-8225 |
| Tran | Samuel | 7888 Quail Run | Portland | OR | 97207 503-555-4587 |
| Chen | Keng | 11211 Benning St. | Houston | TX | 77045 713-555-8596 |
| Chavez | Patricia | 8655 Flamingo Ln. | Miami | FL | 33124 315-555-9887 |
| Hebert | Thomas | 353 Marsh Rd. | Baton Rouge | LA | 70803 504-555-4446 |
| Russell | William | 2864 Holden Rd. | Boston | MA | 02215 617-555-8822 |
| Alexander | Barbara | 3425 Murphy St. | St. Louis | MO | 63108 314-555-9317 |
| Novak | Art | 875 Wheeler Ave. | Baltimore | MD | 21210 301-555-8731 |
| Smith | Steve | 8894 Stone Ave. | Denver | CO | 80204 303-555-2548 |
| Barnes | Alice | 713 Columbia St. | Providence | RI | 02918 401-555-8647 |
| Straw | Stacy | 265 Randall Rd. | Richmond | VA | 23173 804-555-8878 |
| Garner | Cindy | 8775 Payne Blvd. | Chicago | IL | 60605 312-555-2536 |
| Mitchell | Gary | 5251 Winter St. | Columbia | SC | 29208 803-555-1212 |
| Chester | Tom | 3584 Daisy St. | Washington | DC | 20549 202-555-8789 |

Last Name: Hernandez

First Name: Rodrigo

Address: 7826 Cactus Trail

City: Albuquerque

State: NM

ZIP Code: 87131

Phone No.: 505-555-8588

# Saving and Exiting a Database

**Y**ou save a file and exit the database in the same way you perform these operations in the word processor or the spreadsheet. Both the Save command and the Close command appear in the File menu. The Save button on the toolbar can be used to save a file by its current name.

**ACTIVITY**

## Saving and Closing a Database

In this activity, you will save and exit the file *Activity 11-1*, which should be on your screen in Form view.

1. Choose **Save As** from the **File** menu. The Save As dialog box will appear.

2. Key **Address** in the **File name** box.

3. Place your data disk in drive A. In the **Save in** box, choose **A:** to select your floppy disk drive.

4. Click **Save.** Works saves the database.

5. Choose **Close** from the **File** menu. The database will disappear from the screen.

# Designing Fields

**T**he arrangement of a database is critical to its usefulness. At the beginning of this chapter, you learned that one advantage of using a database is that it allows you to find information easily. You also learned that records may be sorted quickly in a database. The efficiency of these operations depends on whether or not the fields of the database have been designed carefully.

## Creating Fields

You can create fields in either List view or Form view. When you are creating fields for a new database, you will automatically begin with the Create Database dialog box on screen; for more information, see Chapter 12. To add a single new field to an existing database, you can use the Form Design command from the View menu in List view—doing so will automatically take you into Form view with Form Design engaged. In this section, new fields will be created in Form view.

To create a field in Form view, click the Form Design button on the tool bar. Click to place the cursor at the position you want the field to appear. Choose Field from the Insert menu. The Insert Field dialog box appears. (The Form Design button and Insert Field dialog box are shown in Figure 11-13.) Key the name of the new field in the dialog box. Fields created in Form view will also appear in List view.

**FIGURE 11-13**
To insert a field in Form view, click the Form Design button on the toolbar and name the field in the Insert Field dialog box.

**Form design button**

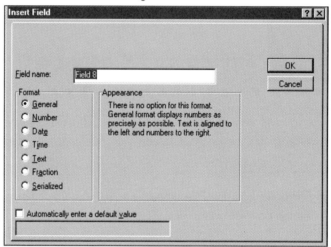

If you would like to move field names, you can drag them to a new location within the record whenever you are in Form Design mode. Works will show you the position of the field name in the Formula Bar.

**ACTIVITY**

## Creating a New Field

In this activity, you will create a new field for the database *Activity 11-8*. This database contains information on national parks in the United States. You would like to use this database to advise travelers of activities available in these parks. Enter an additional field to this database to indicate whether fishing is available in the park by following these steps:

1. Open the file *Activity 11-8* from the template disk.

2. Click the **Form Design** button on the toolbar.

3. Click about two lines below the *A* in the ACRES (000) field.

4. Choose **Field** from the **Insert** menu. The Insert Field dialog box appears.

5. Key **FISHING** in the **Field name** box.

6. Click **OK.**

7. Click the **List view** button to switch to List view.

8. Enter the following data in the newly created FISHING field. You may wish to split the screen to make this task easier.

| | |
|---|---|
| Acadia | **Yes** |
| Badlands | **No** |
| Big Bend | **Yes** |
| Carlsbad Caverns | **No** |
| Denali | **Yes** |
| Everglades | **Yes** |
| Glacier | **Yes** |
| Grand Canyon | **Yes** |
| Haleakala | **No** |
| Hot Springs | **No** |
| Isle Royale | **Yes** |
| Mammoth Cave | **Yes** |
| Olympic | **Yes** |
| Rocky Mountain | **Yes** |
| Shenandoah | **Yes** |
| Yellowstone | **Yes** |
| Yosemite | **Yes** |
| Zion | **No** |

Source: Michael Frome, *The Leading National Park Guide* (Chicago: Rand McNally, 1987); and *National Park Service, National Park System Map and Guide* (Washington, D.C.: U.S. Department of the Interior, 1989).

9. Leave the database *Activity 11-8* on the screen in List view for the next activity.

## Field Size

In the last activity, you created a field in Form view with the default field size of 20 characters. You can change the field size so that it is no larger than the largest entry. However, sometimes you will not be able to determine the field size until you enter data into the field. The field size may be adjusted in either List or Form (Design) view.

In List view, the field size is adjusted in the same way a column width is adjusted in the spreadsheet. If numerical data is wider than the column, a series of number signs (e.g., ######) will appear in the entry. Alphabetical data will be truncated (deleted at the end) if the field is too narrow. You can widen a field by placing the mouse pointer on the boundary of the right edge of the field name. The pointer will turn into a vertical bar with a double-headed arrow with the word *ADJUST* below it. Widen the column by dragging the double-headed arrow to the right until the column is wide enough to show all of the data.

You can also use the Field Width command in the Format menu to specify column width. Like the spreadsheet's Column Width dialog box, the database's Field Width dialog box has a Best Fit option that automatically selects the width that gives the best fit for your data. The Best Fit option is available only in List View. Click the Standard option to change a field width to 10, the standard size.

In Form view, choose Form Design from the View menu or click the Form Design button on the toolbar. Then, adjust the field size by clicking the field entry and pointing to one of the resizing handles, as shown in Figure 11-14. When the pointer turns into a double-headed arrow with the word *RESIZE* below it, drag it to the field size you desire. The field size will be changed for all records.

**FIGURE 11-14**
In Form view with the Form Design button selected, field width is adjusted by dragging the resizing handles.

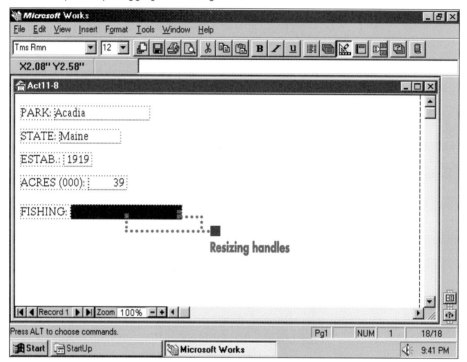

# Changing the Size of a Field

In this activity, you will decrease the size of the FISHING field in Form view of *Activity 11-8*. You will also adjust the width of the PARK field in List view. *Activity 11-8* should be on your screen in List view.

**1.** Select the PARK field by clicking the field name *PARK*. Clicking the field name selects the entire column.

**2.** Choose **Field Width** from the **Format** menu.

**3.** Click **Best Fit.** The field narrows to fit the longest entry.

**4.** Press **F9** to switch to Form view.

**5.** Click the **Form Design** button on the toolbar.

6. Click the entry of the FISHING field to high-light its contents.

7. Point to the resizing handle at the right edge (not the corner) of the field. The pointer will turn into a horizontal arrow with the word *RESIZE* below it.

8. The largest entry of the FISHING field will be three letters (for the word *Yes*). Drag the

double-headed arrow to the left until the field is large enough to fit approximately five letters.

9. Leave the database *Activity 11-8* on the screen in Form view for the next activity.

## Moving a Field in Form View

A field in Form view may be moved to any part of the form. To change the location of the field, click on the Form Design button on the toolbar and then click the field name. The word *DRAG* will appear below the pointer. Press and hold the left mouse button (which causes the word *DRAG* to change to *MOVE*) and drag the field to the location you desire. Changing the location of the field in Form view will not affect the location of the field in List view.

The location of the field will be displayed in the Formula Bar. (See Figure 11-15.) The number after the X indicates where the field appears horizontally, and the number after the Y indicates where the field appears vertically.

**FIGURE 11-15**

In Form view, the position of a field may be changed by dragging the field to a new location.

## Moving a Field

In this activity, you will move a field. The file *Activity 11-8* should be on your screen in Form view with Form Design engaged.

1. Click the *FISHING* field name to select it.

2. Drag the *FISHING* field to the right and down until the X coordinate on the Formula Bar reads 1.50″ and the Y coordinate reads 3.50″.

3. Drag the following fields to the coordinates specified:

| | |
|---|---|
| ACRES | X1.50″ Y3.00″ |
| ESTAB | X1.50″ Y2.50″ |
| STATE | X1.50″ Y2.00″ |
| PARK | X1.50″ Y1.50″ |

4. Leave the database *Activity 11-8* on the screen in Form view for the next activity.

## Field Alignment

Works automatically aligns alphabetical characters to the left side of the field and numerical characters to the right side of a field. You may change the horizontal alignment of field data by highlighting the field (or a field entry) and choosing Alignment from the Format menu. When an alignment is chosen, all the data in the field will be aligned. The alignment will occur in both Form and List view.

You can also change the vertical alignment of field data in the Format dialog box in List view. Data may be aligned at the top, center, or bottom. Although you will not employ this kind of alignment in this text, you may wish to experiment with it on your own.

# ACTIVITY

## Aligning Entries in a Field

In this activity, you will center the data in the FISHING field of database *Activity 11-8*. *Activity 11-8* should be on your screen in Form view with Form Design engaged.

1. Select the contents of the FISHING field. (Do not highlight the field name FISHING. Highlight where *Yes* or *No* appears).

2. Choose **Alignment** from the **Format** menu. The Format dialog box appears with the Alignment section selected, as shown in Figure 11-16.

3. Choose **Center** alignment and click **OK.** The contents of the entry should move to the center.

4. Choose the **List view** button on the toolbar to switch to List view. The contents of the FISHING field should be centered.

5. Leave the database *Activity 11-8* on the screen in List view for the next activity.

**FIGURE 11-16**
Changes made to a field's alignment will affect both Form and List view.

## Font Style

The font style of entries may be changed to boldface, italics, or underline. To change the font style of a field, highlight the field (or a field entry) and click one of the font style buttons on the toolbar. When a style button is clicked, all the data in the field will be changed only in the view you are using—List view or Form view. To alter font style in Form view, select the Form Design button first.

## Database Fonts and Font Sizes

The font and font size can affect the readability of a database on the screen. The number of fonts available is determined by the printer you are using.

To change the font of a field, highlight the field (or a field entry), click the Font Name box arrow on the toolbar, and choose the name of the font you desire. Use the same procedure to specify the font size by clicking the Font Size box arrow. To alter font style in Form view, the Form Design button must be selected first. If you want to change the font of the entire database, highlight all of the fields in List view and then choose the Font Name box.

# *Hiding Fields and Records*

**W**hen databases become large, you may find it easier to view only a portion of the database. Hiding fields and records removes data from view but does not delete data from the database.

## Hiding Fields

Hide a field in List view by dragging the right border of the field to the left border; when the mouse button is released the field name disappears from view. Or you may hide a field by choosing the Field Width command from the Format menu and keying **0** as the field width. To redisplay a field that has been hidden, choose the Go To command from the Edit menu (or press F5) and choose the field name. Then choose the Field Width command and increase the field width (which is currently 0). You cannot hide a field in Form view, but you can hide the field name by choosing Show Field Name from the Format menu.

## Hiding Records

Records may be hidden in List view or Form view. In List view, select the record or records you want to hide and choose the Hide Record command from the Record menu.

In Form view, you may hide the record currently on the screen by choosing the Hide Record command from the Record menu. In Form view, you can hide records only one at a time.

To redisplay hidden records in List or Form view, choose Show from the Record menu, then choose 1 All Records.

# ACTIVITY

## 11-12 Hiding Fields and Records

• • • • • • • • • • • • • • • • • • • • • • • • • • • • • • • • • • • • • • •

In this activity, you will hide and redisplay fields and records. The file *Activity 11-8* should be on your screen in List view.

1. Hide the ESTAB. field following these steps:
   a. Select the ESTAB. field. Point to the right side of the field. The pointer will turn into a double-headed arrow with the word *ADJUST* below it.
   b. Click and drag the double-headed arrow to the left until it reaches the left edge of the field. The field's grid line also moves to show the changing field width. Release the mouse button. The ESTAB. field is now hidden.

2. Hide the records for Haleakala and Hot Springs (Records 9 and 10) by following these steps:
   a. Drag from Record 9 to Record 10 along the left side of the screen to select the records for Haleakala and Hot Springs.
   b. Choose **Hide Record** from the **Record** menu. Records 9 and 10 will be hidden.

3. Redisplay the ESTAB. field by following these steps:
   a. Choose **Go To** from the **Edit** menu. The Go To dialog box will appear.
   b. Click **ESTAB.** in the **Select a field** list of field names and click **OK.** You will be returned to List view.
   c. Choose **Field Width** from the **Format** menu. The Field Width dialog box will appear.
   d. Enter **10** in the **Column width** box and click **OK.**
   or
   Click the **Standard** button.
   e. The ESTAB. field will be restored.

4. Redisplay Records 9 and 10 by choosing **Show** from the **Record** menu, then choosing **1 All Records.**

5. Print the entire database from List view.

6. Save the file to your data disk as *Parks* and close the file.

# Summary

■ A database is an automated electronic filing system that stores and retrieves information. It is made up of rows, called records, and columns, called fields. A database typically contains larger amounts of information and involves less computation than a spreadsheet.

■ A database can be viewed in two ways. List view shows several records at once and has a format similar to a spreadsheet. While in List view, a database screen may be split to view several parts of the database on the screen at the same time. Form view displays one record at a time. Records may be added and deleted from a database in either List or Form view.

■ The appearance of fields in a database is critical to its usefulness. Field size, font style (boldface, italics, and underline), and field alignment (left, center, and right justification) may be adjusted to accommodate the needs of the database user.

■ Selected fields and records may be hidden to make it easier to read a large database. Hiding removes the data from view on the screen but does not delete the data from the database.

● ● ● ● ● ● ● ● ● ● ● ● ● ●

# REVIEW ACTIVITIES

## TRUE/FALSE

**Circle T or F to show whether the statement is true or false.**

**T  F**  1. The ability to sort records quickly is an advantage of using an electronic database.

**T  F**  2. A database usually contains less data than a spreadsheet.

**T  F**  3. A record is a row of entries in the database.

**T  F**  4. A field is the smallest unit in a database and contains one piece of information.

**T  F**  5. The List view of the database shows one record at a time.

**T  F**  6. While in Form view, pressing F9 will switch the screen to List view.

**T  F**  7. While in Form view, choosing the List command in the View menu will switch the screen to List view.

**T  F**  8. The Undo command cannot bring back a deleted record.

**T  F**  9. Works allows only one font in List view and one font in Form view of a database.

**T  F**  10. Hiding a field in the database will erase the field.

## COMPLETION

**Write the correct answer in the space provided.**

1. What is a row of field entries in a database called?

_____

_____

2. What is a column of database information called?

_____

_____

3. In Form view, what buttons are clicked to move to the first, previous, next, or last record in the database?

_____

_____

4. In Form view, what combination of keys is pressed to move to the first record in a database?

_____

_____

5. In what menu is the Delete Record command found?

_____

_____

6. What happens if the Print button on the toolbar is clicked while in Form view?

_____

_____

7. What option must be chosen in the Print dialog box in order to print an individual record in Form view?

_____

_____

8. What is the effect of setting a field width at 0 (zero) in List view?

_____

_____

9. What command in the Record menu will hide a record in a database?

_____

_____

10. What command restores hidden records in a database?

_____

_____

*application   11-1*

## MATCHING

In the blank space, write the letter of the keystroke that matches the highlight movement in the Form view of the database.

| Highlight Movement | Keystroke |
|---|---|
| ___ **1.** Up one line | **a.** Shift+Tab |
| ___ **2.** Down one line | **b.** Up arrow |
| ___ **3.** Up one window | **c.** Ctrl+End |
| ___ **4.** Down one window | **d.** Down arrow |
| ___ **5.** To the next field | **e.** Tab |
| ___ **6.** To the previous field | **f.** Ctrl+Page Down |
| | **g.** Page Up |
| ___ **7.** To the first field | **h.** Ctrl+Page Up |
| ___ **8.** To the last field | **i.** Ctrl+Home |
| ___ **9.** First record | **j.** End |
| ___**10.** Last record | **k.** Home |
| ___**11.** Next record | **l.** Page Down |
| ___**12.** Previous record | |

*a p p l i c a t i o n    1 1 - 2*

## MATCHING

**In the blank space, write the letter of the keystroke that matches the highlight movement in the List view of the database.**

| Highlight Movement | Keystroke |
|---|---|
| ___ 1. Left one field | a.  Ctrl+End |
| ___ 2. Right one field | b.  Ctrl+Page Down |
| ___ 3. Up one record | c.  Down arrow |
| ___ 4. Down one record | d.  Left arrow |
| ___ 5. To the first field of a record | e.  End |
| | f.  Home |
| ___ 6. To the last field of a record | g.  Ctrl+Page Up |
| | h.  Page Up |
| ___ 7. To the first field of the first record | i.  Right arrow |
| ___ 8. To the last field of the last record | j.  Ctrl+Home |
| | k.  Up arrow |
| ___ 9. Up one window | l.  Page Down |
| ___ 10. Down one window | |
| ___ 11. Left one window | |
| ___ 12. Right to last window | |

*a p p l i c a t i o n   1 1 - 3*

## MATCHING

**In the blank space, write the letter of the appropriate database key or mouse procedure that matches the database operations. You may use the items in the right column more than once if necessary. For some questions, more than one answer may be correct; however, you are required to identify only one of the correct answers.**

**Database Operation**

____ 1. Open an existing database file

____ 2. Switch to Form view

____ 3. Switch to List view

____ 4. Split the List view

____ 5. Move to the next record in Form view

____ 6. Move to the first record while in Form view

____ 7. Move up one record in List view

____ 8. Move to the last field of the last record in List view

____ 9. Widen a field in List view

____ 10. Widen a field in Form view

____ 11. Hide a field in List view

____ 12. Redisplay a record in List view

____ 13. Save a database file

____ 14. Exit Works

**Key or Mouse Procedure**

a. Press the F9 key

b. Click a navigation button

c. Press Ctrl+Page Down

d. Double-click the split box

e. Press Ctrl+End

f. Drag from the right boundary of the field name

g. Click a button on the toolbar

h. Press Ctrl+Home

i. Choose a command from the Format menu

j. Press Up arrow

k. Choose a command from the File menu

l. Press Ctrl+Right arrow

m. Drag from the right side of the field name

n. Choose a command from the Record menu

*a p p l i c a t i o n   1 1 - 4*

**The file *Application 11-4* is a database of population statistics for selected countries. The database currently contains the following fields:**

Country

Population (for the year 1990)

Birth Rate (per 1,000 of the population)

Death Rate (per 1,000 of the population)

Perform the following operations to change the fields of the database:

1. Open *Application 11-4*.

2. Narrow the entries to the right of the field names in Form view to eliminate excess space.

3. Switch to List view and widen the fields to show all field names and entry contents if necessary.

4. Add a new field in Form View entitled *Life Expectancy* that will appear as the last field, adjust the width as necessary, and enter the following data in the field:

| Country | Life Expectancy |
|---|---|
| Australia | 76 |
| Brazil | 66 |
| China | 70 |
| Cuba | 74 |
| Egypt | 63 |
| Ethiopia | 43 |
| France | 76 |
| India | 60 |
| Indonesia | 58 |
| Italy | 76 |
| Mexico | 70 |
| Nigeria | 52 |
| Poland | 71 |
| Turkey | 66 |
| United Kingdom | 76 |
| United States | 76 |
| USSR | 70 |
| West Germany | 75 |
| Zaire | 54 |

Source: *United Nations Population Fund* (UNFPA), *The State of the World Population 1990* (1990).

5. Center the contents of the Birth Rate, Death Rate, and Life Expectancy fields.

6. Print the database from List view.

7. Save the file to your data disk as *Population* and close the file.

*application   11 - 5*

**In this application, you will enter an additional record and delete obsolete records from the file created in Application 11-4.**

1. Retrieve the file *Population* created in Application 11-4.

2. The countries of West Germany and the USSR no longer exist by those names, nor are they constituted by the same land areas. Delete these records from the database.

3. Add the following record for the unified Germany to the bottom of the database:

| Country | Population | Birth Rate | Death Rate | Life Expectancy |
|---------|-----------|-----------|-----------|-----------------|
| Germany | 77,188,000 | 10 | 11 | 75 |

4. Print the individual record for Germany from Form view.

5. Save the file as *Population 2* and close the file.


*application   11 - 6*

**The file *Application 11-6* is a database of dog breeds and their characteristics. The purpose of the database is to assist in selecting a breed for a pet. The database exceeds the size of the screen. Perform the following operations to make viewing the database more manageable:**

1. Open *Application 11-6*.

2. Center the contents of the Height and Weight fields.

3. Split the screen horizontally so that the top and bottom of the database may be viewed simultaneously.

4. Suppose you are not interested in the height of the breed. Hide this field from view.

5. Suppose you are not interested in breeds in the Toy Group. Hide the records in the Toy Group.

6. Return the screen to full size—being sure to work from the part of the window in which you made changes.

7. Save the database to your data disk as *Short*.

8. Print the shortened database from List view.

9. Restore the hidden records and fields.

10. Save the database to your data disk as *Long* and exit Works.

Source: Patricia Sylvester, ed., *The Reader's Digest Illustrated Book of Dogs,* rev. ed. (The Readers' Digest Association, Inc., 1989); heights and weights are minimums required by various kennel associations.

# STRENGTHENING DATABASE SKILLS

CHAPTER

*12*

## OBJECTIVES
### When you complete this chapter, you will be able to:

1. Create a new database.

2. Copy data to other entries.

3. Insert a record in a database.

4. Move data to other entries.

5. Format a database field.

6. Insert dates and times in a database.

7. Perform calculations in a database.

8. Protect or hide parts of a database.

# *Creating a New Database*

**A** new database is created by clicking the Database button in the Works Tools dialog box of the Works Task Launcher as shown in Figure 12-1. If Works is already running, you can create a new database by choosing the New command from the File menu and then clicking the Database button in the Works Tools dialog box. In either case, the Create Database dialog box will appear (see Figure 12-2A on page 280). When you have entered your fields and saved the database, you will have created a new database file.

You can switch to Form view with Form Design engaged (Form Design view) to adjust field widths and field placement in the design of records. Field widths may be adjusted to exact sizes by choosing the Field Size command from the Format menu, keying a number in the Width box, and clicking OK.

**NOTE:** *A First-time Help dialog box appears the first time that you select the Database button from the Works Tools dialog box. This help box offers two icons: the first, Quick tour of creating databases, offers an overview of the way the function works; the second icon takes you directly to the Create Database dialog box, but opens a help menu to the right of the screen with creating database directions displayed on it.*

**FIGURE 12-1**

Click the Database button in the Works Tools dialog box
of the Works Task Launcher to create a new database.

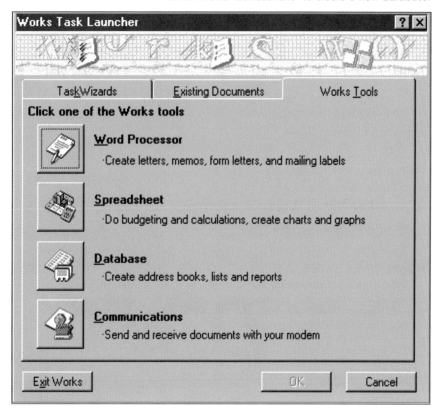

## ACTIVITY

# 12-1 Creating a New Database

In this activity, you will create a new database for membership records for the Future Entrepreneurs by following these steps:

1. Start Works on your computer. The Works

Task Launcher appears.

2. Click on **Works Tools.** Then, click the **Database** icon. The Create Database dialog box will appear.

**3.** Create the following fields by keying each name in the **Field name** box, and then clicking **Add** (Or press **Enter** to finish the task faster). When you have entered all of the field names, click **Done.** The new database will appear in List view.

| Field | Field Name |
|---|---|
| 1 | Last Name |
| 2 | First Name |
| 3 | Address |
| 4 | City |
| 5 | ZIP Code |
| 6 | Interest |

**HINT:** *After keying* Interest, *you must click A*d*d before clicking D*o*ne.*

**4.** Switch to Form Design view by clicking the **Form Design** button. Move the highlight to the first field name (Last Name). When you select a field, its location will be displayed at the left side of the Formula Bar. Move the fields to the following X and Y locations. When you have moved the fields, your screen should look similar to the Form view screen illustrated in Figure 12-2B. Next, adjust the field widths as indicated by highlighting the blank content area after the field name and then performing the same commands for each field name: choose **Field Size** from the **Format** menu, key the size in the **Width** box, and click **OK.** (The contents of the field named *Interest* is already 20, since 20 is the default setting for width.)

| Field Name | X | Y | Width |
|---|---|---|---|
| Last Name | 1.33" | 1.17" | 15 |
| First Name | 3.67" | 1.17" | 15 |
| Address | 1.33" | 1.50" | 22 |
| City | 3.67" | 1.50" | 10 |
| ZIP Code | 5.08" | 1.50" | 10 |
| Interest | 1.33" | 2.00" | 20 |

**FIGURE 12-2A**
Use the Create Database dialog box to create the fields in a new database.

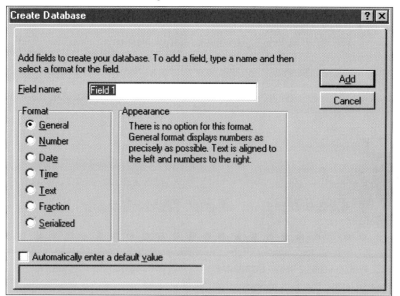

**FIGURE 12-2B**
Activate the Form Design button to adjust your fields in
Form view with Form Design engaged (Form Design view).

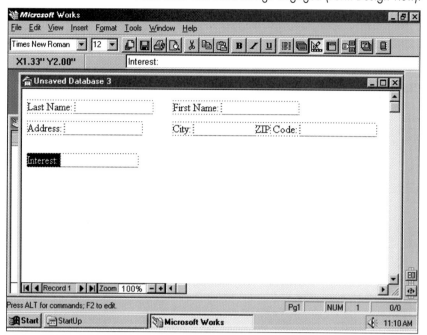

5. Switch to List view.

6. Enter the data below in the database. Do not enter any data for the city at this time.

7. Adjust the field width in List view so that all entry contents are visible on screen. Adjust the Address field and Interest field to prevent data from spilling over into the next

| Last Name | First Name | Address | ZIP Code | Interest |
|-----------|-----------|---------|----------|----------|
| Berry | Kevin | 5902 Sierra St. | 80231 | Plumbing |
| Cheng | Lana | 618 Poplar Pt. | 80266 | Insurance |
| Fisher | Carl | 87 Stone Dr. | 80244 | Furniture |
| Fleming | Jane | 2816 Indigo St. | 80255 | Appliance Repair |
| Foley | David | 1254 Cherry Dr. | 80274 | Locksmith |
| Gordon | Tara | 265 Briar Ln. | 80206 | Clothing |
| Johnston | Betty | 7822 West Ave. | 80231 | Restaurant |
| Knight | Curt | 2822 Echo Ln. | 80266 | Bakery |
| Matthews | Alan | 846 Center Ave. | 80240 | Frozen Foods |
| Mitchell | Jose | 762 Hill St. | 80255 | Convenience Stores |
| Padilla | Phillip | 630 Rosebud St. | 80245 | Restaurant |
| Ross | Ellen | 8401 Harbor Rd. | 80244 | Cabinetry |
| Simon | Heather | 879 Clear Creek Dr. | 80228 | Dry Cleaning |

field. Your screen should appear similar to Figure 12-3.

8. Save the database to your data disk as *Future Entrepreneurs*.

9. Leave *Future Entrepreneurs* on the screen for the next activity.

**FIGURE 12-3**
List view displays the entire database.

# *Copying Data*

**R**epetitive keying is unnecessary if you copy common data from one entry to another. Just as you learned in the spreadsheet chapters, you can copy data using Copy and Paste, Fill Down, or the drag and drop method.

## Copying and Pasting

The first way to copy data from one part of the database to another is to use the Copy and Paste commands located in the Edit menu. Copying and pasting in the database are the same operations as copying and pasting in the word processor or the spreadsheet. The Copy and Paste commands can also be chosen by clicking the Copy and Paste buttons on the toolbar.

# ACTIVITY

## Copying and Pasting

● ● ● ● ● ● ● ● ● ● ● ● ● ● ● ● ● ● ● ● ● ● ● ● ● ● ● ● ● ● ● ● ● ●

In this activity, you will copy a record in the database that you have just created. Your screen should show the database you saved as *Future Entrepreneurs* in List view. David Foley's brother John recently joined the Future Entrepreneurs. His address, ZIP Code, and interest are the same as his brother's. Copy the record for David Foley and change the first name to John by following these steps:

1. Select **Record 5** (David Foley) by clicking 5 in the record number box. The entire record will be highlighted.

2. Choose **Copy** from the **Edit** menu.

3. Click **14** in the record number box to select the empty record at the bottom of the database. The empty record will be highlighted.

4. Choose **Paste** from the **Edit** menu. The record for David Foley will be copied into Record 14.

5. Click the **First Name** field of Record 14. (The field contains the name *David.*)

6. Enter **John** in the First Name field. Your screen should appear similar to Figure 12-4.

7. Save *Future Entrepreneurs* and leave it on the screen for the next activity.

**FIGURE 12-4**

Copy and Paste can be used to copy data from one part of the database to another.

## Filling Down

*Filling down* copies data from an original entry to an entry or entries directly below the original. Filling down is performed by selecting the entry containing the original data and dragging over the entries to be filled with the copied data. When the Fill Down command is chosen from the Edit menu, the contents of the original will be copied to the empty entries.

ACTIVITY

## 12-3 Filling Down

In this activity, you will use the Fill Down command to copy an entry into several fields. Your screen should show the database *Future Entrepreneurs* in List view. Key and then copy the name of the city throughout the entire field by following these steps:

1. Highlight the entry in the City field of Record 1.

2. Key **Denver** and press **Enter.**

3. Drag from the entry in which you entered data to the last entry (Record 14) of the City field.

4. Choose **Fill Down** from the **Edit** menu. The name *Denver* will appear in the empty entries. Your screen should appear similar to Figure 12-5.

5. Save *Future Entrepreneurs* and leave it on the screen for the next activity.

**FIGURE 12-5**
Filling down saves time when the same entry is required in many records.

## Using the Drag and Drop Method

Like the word processor and spreadsheet, the database allows you to copy entries and records quickly using the drag and drop method. First, highlight the entries you want to copy. Then, while holding down the Ctrl key, drag the data to a new location and release the mouse button. As when using drag and drop in the spreadsheet, you must drag from the border of the highlighted data. You will know you are pointing to the correct place when the word *DRAG* appears below the pointer.

# Inserting a Record

In the last chapter, you learned to enter a record at the bottom of a database. You may, however, want to insert a record within the List view of the database. Choosing the Insert Record command from the Record menu, or clicking the Insert Record button shown in Figure 12-6, will place an empty record above a selected record in the database.

**FIGURE 12-6**
The Insert Record button will place an empty
record above a selected record in the database.

■ **Insert record button**

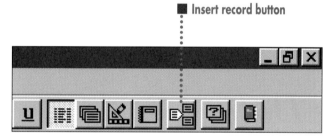

## ACTIVITY 12-4 Inserting a Record in List View

In this activity, you will insert an empty record in the database that you have created. Your screen should show the database *Future Entrepreneurs* in List view. Follow these steps to insert a record in List view:

1. Place the highlight anywhere in Record 6 (Tara Gordon).

2. Click the **Insert Record** button. An empty record will appear as Record 6. The record

for Tara Gordon will be moved down to Record 7, as shown in Figure 12-7.

3. Save *Future Entrepreneurs* and leave it on the screen for the next activity.

**FIGURE 12-7**
When the new record is inserted, each record from the insertion point to the end of the database moves down to make room for the new record.

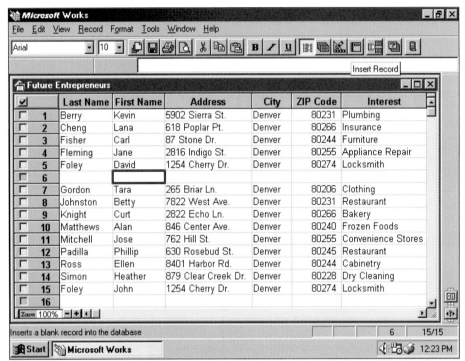

# *Moving Data*

To move data in a database, you can use the Cut and Paste commands from the Edit menu or the drag and drop method. The Cut and Paste commands also are available as buttons on the toolbar. Remember, the cut and paste process is similar to the copy and paste process you learned earlier except that the Cut command removes data from its original position in the database.

ACTIVITY

## Moving Data in a Database

In this activity, you will move the record for John Foley from the bottom of the database to Record 6 in the middle of the database using the drag and drop method. Your screen should show the database *Future Entrepreneurs* in List view.

1. Remove the empty record (Record 6) by highlighting the record and choosing **Delete Record** from the **Record** menu.

**N O T E :** *If you do not remove the empty record it will remain as Record 6 and the record you drag will become Record 7. Works automatically creates a new record space when you drag and drop a record.*

2. Select the contents of Record 14 (John Foley).

3. Position the pointer at the top edge of the highlighted record. You will know you are pointing to the correct place when the word *DRAG* appears below the pointer. Click and hold the pointer and the word *MOVE* appears below the pointer.

4. Drag to the line between Record 5 and Record 6 (which should now be Tara Gordon) and release the mouse button. The record for John Foley will appear in Record 6. Your screen should appear similar to Figure 12-8.

5. Save *Future Entrepreneurs* and leave it on the screen for the next activity.

**FIGURE 12-8**
The drag and drop method allows you to move data quickly without choosing a menu command or clicking the toolbar.

# Field Formats

**F**ield formats determine how data is presented in a column of a database. The formats available are the same as those available in the spreadsheet. However, in the spreadsheet you were able to format individual cells; in a database, all entries within a field must have the same format.

## Formats in the Database

The default format is called **general format,** which works with both text and numerical data. Other available formats are shown in Table 12-1. To format a field, select an entry within the field, choose Field from the Format menu, and choose one of the formats from the Field dialog box shown in Figure 12-9. A field may be formatted in either Form Design view or List view.

**FIGURE 12-9**
The Field dialog box allows you to format data in a field.

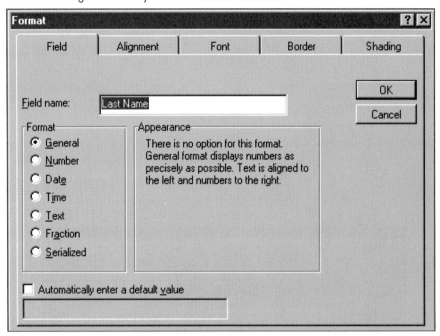

**TABLE 12-1**
Fields of a database may be formatted in several ways.

## DATABASE FIELD FORMATS

| FORMAT | DESCRIPTION |
| --- | --- |
| General | The default format; displays both text and numerical data as keyed |
| Number | |
|   Fixed | Displays numerical data with a fixed amount of places to the right of the decimal point |
|   Comma | Displays numerical data with commas every third decimal place |
|   Currency | Displays numerical data preceded by a dollar sign |
|   Percent | Displays numerical data followed by a percent sign |
|   Exponential | Displays numerical data in scientific notation |
|   Leading zeros | Displays numerical data with a specified number of decimal places to the left of the decimal |
| Date | Displays the text and numerical data as dates |
| Time | Displays the text and numerical data as times |
| Text | Displays values as text; used for sorting entries that contain special characters such as hyphens |
| Fraction | Displays numerical values as fractions |
| Serialized | Assigns a unique number to each record; the number assigned stays with the record even if that record is moved, cut, pasted, or sorted |

# 12-6

## Formatting a Database Field

In this activity, you will create fields for the dues owed to the club and dues paid to the club. You will then format the fields for currency. Your screen should show the database *Future Entrepreneurs* in List view.

1. Switch to **Form Design view,** and create the following fields:

| Field | Field Width | Location (or Approximate Location) in the Form |
|---|---|---|
| Dues Owed | 10 | X1.33" Y2.50" |
| Dues Paid | 10 | X1.33" Y2.83" |
| Balance | 10 | X1.33" Y3.17" |

2. Click the area to the right of the colon in the Dues Owed field. A darkened box will appear to indicate the field is selected.

3. Choose **Field** from the **Format** menu. The Field section of the Format dialog box appears. Choose **Number** from the Format option. The Number selections are displayed in the Appearance box. Choose the currency format—**$1,234.56**—from the selections.

4. You have the option to set the number of decimal places. Since 2 is the default and what you want, click **OK.**

5. Switch to **List view.**

6. Scroll to the three new fields you have created and adjust the column widths so that the entire headings can be seen on screen.

7. Select the **Dues Paid** and **Balance** fields by dragging the field names at the top of the columns.

8. Set the Dues Paid and Balance fields to currency in the Number format.

9. Enter the following data in the Dues Owed and Dues Paid fields. You will enter data into the Balance field in another activity. Your screen should appear similar to Figure 12-10.

| Record Number | Dues Owed | Dues Paid |
|---|---|---|
| 1 | 20 | 20 |
| 2 | 20 | 20 |
| 3 | 20 | 20 |
| 4 | 20 | 0 |
| 5 | 20 | 20 |
| 6 | 10 | 10 |
| 7 | 20 | 0 |
| 8 | 20 | 10 |
| 9 | 20 | 20 |
| 10 | 20 | 20 |
| 11 | 20 | 20 |
| 12 | 20 | 20 |
| 13 | 20 | 20 |
| 14 | 20 | 0 |

10. Save *Future Entrepreneurs* and leave it on the screen for the next activity.

**FIGURE 12-10**
The currency selection in the Number format places a dollar sign in front
of the data and designates the number of decimal places you desire.

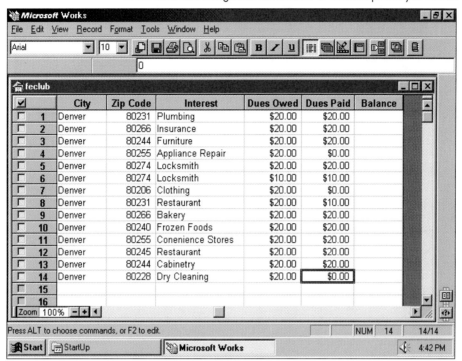

# *Time and Date Format*

**T**imes and dates are sometimes entered as data in a database. Works has special formats for times and dates that permit them to be used in formulas and to be displayed in the formats shown in Table 12-2 (page 292). Format a field in the database for a time or date by selecting a field and choosing a Time or Date format, respectively, from the Field dialog box.

**TABLE 12-2**
Times and dates can be displayed in several ways.

| THIS FORMAT | | WILL DISPLAY |
|---|---|---|
| *Time Formats* | | |
| Hour, minute | 3:00 PM | |
| 12 hours | Hour, minute, second | 3:00:00 PM |
| 24 hours | Hour, minute | 15:00 |
| | Hour, minute, second | 15:00:00 |
| *Date Formats* | | |
| Short | Month, day, year | 9/15/95 |
| | Month, day | 9/15 |
| | Month, year | 9/95 |
| Long | Month, day, year | September 15, 1995 |
| | Month, year | September 1995 |
| | Month, day | September 15 |
| | Month only | September |

ACTIVITY

# Entering Times and Dates in a Database

In this activity, you will enter a field formatted for dates in the database that you have created. Your screen should show the database *Future Entrepreneurs* in List view.

1.  Switch to **Form Design view,** and create a field located at X 1.33″, Y 3.67″ entitled **Date Joined.** When the Insert Field dialog box appears, format the Date Joined field

by following these steps:
a. Choose **Dat̲e.**
b. Choose the default option, which shows the **month/day/year** in short form.
c. Choose **OK.**

2.  Allow the field width to remain at 20 spaces, the default setting. Your screen should look similar to Figure 12-11.

**FIGURE 12-11**

The Date Joined field may be formatted in a number of date formats.

3. Switch to **List view** and enter the data given in the table below in the Date Joined field. You may have to adjust field widths to make the field name or field contents visible.

| Record Number | Date Joined |
|---|---|
| 1 | 1/11/95 |
| 2 | 2/15/95 |
| 3 | 9/30/95 |
| 4 | 1/11/95 |
| 5 | 7/18/95 |
| 6 | 2/1/95 |

| Record Number | Date Joined |
|---|---|
| 7 | 9/2/95 |
| 8 | 1/11/95 |
| 9 | 1/11/95 |
| 10 | 2/15/95 |
| 11 | 1/11/95 |
| 12 | 3/25/95 |
| 13 | 1/11/95 |
| 14 | 11/4/95 |

4. Leave *Future Entrepreneurs* on the screen for the next activity.

Most computers contain an internal clock that keeps track of the current time and date. Works will insert the current time or date in your database or spreadsheet. To do this, select an entry or cell and perform the following keystrokes:

| To Enter The Current | Press |
|---|---|
| Time | Ctrl+Shift+; |
| Date | Ctrl+; |

# Calculating in the Database

The database is not used as extensively for calculation as is the spreadsheet. However, the same mathematical and function formulas available for use in the spreadsheet are also available in the database.

Because the database does not use cell references, formulas in the database use field names to calculate values. For example, Figure 12-12 shows a database containing product prices, sales volumes, and the amount of total sales. Total sales were calculated by a formula designating the product of the price and volume (=Volume*Price). The formula is displayed in the Formula Bar. The formula results are displayed in the Sales field. Note that an equal sign is entered first, just as in the spreadsheet, to tell Works to expect a formula.

**FIGURE 12-12**
The values in the Sales field were determined by the product of the values in the Volume and Price fields.

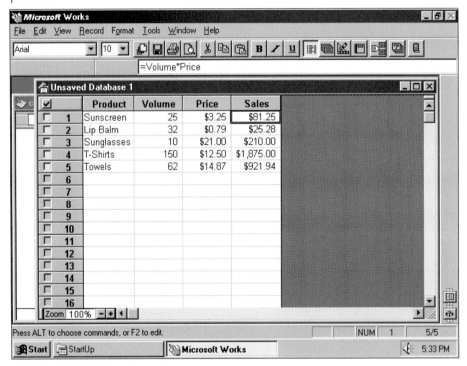

A database formula consists of two types of characters: operands and operators. An *operand* is the field name used in formulas. An *operator* tells Works what to do with the operands. The operators used in formulas are shown in Table 12-3. The sequence in which a formula will perform calculations is the same as the order followed for formulas in the spreadsheet.

**TABLE 12-3**
Operators tell Works what to do with operands.

### FORMULA OPERATORS

| OPERATOR | OPERATION |
|----------|-----------|
| + | Addition |
| – | Subtraction |
| * | Multiplication |
| / | Division |
| ^ | Exponentiation |

**ACTIVITY**

## Calculating in a Database

In this activity, you will enter a field formula to calculate the balance of the dues owed by each member to the club. Your screen should show the database *Future Entrepreneurs* in List view.

1. Place the highlight in any entry in the Balance field.

2. Key **=Dues Owed-Dues Paid**. (Do not key the period.)

3. Press **Enter.** The calculated values will appear in the Balance field. Your completed database should appear similar to Figure 12-13 (page 296).

4. Save *Future Entrepreneurs* and leave it on the screen for the next activity.

**FIGURE 12-13**
The formula has calculated the amounts due in the Balance field.

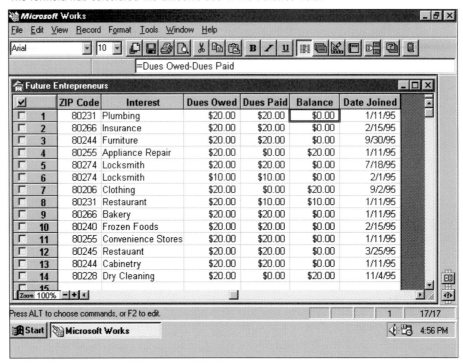

# Protecting Parts of the Database and Hiding Field Names

**P**rotecting data is particularly important in the database because you may want to store data for a long period of time without making any changes to it. By protecting your data, you prevent anyone from making changes accidentally. In other words, the entry becomes "locked" until someone removes the protection. In the database, you can protect data by protecting fields. Although you cannot protect the form of database, you can hide field names in Form view so that they are more difficult to change accidentally.

## Protecting Fields

To protect fields in the database, select an entry in the field you want to protect; then, choose the Protection command from the Format menu. Next, turn on the Protect field check box in the Format Protection dialog box, shown in Figure 12-14. Choose OK and the data in the field will be locked.

If you attempt to change the data in the entries of a field after they have been protected, Works will display a dialog box telling you the data cannot be changed (see Figure 12-15). If you intend to change the data, you must first unprotect it.

**FIGURE 12-14**
The Protect field check box in the Format Protection dialog box locks the field or fields you have selected.

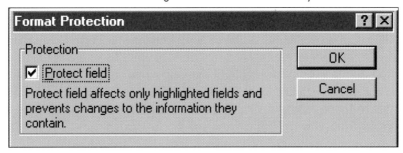

**FIGURE 12-15**
Works displays this message if you attempt to change data in a field that has been protected.

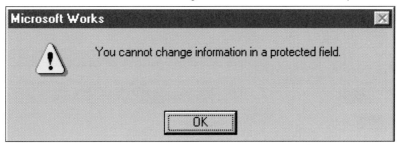

## ACTIVITY

# *12-9* Protecting Fields

In this activity, you will protect the Last Name and First Name fields in the database. Your screen should show the database *Future Entrepreneurs* in List view.

1. Select the **Last Name** and **First Name** of any record.

2. Lock the fields:
   a. Choose **Protection** from the **Format** menu.
   b. In the Format Protection dialog box, click the **Protect field** check box so that a check mark appears.
   c. Click **OK.** The Last Name and First Name fields are now protected.

3. Check the protection of the fields by attempting to enter data in the Last Name field. A dialog box should appear indicating that the field is locked (see Figure 12-15 on page 297). Click **OK** to remove the box.

4. Save *Future Entrepreneurs* and leave it on the screen for the next activity.

## Hiding Field Names

After you have worked with a particular database, you may become comfortable with the database form. Although you cannot protect the form from being altered, you may decide to hide the field names in Form Design view so that no one will accidentally change a field name. To exercise this option: switch to Form Design view, highlight the field name or entry of the field name that you want to hide, and choose Show Field Name from the Format menu (see Figure 12-16 for an example). The field name for the field you highlighted will be removed from view in Form view and Form Design view, but not in List view. To cause the field name to reappear, repeat the procedure.

**FIGURE 12-16**
From Form Design view, you may remove a field name from view in order to protect it from accidental changes.

## ACTIVITY

# 12-10 Hiding Field Names

In this activity, you will hide the names of two fields in Form Design view so that they cannot be accidentally changed. Your screen should show the database *Future Entrepreneurs* in List view.

1. Switch to **Form Design view.**

2. Move the highlight to the **Last Name** field name.

3. Choose **Show Field Name** from the **Format** menu as shown in Figure 12-16.

The Last Name field name will no longer be visible on the Form Design view screen (or on the Form view screen).

4. Remove the **First Name** field name from view.

5. Save and close the file.

# *Summary*

- Data can be moved or copied in the database by using the Cut, Copy, Paste, and Fill Down commands from the Edit menu. The drag and drop method can be used to avoid choosing commands.

- Field formats determine the appearance of data in a column of a database. These formats are designed to accommodate alphabetical data, numerical data (including money and percentages), times of day, and dates. A field format will apply to all entries within the field.

- The same mathematical and function formulas available in the spreadsheet are also available to determine calculated values in the database. Because the database does not contain cell references, variables in a database formula are represented by field names.

- Fields in the database may be protected from accidental change by choosing the Protection command from the Format menu. Although the form of a database cannot be protected or "locked" the way that field information can, it is possible to hide field names in Form Design view so that a deliberate effort must be made to change them. Hiding is accomplished using the Show Field Name command in the Format menu of a database in Form Design view.

● ● ● ● ● ● ● ● ● ● ● ● ●

# REVIEW ACTIVITIES

## TRUE/FALSE

**Circle T or F to show whether the statement is true or false.**

**T   F**   1. When the Database button is clicked in the Works Tools dialog box, a database in Form view will appear.

**T   F**   2. The original data will not be affected when the Copy command is chosen.

**T   F**   3. The Fill Down command copies data to entries directly below the original data.

**T   F**   4. The Insert Record button on the toolbar will place an empty record directly below a record selected in a database.

**T   F**   5. The Cut command is used to move data in the database.

**T   F**   6. Fields may be formatted in the Form view (with Form Design selected) of the database but not in List view.

**T   F**   7. General format may be used for alphabetical data only.

**T   F**   8. Some date formats will show the name of the month spelled out rather than in numerical form.

**T   F**   9. In a database, the field names act as operands in a field formula.

**T   F**   10. The Protect field option in the Protection dialog box will prevent data from being entered in a locked field.

## COMPLETION

**Write the correct answer in the space provided.**

1. What command will cause data that has been copied or cut to appear?

_____

_____

2. What toolbar button is used to copy data to entries?

_____

_____

3. What toolbar button may be used to place an empty record in the middle of a database?

_____

_____

**4.** What are two ways to move data in a database?

_____

_____

**5.** Which field format will place a dollar sign in front of numerical data in the database?

_____

_____

**6.** Which field format is a default format that accommodates both alphabetical and numerical data?

_____

_____

**7.** Which field format may be used to convert an entry of 1/3/96 to January 3, 1996?

_____

_____

**8.** What keystrokes will insert the current time in an entry of a database?

_____

_____

**9.** What term describes the symbols contained in a field formula of a database that tell Works what to do with the operands?

_____

_____

**10.** What is the process for protecting a field?

_____

_____

## REINFORCEMENT APPLICATIONS

*application 12-1*

You have been collecting compact discs (CDs) for your stereo for the last year. The CDs have ranged in cost from $7.99 to $19.87. Each CD may have as many as 21 tracks (songs). Your interest in music includes rock and roll, country, classical, and other types of music.

You would like to create a database to keep track of the CDs you own. The database should contain at least six fields that will distinguish your CDs from one another.

1. In the Field Name column below, identify fields you would include in the database.

2. In the Format column below, designate which field format you would use.

**Field Name**                    **Format**

_____          _____

_____          _____

_____          _____

_____          _____

_____          _____

_____          _____

# *application 12-2*

**The file *Application 12-2* contains financial data for a small corporation. In this application, you will format fields, create a field formula, and add new records.**

1. Retrieve the file *Application 12-2.*

2. Format the Assets, Sales, and Expenses fields for currency. There should be no digits to the right of the decimal point (e.g., 0 decimal places).

3. Switch to Form Design view and add a new field called *Income* after the Expenses field. Format the Income field for currency with no digits to the right of the decimal point.

4. Switch to List view and create a field formula to determine the value in the Income field. Income is determined by the difference between Sales and Expenses.

5. Add a record for the most current year, 1994, for which you have data:

   | | |
   |---|---|
   | Assets | 20,123 |
   | Sales | 55,876 |
   | Expenses | 50,629 |

6. Insert a record for the missing year, 1986:

   | | |
   |---|---|
   | Assets | 3,104 |
   | Sales | 8,456 |
   | Expenses | 7,821 |

7. Protect data in all fields.

8. Switch to **Form Design view** and hide the field name **Year.**

9. Switch to **List view** and save the file to your data disk as *Income.*

10. Print the database.

11. Close the file.

# application 12-3

**In this application, you will prepare a database to help you decide which college you would like to attend.**

1. Open an untitled database.

2. Enter and format the following fields:

| Field Contents | Field Name | Format | Alignment |
|---|---|---|---|
| College or University | School | General | Left |
| Miles from Home | Miles | General | Right |
| Tuition per Semester | Tuition | Currency (with 2 decimals) | Right |
| Dorm Fee per Semester | Dorm | Currency (with 2 decimals) | Right |
| Quality of School | Quality | General | Center |
| Friends at School | Friends | General | Center |

3. Using Copy wherever possible, enter the following data into the database and adjust field widths as necessary:

| School | Miles | Tuition | Dorm | Quality | Friends |
|---|---|---|---|---|---|
| Univ. of Aston | 15 | 500 | 1,500 | C | 5 |
| Bering Univ. | 100 | 1,500 | 3,000 | A | 2 |
| Cochise St. | 150 | 1,000 | 2,000 | B | 1 |
| Denton College | 60 | 2,000 | 2,000 | C | 7 |
| Univ. of Elgin | 300 | 1,000 | 1,000 | A | 0 |
| Franklin College | 20 | 750 | 1,200 | B | 3 |

4. Move Record 5, Univ. of Elgin, to between Record 2 and Record 3 so that all of the universities will be listed together.

5. Save the database to your data disk as *College*.

6. Print the database.

7. Close the file.

**Create a database of the addresses and telephone numbers of some of your friends and relatives.**

1. Create a database containing the following fields: Last Name, First Name, Address, City, ZIP Code, Phone No.

2. Enter the names, addresses, and phone numbers of six of your friends or relatives. Adjust field widths as necessary.

3. Use a key command to insert the current date in the last entry of the last field in the first blank record of your database.

4. Save the database to your data disk as *Directory.*

5. Print the database.

6. Close the file.

# ADVANCED DATABASE OPERATIONS

## OBJECTIVES
### When you complete this chapter, you will be able to:

1. Search a database.

2. Sort data in a database.

3. Use a filter in a database to display particular records that meet certain criteria.

# Searching a Database

As a database becomes large, you will not be able to see the entire database on screen at once. As a result, you may find it difficult to find the specific records with which you want to work. One way to find the records you need is to search the database. *Searching* locates specific data in a database. For example, in a directory of names and addresses, you may want to search for someone whose last name is Johnson and who lives in the ZIP Code area of 77042. Search criteria are specified in the Find dialog box, shown in Figure 13-1 (page 308), and accessed by choosing the Find command from the Edit menu.

Works will perform two types of searches in a database. A *Next record search* finds the first record after the highlight in which the specified data is present and moves the highlight to that information in that record. An *All records search* displays on the screen only those records containing the specified data.

**FIGURE 13-1**
Search criteria are specified in the Find dialog box.

## Searching Next Records

A Next record search looks for entries that match data specified in the Find what box of the Find dialog box. Works looks for the first occurrence of the data following the current location of the highlight. Therefore, if you want to search the entire database, you should begin the search by placing the highlight in the first entry of the database.

You may repeat a Next record search by pressing Shift+F4, the Repeat key. The Find dialog box will not appear because Works assumes you are searching for the same data keyed in the Find what box in the previous search.

ACTIVITY

## *13-1*  Searching Next Records

● ● ● ● ● ● ● ● ● ● ● ● ● ● ● ● ● ● ● ● ● ● ● ● ● ● ● ● ● ● ● ● ● ● ● ● ●

In this activity, you will practice Next record searches. The file *Activity 13-1* contains prices and specifications of several computer products listed for sale. The database contains fields for brand, model, price, CPU (central processing unit), RAM (random access memory), clock speed, hard disk storage, and availability of a mouse. Find the records of computers with the brand name *Ultra* by following these steps:

1. Open the file *Activity 13-1* from your template disk.

2. Place the highlight in the first entry of the Brand field if it is not there already.

3. Choose **Find** from the **Edit** menu. The Find dialog box will appear.

4. Key **Ultra** in the Find what box.

5. Click the **Next record** option button if it is not already selected.

6. Click **OK.** The highlight will appear in the Brand field of Record 22, the first occurrence of the word *Ultra* in the database.

7. Press **Shift+F4** (the Repeat key). The highlight will appear in the Brand field of Record 23, the second occurrence of the word *Ultra* in the database.

8. Press **Shift+F4** again. The highlight will appear in the Brand field of Record 24, the third occurrence of the word *Ultra* in the database. Your screen should appear similar to Figure 13-2.

9. Leave the database *Activity 13-1* on your screen for the next activity.

**FIGURE 13-2**
The Shift+F4 key repeats a Next record search.

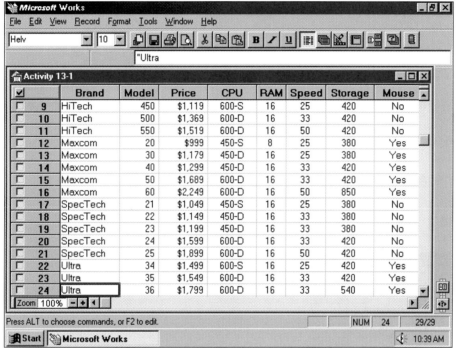

## Searching All Records

An All records search will display all records containing data specified in the Find what box. Records not containing the specified data will be hidden. After you have completed the search, you can see what portion of the records is displayed by looking at the far right of the status line. The fraction at the right side of the status line indicates the number of records displayed and the total number of records in the database.

# ACTIVITY

## *13-2* Searching All Records

• • • • • • • • • • • • • • • • • • • • • • • • • • • • • • • •

In this activity, you will practice searching All records. Your screen should show the database *Activity 13-1*. Suppose you want to view on the screen only those records of computers with a 450-S CPU. Perform an All records search by following these steps:

1. Choose **Find** from the **Edit** menu.

2. Key **450-S** in the Find what box.

3. Click the **All records** option button.

4. Click **OK.** Your screen should appear similar to Figure 13-3. All records containing *450-S* appear on screen. Records that do not contain *450-S* are hidden from view. The fraction *6/29* at the right side of the status line indicates that there are 29 records in the database and that 6 of those records are currently displayed.

5. Leave the database *Activity 13-1* on the screen for the next activity.

**FIGURE 13-3**
The fraction in the status line indicates that 6 of the 29 records in the database are displayed.

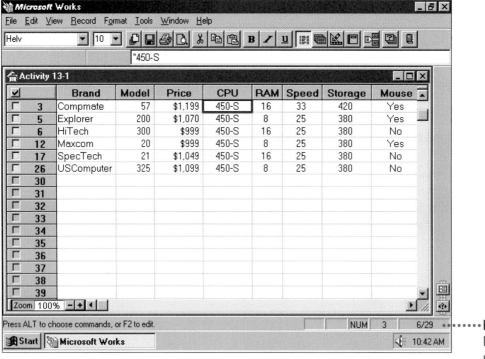

Number of records found out of total records

## Redisplaying Records

Hidden records may be redisplayed in two ways. Choosing the Show, 4 Hidden Records, command from the Record menu will hide records currently displayed and display those records hidden. Choosing the Show, 1 All Records, command from the Record menu will display all the records contained in the database.

## 13-3 Redisplaying Hidden Records

In this activity, you will redisplay hidden records. Your screen should show the database *Activity 13-1*. Suppose you want to view only those records currently hidden. Redisplay the hidden records and hide the currently visible records by following these steps:

1.  Choose the command **4 Hidden Records** from the **Show** command from the **Record** menu. The records that do not contain *450-S* will be displayed on screen. The fraction *23/29* should appear in the status line to in-dicate that 23 of the 29 records in the data-base are displayed on screen.

2.  Choose the command **1 All Records** from the **Show** command from the **Record** menu. All the records in the database will be displayed. The fraction *29/29* should appear in the status line.

3.  Leave the database *Activity 13-1* on the screen for the next activity.

## Searching with Wildcards

Suppose you want to find a particular record in your database but cannot remember enough information to use the Find command. For example, you know the last name of the person is either Jenson or Jonson. Rather than per-form two searches to try to find the record, you can use a *wildcard* character to help you retrieve the record you want.

The Works wildcard character is an asterisk (*) or a question mark (?). The asterisk can represent one or several characters—either letters or numbers—and may be placed in any part of a word for a search; the question mark can, likewise, be placed anywhere but represents only one character. To find the record men-tioned above, you would key *J\*nson* in the Find what box. Works will find all names that begin with *J* and end with *-nson*. It will find not only Jenson and Jonson, but also Johanson and Johnson. If you key *J?nson*, Works will find Jenson and Jonson, but not Johanson and Johnson. Table 13-1, on the following page, shows examples of how the wildcard character may be used to search for data.

**TABLE 13-1**
Wildcard searches look for data similar to but not
exactly like the characters entered in the search.

| SEARCHING WITH WILDCARDS | |
|---|---|
| **THESE WILDCARD SEARCHES** | **WILL FIND** |
| Will* | William, Will, Willy, Willard |
| *ness | lness, kindness, tenderness, selfishness |
| b*p | bop, bump, bishop, blimp |
| Will? | Willy |
| ?ness | lness |
| b?p | bop |

## ACTIVITY

### 13-4 Wildcard Searches

In this activity, you will perform a wildcard
search. Your screen should show the database
*Activity 13-1.* Suppose you want to view records
of computers priced in the range of $2,000 to
$2,999. Search for these records by following
these steps:

1. Choose **Find** from the **Edit** menu. The Find
   dialog box will appear.

2. Key **$2\*** in the Find what box.

3. Click the **All records** option button.

4. Click **OK.** All records containing computers
   in the price range of $2,000 to $2,999 will
   appear on the screen. Your screen should
   appear similar to Figure 13-4.

5. Choose the command **1 All Records** from
   the **Show** command from the **Record**
   menu. All the records of the database will
   be redisplayed.

6. Leave the database *Activity 13-1* on the
   screen for the next activity.

**FIGURE 13-4**
Wildcard searches can help you find data similar to
but not exactly like the characters entered in the search.

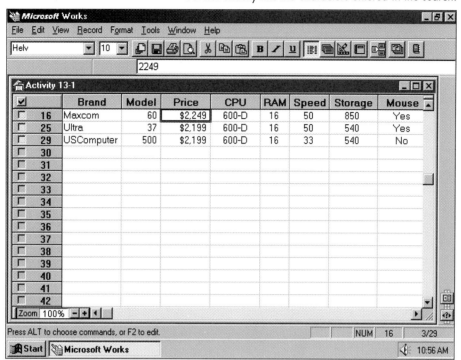

**FIGURE 13-4**
Wildcard searches can help you find data similar to
but not exactly like the characters entered in the search.

# *Sorting a Database*

**S**orting arranges records in a specific sequence. For example, a directory of names, addresses, and phone numbers may be sorted in many ways. Directories, including telephone directories, are usually sorted in alphabetical order according to last names. However, you may want to sort a directory in other ways. You could sort a directory of addresses geographically by state or by ZIP Code. If birthdays are entered in a directory, you could sort the directory by the birth date of the person described in the record.

You sort a database by selecting the Sort Records command from the Record menu. When the Sort Records dialog box appears, the sort field and order (ascending or descending) are designated (see Figure 13-5 on the following page). A second field may be designated if more than one record contains the same data in the first field. For example, if you would like to sort a directory geographically, you could sort first by the state. Because some records may contain the same state, a second field sort will order by the city within each state. You can even sort by a third field if necessary.

**NOTE:** *A First-time Help dialog box appears the first time that you select the Sort Records command from the Record menu. This box offers two icons: the first, Quick tour of sorting, offers an overview of the way the function works; the second icon takes you directly to the Sort Records dialog box, but opens a help menu to the right of the screen with sort directions displayed on it.*

**FIGURE 13-5**
The sort field and sort order are designated in the Sort Records dialog box.

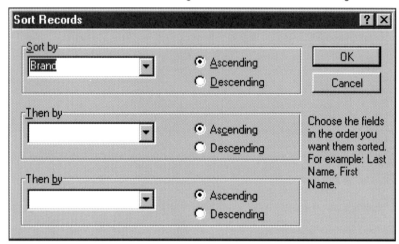

Table 13-2 shows the order in which records will be sorted. In an ascending sort, text will be sorted from A to Z and numerical data from smallest to largest. In mixed input, numbers sort before text. In a descending sort, text will be sorted from Z to A and numerical data from largest to smallest. Works will also sort times and dates.

**TABLE 13-2**
The Ascending or Descending option buttons determine the order of the sort.

| SORTING | | |
| --- | --- | --- |
| **SORT** | **DATA** | **DIRECTION OF SORT** |
| Ascending | Text | A to Z |
| | Numbers | Smaller to larger |
| | Times | Earlier to later |
| | Dates | Past to recent |
| Descending | Text | Z to A |
| | Numbers | Larger to smaller |
| | Times | Later to earlier |
| | Dates | Recent to past |

## ACTIVITY

 *13-5* **Sorting a Database**

● ● ● ● ● ● ● ● ● ● ● ● ● ● ● ● ● ● ● ● ● ● ● ● ● ● ● ● ● ● ● ●

In this activity, you will sort the database in several different orders. Your screen should show the database *Activity 13-1* in List view. To help you decide which computer to purchase, you want to sort the records in certain orders based on the contents of certain fields.

1. Sort the records by price from least expensive to most expensive:
   a. Choose **Sort Records** from the **Record** menu.
   b. In the S̲ort by box, choose **Price** from the list that appears when you click the down arrow beside the field.
   c. Click the **Ascending** option button in the S̲ort by box if it is not already selected.
   d. Click **OK.** The records will be sorted from least expensive to most expensive.

2. Sort the records by price from most expensive to least expensive:
   a. Choose **Sort Records** from the **Record** menu. *Price* should already be displayed in the S̲ort by box.
   b. Click the **Descending** option button in the S̲ort by box.
   c. Click **OK.** The records will be sorted from most expensive to least expensive.

3. Sort the records by most to least hard disk storage:
   a. Choose **Sort Records** from the **Record** menu.
   b. Scroll down to and choose **Storage** in the S̲ort by box.
   c. Click the **Descending** option button in the S̲ort by box if it is not already selected.
   d. Click **OK.** The records will be sorted from most storage to least storage.

4. Sort the records by brand name and then by model number:
   a. Choose **Sort Records** from the **Record** menu.
   b. Scroll up and choose **Brand** in the S̲ort by box.
   c. Click the **Ascending** option button in the S̲ort by box.
   d. Choose **Model** in the T̲hen by box.
   e. Click the **Ascending** option button in the T̲hen by box if it is not already selected.
   f. Click **OK.** The records will be sorted by brand name and model number within the brand name.

5. Leave the database *Activity 13-1* on your screen for the next activity.

# Using Filters in a Database

**D**atabase *filters* display records meeting specific criteria. Using filters differs from All records searches in two ways. First, filters look for a match in a specific field; whereas, searches look for matches in any part of the database. Second, filters can match records that fit into a range. For example, in a database of names and addresses, you may request all records with a ZIP Code greater than 50000 or last names beginning with the letters G through K. Wildcards may be used in filters in the same way that they are used in searches.

To create a filter, choose Filters from the Tools menu or use the Filters button on the toolbar (see Figure 13-6). The Filter dialog box appears (see Figure 13-7) with the Filter Name dialog box on top of it, as shown in Figure 13-7. In the Filter Name dialog box, you can give the filter a name or accept the one Works provides automatically (e.g., Filter 1). Once you have named the filter, you have access to the Filter dialog box, itself. A filter can include up to five criteria. When setting up filter criteria, you specify a field that the comparison will affect, the kind of comparison, and the value to which the field will be compared. Clicking the Apply Filter button displays the records that match the criteria of the filter.

**N O T E :** *A First-time Help dialog box appears the first time that you select the Filters command from the Tools menu. This box offers two icons: the first, Quick tour of filters, offers an overview of the way the function works; the second icon takes you directly to the Filter Name and Filter dialog boxes, but opens a help menu to the right of the screen with filter directions displayed on it.*

**FIGURE 13-6**
Access the filters by using the menu or toolbar command.

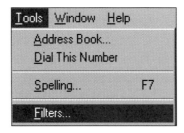

**FIGURE 13-7**
The Filter dialog box is where the criteria for a filter are entered.
The Filter Name dialog box appears overlaid as you begin a
new filter so that you name it before you begin to select criteria.

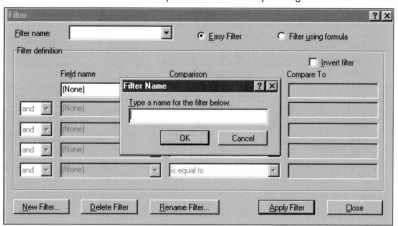

# Filters Based on a Single Criterion

The easiest kind of filter is based on a single criterion. In other words, the filter considers the values in only one field.

**ACTIVITY**

## 13-6 Creating a Single Criterion Filter

In this activity, you will display only the records of computers listed in *Activity 13-1* that have a speed of 33 by following these steps:

1. Choose **Filters** from the **Tools** menu. The Filter Name dialog box appears (on top of the Filter dialog box, which also appears).

2. Key **Speed 33** as the name of the filter. Click **OK.**

3. In the Filter dialog box, which is now available, scroll down to and choose **Speed** in the Field name box.

4. The Comparison box should already read "is equal to." Key **33** in the Compare To box. Your dialog box should appear similar to Figure 13-8 shown on the following page.

5. Click **Apply Filter.** Only the records showing a speed of 33 appear. The fraction at the bottom of the page in the status line should be *12/29*, indicating that 12 of 29 computers have a speed of 33.

6. Leave the database *Activity 13-1* on the screen for the next activity.

**FIGURE 13-8**
This simple filter considers only one field in the comparison.

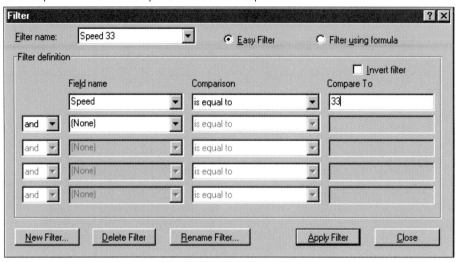

Numerical filters may request data occurring within a range. For example, you may request records with data less than or greater than a certain value.

## ACTIVITY

# 13-7 Using a Numerical Range in a Filter

● ● ● ● ● ● ● ● ● ● ● ● ● ● ● ● ● ● ● ● ● ● ● ● ● ● ● ● ● ● ● ● ● ● ● ● ● ● ● ●

In this activity, you will display only the records of computers costing less than $1,500. Your screen should show the database *Activity 13-1* in List view with the Speed 33 filter applied.

1. Choose **Filters** from the **Tools** menu. The Filter dialog box appears.

2. Click **New Filter.** The Filter Name dialog box appears.

3. Key **Price < 1500** as the name of the filter. Click **OK.**

4. In the Filter dialog box, choose **Price** in the Field name box.

5. Choose **is less than** in the Comparison box.

6. Key **1500** in the Compare To box. (Do not include a dollar sign in the filter.)

7. Click **Apply Filter.** Only the records for computers costing less than $1,500 appear. The fraction at the bottom of the page in the status line should be *16/29*, indicating that 16 of 29 computers cost less than $1,500.

8. Leave the database *Activity 13-1* on the screen for the next activity.

## Filters Based on Multiple Criteria

A *multiple selection filter*, or multiple criteria filter, will make several comparisons simultaneously in the database. The comparisons are linked with the operators *and* or *or*. For example, you might use a filter to show computers that cost less than $1,500 and have a speed of at least 33 MHz.

**A C T I V I T Y**

## *13-8* Multiple Selection Filters

In this activity, you will use a filter in database *Activity 13-1* to identify the computers meeting very specific qualities. Suppose you have decided you would like to buy a computer with the following characteristics:

■ The computer should have at least 16 megabytes of RAM.

■ The hard disk should have at least 540 megabytes of storage.

■ The computer should cost less than $1800.

Display the records of computers meeting these criteria by following these steps:

1. Choose **Filters** from the **Tools** menu. The

Filter dialog box appears.

2. Click **New Filter.** The Filter Name dialog box appears.

3. Key **My Computer** as the name of the filter.

4. In the Filter dialog box, make your selections and key values into the Filter dialog box so that it matches Figure 13-9. **And** should brighten in intensity for the next row of criteria as you complete the one before (the *and* option is the default; you do not want to choose the alternative *or* option).

**FIGURE 13-9**
The Filter dialog box allows you to create a filter with up to five criteria.

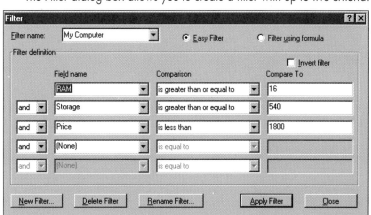

**5.** Click **Apply Filter.** Only the records of computers with at least 16 megabytes of RAM, with at least 540 megabytes of storage, and with a cost less than $1,800 appear. The fraction at the bottom of the page in the status line should be *3/29*, indicating that 3 of 29 computers meet the criteria.

**6.** Save the database to your data disk as *Computer.* Your screen should appear similar to Figure 13-10.

**7.** Close the file.

**FIGURE 13-10**
The multiple criteria filter reveals that 3 of the 29 computers in the database meet your needs.

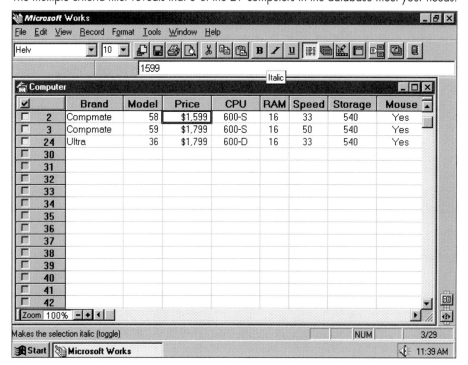

# *Summary*

■ As a database becomes large, it is impossible to see the entire database on screen at once. Searching locates specific data in a database when you are not sure of its location. You may search for the next record in the database containing data you specify using a Next record search. An All records search will display only the records containing data specified.

■ Sorting a database arranges records in the database in a specific order (such as alphabetically or largest to smallest). Database sorts can also arrange times and dates.

■ Using a filter in a database displays only records with certain qualities. Filters differ from All records searches by matching data to a specific field and by matching records that fit into a range.

● ● ● ● ● ● ● ● ● ● ● ● ●

# REVIEW ACTIVITIES

## TRUE/FALSE

**Circle T or F to show whether the statement is true or false.**

T  F    1. A Next record search will hide all records that do not contain specific data.

T  F    2. A Next record search may be repeated by pressing the F9 key.

T  F    3. An All records search will display all records in the database.

T  F    4. The Show, 1 All Records, command in the Record menu will redisplay all of the records that are currently hidden in place of the records currently displayed.

T  F    5. Wildcard characters aid in locating data that is similar, but not identical, to the data entered into the search.

T  F    6. If *child** is entered in the Find what box, Works will search for both the words *child* and *children*.

T  F    7. Sorting will locate specific data within a database.

T  F    8. A descending sort arranges dates from the most recent to the past.

T  F    9. A database filter does not look for data in a specific field.

T  F    10. Filters can match data that fit into a range.

## COMPLETION

**Write the correct answer in the space provided.**

1. What kind of search indicates the first record after the highlight in which specified data is present?

_____

_____

2. What kind of search displays on the screen only those records containing the specified data?

_____

_____

3. What command will display records previously hidden and hide records currently displayed?

_____

_____

4. What command will display all the records in the database?

_____

_____

5. What key(s) will repeat a Next record search?

_____

_____

6. What is the effect of specifying a second sort field?

_____

_____

7. What type of sort will arrange alphabetical data from Z to A?

_____

_____

8. What term describes a filter that makes several comparisons simultaneously?

_____

_____

9. What is the maximum number of comparisons that can be entered in the Filter dialog box?

_____

_____

10. What does the fraction 7/52 in the status line of the List view in a database indicate?

_____

_____

# REINFORCEMENT APPLICATIONS

## application 13-1

The file *Application 13-1* is a database of the planets in our solar system. It contains some statistics about each planet. Perform the following database sorts to answer the following questions:

1. Open *Application 13-1* from your template disk.

   a. Sort the database by **distance** in ascending order. Which planet is closest to the sun?

   b. Sort the database by **distance** in descending order. Which planet is farthest from the sun?

   c. Sort the database by **revolution** in descending order. Which planet takes longest to revolve around the sun?

   d. Sort the database by **rotation** in ascending order. Which planet takes the shortest time to rotate around its axis?

   e. Sort the database by **diameter** in descending order. Which planet is the largest?

   f. Sort the database by **moons** in descending order. Which planet has the most moons?

2. Close the file without saving.

## application 13-2

The file *Application 13-2* is a database of zoo animals, their classifications, and their continents of origin. The database also contains the location of the animals in the zoo (W is west, E is east, C is central, N is north, S is south) and the number of animals in the exhibit.

1. Open *Application 13-2* from your template disk.

   a. Sort the database alphabetically by **animal.** What is the first animal in alphabetical order?

   b. Sort the database alphabetically by **classification.** What is the first classification to be listed in the database?

   c. Sort the database alphabetically by **zoo location.** What is the first zoo location to be listed?

   d. Sort the database in descending order of the **number** of animals in the exhibit. What is the most common animal in the zoo?

   e. Sort the database in ascending order of the **number** of animals in the exhibit. How many animals in the zoo occur in twos?

   f. Sort the database alphabetically by **zoo location** and alphabetically by **animal** within zoo location. How many different animals are in the central location?

   g. Sort the database alphabetically by **continent,** then alphabetically by **classification** within continent and alphabetically by **animal** within classification. How many different animals are from Asia?

2. Close the file without saving.

# application 13-3

**The file *Application 13-3* is a database of restaurants in a city. The database has been developed by a hotel to aid guests in selecting a restaurant that meets their needs.**

1. Open *Application 13-3* from your template disk.

2. Perform filters to identify the restaurants that satisfy the following guest requests: (Each time the Filter Name box appears you may accept the name given automatically by Works by choosing OK. After the first filter has been created, do not forget to choose <u>N</u>ew Filter to create the next one.)

   a. What are the names of restaurants that serve Chinese food?

   b. What are the names of restaurants in the western part of town?

   c. Is Frank's open for dinner?

   d. What are the names of restaurants that serve either barbecue or hamburgers?

   e. What are the inexpensive restaurants downtown?

   f. What restaurants serve lunch in the southern or southwestern section of town?

3. Close the file without saving.

# application 13-4

**The file *Application 13-4* is a database for a mail order catalog business called The Night Shop. The store specializes in bedding and nightclothes. Many merchandise requests come over the telephone and require quick answers. Use search, sort, and filter techniques to respond to the following customer requests:**

1. Open *Application 13-4* from your template disk.

   a. How much does item 21-74-3 cost? (*Hint:* Do a search.)

   b. How many of Item No. 18-73-2 are available? (*Hint:* Do a search.)

   c. What types of articles are available in pink? (*Hint:* Do a search.)

   d. What is the name of the least expensive type of items in the store? (*Hint:* Sort the database. Don't forget to show all of the records before you begin the sort.)

   e. What sizes of sheets are available in solid blue? (*Hint:* Use a filter.)

   f. What types of sheets are available in gray? (*Hint:* Use a filter.)

   g. What sizes of terry robes are available in white? (*Hint:* Use a filter.)

2. Close the file without saving.

*application   1 3 - 5*

**In Application 12-4, you created a directory of friends and relatives and saved the database as *Directory*.**

1. Open the database *Directory* that you created.

2. Sort the directory of friends and relatives by last name and then by first name.

3. Close the file without saving.

# DATABASE
# REPORTING

CHAPTER

*14*

## OBJECTIVES
### When you complete this chapter, you will be able to:

1. Create a database report.

2. Change the appearance of a database report.

3. Sort and group records in a database report.

4. Use filters in a database report.

5. Preview and print a database report.

6. Name and rename a database report.

7. Save a database report.

Databases can become large as additional records are added. Because of the size, an entire database is rarely printed. By creating a ***database report***, you may organize, summarize, and print a portion of a database. The report organizes by placing records, or portions of records, in a certain order or in groups. Reports can summarize data by inserting subtotals, totals, and statistics between groups or at the end of reports. For example, the report in Figure 14-1 (on page 328) was created from the database shown in Figure 14-2 (on page 329). The report contains six of the nine fields in the database. The report also sums the contents of two of the fields.

## FIGURE 14-1
Database reports organize, summarize, and print a portion of a large database.

| **REORDER REPORT** | | | | | |
|---|---|---|---|---|---|
| **MANUFACTURER** | **MODEL** | **COLOR** | **QUANT** | **ORDER** | **COST** |
| Bye-cycles | 50 | Blue | 7 | 5 | $112.50 |
| Bye-cycles | 50 | Red | 8 | 4 | $112.50 |
| Bye-cycles | 70 | Blue | 5 | 4 | $142.50 |
| Bye-cycles | 70 | Red | 4 | 4 | $142.50 |
| Two Wheeler | Sizzle | Green | 3 | 4 | $125.00 |
| Two Wheeler | Sizzle | Red | 2 | 4 | $125.00 |
| Two Wheeler | Zip | Blue | 3 | 4 | $135.00 |
| Two Wheeler | Zip | Red | 3 | 4 | $135.00 |
| Spokes | 101 | Green | 4 | 3 | $157.50 |
| Spokes | 101 | Red | 2 | 3 | $157.50 |
| Spokes | 103 | Green | 1 | 3 | $187.50 |
| Spokes | 103 | Red | 3 | 3 | $187.50 |
| Spokes | 103 | Blue | 6 | 3 | $187.50 |
| Edison | Dart | Orange | 5 | 5 | $180.00 |
| Edison | Dart | Yellow | 7 | 5 | $180.00 |
| Edison | Sierra | Green | 2 | 5 | $190.00 |
| Edison | Sierra | Red | 3 | 5 | $190.00 |
| Edison | Sierra | Orange | 2 | 5 | $190.00 |
| Star | Spica | Black | 10 | 8 | $220.00 |
| Star | Mira | Yellow | 6 | 8 | $230.00 |
| | | **TOTAL** | **86** | **89** | |

A number of reports may be created from one database. For example, in this chapter you will create and print several database reports from the inventory of a bicycle shop named Mike's Bikes (see Figure 14-3). The bicycle shop uses database reports to inform

■ The owner of when to order more bicycles from the manufacturer,

■ Salespersons of whether a specific model is in stock,

■ The accountant of the value of the bicycle inventory, and

■ Customers of the price of the bicycles in stock.

**FIGURE 14-2**

A database report is created from an existing database. This illustration shows the database reduced, using the Zoom feature, so that you can see all of the data.

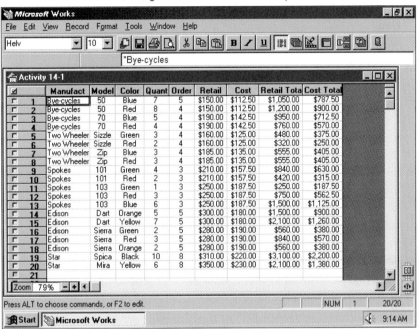

**FIGURE 14-3**

More than one report may be created from one database.

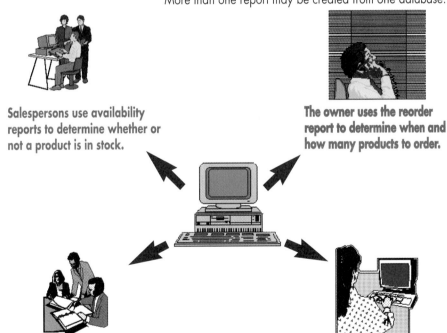

Salespersons use availability reports to determine whether or not a product is in stock.

The owner uses the reorder report to determine when and how many products to order.

Customers use price lists to determine which product they would like to buy.

Accountants use inventory reports to value inventories for financial reporting.

# Creating and Naming a Database Report

**D**atabase reports are named in the Report Name box; the reports are created in the ReportCreator dialog box. The Title section of the ReportCreator dialog box allows you to title the report and to change the orientation for printing and to change the font and font size. The Fields section of the Report-Creator dialog box is where you specify the fields to be included in a report. At any point after the fields have been selected, you may click Done (available in all of the sections of the ReportCreator dialog box) to create the report. However, there are numerous kinds of input you may wish to make to the report before doing so. For instance, the Summary section of the ReportCreator dialog box allows you to specify statistics (such as sums, averages, minimums, and maximums) that summarize numerical data in the database report.

## Choosing Fields for a Report

The ReportCreator feature is accessed by choosing the ReportCreator command from the Tools menu. The Report Name dialog box appears first and allows you to name the report using up to 15 characters. Next, the ReportCreator dialog box appears, open to the Title section. After you have titled the report (not to be confused with naming the report: the title is what prints; the name is how you access the report on screen) and verified orientation and font and font size, you may click Next>. The Fields section of the ReportCreator box, which now appears, is where you designate the fields to be included in the report by selecting each field from the Fields available box and clicking the Add> button (or to include all of the fields, by clicking Add All>>). If you change your mind about a field you have already added, select the field in the Field order box and click the <Remove button; to remove all of the fields selected, click <<Remove All. The Report Name dialog box, the Title section of the ReportCreator dialog box, and the Fields section of the ReportCreator dialog box are shown in Figure 14-4.

**NOTE:** *A First-time Help dialog box appears the first time that you select the ReportCreator command from the Tools menu. This box offers two icons: the first, Quick tour of reports, offers an overview of the way the function works; the second icon takes you directly to the Report Name dialog box, but opens a help menu to the right of the screen with report directions displayed on it.*

**FIGURE 14-4**
The Report Name dialog box is used to name the report, and the ReportCreator dialog box is used to title the report, designate fields to be included in the report, and specify other information.

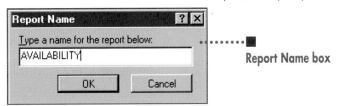

**Report Name box**

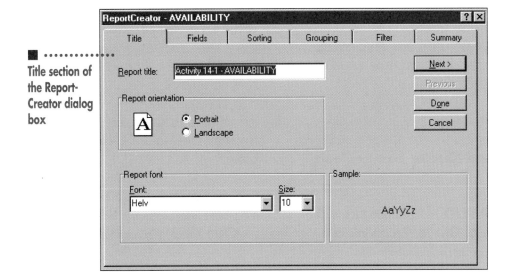

**Title section of the Report-Creator dialog box**

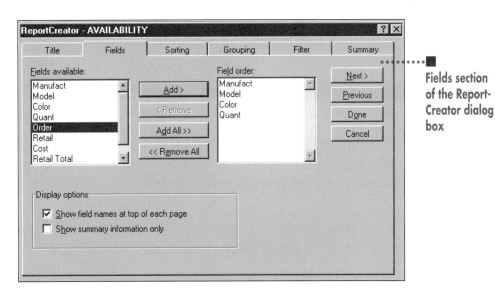

**Fields section of the Report-Creator dialog box**

## ACTIVITY

# 14-1

## Creating and Naming a New Report

● ● ● ● ● ● ● ● ● ● ● ● ● ● ● ● ● ● ● ● ● ● ● ● ● ● ● ● ● ● ● ● ● ● ● ● ●

In this activity, you will create and name a database report. The file *Activity 14-1* is a database that contains an inventory for a bicycle shop. You will create an Availability Report to help the salespeople determine which bicycles are available for sale. Title the report and designate the fields to be included in the report by following these steps:

1. Open *Activity 14-1* from the template disk.

2. Choose **ReportCreator** from the **Tools** menu.

3. Key **AVAILABILITY** in the Report Name dialog box. Click **OK.** The ReportCreator dialog box appears.

4. Key **AVAILABILITY REPORT** in the Report title box of the Title section.

5. Click **Next>.** The Fields section of the ReportCreator dialog box appears.

6. In the Fields available box, select **Manufact** if it is not already selected.

7. Click **Add>.** *Manufact* will appear in the Field order box.

8. Include **Model, Color,** and **Quant** in the report by selecting and clicking the **Add>** button.

9. Click the **Summary** tab at the top of the dialog box. The Summary section of the ReportCreator dialog box will appear.

10. Leave this section of the ReportCreator dialog box on screen for the next activity.

## Placing Statistics in a Report

Statistics summarize numerical data. The Summary section of the Report-Creator dialog box, shown in Figure 14-5, is used to specify statistics for numerical data in the report. For example, at the bottom of a report containing the salaries of employees of a department, you may want to show the number of employees, the average salary, the largest salary, and the smallest salary.

FIGURE 14-5
The Summary section of the ReportCreator dialog box is used to
specify statistics that summarize numerical data in the database report.

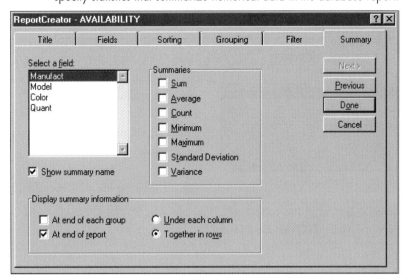

There are seven statistics available in the Summaries list. You may place
the statistics under the column of the field or group the statistics together in
rows at the bottom of the report. After you select the statistics you want, click
Done.

ACTIVITY

## Placing Statistics in a Report

In this activity, you will add statistics to your report. Your screen should show the Summary section of the ReportCreator dialog box for the
report you are creating in the file *Activity 14-1*.
One of the fields, Quant, contains numerical
data. You will sum the field at the bottom of the
report by following these steps:

1. Select **Quant** in the Select a field box.

2. Click the **Sum** box in the Summaries box.

3. Click **Together in rows** in the Display
summary information box if it is not already
selected.

4. Click **At end of report** in the Display
summary information box if it is not already
selected.

5. Click **Done.** A message similar to Figure 14-6 will appear.

**FIGURE 14-6**
After report statistics have been defined and Done is clicked, a message will appear indicating that the report is complete.

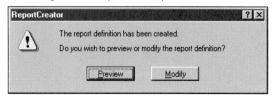

6. Click **Preview** to see what the report will look like when printed. (**NOTE:** *Had you made a mistake in selecting Done or simply wished not to preview the printed report, you could have chosen Modify to take you directly to Report view.*) The report you have created will appear in Print Preview format. View the report more closely by clicking the mouse to zoom in. The report should appear similar to Figure 14-7.

7. Click **Cancel.** Your screen is now in Report view.

8. Leave the file *Activity 14-1* on the screen for the next activity.

**FIGURE 14-7**
The Preview command will show what the database report will look like when it is printed.

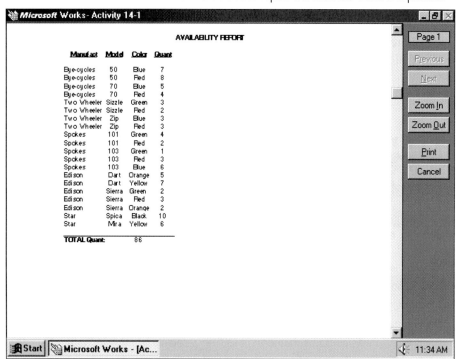

# *Changing the Appearance of a Database Report*

**Y**ou can alter the appearance of the database report by making changes in the ***Report view*** of the database, an example of which is shown in Figure 14-8. The Report view determines what information will be included in the report, how the information will be presented, and how the information will be printed.

The ***row labels*** that appear on the left side of the Report view instruct Works on how the report will appear. The report in Figure 14-8 and the report you just created have row labels for the title, headings, records, and summaries. Table 14-1 (on page 336) describes the purpose of each row label available in Report view.

**FIGURE 14-8**

The appearance of a database report is changed in Report view.

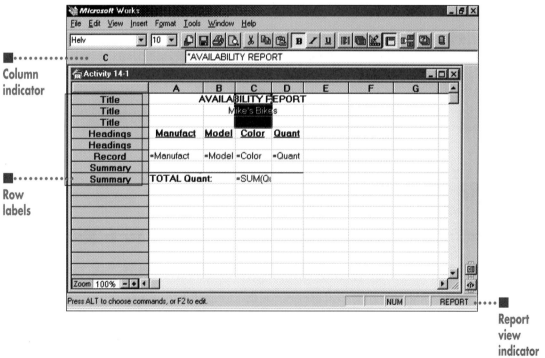

Column indicator

Row labels

Report view indicator

**TABLE 14-1**
Row labels determine the format of a database report.

| ROW LABELS | |
|---|---|
| **ROW LABEL** | **FUNCTION** |
| Title | Prints a title on the first page of the report |
| Headings | Prints a heading at the top of each column |
| Record | Indicates which fields will be printed in the report |
| Summary | Indicates which statistic(s) will be printed in the report |
| Intr *field name* | Inserts a heading between groups of records in a sorted report |
| Summ *field name* | Indicates which statistics will be printed after each group of records in a sorted report or simply enables grouping |

## Placing Additional Titles in a Report

The Title section of the ReportCreator dialog box permits you to enter one title line in the database report. For example, in Activity 14-1, you entered AVAILABILITY REPORT in the Report Title box. If you would like to change that title or add an additional title, you may do so in Report view. Titles are added and changed in rows with Title labels.

In this activity, you will insert an additional title in file *Activity 14-1* and insert a blank line under the title by following these steps:

1. In the second row, select the entry in Column E.

2. Key **Mike's Bikes**.

3. Press **Enter.**

4. Click the first appearance of the word **Headings** in the row label column in the left part of the screen. The entire row will be highlighted.

5. Choose **Insert Row** from the **Insert** menu. The Insert Row dialog box will appear.

6. Click **Title.**

7. Click **Insert.** A Title row label will be inserted in the Report view screen.

8. Center the title over the data in the report by following these steps:
   a. Select the three title rows in Column E.
   b. Choose **Cut** from the **Edit** menu.
   c. Select the first entry in Column C.
   d. Choose **Paste** from the **Edit** menu.

   e. With the three rows still selected, choose **Alignment** from the **Format** menu.
   f. Choose **Center** from the Horizontal alignment box. (Do not use the Vertical alignment box.) Click **OK.**

9. Leave the file *Activity 14-1* on the screen in Report view for the next activity.

## Changing Heading Names

Heading names are contained in the rows with Headings row labels in Report view. The default heading will be the name of the field as it appears in the database. The field name is often abbreviated to fit the limited space in the database. If you prefer a different name, you must edit the field name as it appears in the row with the Headings row label.

ACTIVITY

## Changing the Names of Headings

In this activity, you will change the names of the two headings in *Activity 14-1* that are now abbreviated by following these steps:

1. Select **Manufact** in Column A of the Headings row.

2. Enter **Manufacturer**.

3. Widen the column so that the entire word fits on one line.

4. Select **Quant** in Column D of the Headings row.

5. Enter **Quantity**.

6. Widen the column so that you can see the entire entry.

7. Select **TOTAL Quant:** in Column A of the Summary row.

8. Enter **Total Bikes in Stock**.

9. Examine your changes by clicking the **Print Preview** button in the toolbar. When you have finished, click **Cancel** to return to Report view.

10. Leave the file *Activity 14-1* on the screen in Report view for the next activity.

# Including Additional Fields in a Report

In most cases, fields to be included in a database report will be specified in the Fields section of the ReportCreator dialog box when the report is created. However, if you want to add additional fields, they may be added in Record rows in Report view.

## Adding an Additional Field to a Report

In this activity, you will include the retail cost of the bicycle model in the *Activity 14-1* report.

1. Select the entry in Column E of the Record row.

2. Key **=Retail**.

3. Press **Enter.**

4. Format the =Retail report data as currency by following these steps:
   a. Choose **Number** from the **Format** menu.
   b. Choose **Currency** format.
   c. Click **OK.**

5. Select Column E of the first Headings row.

6. Key **Price**.

7. Press **Enter.**

8. Format the Price heading by following these steps:
   a. Click the **Bold** button in the toolbar.
   b. Click the **Underline** button in the toolbar.
   c. Choose **Alignment** from the **Format** menu. Choose **Center** from the Horizontal alignment box.
   d. Click **OK.**

9. Examine your changes by clicking the **Print Preview** button in the toolbar. When you have finished, return to Report view.

10. Leave the file *Activity 14-1* on the screen in Report view for the next activity.

# *Sorting and Grouping Records in a Report*

**Y**ou can sort the records in a database report in the same way you would sort records in the full database. When you choose the Report Sorting command from the Tools menu, the Sorting section of the Report Settings dialog box, as shown in Figure 14-9, will appear. (This section is the same as the Sorting section of the ReportCreator dialog box, which is available when you first create a report.)

**FIGURE 14-9**

The Sorting section of the Report Settings dialog box lets you indicate how to sort records in your report. The Grouping section of the Report Settings dialog box lets you indicate how to group records in your report.

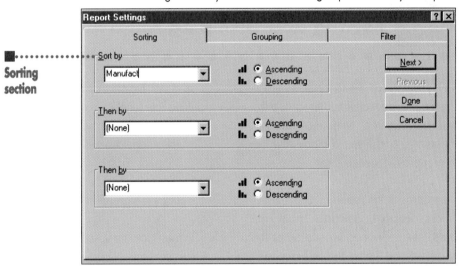

**Sorting section**

**Grouping section**

Grouping identifies records that have similar field contents. For example, if you are sorting by color, Works will "break" between each group of colors in a sorted database report. To group records, select the When contents change option in the Grouping section of the Report Settings dialog box. Works will insert a Summ *field name* row after the records row. If you also select the Show group heading option, Works will insert an Intr *field name* row before the records row. This new row will provide the field name for each group of records. The Grouping section of the Report Settings dialog box may be reached by choosing Report Grouping from the Tools menu or by clicking Next> after making sorting selections.

# Sorting and Grouping Records in a Report

In this activity, you will sort the records in file *Activity 14-1* by the bicycle manufacturer, group the records by manufacturer with manufacturer names as headings, and insert a blank row between each group by following these steps:

1. Sort the records in the report:
   a. Choose **Report Sorting** from the **Tools** menu. The Sorting section of the Report Settings dialog box will appear.
   b. In the Sort by box, click the arrow next to the box and choose **Manufact** from the drop-down list.
   c. Click the **Ascending** button if it is not already selected.
   d. Click **Next>** to switch to the Grouping section of the Report Settings dialog box.
   e. Click **When contents change** in the Group by: Manufact box.
   f. Click **Show group heading** in the Group by: Manufact box.

   g. Click **Done.** A new row will appear with a row label of *Summ Manufact* to indicate that there will be a blank row between headings. An *Intr Manufact* row will also appear to show that sorted groups will have the bicycle manufacturer by which they are grouped as their heading.

2. Widen Column C so that you can view all of the contents. Your screen should appear similar to Figure 14-10.

3. View the database report by clicking the **Print Preview** button on the toolbar. Notice that the database has been sorted alphabetically and grouped by manufacturer and that headings divide each group. When you have finished viewing the report, return to Report view by clicking the **Cancel** button.

4. Leave the file *Activity 14-1* on the screen in Report view for the next activity.

**FIGURE 14-10**
The Report view determines how information will appear in the database report.

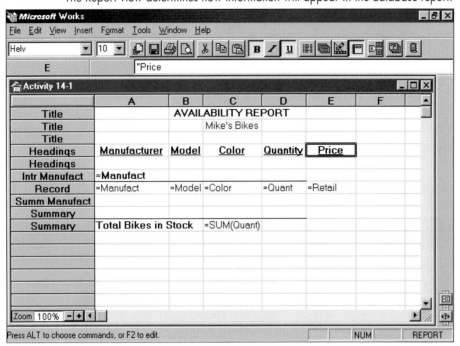

In Activity 14-2, you placed statistics at the end of a report by creating a Summary row. The Summ *field name* row is used to place statistics after each group of records in a sorted report.

**ACTIVITY**

## Placing Summary Statistics after a Group

In this activity, you will prepare statistics to indicate the number of models and the number of bicycles currently in stock for each of the manufacturers. Your screen should show the file *Activity 14-1* in Report view. All the following entries will be made in the row with the row label *Summ Manufact.*

1. Enter a label to indicate the number of models supplied by each manufacturer:
   a. Enter **No. of Models:** in Column A.
   b. Click the **Bold** button in the toolbar.
   c. Widen the column to fit the new data.

d. Right align the label.

2. Enter summary statistics to determine the number of models supplied by each manufacturer:
   a. Enter **=COUNT(Model)** in Column B.
   b. Boldface and left align the label.
   c. Widen the column to fit the new data.

3. Enter a label to indicate the number of models supplied by each manufacturer that are in stock:

**a.** Enter **In Stock:** in Column C.

**b.** Boldface and right align the label.

**4.** Enter summary statistics to determine the number of models supplied by each manufacturer that are in stock:

**a.** Enter **=SUM(Quant)** in Column D.

**b.** Boldface and left align the label.

**c.** Widen the column to accommodate the new data.

**5.** When you have completed step 4, the Report view screen should appear similar to Figure 14-11. Examine the changes you have created once more by clicking the **Print Preview** button.

**6.** Click **Cancel.**

**7.** Leave the file *Activity 14-1* on the screen in Report view for the next activity.

**FIGURE 14-11**
The Report view in this figure contains all six types of row labels.

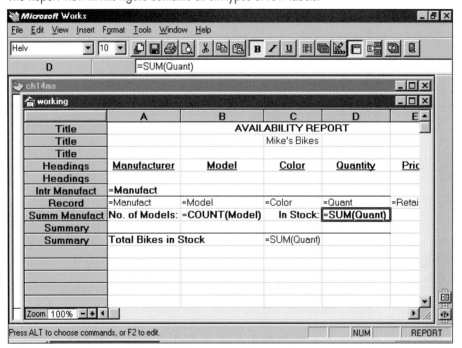

# *Using Filters in a Database Report*

Y ou can use filters in a database report in the same way you would use them in the full database. When you choose the Report Filter command from the Tools menu, the Filter section of the Report Settings dialog box, as shown in

Figure 14-12, will appear. (This section is the same as the filter section of the ReportCreator dialog box, which is available when you first create a report.) Once you click on Create New Filter, you get the same Filter Name dialog box and then Filter dialog box as you learned about in Chapter 13 when creating filters in a full database.

**FIGURE 14-12**

The Filter section of the Report Settings dialog box.

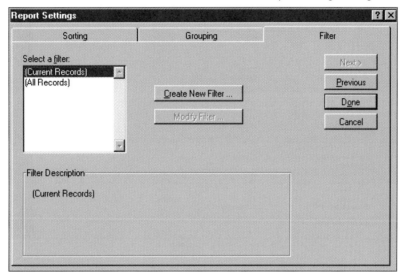

ACTIVITY

## Using a Filter in a Report

In this activity, you will use a filter in the database report you have prepared following these steps:

1. Choose **Report Filter** from the **Tools** menu. The Filter section of the Report Settings dialog box appears.

2. Click on **Create New Filter.**

3. In the Filter Name dialog box, key **Quantity**.

4. Click **OK.**

5. In the Filter dialog box, create a filter that will show all models for which there are more than one available.

6. Click **OK.**

7. In the Filter section of the Report Settings dialog box, click **Done.**

8. When you have completed the activity, use the **Print Preview** button to view your work. Use the **Zoom In** button to make the

**FIGURE 14-13**
A filter in a report allows you to show only those records that meet certain criteria. This report shows only those models for which the company has more than one available.

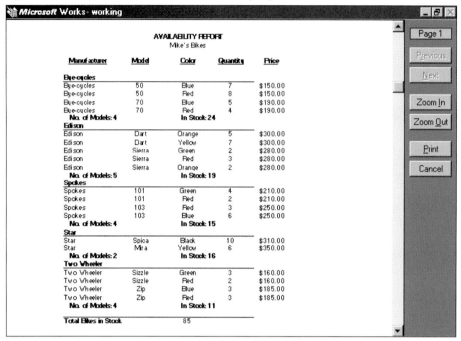

preview more readable. Your screen should look like Figure 14-13.

9. Click **Cancel.**

10. Leave the file *Activity 14-1* on the screen in Report view for the next activity.

# *Printing a Database Report*

Throughout this chapter, you have previewed the database to see what it will look like when you print. You may print the database report by choosing Print from the File menu, clicking the Print button on the toolbar, or clicking the Print button in the Print Preview screen. The Print dialog box will appear only if you choose Print from the File menu. The Print button on the toolbar and the Print button in Print Preview cause printing to start immediately.

**ACTIVITY**

**14-9**  **Printing a Report**

● ● ● ● ● ● ● ● ● ● ● ● ● ● ● ● ● ● ● ● ● ● ● ● ● ● ● ● ● ●

In this activity, you will print the database report you have prepared following these steps:

1. Choose **Print** from the **File** menu. The Print dialog box will appear. The options now indicate that one copy of all pages will be printed.

2. Choose **OK.** The database report will be printed.

3. Leave the file *Activity 14-1* on the screen for the next activity.

# *Naming and Renaming Reports in a Database*

**W**orks will automatically name database reports as you create them. The first report will be called Report 1; the second, Report 2; and so on. A maximum of eight reports may be created for each database. You may choose to give the report its own name in the Report Name dialog box, which appears when you select ReportCreator from the Tools menu, as you did in Activity 14-1.

You may rename a report by choosing the Rename Report command from the Tools menu. The Rename Report dialog box, shown in Figure 14-14, will appear. If there is more than one report, select the report to be named by clicking the name in the Select a report box; then, key the new name in the Type a name below box and click the Rename button. A report name is limited to 15 characters.

**FIGURE 14-14**
The Rename Report dialog box contains a list of all reports existing for the database.

| Rename Report | ? X |
|---|---|
| <u>S</u>elect a report: | OK |
| AVAILABILITY | Cancel |
| <u>T</u>ype a name below: | |
| Avail Report | <u>R</u>ename |

## ACTIVITY

# 14-10 Renaming a Database Report

In this activity, you will name the database report you have prepared by following these steps:

1. Choose **Rename Report** from the **Tools** menu. The Rename Report dialog box will appear and *AVAILABILITY* will be highlighted in the Select a report box.

2. Key **Avail Report** in the Type a name below box.

3. Click **Rename.**

4. Click **OK.**

5. Choose **Report** from the **View** menu. Notice the name *Avail Report* appears in the View Report dialog box. (You may access the Report view for any report you have created by choosing Report from the View menu.) Click **Cancel.**

6. Leave the file *Activity 14-1* on the screen for the next activity.

# *Saving Reports in a Database*

You may create and save as many as eight reports per database. When you save the database, you will save all of the reports you have created from the database. You need not return to the full database to save. However when you reopen the database after saving and closing, it will be in List view; you will have to use the View menu to access the report or reports you have created.

The database reports you save become an integral part of the database. In other words, the report depends on the data saved in the database. If the database is changed, the presentation of the report will also be changed to reflect the new data in the database.

## ACTIVITY

# 14-11 Saving Reports in a Database

In this activity, you will save the database and report you created in the database by following these steps:

1. Save the file to your data disk as *Mike's*

*Bikes*. The database and the report you have created will be saved.

2. Close the file.

# *Summary*

- An entire database is rarely printed because of its large size. Instead, database reports, which organize and summarize database information, are printed. Database reports are created in the ReportCreator dialog box. Within this dialog box are sections in which you may perform the following tasks on your report: title, change the orientation, and change the font (Title); specify fields (Fields); sort (Sorting); group (Grouping); create filters (Filter); and summarize material statistically (Summary). The new database report may be changed in the Report view of the database.

- Records in a database report may be sorted in the same way you would sort records in the full database. Sorted database reports may also be grouped, with a row containing statistics printed after each group of records in a sorted report. Sorting and grouping may be accomplished when the report is created or at a later date using the Report Sorting and Report Grouping commands, respectively, from the Tools menu.

- You may also use filters in a database report just as you would in a full database. Filters may be created when the report is created or at a later date using the Report Filter command from the Tools menu.

- Database reports are printed by choosing Print from the File menu, by choosing Print in the Print Preview screen, or by clicking the Print button in the toolbar.

- You may create and save as many as eight reports per database. Each report may be named to indicate what is contained in the report. Otherwise, Works will automatically name the database report as it is created. When you save the database, you will save all of the database reports you have created from the database.

● ● ● ● ● ● ● ● ● ● ● ● ● ●

# REVIEW ACTIVITIES

## TRUE/FALSE

**Circle T or F to show whether the statement is true or false.**

**T   F**   1. The purpose of the database report is to print the entire database as it appears on screen.

**T   F**   2. You may create as many reports as you like from a single database.

**T   F**   3. The Summary row label indicates which statistic will be printed at the bottom of the report.

**T   F**   4. Row labels determine the type of information that will appear in a database report.

**T   F**   5. The Headings row label indicates the title that will be printed at the top of the database report.

**T   F**   6. Statistics summarizing the data in a report may be placed under the column in which the data appears or grouped together in rows at the bottom of the report.

**T   F**   7. The procedure to sort records in a database report is similar to the procedure for sorting records in a full database.

**T   F**   8. Using filters in a database report is very different from using filters in a full database.

**T   F**   9. Works will automatically name database reports if you do not assign a name.

**T   F**   10. Database reports must be saved separately before you exit a database.

## COMPLETION

**Write the correct answer in the space provided.**

1. Which menu is accessed to perform database reporting functions, such as creating and naming a report?

_____

_____

2. Identify three of the operations that take place in the ReportCreator dialog box.

_____

_____

3. In which view may one make changes to a database report?

_____

_____

4. Which Report view row label determines the title appearing at the top of the first page of a database report?

_____

_____

5. Which Report view row label determines which fields will be printed in the report?

_____

_____

6. Once a new database report has been created, how do you add additional fields to the report?

_____

_____

7. Identify two statistics that may be used in a database report.

_____

_____

8. What command will allow you to place records in a database report in a specified order?

_____

_____

9. Which section in the ReportCreator dialog box will later allow you to insert statistics after each group of records in a sort?

_____

_____

10. What is the maximum number of database reports that may be saved with a single database?

_____

_____

# REINFORCEMENT APPLICATIONS

## application 14-1

The file *Application 14-1* contains a database of bicycles for Mike's Bikes (similar to the database used in the chapter). In this application, you will prepare a database report that answers the questions of the accountant for Mike's Bikes. Specifically, the accountant would like to know the number of bicycles in the inventory and the value of the inventory at cost.

1. Open *Application 14-1*.

2. In the ReportCreator dialog box, designate the following:
   a. Accept the report name *Report 1* (in the Report Name box) for now.
   b. Title the report **Year End Inventory**.
   c. Include the following fields in the report: Manufact, Model, Quant, Cost, and Cost Total.
   d. Do not click Done.

3. In the Summary section of the ReportCreator dialog box, perform the following operations:
   a. Create a Sum statistic for the Quant field.
   b. Create a Sum statistic for the Cost Total field.
   c. Position the statistics under each column.
   d. Choose **Done, Preview** the report, and **Cancel** to return to Report view.

4. In Report view, perform the following steps:
   a. Change the Manufact heading to **Manufacturer**.
   b. Change the Quant heading to **Quantity**.
   c. Widen the columns to fit the expanded headings.
   d. Change the Summary title in Column C to **No. of Bicycles:**
   e. Change the Summary title in Column E to **Value of Inventory:**
   f. Widen Column C and Column E to accommodate the summary statistics.

5. Move the title **Year End Inventory** from Column E to Column C.

6. Print the report.

7. Name the report **INVENTORY**.

8. Save the database to your data disk as *Inventory*.

9. Close the file.

10. Using the information on your printed report, answer the following questions asked by the accountant:
    a. How many bicycles are in the year-end inventory?
    b. What is the value of the inventory at cost?

# application 14-2

The file *Application 14-2* contains a database of bicycles for Mike's Bikes (similar to the database used in the chapter). In this application, you will prepare a database report that will be provided to customers so that they may know the retail prices for each bicycle model.

1. Open *Application 14-2* and prepare a database report with the following characteristics:
   a. The report name will be *Price List.*
   b. The report title will be PRICE LIST.
   c. The fields to be included in the report include Manufact, Model, Color, and Retail.
   d. The report should contain no summary statistics.
   e. The records should be sorted by price (the Retail field), from the least expensive to the most expensive.
   f. The heading for Manufact should be changed to Manufacturer.
   g. The title of the report should be centered over the report contents. (*Hint:* Move the title from Column E to Column B in Report view.)

2. Print the report.

3. Save the database to your data disk as *Price.*

4. Close the file.


# application 14-3

The file *Application 14-3* contains grades recorded for three tests and a final examination by a course instructor. The database is currently sorted by grades made on the final examination.

1. Prepare a report that indicates test averages, the highest grade for each test, and the lowest grade for each test. The database report should be named *Exam Summary* and entitled *EXAMINATION SUMMARY* and appear similar to the following:

## EXAMINATION SUMMARY

| Name | Test 1 | Test 2 | Test 3 | Final Exam |
|------|--------|--------|--------|------------|
| Appleby | 85 | 86 | 90 | 91 |
| Barnett | 95 | 92 | 87 | 90 |
| Chandler | 77 | 74 | 73 | 70 |
| Dawson | 68 | 66 | 71 | 66 |
| Ellington | 75 | 74 | 78 | 72 |
| Fowler | 81 | 83 | 85 | 90 |
| Getz | 83 | 84 | 85 | 85 |
| Harrington | 74 | 78 | 76 | 79 |
| Ingram | 72 | 71 | 73 | 77 |
| Jones | 75 | 80 | 75 | 85 |
| Kinslow | 82 | 81 | 89 | 87 |

| Name | Test 1 | Test 2 | Test 3 | Final Exam |
|------|--------|--------|--------|------------|
| Lowe | 74 | 75 | 76 | 79 |
| Martinez | 95 | 98 | 94 | 88 |
| Newsom | 83 | 88 | 90 | 82 |
| | AVG: | AVG: | AVG: | AVG: |
| | 79.93 | 80.71 | 81.57 | 81.50 |
| | MIN: | MIN: | MIN: | MIN: |
| | 68 | 66 | 71 | 66 |
| | MAX: | MAX: | MAX: | MAX: |
| | 95 | 98 | 94 | 91 |

*Hints:*

   **a.** Make sure you position the report statistics under each column.

   **b.** Format the test averages as fixed with two decimal digits. (*Hint:* Use the <u>N</u>umber command in the F<u>o</u>rmat menu.)

   **c.** Move the title of the report to Column C.

   **d.** Sort the database report alphabetically by name.

**2.** Rename the report *Stats.*

**3.** Print the database report.

**4.** Save the file to your data disk as *Examination* and close the file.

# application 14 - 4

**In this application, you will create two reports from the database *Directory,* which you created in Application 12-4 and revised in Application 13-5. Feel free to add more names, addresses, and phone numbers if you desire.**

**1.** Open *Directory.*

**2.** Create a database report that acts as a phone list of your friends and relatives. The report will be named *Phone Directory* and have the following characteristics:

   **a.** The report should include the fields Last Name, First Name, and Phone No.

   **b.** The list should be sorted alphabetically by Last Name.

**3.** Create a database report that lists the names and addresses of your friends and relatives by geographical area. The report should be named *Addresses* and have the following characteristics:

   **a.** The report should include the fields Last Name, First Name, Address, City, and ZIP Code.

   **b.** The list should be sorted by ZIP Code.

**4.** Print both reports.

**5.** Save *Directory* and close the file.

U N I T

5

# TASK WIZARDS AND COMMUNICATIONS

# WORKS
# TASKWIZARDS

**OBJECTIVES**

**When you complete this chapter, you will be able to:**

1. Describe a TaskWizard.

2. Use a TaskWizard to create an address book.

3. Use a TaskWizard to create a personal letterhead.

4. Use a TaskWizard to create a time sheet.

5. Use a TaskWizard to create a resume.

# *Meet the Works TaskWizards*

**Y**ou have probably noticed the TaskWizards section of the Task Launcher and wondered what a Wizard is. *TaskWizards* are programs within Works that automate certain common Works tasks, such as creating address lists and form letters. Think of a TaskWizard as an expert that follows your orders to set up a database or document and then, almost magically, does the work before your eyes. Using one of Works' 39 TaskWizards is the easiest and fastest way to create a document.

To start a TaskWizard, click the Task Launcher button on the toolbar. Then, click the TaskWizards tab in the Works Task Launcher. In the TaskWizards section, the Wizards are arranged in categories such as Common Tasks and Business Management, as shown in Figure 15-1. Click the category to see the Wizards that are available within it. Then, choose the Wizard you want. While you are working in a Wizard, you can click Cancel to stop at any time and return to the Task Launcher.

**FIGURE 15-1**
The TaskWizards section of the Works Task
Launcher allows you to choose a TaskWizard.

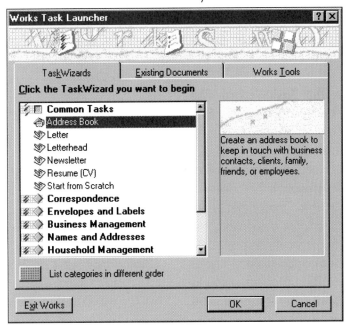

# Using a TaskWizard to Create an Address Book

The Address Book TaskWizard can create several types of address books. You will create a personal address book that can include all of your friends' and family's phone numbers, addresses, birthdays, and anniversaries. The Wizard will ask you some questions to customize your address book, and then the Wizard will create it for you. Once this database is created, you can add and delete records like you would in any database.

**ACTIVITY**

## 15-1 Create an Address Book

In this activity, you will use a TaskWizard to create an address book. This activity assumes

Works is running and the Task Launcher is on your screen.

1. Click the **TaskWizards** tab if it is not already selected.

2. Click **Address Book.** Read the description of the address book at the right side of the dialog box. Click **OK.**

3. Click **Yes, run the TaskWizard.** The screen shown in Figure 15-2 appears.

4. Click the **Personal** address book if it is not already selected. Notice the explanation of this kind of address book at the bottom of the window. Click on the other types of address books and read their descriptions.

5. Click the **Personal** address book again. Click **Next.** The Next button takes you to the next screen where you will have more choices for customizing your address book.

6. Read the list of fields that will be in your address book. Notice the Back button, which allows you to go back to the previous screen.

Click **Next** to go on to the next screen.

7. Click the arrow beside *Additional Fields.*

8. You want to add one of these fields. Click in the box beside *Personal Information* and click **OK.**

9. Click the arrow beside *Your Own Fields.*

10. You will add a field, so click in the box beside *Field 1.* Key **Grade** as the field name. Click **OK.**

11. Click the arrow beside *Reports.*

12. You may want an alphabetical report, so click in the box beside *Alphabetized Directory.* Click **OK.**

13. Click **Create It!** The Checklist screen, shown in Figure 15-3, appears. It lists all the choices you made in the Address Book TaskWizard.

**FIGURE 15-2**
Screens like this one guide you through the creation of the address book.

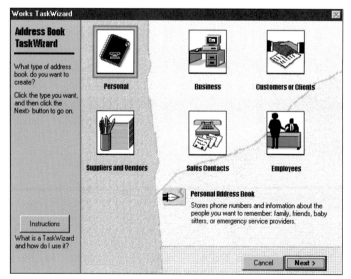

**FIGURE 15-3**
When all of the TaskWizard's questions have
been answered, the Checklist screen will appear.

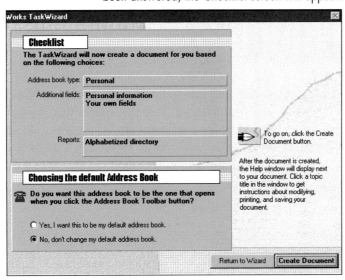

14. Under *Choosing the default Address Book,* choose **No** if it is not already selected.

15. Notice the Return to Wizard button, which allows you to go back and change any of your choices. Click **Create Document.** After a few moments, your address book will appear on screen. The TaskWizard's work is done, and you can enter information into your address book.

16. Enter your own name and information as the first record. Use the Tab key to move to each entry.

17. Enter a friend's or relative's information as the second record.

18. Save the database as *Address Book* on your data disk just as you would save any file. You can open this database at any time and add more records to your address book.

19. Close the database just as you would close any file.

The database created by the TaskWizard is just like other databases you have worked with throughout the book. Add data to the address book in the same way you have in earlier chapters. Remember, the TaskWizard helps you create the database quickly, but once created, the database does not need the TaskWizard.

# Using a TaskWizard to Create a Personal Letterhead

**W**orks has a TaskWizard that helps you create letterheads for personal or professional use. As with the Address Book Wizard, you will make several selections to customize your letterhead. In addition, Works contains sample text you can use in your letters to help you get started. For example, one sample text is a thank you letter for a gift. Not only is the letter already written, but the content also gives hints about what to include in a thank you letter so that you can revise the content to fit what you want to say.

## ACTIVITY

## 15-2 Create a Personal Letterhead

● ● ● ● ● ● ● ● ● ● ● ● ● ● ● ● ● ● ● ● ● ● ● ● ● ● ● ● ● ● ● ● ● ● ● ● ● ●

In this activity, you will use the TaskWizard to create a personal letterhead and letter. The Works Task Launcher should be on your screen.

1. Click the **TaskWizards** tab if it is not already selected.

2. Click **Letterhead** under *Common Tasks*.

Click **OK.**

3. Click **Yes, run the TaskWizard.**

4. Choose the **Simple** layout type of letterhead and click **Next.** Your screen should look like Figure 15-4.

**FIGURE 15-4**

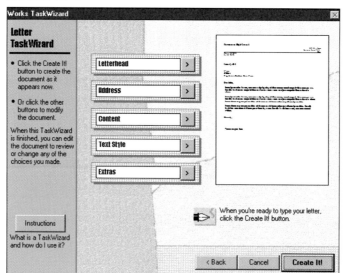

5. Click the arrow beside *Letterhead.* Choose **I want to design my own** if it is not already selected and click **Next.**

6. Choose the **Art Deco** letterhead style and click **Next.**

7. Click **Company name** to remove the X. Click **Personal name** and key your name in the space provided. Click **Next.**

8. Fill in your own address in the spaces provided and click **Next.** (If your address has only one line, then you will not key in the Address 2 line.)

9. Click to remove the phone numbers you do not want. Key the phone numbers and/or e-mail address you do want and click **Next.**

10. Choose **OK.**

11. Click the arrow beside *Address.* Choose **I want to type a single address** if it is not already selected and click **Next.**

12. Key the following in the space provided:

   **Mr. Jeremy Willis**
   **5669 Oak Hill Drive**
   **Atlanta, Georgia 30369-0556**

13. Click **Next.**

14. In the greeting beside *Dear,* key **Jeremy** and click **Next.**

15. Click **OK.**

16. Click the arrow beside *Content.*

17. Here you will choose the content you want to use for your letter. Scroll down to the bottom of the list and choose **Thank you for the party invitation.** Click **OK.**

18. Click the arrow beside *Text Style.*

19. Choose the **Contemporary** text style and click **OK.**

20. Click the arrow beside *Extras.* You don't need any of the extras in your letter, so click **OK** without choosing any of the options.

21. Choose **Create It!** The Checklist screen appears.

22. Click **Create Document.** The Wizard creates your letterhead and letter.

23. Read the letter.

24. This time, you won't change anything in the letter, so delete the two paragraphs about letter-writing tips.

25. Highlight *Your name goes here,* and key your name.

26. Save the document as *Personal Letterhead* on your data disk.

27. Print as you would print any document, and close.

# Using a TaskWizard to Create a Time Sheet

**W**orks has many TaskWizards that can help you do a variety of different tasks. In the next activity, you will use a spreadsheet Wizard to figure hours worked and wages for a week. This Wizard saves you time and effort because the document you create will already contain the formulas needed to compute total hours worked and wages. After learning this Wizard, you can modify it to keep track of your own work schedule and wages.

**ACTIVITY**

## Creating a Time Sheet

In this activity, you will use the TaskWizard to create a time sheet. The Task Launcher should be on your screen.

1. Click the **TaskWizards** tab if it is not already selected.

2. Scroll down and click the **Employment** category. A list of documents in that category appears.

3. Click **Employee Time Sheet.**

4. Click **OK.**

5. Click **Yes, run the TaskWizard.**

6. Click the **Weekly Time Sheet** if it is not already selected and click **Create It!** The Time Sheet spreadsheet appears.

7. In Cell A2, key **Cool Ice Cream Cafe**, which is the place of employment.

8. In Cell B5, key **Jordan Hall**. This is the employee's name.

9. In Cell B6, key **Customer Service**, which is Jordan's department.

10. In Cell B7, key **Kokomo, Indiana**, the city where the ice cream cafe is located.

11. In Cell B8, key **June 23, 199-** for the date.

12. in Cell G5, key **cashier** as Jordan's title and in Cell G6 key **555-090-2002** as his social security number.

13. In Cell C12, key **10 am** and in Cell C13, key **3:30 pm**. These are Jordan's hours of work for June 23. The hours subtotal will be calculated automatically.

14. Copy Cells C12 and C13 to Cells E12 and E13 and to Cells G12 and G13.

**15.** In Cell D15, key **3 pm** and in Cell D16, key **9 pm**.

**16.** Copy Cells D15 and D16 to Cells H15 and H16.

**17.** In Cell B34, key **5**. This is Jordan's amount

of pay per hour. The total wages and total hours are calculated automatically.

**18.** Save the document as *Time Sheet* on your data disk.

**19.** Print and close.

# *Using a TaskWizard to Create a Resume*

**A**n attractive resume will help you get a job. A *resume* is a professional document that lists concise information about you. The information on a resume helps an employer decide if he or she wants to grant an interview. Therefore, you want to create an attractive resume that makes a good impression. In the next activity, you will create a chronological resume using a TaskWizard.

**ACTIVITY**

**15-4 Creating a Resume**

In this activity, you will use the TaskWizard to create a resume. The Task Launcher should be on your screen.

**1.** Click the **Tas_kWizards** tab if it is not already selected.

**2.** Choose **Resume (CV)** (CV stands for Curriculum Vitae, which you will read about in this activity) from the **Students and Teachers** category.

**3.** Click **OK**.

**4.** Click **Y̲es, run the TaskWizard.**

**5.** Click the **Chronological** resume style if it is not already selected. Read the description below the sample document. Click on the **Qualifications** and **Curriculum Vitae** resumes and read their descriptions.

**6.** Click the **Chronological** resume style again if it is not already selected and click **Next.**

**7.** Click the arrow beside *Letterhead*.

**8.** Click **I want to design my own** if it is not already selected and click **Next.**

9. Choose the **Contemporary** letterhead style. Notice the < and |< buttons. Click < to go back to the previous screen; click |< to go back to the first screen of this section, Letterhead. Click **Next.**

10. Click to put an X beside *Personal name* if it is not already selected. Key **Felecia Thomas**.

11. Click to remove the X (if there is one) from *Company name* and click **Next.**

12. In the address lines provided (do not key in Address line 2 or Country), key the following:

   **734 West Shiloh**
   **Wichita, Kansas 67290-0734**

13. Click **Next.**

14. Key the home phone number **316-555-9099** and the e-mail address **FeleciaT@mailbox.com**.

15. Click **Next** and then **OK.**

16. Click the arrow next to *Layout*.

17. Choose **Contemporary Headings** and click **OK.**

18. Click the arrow beside *Headings*.

19. Click the headings **Objective, Interests & Activities, Computer Skills,** and **Awards Received,** then click **OK.** Note that certain headings are already made for you by default. These are *Summary, Work History,* and *Education.* If these headings are not already selected, click on them with your mouse.

20. Click the arrow beside *Entries*.

21. Choose to show two jobs on your resume and one education entry, and click **OK.**

22. Choose **Create It!** The Checklist screen appears.

23. Click **Return to Wizard.**

24. Click the arrow beside *Heading* and remove the X from *Summary.* Click **OK.**

25. Click **Create It!** The Checklist screen appears.

26. Click **Create Document.** After a few moments, your document will appear.

27. Notice the text below each heading. These *placeholders* help you key in the right place and help you to write appropriate text by giving you hints about the kind of information to include in each section. Key the information in the resume as shown in Figure 15-5.

28. Save as *Felecia Resume* on your data disk.

29. Print and close.

**FIGURE 15-5**

CHAPTER 15: Works TaskWizards

---

### Felecia Thomas

734 West Shiloh ◆ Wichita, Kansas 67290-0734
Home Phone 316-555-9099 ◆ email FeleciaT@mailbox.com

**O B J E C T I V E**

Seeking a part-time job on the campus of State University where I can utilize my computer abilities and customer service skills.

**W O R K   H I S T O R Y**

*Sales Associate, Miller's Department Store*          *1996- 1997*

Informed customers about types of shoes and recommended styles they might like. Helped customers choose shoes for specific outfits and helped customers find shoes that fit comfortably.  Was responsible for my cash drawer and for reordering children's shoes.

*Cashier, Apple Core Superstore*          *1995- 1996*

Used the cash register to check out customer purchases. Bagged groceries and helped stock candy and gum displays. Trained new cashiers.

**E D U C A T I O N**

Middleton High School, 1997
Wichita, Kansas
G.P.A.: 3.6
Class Ranking: Top Quarter

Will attend State University next semester, majoring in Architecture.

**I N T E R E S T S   &   A C T I V I T I E S**

- In high school, I was on the tennis team and still enjoy playing tennis with friends. I played the saxophone in the band.
- I enjoy music, reading, and computers. I am a volunteer assistant leader in the local council of Girl Scouts of the U.S.A. I am a member of Future Entrepreneurs of Wichita.

**C O M P U T E R   S K I L L S**

- I am familiar with many types of software; however, I have extensive experience with Works 4.0 for Windows 95. I also have experience with Aldus PageMaker 5.0, which I use to do the quarterly newsletter for Future Entrepreneurs of Wichita.  I also use Microsoft Money for personal financial management.
- I have used computers for three years.  In high school, I took three different computer courses including Beginning Computers, Computer Applications, and Document Design. My family bought a computer one year ago, and I spend lots of time using it to explore the Internet.

**A W A R D S   R E C E I V E D**

- English award, 1994.
- Beginning Computers award, 1995.
- District winner, doubles tennis, 1996.
- Second place, Division 1 Saxophone solo, 1996.
- Special Volunteer award, Wichita Girl Scout Council, 1996.
- Employee of the Month, Miller's Department Store, October 1996.

# *Other TaskWizards*

**W**orks includes TaskWizards to assist you in creating other documents such as school reports and schedules. In addition, Works contains many Wizards business people can use. If there is no wizard listed for the type of document you want to create, you can choose the Start from Scratch TaskWizard to help you get started. For a complete list of the TaskWizards, see Appendix A.

# Summary

- Works contains many TaskWizards that can create and customize documents for you. Once created, you don't need the Wizard anymore. You can edit and format a document just as you've done with other documents throughout this book.

• • • • • • • • • • • • • •

# REVIEW ACTIVITIES

## TRUE/FALSE

**Circle T or F to show whether the statement is true or false.**

**T   F**   1. Works TaskWizards are accessed through the Task Launcher.

**T   F**   2. Creating a document on your own is the easiest way to create a document in Works.

**T   F**   3. Once a database is created by a TaskWizard, you can add and delete records just as you would in any database.

**T   F**   4. After a document is created with a TaskWizard, you cannot make changes to it.

**T   F**   5. In the Address Book TaskWizard, you cannot create your own fields.

**T   F**   6. While answering questions in a TaskWizard, you can always go back and change your choices.

**T   F**   7. Click Back to go to the next screen.

**T   F**   8. Works contains sample text you can use in your letters.

**T   F**   9. In the Time Sheet TaskWizard, you must enter formulas to figure total hours and wages.

**T   F**   10. In the Resume TaskWizard, you can choose the headings you want.

## COMPLETION

**Write the correct answer in the space provided.**

1. What is a TaskWizard?

_____

_____

2. How do you stop a TaskWizard?

_____

_____

3. What happens when you click the Next button?

_____

_____

4. What are the steps for saving a document created by a TaskWizard?

_____

_____

5. What screen shows the choices you made using the TaskWizard?

_____

6. What are two of the five Extra elements you can use in a letter?

_____

7. Why does the Time Sheet Wizard save you time and effort?

_____

8. What kind of resume did you create in this chapter?

_____

9. What are the two purposes of placeholders?

_____

_____

10. Which Wizard do you use if you want to create a type of document for which there is no TaskWizard?

_____

## application 15 - 1

**In this application, you will use the Resume TaskWizard to create your resume.**

1. Create your own resume.

2. Save the document as *Resume* on your data disk.

3. Print and close.

## application 15 - 2

**In this application, you will create a certificate using the Certificate TaskWizard from the Students and Teachers category.**

1. Use the Classic layout to create the certificate shown in Figure 15-6. Insert your name in place of *Student's Name*.

**FIGURE 15-6**

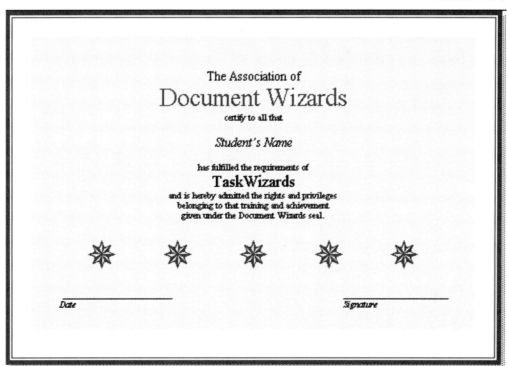

2. Save the document as *Certificate* on your data disk.

3. Print and close.

# COMMUNICATION BASICS

## OBJECTIVES
### When you complete this chapter, you will be able to:

1. Explain the concepts of modem communication.
2. Use the Works Communications tool.

# *Concepts of Modem Communications*

**W**orking alone, a computer is a powerful tool. Your computer, however, becomes even more powerful when it shares information with other computers. In this chapter, you will discover how modem communication can expand the capabilities and increase the usefulness of your computer.

*Modem communication* is the process of transmitting information from one computer to another over telephone lines. Modem communication is a form of telecommunication. *Telecommunication* is the transfer of information from one place to another electronically. Using the telephone to call a friend is another form of telecommunication.

# *The Modem*

**T**he device needed for modem communication is the *modem.* A modem converts computer signals so that they can be transmitted and received over phone lines. This conversion of signals is called *modulating* and *demodulating.* Modulating is the process of converting signals so that they can be sent over a phone line. Demodulating is the process of converting signals so that they can be received through a phone line. The word *modem* is a short form of *modulator/dem*odulator. Modems are available in different speeds and with a variety of optional features.

The speed at which a modem modulates signals is measured in **baud.** Another measurement, ***bits per second (BPS),*** is more descriptive because it is a measure of the usable bits that the modem sends or receives in a second. A ***bit*** is a single electronic signal that is either on or off. One bit alone cannot do much. But in groups, bits do practically everything in your computer. Each character is represented by a unique combination of eight bits, called a ***byte.*** Every time you key a character in the word processor, each of the eight bits that identify that character is assigned to be either on or off.

Some modems, particularly older ones, transmit one bit per baud. Because of this, many people think of baud and BPS as interchangeable. Because newer modems sometimes squeeze four or more bits into one baud, baud and BPS can no longer be thought of as the same thing.

Common modem speeds range from 2,400 up to 28,800 BPS. In its standard mode, a 2,400-BPS modem can transmit about 240 characters per second. The speed at which a modem can transmit data is an important factor when you are communicating over long-distance phone lines.

Modems may be installed inside the computer or connected to the computer by a cable. Modems installed inside the computer are called *internal modems.* An internal modem is a circuit card that plugs into one of the connectors inside the computer. An *external modem* connects to the computer by a cable that plugs into a port on the back of the computer. Figure 16-1 illustrates an external modem.

**FIGURE 16-1**
An external modem is attached to the computer with a cable.

# Host and Terminal

When you place a call with a modem, the computer you connect with is the *host computer.* When connected to a host computer, your computer becomes a *terminal.*

*Terminal emulation* is the way text coming over the modem is presented on the screen. Emulations like VT100 were developed so that text coming over a modem could be placed at any location on the screen and support a special set of graphic characters.

# Why Communicate?

Modems open the door to a whole world of information and communication. Let's look at some of the things you can do with a modem and a personal computer.

### CONNECTING TWO COMPUTERS DIRECTLY

In one form of modem communication, two computer users use their modems to connect their computers in order to transfer a file. Suppose that a student named Brian has just written a letter to a company inquiring about a job opening. Brian composed the letter in Microsoft Works, but he has not yet printed it. Brian's friend Kelsey, on the other side of town, volunteers to edit the letter before Brian prints it. Brian and Kelsey use their modems to connect their computers, and Brian sends his letter to Kelsey's computer. Not only can Kelsey read it, she can also make revisions to it and send the revised letter back to Brian.

### BULLETIN BOARD SYSTEMS

A *bulletin board system,* commonly called a BBS, is a service run by an individual, college, club, or business. BBSs provide a place to post messages for other users to read. In addition, BBSs may offer private mail, files to transfer, and even games that can be played over the modem. Some BBSs are local systems with one phone line used primarily by local callers. Other BBSs, however, have multiple phone lines and attract callers from all over the world.

Many BBSs are part of networks that transmit messages from local systems to other systems all over the nation and in some cases to other countries. These networks can exchange information with other computer users nationwide with a local phone call.

### ON-LINE SERVICES

Larger, commercial versions of BBSs are known as *on-line services,* or electronic information services. America Online, CompuServe, and Prodigy are three popular on-line services. Others are joining this list, such as Microsoft Network. These services charge for access. On-line services allow you to check stock prices and up-to-the-minute news and weather and perform encyclopedia searches. You can make airline and hotel reservations, shop for almost anything, and in some cases do your banking. You can send messages to software publishers, such as Microsoft, and sometimes get updates to software products.

## Transferring Text and Files

Many of the features of BBSs and on-line services are accessed through interaction with simple text. For example, reading a message from a BBS requires that the host computer send the text of the message to your computer. Making travel reservations, playing an on-line game, and searching an encyclopedia for a specific topic can all be accomplished by exchanging text between computers.

If you want to send a program or data file between computers, however, a special process known as a *file transfer* is used. During a file transfer, data is sent over the modem but does not appear on your screen. The data is transferred without appearing on your screen because programs and most data files are in a binary format, which means that they are in a form that only computers understand. The communications software directs the transfer.

The data is checked for errors by a file transfer protocol. A *file transfer protocol* encodes the data in such a way that if a bad connection or faulty modem causes an error in the data, the communications software will recognize that fact and re-transmit the data. An exception is the case of a text file transfer protocol. Text transfers do not check for errors. For this reason, even when transferring a text file, a binary file transfer protocol should be used.

## Parity and Bits

A modem is very flexible in the way it can modulate and demodulate data. Therefore, the user must know the format of the data being transferred.

To transfer a character over the modem, a group of bits is sent over the phone line one at a time. Some of the bits (usually 8 of them) are used to identify the character being transferred. The bits used to transfer the character are called *data bits.*

Sometimes an extra bit (called a parity bit) is transferred. A *parity bit* allows the modem software to verify that the character was transferred without error. *Stop bits* are necessary to signal the end of the character's transfer. The number of stop bits is usually 1, 1.5, or 2.

Because the transfer of every bit takes time, it is desirable to keep the number of bits to a minimum. Most systems, therefore, do not use a parity bit and use only one stop bit. When files are transferred using a file transfer protocol, error checking is done within the protocol, and a parity bit is not necessary. When text is being transferred without a parity bit, occasionally a character may be incorrect because of line noise or other hardware error. Because most of the text that is transferred is used only to interact with the user, it is rare for an error to cause problems.

## Serial Ports

You have learned that modems send and receive bits one at a time. Devices that deal with bits one at a time are called *serial* devices. Thus, the port to which the modem is attached is a *serial port.* Most serial ports can transfer data much faster than a modem can modulate it.

# The Communication Tool

**E**ach computer that participates in modem communication must be equipped with a modem, have access to a phone line, and have special software for communications. Works provides the special software necessary to communicate over a modem.

The Works Communications tool is a program that allows your computer to connect over a modem to a host computer. The Works Tools tab in the Works Task Launcher dialog box can be used to start the Communications tool. Before you connect to a host computer, you must set up the Communications tool to dial the number and to communicate with the other computer. The files created by the Communications tool save communications settings and phone numbers. Therefore, the Open dialog box can be used to open a communications file to quickly set up the tool.

When the Communications tool is started, the Easy Connect dialog box appears, as shown in Figure 16-2. You can also access the Easy Connect dialog box by clicking the Easy Connect button on the toolbar. Table 16-1 details the contents of the Easy Connect dialog box.

**FIGURE 16-2**
In the Easy Connect dialog box, you enter the country code, area code, phone number, and name of the service you are calling.

| Easy Connect | ? X |
| --- | --- |

To connect to another computer, type in the phone number (with the prefix if necessary), then click OK. Name the service to identify it for future use. When you save this file, it will appear in the list below.

Country code: United States of America (1)    OK

Area code:    Cancel

Phone number:

Name of service:

_____ Or _____

Select one of the services below, and then click OK.
Services:

Delete

Receive an incoming call

**TABLE 16-1**
Contents of the Easy Connect dialog box.

## EASY CONNECT DIALOG BOX

| SETTINGS | DESCRIPTION |
|---|---|
| Country code | Lists the available country codes for international dialing. |
| Area code | Enter the area code of the number you are calling. |
| Phone number | Enter the number of the service or other computer you want to call. |
| Name of service | Enter a name to identify the number. For example, if you are entering a CompuServe access number, enter CompuServe as the Name of service. |
| Services | After you have saved the file, the Name of service appears in the Services box so you can choose it again later to easily dial the same computer. |

ACTIVITY

16-1 **Starting the Communications Tool**

In this activity, you will start the Communications tool.

1. Choose **New** from the **File** menu. The Works Task Launcher appears.

2. Click the **Works Tools** tab.

3. Click the **Communications** button. The Communications tool starts and the Easy Connect dialog box appears, as shown in Figure 16-2.

4. If you are dialing a number within the United States, the Country code box should read *United States of America (1)*. If it does not, click the down arrow at the right of the box and select it from the list.

5. Enter the area code of the number you want to dial in the Area code box. (If the computer has been used before to communicate, your area code may already be present.)

6. Enter the phone number you want to dial in the Phone number box. Include any other numbers necessary, such as a 9 to get an outside line or a 1 for long-distance calls. You can key hyphens, spaces, or parentheses between parts of the number to make it more readable, but they are not necessary. You can also insert commas to create a short pause in dialing. For example, if you must dial 9 to get an outside phone line, you might key the number 9 and a comma as in the following sample phone number entry: 9,555-1234.

**7.** Enter the name of the service in the Name of service box.

**8.** Choose **OK.** The Dial dialog box appears. Choose Cancel so you can change settings before you dial.

**9.** A file in the Communications tool is dis-

played, as shown in Figure 16-3. The title of the file is whatever you entered in the Name of service box. If you don't enter a service then the file name is the phone number.

**10.** Leave the Communications tool open for the next activity.

**FIGURE 16-3**
The Communications tool has its own menus and toolbar used to change communications settings and control communications while connected to another computer.

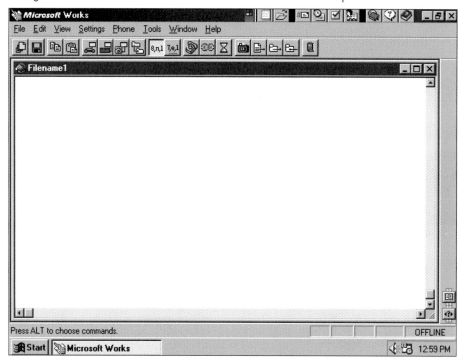

## Changing Settings

A new communications file has default settings that are appropriate in most cases. You may, however, need to change some of these settings to match your equipment or to adapt to the system you are calling.

An almost overwhelming number of settings are available. The major categories of settings are phone, communication, terminal, and transfer. The Settings menu provides a command for each of the categories. There is also a button on the toolbar for each of the four commands. All four commands, however, access the Settings dialog box, shown in Figure 16-4. The Settings dialog box is divided into sections, similar to other dialog boxes you have used in Works.

FIGURE 16-4
The Settings dialog box can be accessed by four different commands.

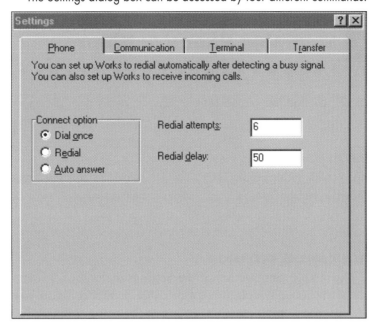

## PHONE SETTINGS

The Phone section of the Settings dialog box, shown in Figure 16-4, allows you to set the phone settings. You can access the Phone section of the Settings dialog box directly by clicking the Phone Settings button on the toolbar. Table 16-2 details the Phone settings.

**TABLE 16-2**
Contents of the Phone section of the Settings dialog box.

| PHONE SETTINGS | |
| --- | --- |
| **SETTING** | **DESCRIPTION** |
| Connect option | Allows you to choose whether you want to automatically redial if the line is busy. You can also set the modem to answer a call. |
| Redial attempts | If Redial is on, this setting specifies the number of times Works will retry the number. |
| Redial delay | If Redial is on, this setting specifies the number of seconds Works will wait between dial attempts. |

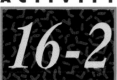

# Changing Phone Settings

In this activity, you will change the phone settings.

1. Choose **Phone** from the **Settings** menu. The Phone section of the Settings dialog box appears, as shown in Figure 16-4.

2. If necessary, change the settings. Your teacher will provide you with the necessary settings.

3. Leave the Settings dialog box open for the next activity.

## COMMUNICATION SETTINGS

The Communication section of the Settings dialog box has an Available devices box to choose which modem or cable connection you want to use. You can access the Communication section of the Settings dialog box directly by clicking the Communication Settings button on the toolbar. Click on Properties to bring up a dialog box with Port Settings, as shown in Figure 16-5. Table 16-3 details the Port Settings.

**FIGURE 16-5**
The Port Settings section in the Communication section of the Settings dialog box allows you to set communications settings, such as the bits per second.

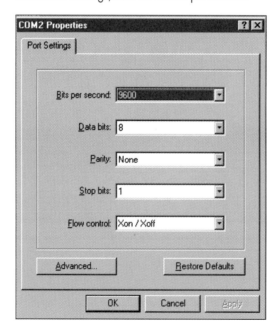

**TABLE 16-3**

Contents of the Port Setting section of the Communication section of the Settings dialog box.

## COMMUNICATION SETTINGS

| SETTING | DESCRIPTION |
|---|---|
| Bits per second | Enter the highest baud rate that your modem and the modem you are calling support. |
| Data bits | Choose the number that matches the computer you are calling. Usually, data bits are set to 8. |
| Parity | Usually, Parity is set to None. |
| Stop bits | Choose the number that matches the computer you are calling. Usually, stop bits are set to 1. |
| Flow control | Flow control, also known as handshaking, is a setting that regulates the way connected computers take turns sending and receiving data. Choose Xon/Xoff when using a modem. If you are connected directly to another computer, choose Hardware. If problems occur with Xon/Xoff while on the modem, try choosing None. |

## ACTIVITY

# 16-3 Changing Communication Settings

In this activity, you will change the communications settings.

1. Click the **Communication** tab in the Settings dialog box.

2. Click **Properties.** The Properties dialog box with the Port Settings section appears, as shown in Figure 16-5.

3. Choose the settings necessary to match the host computer you will be calling. Your teacher will provide you with the necessary settings.

4. Click **OK** to return to the Settings dialog box. Leave it open for the next activity.

### TERMINAL SETTINGS

The Terminal section of the Settings dialog box is shown in Figure 16-6. You can access the Terminal section of the Settings dialog box directly by clicking the Terminal Settings button on the toolbar. Table 16-4 details the Terminal settings.

**FIGURE 16-6**
The Terminal section of the Settings dialog box allows you to specify how the screen will handle the data coming over the modem.

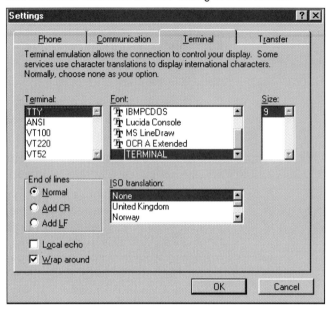

**TABLE 16-4**
Selected options in the Terminal section of the Settings dialog box.

## TERMINAL SETTINGS

| SETTING | DESCRIPTION |
| --- | --- |
| Terminal | Choose either VT100 or ANSI emulation. If the default of VT100 does not work, choose ANSI. If the system you are calling does not support any emulation, choose TTY. |
| End of Lines | If lines of text coming over the modem do not always begin at the left margin, choose Add CR. If the lines overwrite one another, choose Add LF to add a line feed code to each line. |
| Local echo | If what you key when connected to another computer does not appear on your screen, turn this option on. If each character you key appears twice, turn this option off. |
| Wrap around | This option should normally be on. When the option is on, any text that happens to extend past the right edge of the window will wrap to the next line so that it can be seen. |
| ISO Translation | This option is available to automatically translate special international characters if you are connecting to a computer in a foreign country. |
| Font | List of fonts you can use to display information on the screen. |
| Size | List of font sizes you can use to display information on the screen. |

ACTIVITY

# 16-4 Changing Terminal Settings

● ● ● ● ● ● ● ● ● ● ● ● ● ● ● ● ● ● ● ● ● ● ● ● ● ● ● ● ● ● ● ● ● ● ●

In this activity, you will change the terminal settings.

**1.** Click the **Terminal** tab of the Settings dialog box.

**2.** Choose the settings that your teacher provides for you.

**3.** Choose **OK.** You will use the Transfer section of the dialog box later in the chapter.

**4.** Leave the Communications tool open for the next activity.

## Connecting

After the settings are correct, you can place the call and connect to the other computer. To place the call, click the Dial/Hangup button on the toolbar; then, choose Dial in the Dial dialog box (shown in Figure 16-7.) The Dial Status box appears (similar to Figure 16-8) as the modem dials the phone and waits for a connection. Your modem should have a speaker that lets you listen to the dialing and connection. When the computer you are calling answers, you will hear a mixture of tones coming from both ends of the line. After the connection is made, the speaker will turn off and you will see text on the screen coming from the computer you have called.

Most BBSs and on-line services will prompt you for your name and a password for identification. Entering this information is called *logging on* to a system. In most cases, the process of logging on will be followed by a menu to guide your use of the system.

Disconnecting from a host computer involves letting the host know you are hanging up and then closing the connection from the Communications tool. If you are connected to a friend's computer rather than to a BBS or an on-line service, you can again click the Dial/Hangup button on the toolbar to disconnect. If you are connected to a BBS or an on-line service, however, you should follow the disconnect procedure provided by the system you have called. Disconnecting is sometimes referred to as *logging off* or signing off.

It is more courteous to log off rather than just hang up. Logging off ensures that the host system properly resets for the next caller. In addition, if you are paying for access to the host system, logging off ensures that you are not charged for time after you hang up.

ACTIVITY

# *16-5*  Connecting, Logging On, and Logging Off

● ● ● ● ● ● ● ● ● ● ● ● ● ● ● ● ● ● ● ● ● ● ● ● ● ● ● ● ● ● ●

In this activity, you will connect to a host computer, interact with it, and log off.

1. Click the **Dial/Hangup** button on the toolbar. The Dial dialog box appears, similar to the one in Figure 16-7.

2. Click **Dial.**

3. A Dial Status dialog box appears, similar to the one shown in Figure 16-8, as the modem dials the number and waits for a connection.

4. If the connection was properly made, you will see text appearing in the communications window coming from the host computer. Text you key in response to prompts from the host should also be visible on your screen. Follow the prompting of the host computer.

5. When you have finished using the system you called, follow that system's procedure for logging off. Most systems provide a menu option for logging off or require that you key **BYE**. Choose the option and allow the host computer to begin logging you off.

6. When the system appears to have stopped sending text, NO CARRIER has appeared

**FIGURE 16-7**
The Dial dialog box appears so you can verify the phone number that you are dialing.

**FIGURE 16-8**
The Dial Status dialog box appears and shows the status of the call as the modem makes a connection to the host computer.

on your screen, or the lights on the modem indicate that the modems are no longer connected, click the **Dial/Hangup** button. A dialog box will appear asking if it is okay to disconnect. Click **OK.**

7. Leave the Communications tool open for the next activity.

## Saving a Communications File

Saving a communications file is the same as saving any other Works file. A communications file does not store visible data for you like a word processor, spreadsheet, or database document does. A communications file stores the settings for a particular kind of task you do with your modem. For example, suppose you regularly call a certain local BBS. You can enter the phone number and other required settings one time and save the settings as a communications file. Each time you want to connect to that BBS, you can open that communications file and be ready to dial.

ACTIVITY

 **Saving a Communications File**

● ● ● ● ● ● ● ● ● ● ● ● ● ● ● ● ● ● ● ● ● ● ● ● ● ● ● ● ● ● ● ●

In this activity, you will save the current settings by saving the file.

1. Choose **Save As** from the **File** menu. The Save As dialog box appears.

2. Save the file using a name that describes the host system to which you connected.

3. Close the file.

## Sending and Receiving Files

Sending a data file or program to another computer requires that a file transfer be used. Earlier in this chapter, you learned that files are transferred using file transfer protocols.

The Communications tool provides four protocols: Kermit, XModem/CRC, YModem, and ZModem. These protocols will transfer text or binary files and will correct any errors detected in the transfer.

Before sending or receiving a file, choose the protocol you want to use from the Transfer section of the Settings dialog box, shown in Figure 16-9. You can access the Transfer section of the Settings dialog box directly by clicking the Transfer Settings button on the toolbar.

**FIGURE 16-9**
Choose a transfer protocol that is
supported by the system you are calling.

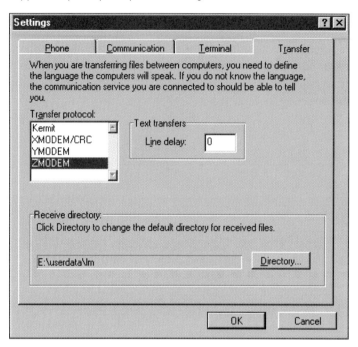

Sending a file is called ***uploading.*** To send a file, choose Send File from the Tools menu or click the Send Binary File button on the toolbar. A dialog box will appear to allow you to choose the file you want to send. When you choose a file, the sending begins. During the transfer, you will be able to see the progress.

Receiving a file is called ***downloading.*** To receive a file, choose Receive File from the Tools menu or click the Receive Binary File button on the toolbar. The software will immediately wait to receive a file, and the Receive File status box like the one in Figure 16-10 will appear.

To download a file to a disk or a directory other than the default one, you need to choose the path of the incoming file. Choose Transfer from the Settings menu. Then, click Directory and choose the location where you want to save the file you are downloading.

You must be careful not to use the modem to transfer or distribute programs or data illegally. It is illegal to give a copy of a program to another computer user unless you have the permission of the program's author to do so. The same rule may apply to some data. Programs like Microsoft Works are protected by copyright law. There are severe penalties for distributing programs illegally, whether by modem or disk.

**FIGURE 16-10**
The Receive File status box displayed during a
download gives the same status information as
the Send File status box displayed during an upload.

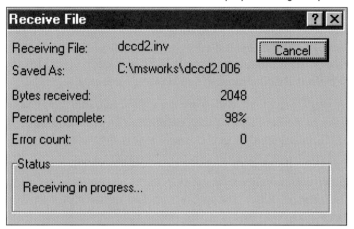

# Capturing Text

**A**s you have learned, much of the interaction with a host computer involves text flowing onto your screen. Sometimes there may be long messages that you want to read or print out to read later. *Capturing text* will let you gather all the text of a communications session into one file. After the session is over, the text can be loaded into a word processor where you can read, edit, or print it.

Capturing text is a good way to keep a record of a communications session. For example, if you need up-to-date stock prices for a report, you can access the stock prices from an on-line service, capture the text, load the captured text into your word processor, and copy the numbers you need for your report without rekeying them. The task is made quicker and more accurate because of text capturing.

Choose Capture Text from the Tools menu. You will be prompted for a filename for the captured text. From that point on in the session, the text shown in the communications window will be saved to the text file. When you are ready to quit saving the text, choose End Capture Text from the Tools menu or click the Capture Text button on the toolbar.

# Summary

■ Modem communication is the process of transmitting information from computer to computer over telephone lines. The device at the heart of modem communication is the modem, which converts computer signals so that they can be transmitted over phone lines. Baud rate is the speed at which a modem modulates signals. Bits per second (BPS) is the measure of usable bits that the modem sends or receives in a second.

■ When you place a call with a modem, the computer you connect with is the host computer. The calling computer, or your computer, is the terminal. Terminal emulation is the way text is displayed on the screen.

■ Modems can be used to connect two computers directly, to connect one computer with a bulletin board system, or to connect one computer to an on-line service. When sending a file, file transfer protocols encode the data in such a way that if a bad connection or faulty modem causes an error in the data, the error will be corrected. When data is transferred over a modem, bits are sent one at a time. Some of the bits are data bits, some are parity bits, and some are stop bits.

■ The Works Communications tool allows a computer equipped with a modem to connect to a host computer. A new communications file has default settings that are appropriate in most cases. You can, however, change terminal, communication, and phone settings.

■ Saving a communications file is the same as saving any other Works file. Files are sent and received using file transfer protocols. Text can be captured during a communications session.

● ● ● ● ● ● ● ● ● ● ● ●

## TRUE/FALSE

**Circle T or F to show whether the statement is true or false.**

**T    F    1.** Modem communication is the process of transmitting information from one computer to another over telephone lines.

**T    F    2.** The word modem is a short form of modulator/demodulator.

**T    F    3.** A file transfer is used to regulate the way connected computers take turns sending and receiving information.

**T    F    4.** Parity bits allow the modem software to verify that characters are transferred without error.

**T    F    5.** Serial describes a device that sends data eight bits at a time.

**T    F    6.** The phone number the modem is to dial is entered in the Easy Connect dialog box.

**T    F    7.** One type of terminal emulation is VT100.

**T    F    8.** You save a communications file by choosing Save File from the Settings menu.

**T    F    9.** Sending a file to a host computer is called downloading.

**T    F    10.** Capturing text will let you gather all the text of a communications session into one file.

## COMPLETION

**Write the correct answer in the space provided.**

1. What is telecommunication?

_____

_____

2. Which is more descriptive from a computer user's standpoint, bits per second or baud?

_____

_____

3. Name two things you can do by accessing a typical on-line service.

_____

_____

4. What does a file transfer protocol do?

_____

_____

5. What are the bits that transfer actual characters called?

_____

_____

6. Name two ways you can access the Phone section of the Settings dialog box.

_____

_____

7. What character can be inserted in a phone number in the Phone dialog box to create a pause in the dialing?

_____

_____

8. What is the term used for disconnecting from a bulletin board system or an on-line service?

_____

_____

9. List three of the four file transfer protocols supported by the Works Communications tool.

_____

_____

10. When might you want to capture the text of a communications session into a file?

_____

_____

# INTEGRATION AND SIMULATION

# INTEGRATION BASICS

## OBJECTIVES
### When you complete this chapter, you will be able to:

1.  Understand the concept of integration.

2.  Cut, copy, and paste among documents.

3.  Use linking to integrate documents.

4.  Create a form letter.

5.  Create mailing labels.

# *Introduction to Integration*

**A**s you have already learned earlier in this text, Works 4.0 for Windows 95 is an integrated program. *Integration* refers to using more than one Works tool to complete a project. This means that you can use information created in a spreadsheet to complete a report in the word processor. Or you can use information from a database to create form letters in the word processor. Tables from the word processor can become spreadsheet data. It is just as easy to transfer data from a database to a spreadsheet as to transfer it to another database document.

The value of an integrated program like Works is that sharing data among tools is easy. In this chapter, you will explore several ways to share data among the Works tools. The easiest approach is simply to cut, copy, and paste among the tools. Works also allows you to use a process called *linking* to integrate data between the spreadsheet and the word processor. When you use linking to insert data from a spreadsheet into a word processor document, any change to the spreadsheet will be reflected in the word processor document as well. Finally, you will explore how easy it is to create form letters and mailing labels by using database information in a word processor document.

# *Moving and Copying Data between Documents*

**Y**ou have already learned how easy it is to move and copy data among documents created in any one of the Works tools using the Cut, Copy, and Paste commands. However, the process of moving data among different tools varies, depending on what tools are involved. Word processor, spreadsheet, and database documents have unique formats. For example, data from a spreadsheet is arranged in cells, information in a database is collected in fields, and text in a word processor document does not follow any particular format. When you move data among tools, Works changes the format of the information you are moving so that it may be used in the destination document.

## Spreadsheet to Word Processor

A common integration operation is to paste numbers from a spreadsheet into a word processor document. When spreadsheet data is copied to a word processor document, Works automatically uses tabs to separate the spreadsheet information into columns.

**ACTIVITY**

## Copying from the Spreadsheet to the Word Processor

Your template disk contains two files relating to a ski trip that Stephen and Gabriel are planning. In this activity, you will copy the spreadsheet data from the *Ski cost* spreadsheet and paste it into the *Ski trip* letter. By integrating the documents, Stephen can send one page instead of two pages to Gabriel.

1. From your template disk, open *Ski trip* from the *Gabriel* folder, which is in the *Letters* folder.

2. Choose **Open** from the **File** menu.

3. Open *Ski cost*, also in the *Gabriel* folder. Your screen should resemble Figure 17-1.

4. Highlight the data in the spreadsheet from Cell A1 to Cell C14.

5. Click the **Copy** button on the toolbar.

6. To bring the letter to Gabriel to the front, choose **1 Ski trip** from the Window menu.

7. Place the cursor between the first and second paragraphs.

8. Click the **Paste** button on the toolbar. The data from the spreadsheet appears in the letter.

9. Insert a blank line before and after the spreadsheet data.

**10.** Save *Ski trip* on your data disk as *Ski letter.*

**11.** Print *Ski letter* and close it.

**12.** Save *Ski cost* on your data disk as *Ski data* and leave it on the screen for the next activity.

**FIGURE 17-1**
In preparation for integrating data from a spreadsheet to a word processor document, both documents are opened.

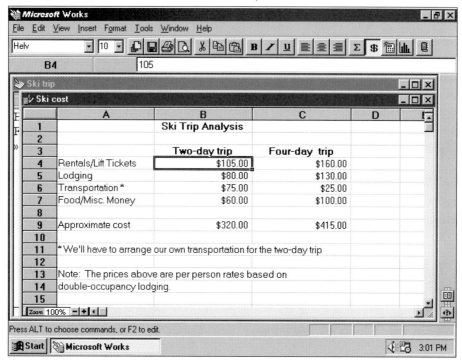

## Word Processor to Spreadsheet

Suppose you want to move data from a table in a report to the spreadsheet in order to make calculations using the data. Works handles pasting into a spreadsheet from the word processor in one of two ways. If the text from the word processor is set up as a table, with data separated by tabs, the spreadsheet will separate the text into separate cells in the spreadsheet. If the text is in a single block, all of the text will be pasted into the currently highlighted cell of the spreadsheet.

## Word Processor to Database

Suppose you have been given a list of names and addresses in a word processor file. The names need to be entered into a database. Pasting into a database from the word processor is similar to pasting into a spreadsheet from the word processor. If the text from the word processor is set up as a table, with data separated by tabs, the database will separate the text into fields. Each line will be entered as a separate record. If the text is in a single block, all of the text will be pasted into the currently highlighted field.

## Spreadsheet to Database

Pasting into a database from a spreadsheet is essentially the same as pasting from a spreadsheet to a spreadsheet. The cells cut or copied from the spreadsheet will appear in the database beginning with the highlighted entry.

## Database to Spreadsheet

When you paste into a spreadsheet from a database, the field entries will be pasted into the spreadsheet columns, and the records will be pasted into the rows.

## Database to Word Processor

Data from a database is pasted into the word processor the same way spreadsheet data is pasted into the word processor. The data is formatted with tabs when it enters the word processor. This feature could be used to create a table in the word processor, based on data in a database.

# *The Missing Link*

**P**asting data from one document into another can be useful. There will be times, however, when the data you are pasting may change periodically. Suppose it is your job as treasurer of an organization to file a monthly financial report. Your report is basically the same each month except for the month's cash flow numbers. You keep the cash flow data up to date in a spreadsheet. Using the copying and pasting techniques discussed above, you would have to copy the latest spreadsheet numbers and paste them into your word processor document each month.

There is an easier way. Instead of pasting the data manually each time, the Paste Special command can be used to link the two documents. *Linking* will automatically paste the latest figures from your spreadsheet into your report. Each time the word processor document is opened, you have the opportunity to update the document with the latest spreadsheet data.

Figure 17-2 shows the Paste Special dialog box that appears when data from a Works spreadsheet is pasted into a word processor document. The Paste Link option places the spreadsheet data into the document and creates the link to the actual spreadsheet.

**FIGURE 17-2**
The Paste Special dialog box allows spreadsheet
data to be pasted into a word processor document.

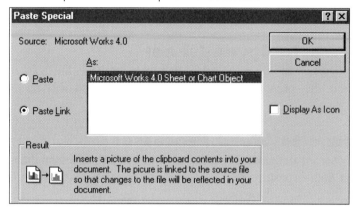

 **Linking**

In this activity, you will link the data from the *Ski data* spreadsheet into the *Ski trip* document. *Ski data* should be on your screen.

1. Open *Ski trip* from the *Gabriel* folder in the *Letters* folder of your template disk.

2. Switch to *Ski data* and highlight Cells A1 through C14, if they are not already highlighted. Copy the cells and switch back to *Ski trip*.

3. Place the cursor between the first and second paragraphs.

4. Choose **Paste Special** from the **Edit** menu. The Paste Special dialog box appears.

5. Click **Paste Link.** The Paste Special dialog box should look similar to Figure 17-2.

6. Click **OK.** The spreadsheet data appears in the document. The data is linked to *Ski data*. Any changes made to *Ski data* will be reflected in *Ski trip*.

7. Insert one blank line above and one blank line below the linked data.

8. Save *Ski trip* on your data disk as *Ski link*.

9. Print *Ski link* and close it.

10. Save *Ski data* and leave it on the screen for the next activity.

Changes made in the *Ski data* spreadsheet can become a part of the *Ski link* letter when the letter is opened. When you open *Ski link,* you will have the opportunity to update the document with the latest spreadsheet data.

## ACTIVITY 17-3 **Updating a Linked Document**

In this activity, you will update the *Ski data* spreadsheet data. You will then open *Ski link* and update the letter to Gabriel with the new data. *Ski data* should be on your screen.

1. Change the cost of transportation to $95 for the two-day trip and $35 for the four-day trip.

2. Save *Ski data*.

3. Open *Ski link* from your data disk. You will be asked whether you want to update links.

4. Click **Yes.** *Ski link* appears.

5. Save as *Ski link 2* and print. Look at the printout to see that the transportation costs were updated.

6. Open *Ski letter.* Scroll down until the transportation costs are in view. The data was not updated in *Ski letter* because the data was not linked.

7. Close all three files.

# Form Letters

**A**nother way to integrate Works tools is to print form letters. A ***form letter*** is a word processor document that uses information from a database in specified areas to personalize a document.

For example, you might send a letter to all of the members of a club using a form letter. The information is the same in each letter, but the names will be different in each case. Each printed letter will carry the name of a different member of the club. One letter may begin "Dear Michael" and another "Dear Kari."

## Creating a Form Letter

To create form letters, you integrate information from a database with a document from the word processor. You then insert the field names in the word processor document where you want to print the information from the database. The field names you place in the word processing document are enclosed in angle brackets (<< Field Name >>), as shown in Figure 17-3.

**FIGURE 17-3**
Database fields can be inserted anywhere in a word processor document.

Works ——————

Users of ——————

Maryland ——————————
678 Thornfield Rd.
Baltimore, MD 21229


February 13, 19--

<<Title>> <<First Name>> <<Last Name>>
<<Address>>
<<City>>, <<St>> <<ZIP Code>>

Dear <<First Name>>:

I know I do not have to tell you the benefits of membership in WUM. The growth our group has experienced in the last year is evidence of the value WUM offers users of integrated programs.

Now WUM is an even better value! Because of the success of the group, dues have been lowered. You will continue to receive our award-winning newsletter, *A WUM Response*, and access to our 24-hour computer bulletin board system. All of the quality services you have come to expect from WUM have not changed. Only the price is on the decline.

Dues this year are <<Dues>>. Our records indicate that you have paid <<Paid>> and owe a balance of <<Balance>>. Please remit the balance to the address on this letterhead as soon as possible.

We expect our lower dues to attract even more members. Remember to give our new members a WUM welcome!

Yours truly,


Shae Bradshaw
President

**ACTIVITY**

*17-4*

## Loading Documents for a Form Letter

In this activity, you will load a database and a word processor document to be used for form letters.

1. Open *Activity 17-4 DB* from your template disk.

**2.** Use the scroll bars to view all of the fields in the database.

**3.** Open *Activity 17-4 WP* from your template disk. Figure 17-3 shows where database

fields have been inserted.

**4.** Leave both files on the screen for the next activity.

To insert a field from the database, choose the Database Field command from the Insert menu. The Insert Field dialog box will appear, as shown in Figure 17-4. The bottom of the dialog box allows you to choose the database from which the form letter will draw its information. The top of the dialog box allows you to choose which field from the database you want to insert.

**FIGURE 17-4**

The Insert Field dialog box inserts database fields into a word processor document.

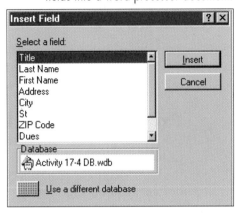

# Inserting Database Fields

In this activity, you will insert additional database fields into the form letter. *Activity 17-4 WP* should be displayed on your screen.

**1.** Position the cursor immediately before the word *We* in the first sentence of the last paragraph in the letter.

**2.** Start a new paragraph before the last paragraph by keying **Dues this year are**. (Do not key the period.)

**3.** Choose **Database Field** from the **Insert** menu. (If a First-time Help screen appears,

click OK.) The Insert Field dialog box appears.

**4.** Click **Use a different database.**

**5.** In the Select a database box, highlight **Activity 17-4 DB.wdb** and click **OK.**

**6.** The fields from *Activity 17-4 DB* appear, as shown in Figure 17-4.

**7.** In the Select a field box, highlight **Dues** and click **Insert.** The field will appear in your document as <<Dues>>. Click **Close.**

**8.** Backspace to delete the space after <<Dues>> and key a period to end the sentence. Key a space. Then key **Our records indicate that you have paid**. (Do not key a period.)

**9.** Choose **Database Field** from the **Insert** menu. Scroll down in the <u>S</u>elect a field box to click **Paid.** Click <u>I</u>**nsert.** Click **Close.**

**10.** Key **and owe a balance of**. (Do not key a period.)

**11.** Insert the Balance field.

**12.** Backspace to delete the space after <<Balance>>. Then key a period after the Balance field. Key a space. Key the following sentence (and the period) to complete the paragraph: **Please remit the balance to the address on this letterhead as soon as possible.**

**13.** Press **Enter** twice. Adjust the spacing around the paragraph if necessary.

**14.** Save the document on your data disk as *WUM*. Leave *WUM* on the screen for the next activity.

## Previewing and Printing the Form Letters

After the fields are inserted, the form letters are ready to print. The Print dialog box, shown in Figure 17-5, has a check box called *Print Merge*. When the Print Merge check box is chosen, data from the database is inserted into the document during printing.

**FIGURE 17-5**
The Print dialog box's Print Merge check box is used when printing form letters.

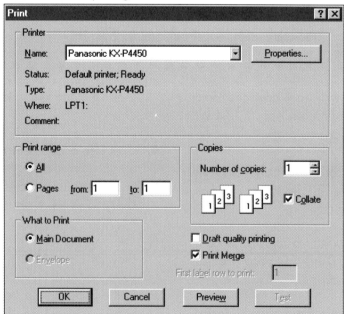

**ACTIVITY**

# 17-6

## Previewing and Printing Form Letters

• • • • • • • • • • • • • • • • • • • • • • • • • • • • • • • • • • • • •

In this activity, you will preview and print the form letters. *WUM* should be on your screen.

1.  Choose **Print** from the **File** menu.

2.  Click the **Preview** button. A prompt appears asking if you want to preview all records in the database.

3.  Click **OK.** The first letter appears on the screen.

4.  Click **Zoom In** twice. Your screen should look similar to Figure 17-6.

5.  Click the **Next** button to see the next letter.

Notice that the name, address, and payment information changes with each letter.

6.  Click the **Next** button again to see the last letter.

7.  Click **Print.** The Print dialog box appears with the Print Merge option checked. (See Figure 17-5.)

8.  Click **OK** to print the form letters. When a prompt appears asking if you want to print all records, click **OK.**

9.  Save and close *WUM.* Leave *Activity 17-4 DB* on the screen for the next activity.

**FIGURE 17-6**
Form letters can be previewed before printing.

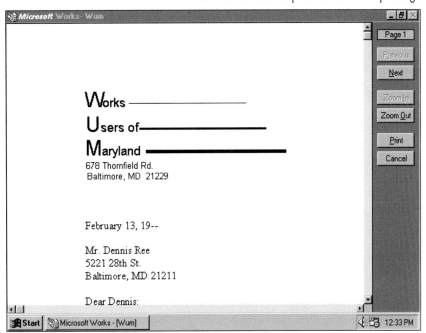

# *Mailing Labels*

**W**orks makes it easy to create mailing labels from any database that has name and address information. Creating mailing labels involves integrating the word processor and database tools. In fact, creating mailing labels is very similar to creating form letters. The main difference is that mailing labels place information from more than one record on the same word processor page. This is because mailing labels usually come in sheets that have as many as 30 labels per page.

Works provides special dialog boxes for creating mailing labels. The Labels dialog box, shown in Figure 17-7, lets you choose whether you will be creating labels with different information or multiple copies of the same label. When you make your choice, the Labels: Unsaved Document dialog box appears, similar to Figure 17-8. Works will create your mailing labels based on the information you provide in this dialog box, such as label type and fields.

**FIGURE 17-7**
In the Labels dialog box you can choose the type of label you want.

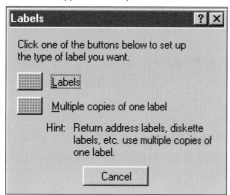

**FIGURE 17-8**
The Labels: Unsaved Document dialog box helps set up and create your mailing labels.

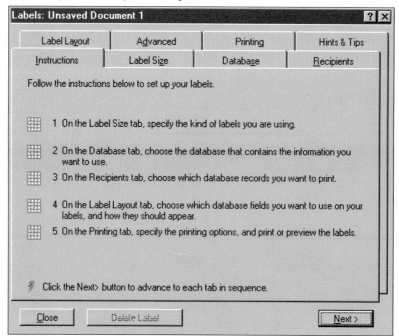

## ACTIVITY

# 17-7 Creating Mailing Labels

In this activity, you will create mailing labels using the Labels dialog boxes. *Activity 17-4 DB* should be on your screen.

1. Choose **Labels** from the **Tools** menu. A new word processing document opens and the Labels dialog box appears.

2. Click **Labels.** The Labels: Unsaved Document 1 dialog box appears.

3. Click the **Label Size** tab.

4. In the Choose a label size box, scroll down to highlight **Avery 5160 (2 5/8" x 1"),** as shown in Figure 17-9.

5. Click the **Recipients** tab. **All records in the database** should be chosen.

6. Click the **Label Layout** tab.

7. **Title** should be highlighted in the Choose a field box. Click **Add Field.**

**FIGURE 17-9**
You can print mailing labels on any size label you choose.

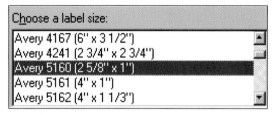

8. Highlight **First Name** in the Choose a field box. Click **Add Field.**

9. Highlight **Last Name** and click **Add Field.**

10. Click **New Line** to move the cursor to the next line in the Label Layout box.

11. Continue to add fields to make the Label layout box look similar to Figure 17-10. After you have added all the fields, add a comma between the City and St fields.

**FIGURE 17-10**
Fields selected in the Choose a field box appear in the Label layout box.

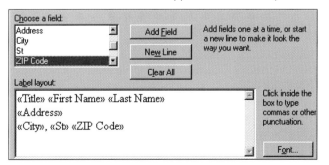

**12.** Click the **Printing** tab. Click **Preview** to preview the labels. A prompt appears asking if you want to preview all records in the database. Click **OK.**

**13.** Click **Zoom In** to view the labels more clearly.

**14.** Click **Print.** The Print dialog box appears. Click **OK.**

**15.** A prompt appears asking if you want to print all the records. Click **OK.**

**16.** Click **Close.** The Unsaved Document appears with a label on it. Save the *Unsaved Document* on your data disk as *Labels* and close. Close *Activity 17-4 DB* without saving changes.

# *Summary*

- Integration refers to using more than one of the Works tools to create a document. Data can be copied and pasted among documents or linked to ensure that data is up to date.

- A common form of integration is to paste numbers from a spreadsheet into a word processor document. Data can be copied and pasted between other types of documents as well. Works performs special operations to give you the best conversion of your data.

- Spreadsheet data can be linked to a word processor document using the Paste Special command. Each time the word processor document is opened, you have the opportunity to update the document with the latest spreadsheet data.

- Form letters combine data from a database into word processor documents. Works allows you to insert fields from a database anywhere in a word processor document. You can then print a document for each entry in your database.

- Mailing labels are created in a way similar to form letters. The Labels dialog boxes help you create the label and format the page to match your label style.

● ● ● ● ● ● ● ● ● ● ● ● ●

# REVIEW ACTIVITIES

## TRUE/FALSE

**Circle T or F to show whether the statement is true or false.**

T  F  1. Copying spreadsheet data into a word processor document is one example of integration.

T  F  2. The value of an integrated program like Works is that sharing data among the tools is easy.

T  F  3. Data can be copied and pasted among any of the Works tools.

T  F  4. Works does not change the format of data copied and pasted among the tools.

T  F  5. Linking is performed using the Copy Special command.

T  F  6. Linking always updates the link when the document with the link is opened.

T  F  7. Form letters get their data from spreadsheets.

T  F  8. The Insert Field dialog box is where you choose the fields to be inserted in a form letter.

T  F  9. Form letters can be previewed before being printed.

T  F  10. Creating mailing labels is similar to creating form letters.

## COMPLETION

**Write the correct answer in the space provided.**

1. What is the term for using more than one Works tool to create a document?

_____

_____

2. Give an example of a document that could be created using integration.

_____

_____

3. Give an example of when you might copy data from a word processor document to a spreadsheet.

_____

_____

4. Give an example of when you might copy data from a word processor document to a database.

_____

_____

5. What commands are used to place data from a database into a spreadsheet?

_____

_____

6. What does Works do to spreadsheet data when it is pasted into a word processor document?

_____

_____

7. Give an example of a document that could use linking effectively.

_____

_____

8. What commands allow you to link spreadsheet data into a word processor document?

_____

_____

9. What is a form letter?

_____

_____

10. What tab in the Labels: Unsaved Document dialog box is used to add fields to the labels?

_____

_____

# REINFORCEMENT APPLICATIONS

## application 17-1

**In this application, you will use Cut, Copy, and Paste to move and copy data among documents.**

1. Open *Application 17-1* from your template disk.

2. Highlight the names and addresses of both Oscar Alvarado and Marcy Bell. Do not include their titles or prizes. Highlight only the fields from First Name to ZIP Code. Choose Copy from the Edit menu.

3. Create a new word processor document. Paste the database data into the document. Notice how the fields are separated by tabs.

4. Create a new spreadsheet document. Paste the database data into the spreadsheet. Notice how each field is placed in a separate cell.

5. Close all three files. Do not save the files.

## application 17-2

**In this application, you will use linking to create a report for the members of a science group that is raising funds for a trip.**

1. Open *Application 17-2 SS* from your template disk. The number in Cell D4 of the spreadsheet is the total amount of money raised for the science trip. The money is to be divided among the 11 students who are going on the trip. The spreadsheet takes the total funds raised and divides it by the number of students to calculate the portion of the trip paid for by the fundraiser. Then the remaining balance is calculated to show the students how much of the cost they will be responsible for at the current level of funding. As the total funds raised grow, each student's portion of the cost decreases.

2. Open *Application 17-2 WP* from your template disk.

3. Make *Application 17-2 SS* the active window. Highlight Cell D3. Choose Copy from the Edit menu.

4. Make *Application 17-2 WP* the active window. Position the cursor to the right of the word *are*. Press the spacebar once. Use Paste Special to link the number from the spreadsheet.

5. Key the remainder of the first sentence to match Figure 17-11. Key the rest of the report, inserting the spreadsheet links using the same procedure followed in Steps 3 and 4. Be sure to copy the correct cells from the spreadsheet.

6. Save the word processor document as *Trip report* on your data disk. Save the spreadsheet as *Trip fund* on your data disk. Experiment with changing numbers in the spreadsheet to see the changes reflected in the report. Change the figures back to those in Figure 17-11. Print the report. Save and close both files.

**FIGURE 17-11**

```
 . . . . . . . . 1 . . . . . . . . 2 . . . . . . . . 3 . . . . . . . . 4 . . . . . . . . 5 . . . . . .
```

**Science Trip Fund Raising Report**
***date***

As of today, there are [ 11 ] members planning to attend this year's science trip. Our fundraiser has raised [ $1,256.38 ] to date. Members can now expect to receive [ $114.22 ] of the [ $225.00 ] needed to pay for the trip, leaving [ $110.78 ] to be paid by each attending member.

*a  p  p  l  i  c  a  t  i  o  n        1  7  -  3*

**In this application, you will draft a letter to notify customers in a database that they have won a prize in a promotional drawing. Your template disk includes a database of names, addresses, and prizes to be awarded in a file named *Application 17-1*. You are to complete the following.**

1. Add your own name, address, and the prize you would like to be awarded to the *Application 17-1* database.

2. Create a form letter that notifies the customers in the database of the prizes they have been awarded. Be sure to include the:

   a. name of the business awarding prizes

   b. address where the prize can be claimed

   c. hours of the business

   Make sure you insert the database fields in all appropriate places.

3. Ask your teacher if you should print your form letters or preview them on the screen.

4. Save the database as *Winners* and save the letter as *Prize letter*. Close both files.

# A SIMULATION: NEW YEAR'S EVE DINNER DANCE

CHAPTER *18*

# *Background*

**T**he Evergreen Youth Club has 31 members who work in the community on many different projects. They help keep the city park clean, raise money for local charities, and improve their own leadership skills.

This New Year's Eve, the club is hosting a dinner dance at the Evergreen Community Center. The club members will plan the event, make arrangements for entertainment and food, decorate the community center, and sell tickets and sponsorships. Although the club has organized various types of dinners and leisure activities in the past, this is the first year for the New Year's Eve Dinner Dance. The theme is Hawaiian; therefore, everyone will be encouraged to dress and think Hawaiian.

The purpose of the event is to offer a place for youth to have fun on New Year's Eve without alcohol and without driving on the dangerous streets. Tickets will be $15 each and will include dinner, dancing, refreshments, and New Year's party favors. Money raised from the event will fund the club's trip to the state capital next summer.

You have been elected chair of the event. Your responsibilities are to make sure committees do their jobs, to answer questions, and to take care of last-minute arrangements or problems that arise. Trent Locke is the club's advisor. He will check with you periodically about the progress of the event.

## November 13

Last week at the club's meeting, you circulated a committee sign-up sheet and asked everyone to volunteer to work on a committee or to be a committee chair. Based on the sign-ups, create a committee list to give to committee chairs.

1.  Key a Committee List from the committee sign-up sheet shown in Figure 18-1. Make the changes indicated by the proofreader's marks. If you are unfamiliar with proofreader's marks, see Appendix B for a list of commonly used marks.

**FIGURE 18-1**

---

**Evergreen Youth Club**
New Year's Eve Dinner Dance
Committee Sign-up Sheet

DS

**Ticket sales Committee**
Sell at least 85 tickets. Report ticket sales to Event Chair by (Dec) 2~~0~~. Turn in money to Finance chair.
~~Take up tickets at the event.~~
Chair: *Hunter Aldridge*
1. *Cecilia Haddock*          } delete underlines
2. *Sidney Lewis*
3. *Jude Acker*

**Decorations Committee**
Plan decorations with a Hawaiian theme. Submit expenses to Finance committee. Decorate Community
Center before the event. Clean up decorations after the event.
Chair: *Ashley Wyatt* (and)
1. *Te Yung*
2. *Shane Hunter*          } delete underlines
3. *Erica Katz*

**Program Committee**
Plan the program for the evening by December 1. Get musicians (or disc jockey) and party favors—such as
party hats, confetti, and nonalcoholic champagne. Submit expenses to Finance committee.
Chair: *Paul Sartor*
1. *Danielle Rogers*
2. *Mike Miller*          } delete underlines
3. *Heather Stone*

**Food Committee**
Plan the dinner menu and refreshments by December 10. Get bids from three caterers to submit to Event
committee. Submit expenses to Finance committee.
Chair: *Michelle Poole*
1. *Vera Cortez*
2. *Belinda Mires*          } delete underlines
3. *Doug Johnson*

**Finance Committee**
Accept receipts for reimbursement and pay bills. By January 15, ~~create~~ submit an end report that shows income (to Event Chair)
and expenses.
Chair: *Glenn Glass*
1. *Aubrey Eagle*          } delete underlines
2. *Katie Clements*

**Sponsorship Committee**
By December 10, sign up at least five corporations, businesses, or individuals to sponsor the event with
$200 sponsorships. Buy thank-you gifts for sponsors.
Chair: *Cody Carrizales*
1. *Mia Jackson*
2. *Samantha Bledsoe*          } delete underlines
3. *Simon Rodriguez*

---

2. Save the file as *Committee List.*

3. Change all margins to .75 inches.

4. Adjust font size to make sure all data fits on one page.

5. Save, print, and close.

# November 16

Paul Sartor, chair of the Program Committee, called you to ask about the phone numbers and addresses of the people on his committee. You decide it would be helpful if all committee chairs had this information about their committee members. Use the sign-up sheet and the club's roster to create a database that includes the names, addresses, and phone numbers of all committee members. You can give each committee chair his or her committee list at the meeting on November 20. (Do not enter records for members who are not on a committee.)

1. Create the following fields and format them as indicated.

   | Field | Format |
   |---|---|
   | First Name | General |
   | Last Name | General |
   | Address | General |
   | City | General |
   | State/Province | General |
   | Postal Code | Number, 1234.56, 0 decimals |
   | Telephone | Number, 1234.56, 0 decimals |
   | Committee | General |

2. In List view, enter records from the roster in Figure 18-2. Adjust field widths to best fit. Use Fill Down to enter the city and state data.

3. Save the file as *Committee Members*.

4. Hide the City and State/Province fields.

5. In List view, create a filter named Food to show only members on the Food Committee.

6. Print the list.

7. Create appropriately named filters and print the lists for the other five committees.

8. Save and close.

**FIGURE 18-2**

**Evergreen Youth Club Membership Roster**

Jude Acker *Ticket Sales*
79 Treetop Boulevard
Evergreen, CO 80498-9710
303-555-7700

Hunter Aldridge *Ticket Sales*
9345 Snow Hill
Evergreen, CO 80498-9340
303-555-8779

Samantha Bledsoe *Sponsorship*
4551 Rocky Road
Evergreen, CO 80499-4511
303-555-6632

Cody Carrizales *Sponsorship*
9212 Bear Road
Evergreen, CO 80498-9121
303-555-4739

Paul Chen
3445 West Willow
Evergreen, CO 80498-3334
303-555-9911

Katie Clements *Finance*
8776 Hunter's Way
Evergreen, CO 80499-8771
303-555-0412

Vera Cortez *Food*
456 Bear Road
Evergreen, CO 80498-4600
303-555-8246

Kristi Duncan
8998 Hunter's Way
Evergreen, CO 80498-9988
303-555-1290

Aubrey Eagle *Finance*
78 Beaver Road
Evergreen, CO 80499-7811
303-555-6034

Glenn Glass *Finance*
4423 Pine Alley
Evergreen, CO 80499-4332
303-555-7702

Shane Gunter *Decorations*
5360 Shadow Lane
Evergreen, CO 80498-6030
303-555-7351

Cecilia Haddock *Ticket Sales*
1265 Green Street
Evergreen, CO 80498-1221
303-555-4001

Mia Jackson *Sponsorship*
7832 Hunter's Way
Evergreen, CO 80498-7382
303-555-6092

Doug Johnson *Food*
902 East Lake
Evergreen, CO 80498-9002
303-555-6080

Erica Katz *Decorations*
4077 Sky View
Evergreen, CO 80499-4117
303-555-5910

Sidney Lewis *Ticket Sales*
598 Pine Valley
Evergreen, CO 80499-5800
303-555-4025

Mike Miller *Program*
9090 Wren Avenue
Evergreen, CO 80499-9191
303-555-1209

Belinda Mires *Food*
1009 Elk Crossing
Evergreen, CO 80499-1019
303-555-6978

Michelle Poole *Food*
876 Leaf Avenue
Evergreen, CO 80499-8176
303-555-4826

Simon Rodriguez *Sponsorship*
799 Beaver Road
Evergreen, CO 80499-7990
303-555-7677

Danielle Rogers *Program*
2331 Sunset Street
Evergreen, CO 80498-2113
303-555-5732

Paul Sartor *Program*
8001 Lake View
Evergreen, CO 80499-8010
303-555-1188

Renee Sokora
4590 Elk Crossing
Evergreen, CO 80498-4951
303-555-8004

Heather Stone *Program*
4561 Yucca Avenue
Evergreen, CO 80498-4615
303-555-5294

Evan Strange
6857 Berry Hill
Evergreen, CO 80498-6580
303-555-9843

Melissa Tait
3311 Doe Road
Evergreen, CO 80499-3300
303-555-7998

Tyrone Thomas
3489 Redwood
Evergreen, CO 80499-4839
303-555-2119

Robin Vickers
5776 Brookview
Evergreen, CO 80499-7777
303-555-3223

Nathan Whitaker
807 Pine Alley
Evergreen, CO 80499-8171
303-555-6060

Ashley Wyatt *Decorations*
5055 Eagle Landing
Evergreen, CO 80499-5150
303-555-8712

Te Yung *Decorations*
709 Maple Avenue
Evergreen, CO 80498-7099
303-555-8824

# November 18

You need a budget based on the club's previous dinners and estimates of costs for this year's dinner and dance. Create the following budget to give to all the committee chairs at the next committee meeting.

1. Key the data as shown in Figure 18-3 in a new spreadsheet file.

2. Increase the width of column A to 12 and column B to 18.

3. Format columns C and D for currency with 0 decimals.

FIGURE 18-3

| | A | B | C | D |
|---|---|---|---|---|
| 1 | NEW YEAR'S EVE DINNER DANCE | | | |
| 2 | Budget | | | |
| 3 | | | Estimated | Estimated |
| 4 | Committee | Item | Income | Expenses |
| 5 | Ticket | | | |
| 6 | | 85 Tickets X $15 | $1,275 | |
| 7 | | | | |
| 8 | Sponsorship | | | |
| 9 | | 5 Sponsors X $200 | $1,000 | |
| 10 | | | | |
| 11 | Food | | | |
| 12 | | Meals | | $680 |
| 13 | | Refreshments | | $75 |
| 14 | | Paper Goods | | $25 |
| 15 | | | | |
| 16 | Program | | | |
| 17 | | Music | | $500 |
| 18 | | Party Favors | | $170 |
| 19 | | | | |
| 20 | Decorations | | | |
| 21 | | Decorations | | $150 |
| 22 | | | | |
| 23 | Sponsorship | | | |
| 24 | | Gifts for Sponsors | | $100 |
| 25 | | | | |
| 26 | Event Chair | | | |
| 27 | | Postage | | $15 |
| 28 | | Printing/Copying | | $50 |
| 29 | | | | |
| 30 | Totals | | | |
| 31 | | | | |
| 32 | Estimated | | | |
| 33 | Profit | | | |
| 34 | | | | |

4. Use a function in Cell C30 to get the total income budgeted.

5. Use a function in Cell D30 to get the total expenses budgeted.

6. Create a formula in Cell D33 to subtract the budgeted expenses from budgeted income to get estimated profit.

7. Boldface Cells C30, D30, and D33.

8. Save the file as *Budget*.

9. Print and close.

# November 19

Many topics need to be discussed at the committee meeting tomorrow. Create an agenda so that everyone will be aware of the topics and you won't forget anything.

1. In a new word processing file, key the handwritten data up to the roman numeral one (I).

**FIGURE 18-4**

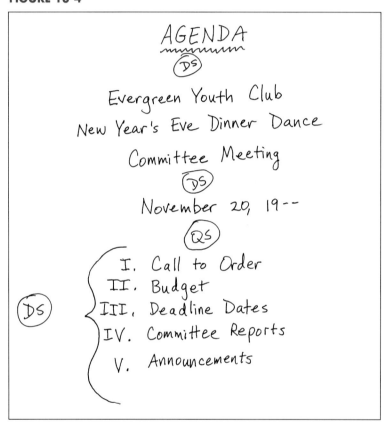

2. Save the file as *Agenda*.

3. Change the top margin to 2.75 inches and the left and right margins to 1.75 inches.

4. Set a right tab at 2 inches and a left tab at 2.25 inches.

5. Key the remaining data using the tabs you set.

6. Save, print, and close.

# November 21

At the committee meeting, it was decided that you should write a memo to all Evergreen Youth Club members. Encourage them to help committees and to buy tickets.

1. Key **MEMORANDUM** centered and boldfaced in a new word processing file.

2. Set a right tab at 1.25 inches and a left tab at 1.5 inches.

3. Key the rest of the memo as shown in Figure 18-5.

**FIGURE 18-5**

**MEMORANDUM**

*TS*

**To:**   All members of the Evergreen Youth Club

**From:**  *Student's Name*

**Date:**  November 21, 19--

**Subject:**  New Year's Eve Dinner Dance

*DS* *TS*

Plans for the New Year's Eve Dinner Dance are underway. Thanks to all of you who signed up and are working on committees. If your committee hasn't met, it will meet soon. Not only is this a chance for you to have fun, it is also a fund-raiser for our club. Any profits we make will go toward our trip to Fun World next summer. Please help all you can.

*DS*

Remember that each member must purchase a ticket to participate in the dinner and dance on New Year's Eve. This year the theme is Hawaiian, so wear your grass skirts and Hawaiian shirts. Ashley Wyatt and her committee will be decorating the community center with coconut trees, sand, and other related items. The dinner menu also will follow the Hawaiian theme, so get ready for some fresh pineapple!

*DS*

Disc jockey Jammin' Jay Jay Jones will be playing Top 40 dance music. He'll also be taking requests. At midnight, everyone will be given confetti to throw, noise makers to use, and nonalcoholic champagne to drink. We'll have dance contests and games. Bring all your friends!

*DS*

New Year's Eve Dinner Dance
December 31
7:00 p.m.
Evergreen Community Center
$15 per person

*DS*

For tickets, call Hunter Aldridge at 303-555-8779.

4. Save the file as *Member Memo*.

5. Change the top margin to 1.5 inches and the left and right margins to 1.5 inches.

6. Save, print, and close.

You need mailing labels to put on all the memo envelopes. Since most of the members are already in the database, you will use it to create the labels. You need to add the members who aren't on a committee to the database.

1. Open *Committee Members*.

2. Redisplay the City and State/Province fields.

3. Insert (in any order) the records of those who are not on a committee. See Figure 18-6.

4. Save as *Membership*.

5. Create and print mailing labels for all the members of the Evergreen Youth Club. Include the fields First Name, Last Name, Address, City, State/Province, and Postal Code. Use Avery 5160 (2 5/8" X 1") labels. Insert a comma after the City field.

6. Save as *Mailing Labels* and close.

7. Close *Membership*.

## November 29

Hunter Aldridge just reported that her committee has already sold 25 tickets. Create a spreadsheet to record ticket sales.

1. Key the data as shown in a new spreadsheet file. Adjust column widths as needed. See Figure 18-7.

2. Save the file as *Tickets*.

3. Use a function in Cell B12 to get the total number of tickets sold.

4. Save, print, and close.

## December 10

The club's advisor, Trent Locke, wants a list of all the sponsors for the dinner and dance. He would also like to know which member on the Sponsorship Committee sold each sponsorship. You call Cody Carrizales, chair of the Sponsorship Committee, to get this information. Create a database of the sponsors.

**FIGURE 18-6**

### Evergreen Youth Club Membership Roster

Jude Acker *Ticket Sales*
79 Treetop Boulevard
Evergreen, CO 80498-9710
303-555-7700

Hunter Aldridge *Ticket Sales*
9345 Snow Hill
Evergreen, CO 80498-9340
303-555-8779

Samantha Bledsoe *Sponsorship*
4551 Rocky Road
Evergreen, CO 80499-4511
303-555-6632

Cody Carrizales *Sponsorship*
9212 Bear Road
Evergreen, CO 80498-9121
303-555-4739

Paul Chen
3445 West Willow
Evergreen, CO 80498-3334
303-555-9911

Katie Clements *Finance*
8776 Hunter's Way
Evergreen, CO 80499-8771
303-555-0412

Vera Cortez *Food*
456 Bear Road
Evergreen, CO 80498-4600
303-555-8246

Kristi Duncan
8998 Hunter's Way
Evergreen, CO 80498-9988
303-555-1290

Aubrey Eagle *Finance*
78 Beaver Road
Evergreen, CO 80499-7811
303-555-6034

Glenn Glass *Finance*
4423 Pine Alley
Evergreen, CO 80499-4332
303-555-7702

Shane Gunter *Decorations*
5360 Shadow Lane
Evergreen, CO 80498-6030
303-555-7351

Cecilia Haddock *Ticket Sales*
1265 Green Street
Evergreen, CO 80498-1221
303-555-4001

Mia Jackson *Sponsorship*
7832 Hunter's Way
Evergreen, CO 80498-7382
303-555-6092

Doug Johnson *Food*
902 East Lake
Evergreen, CO 80498-9002
303-555-6080

Erica Katz *Decorations*
4077 Sky View
Evergreen, CO 80499-4117
303-555-5910

Sidney Lewis *Ticket Sales*
598 Pine Valley
Evergreen, CO 80499-5800
303-555-4025

Mike Miller *Program*
9090 Wren Avenue
Evergreen, CO 80499-9191
303-555-1209

Belinda Mires *Food*
1009 Elk Crossing
Evergreen, CO 80499-1019
303-555-6978

Michelle Poole *Food*
876 Leaf Avenue
Evergreen, CO 80499-8176
303-555-4826

Simon Rodriguez *Sponsorship*
799 Beaver Road
Evergreen, CO 80499-7990
303-555-7677

Danielle Rogers *Program*
2331 Sunset Street
Evergreen, CO 80498-2113
303-555-5732

Paul Sartor *Program*
8001 Lake View
Evergreen, CO 80499-8010
303-555-1188

Renee Sokora
4590 Elk Crossing
Evergreen, CO 80498-4951
303-555-8004

Heather Stone *Program*
4561 Yucca Avenue
Evergreen, CO 80498-4615
303-555-5294

Evan Strange
6857 Berry Hill
Evergreen, CO 80498-6580
303-555-9843

Melissa Tait
3311 Doe Road
Evergreen, CO 80499-3300
303-555-7998

Tyrone Thomas
3489 Redwood
Evergreen, CO 80499-4839
303-555-2119

Robin Vickers
5776 Brookview
Evergreen, CO 80499-7777
303-555-3223

Nathan Whitaker
807 Pine Alley
Evergreen, CO 80499-8171
303-555-6060

Ashley Wyatt *Decorations*
5055 Eagle Landing
Evergreen, CO 80499-5150
303-555-8712

Te Yung *Decorations*
709 Maple Avenue
Evergreen, CO 80498-7099
303-555-8824

**FIGURE 18-7**

|    | A                        | B            | C |
|----|--------------------------|--------------|---|
| 1  | NEW YEAR'S EVE DINNER DANCE |            |   |
| 2  | Ticket Sales             |              |   |
| 3  |                          |              |   |
| 4  | Committee                |              |   |
| 5  | Member                   | Tickets Sold |   |
| 6  |                          |              |   |
| 7  | Hunter Aldridge          | 9            |   |
| 8  | Cecilia Haddock          | 6            |   |
| 9  | Sidney Lewis             | 7            |   |
| 10 | Jude Acker               | 3            |   |
| 11 |                          |              |   |
| 12 | Total                    |              |   |
| 13 |                          |              |   |
| 14 |                          |              |   |

1. Create the following fields and format them as indicated.

| Field | Format |
|---|---|
| Sponsor | General |
| Contact | General |
| Address | General |
| City | General |
| State | General |
| ZIP | Number, 1234.56, 0 decimals |
| Telephone | Number, 1234.56, 0 decimals |
| Amount | Currency, 0 decimals |
| Member | General |

2. Enter the following data, adjusting field widths as necessary. See Figure 18-8.

**FIGURE 18-8**

| Sponsor | Contact | Address | City | State | ZIP | Telephone | Amount | Member |
|---|---|---|---|---|---|---|---|---|
| Miriad T-Shirts | Janice Young | 7895 Lake View | Evergreen | CO | 80498-7811 | 303-555-9006 | $200 | Mia Jackson |
| First Bank | Tanya Rich | 8003 Bear Circle | Evergreen | CO | 80499-8000 | 303-555-8512 | $200 | Samantha Bledsoe |
| Evergreen Style | Pat Corpuz | 102 Main Street | Evergreen | CO | 80498-1021 | 303-555-1030 | $200 | Simon Rodriguez |
| KGRN Radio | Brad Vance | 6071 Elk Crossing | Evergreen | CO | 80499-6070 | 303-555-9999 | $200 | Cody Carrizales |
| EG Computers | Rachel Reid | 599 Pine Plaza | Evergreen | CO | 80499-5992 | 303-555-3030 | $200 | Cody Carrizales |

3. Save the file as *Sponsors*.

4. Hide the City, State, and Amount fields.

5. Make sure all data fits on one page.

6. Save, print, and close.

# December 17

Hunter Aldridge called to give you an update on ticket sales. Update your spreadsheet.

1. Open *Tickets*.

2. Update the spreadsheet with the following information: Hunter has sold a total of 23 tickets, Cecilia has sold 17 total, Sidney has sold 13 total, and Jude has sold 15 total.

3. Save the file as *Tickets 2*.

4.   Key **Goal** in Cell A14.

5.   Key **# To Go** in Cell A16.

6.   Key **85** in Cell B14.

7.   Create a formula in Cell B16 to find how many more tickets need to be sold before the goal is reached.

8.   Save, print, and close.

## December 28

Trent Locke suggested that you write a form letter to the sponsors to thank them for supporting the event.

1.   Open *Sponsors.*

2.   Show the City and State fields.

3.   Key the text shown below in a new word processing file. Insert the database fields where shown in Figure 18-9.

4.   Save the document as *Thanks.*

5.   Change all the margins to 1 inch.

6.   Print the form letters.

7.   Save and close *Thanks.*

8.   Close *Sponsors* without saving the changes.

## December 29

The Ticket Sales Committee has made its final report to you. Update the spreadsheet.

1.   Open *Tickets 2.*

2.   Update the spreadsheet with the following total sales: Hunter sold 30 tickets, Cecilia sold 21, Sidney sold 22, and Jude sold 19.

3.   Save the file as *Tickets 3.*

4.   Key **# Above Goal** in Cell A16.

FIGURE 18-9

**Evergreen Youth Club**
1200 Main Street
Evergreen, CO 80498-1201
303-555-0075

December 28, 19--

<<Sponsor>>
Attention: <<Contact>>
<<Address>>
<<City>>, <<State>> <<ZIP>>

Ladies and Gentlemen:

Thank you for sponsoring our New Year's Eve Dinner Dance. The thoughtfulness and generosity of <<Sponsor>> will help keep the youth of Evergreen safe and alcohol-free on New Year's Eve.

As <<Member>> may have told you, our club continues to give back to the community in many ways. We work one day each month in the Evergreen Park to keep it clean and free of trash. We've also helped the city plant flowers there for the past two years. In addition, the Evergreen Youth Club raises money for local charities by hosting car washes, rummage sales, and bake sales.

We have other fund-raisers to pay for club trips. The money earned from the New Year's Eve Dinner Dance will fund a trip to Denver next summer. During the three-day trip, the club will visit Fun World, attend a youth leadership conference, and be the governor's guests for the day at the state capitol.

Your sponsorship of this event shows that you are interested in today's youth, who will be the leaders of tomorrow. Thank you for your gift.

Sincerely,

*Student's Name*
Event Chair

5. Edit the formula in Cell B16 to subtract B14 from B12 to get a positive number.

6. Save, print, and close.

# December 31

The New Year's Eve Dinner started at 7 p.m. After dinner, everyone mingled, danced, and played games. At midnight, everyone celebrated the new year. The party ended at 1 a.m., and everyone had a good time.

# January 8

You and Glenn Glass, the Finance Committee Chair, reviewed the income and expenses. Now you need to create a Financial Report to submit to the Evergreen Youth Club advisor, Trent Locke.

1. Open *Budget*.

2. Change the subtitle in Cell A2 to **Financial Report, January 8, 19--**.

3. Insert a new column to the right of column C.

4. Key the new data as shown in Figure 18-10.

FIGURE 18-10

| | A | B | C | D | E | F |
|---|---|---|---|---|---|---|
| 1 | | | | | | |
| 2 | | | | | | |
| 3 | | | | Actual | | Actual |
| 4 | | | | Income | | Expenses |
| 5 | | | | | | |
| 6 | | | | 1380 | | |
| 7 | | | | | | |
| 8 | | | | | | |
| 9 | | | | 1000 | | |
| 10 | | | | | | |
| 11 | | | | | | |
| 12 | | | | | | 732 |
| 13 | | | | | | 71.78 |
| 14 | | | | | | 25.4 |
| 15 | | | | | | |
| 16 | | | | | | |
| 17 | | | | | | 395 |
| 18 | | | | | | 168.49 |
| 19 | | | | | | |
| 20 | | | | | | |
| 21 | | | | | | 147.59 |
| 22 | | | | | | |
| 23 | | | | | | |
| 24 | | | | | | 103.75 |
| 25 | | | | | | |
| 26 | | | | | | |
| 27 | | | | | | 10.44 |
| 28 | | | | | | 43.88 |
| 29 | | | | | | |
| 30 | | | | | | |
| 31 | | | | | | |
| 32 | | | | | | |
| 33 | | | | | | |
| 34 | | | | | | |
| 35 | Actual Profit | | | | | |
| 36 | | | | | | |

5.    Save the file as *Budget Report.*

6.    Copy the formula in Cell C30 to Cell D30.

7.    Copy the formula in Cell E30 to Cell F30.

8.    Create a formula in Cell F35 to subtract F30 from D30. Boldface the data in Cell F35.

9.    Format columns D and F for currency with 2 decimals.

10.    Insert two blank rows after row 31.

11.    Key **Difference** boldfaced in Cell A32.

12.    Create a formula in Cell D32 to subtract D30 from C30.

13.    Create a formula in Cell F32 to subtract F30 from E30.

14.    Change the font size of the entire spreadsheet to 10 (if it is 10 already, make it 8) and the left and right margins to 1 inch.

15.    Save.

16.    Open *Member Memo.* Save the file as *TL Report.*

17.    Replace the current data with the new data as shown in Figure 18-11.

18.    Change all the margins to .75 inches.

19.    Copy the financial report from *Budget Report* to *TL Report.* Make sure all data fits on one page.

20.    Save, print, and close *TL Report.*

21.    Close *Budget Report.*

Congratulations! You were a great Event Chair, and the club appreciates you!

**FIGURE 18-11**

**MEMORANDUM**

| | |
|---|---|
| **To:** | Trent Locke |
| **From:** | *Student's name* |
| **Date:** | January 8, 19-- |
| **Subject:** | New Year's Eve Dinner Dance Financial Report |

Here is the financial report for the New Year's Eve event. I think it was a wonderful success. I look forward to meeting with you on January 15 to discuss suggestions for next year's event.

# TASKWIZARDS INCLUDED WITH WORKS

Accounts

Address Book

Bibliography

Bids

Brochure

Business Inventory

Certificate

Customers or Clients

Employee Profile

Employee Timesheet

Envelopes

Fax Cover Sheet

Flyer

Form Letter

Grade Book

Home Inventory

Invoice

Labels

Letter

Letterhead

Memo

Mortgage/Loan Analysis

Newsletter

Order Form

Phone List

Price List

Proposal Forms

Proposal Letter

Quotations

Resume (CV)

Return Address Labels

Sales Contacts

Schedule

School Reports/Thesis

Start from Scratch

Statements

Student and Membership Information

Suppliers and Vendors

Tests

# PROOFREADER'S MARKS

| Revision | Symbol | Edited Copy | Corrected Copy |
|---|---|---|---|
| Boldface | ∿∿∿ | Clearance Sale! | **Clearance Sale!** |
| Capitalize | ≡ | Lisa and chris | Lisa and Chris |
| Center | ⌐⌐ | ⌐Danbury Journal⌐ | Danbury Journal |
| Delete | ℘ | Tony ~~and Shelly~~ swam. | Tony swam. |
| Delete and close up | ℘ | Ice is co͡old. | Ice is cold. |
| Delete and add | ℘ | Use the ~~red~~ ^blue^ paper. | Use the blue paper. |
| Insert | ∧ | He ordered ∧salad. | He ordered egg salad. |
| Insert space | #/ | He#ordered salad. | He ordered salad. |
| Italicize | — (ital) | She read Moby Dick. (ital) | She read *Moby Dick*. |
| Lowercase | / (lc) | The Bell rang. (lc) | The bell rang. |
| Move right | ⌐⌐ | He read, also. | He read, also. |
| Move left | ⌐ | ⌐He read, also. | He read, also. |
| New paragraph | ¶ | ¶It's a nice day for a picnic. | It's a nice day for a picnic. |
| Run together | ⌐ | Kim called earlier.⌐ She left a message. | Kim called earlier. She left a message. |
| Spacing Double (1 blank line between text) | DS | DS {Zephyr High School Administration Office | Zephyr High School  Administration Office |

| Triple (2 blank lines between text) | $TS$ | $TS$ {Zephyr High School / Administration Office | Zephyr High School |
|---|---|---|---|
| | | | Administration Office |
| Quadruple (3 blank lines between text) | $QS$ | $QS$ {Zephyr High School / Administration Office | Zephyr High School |
| | | | Administration Office |
| Spell Out | (SP) | (Jan.) 1 | January 1 |
| Stet | ‹ ‹ › | The car is new. | The car is new. |
| Transpose | ∿ | The car is old. | The car is old. |

## A

**Absolute Cell Reference** A cell reference that does not adjust to the new cell location when copied or moved.

**Active Cell** A highlighted cell in the spreadsheet that is ready for data entry.

**Alignment** Determines how text is aligned at the margins.

**All Records Search** A database search that displays on the screen only those records containing the specified data.

**ASCII** Acronym for American Standard Code for Information Interchange. The ASCII format was developed to provide a standard for communication between different types of programs.

## B

**Backspace Key** Deletes the character to the left of the insertion point.

**Bar Chart** A chart that uses rectangles of varying heights to illustrate values in a spreadsheet.

**Baud** A measure of the speed at which a modem modulates signals.

**Bit** A single electronic signal that is either on or off.

**Bits Per Second (BPS)** A measure of the usable bits that the modem sends or receives in a second.

**Bulletin Board System** A service available by modem that offers private and public messages, files for download, and other services.

**Byte** A group of eight bits.

## C

**Capturing Text** A feature that allows you to gather all the text of a communications session into one file.

**Cell** The intersection of a row and column in a spreadsheet.

**Cell Reference** Identifies a cell by the column letter and row number (for example, A1, B2, C4).

**Chart** A graphical representation of data contained in a spreadsheet.

**Clip Art** Graphics that are already drawn and available for use in documents.

**Clipboard** A temporary storage place in memory.

**Close** Removing a document or window from the screen.

**Close Button** The "X" on the right side of the title bar that closes a window.

**Columns** Appear vertically in a spreadsheet and are identified by letters at the top of the spreadsheet window.

## D

**Data Bits** The bits used to transfer data over a modem.

**Database** An automated electronic filing system that stores and retrieves information.

**Database Report** Allows you to organize, summarize, and print a portion of a database.

**Delete Key** Removes the character to the right of the insertion point.

**Desktop Space** Where your work takes place.

**Directory** A list of files grouped together on a disk.

**Downloading** Receiving a file from a host computer.

## E

**End-of-File Marker** Marks the end of the document.

**Entry** The smallest unit in a database, consisting of one piece of information.

## F

**Field** A category of information in a database.

**Field Format** Determines how data is presented in a column of a database.

**Field Name** A label at the top of a database column that describes the kind of information to be stored in the column.

**File Transfer** A process by which files are sent over a modem.

**File Transfer Protocol** A method of transferring a file that encodes the data in such a way that if a bad connection or faulty modem causes an error in the data, the communications software will know and retransmit the data.

**Filling Down** A process that copies data from an original entry to an entry or entries directly below the original.

**Filters** A database feature that displays records that meet one or more specific criteria.

**Font** The shape of the characters belonging to a particular family of type.

**Footer** Text that is printed at the bottom of each page.

**Footnote** Used to document quotations, figures, summaries, or other text that you do not want to include in the body of your document.

**Form Letter** A word processor document that uses information from a database in specified areas to personalize a document.

**Form View** A window in the database that displays one record at a time; Form view is most appropriately used for entering or editing a specific record.

**Formula** An equation that calculates a new value from existing values.

**Formula Bar** Appears directly below the toolbar in the spreadsheet; the Formula Bar will display a formula when the cell of a spreadsheet or entry of a database contains a calculated value.

**Function Formula** A special formula that does not use operators to calculate a result.

**General Format** The default format that displays both text and numerical data as keyed.

**Graphical User Interface (GUI)** A way of interacting with a computer that involves pictures.

**Graphics** Pictures that help illustrate the meaning of the text or that make the page more attractive or functional.

**Grid Snap** An invisible grid on your screen that allows you to automatically align objects to the nearest grid line.

**Grouping** A database reporting process that inserts a Summ *field name* row after records that constitute each sorted group.

**Handles** Little squares that appear at the edges of a graphic.

**Hanging Indent** The first line of text begins at the left margin and the remaining lines are indented from the left margin.

**Hardware** Physical components of a computer.

**Header** Text that is printed at the top of each page in Page Layout view.

**Header Pane** The top of each new document in page layout view where the text for a header is keyed.

**Highlight** The entry point of a spreadsheet or database; a highlighted cell is indicated by a dark border.

**Host Computer** The computer you connect with when you call a bulletin board system or an on-line service.

I

**I-beam** The shape the mouse pointer assumes in a document window.

**Icon** A small picture that represents an item or object.

**Indent** The space you place between text and a document's margin.

**Insertion Point** Marks your place in the text and shows where the next character you key will appear.

**Integrated Software Package** A computer program that combines common tools into one program.

**Integration** The process of using more than one Works tool to create a document.

## K

**Key Combination** Two keys connected with a plus sign, which indicates that you are to press two keys at the same time.

## L

**Line Chart** A chart that is similar to a bar chart except bars are replaced by points connected by a line.

**Linking** The process of integrating data between the spreadsheet and the word processor.

**List View** A window in the database that is similar in appearance to the spreadsheet; List view is most appropriately used when you want to display several records at once.

**Logging Off** The procedure used to disconnect from a bulletin board system or an on-line service.

**Logging On** Providing a name and password for access to a bulletin board system or an on-line service.

## M

**Margin** The amount of space between the edge of a page and the printed or written text in a document.

**Maximize Button** A button at the right side of the title bar that enlarges a window to its maximum size.

**Menu** A list of options from which to choose.

**Menu Bar** The horizontal bar at the top of the application window that contains menu titles from which you can choose a variety of word processing commands.

**Minimize Button** A button at the right side of the title bar that reduces a window to a button on the taskbar.

**Mixed Cell Reference** A cell reference containing both relative and absolute references.

**Modem** A device that converts computer signals so that they can be transmitted over phone lines.

**Modem Communication** The process of transmitting information from one computer to another over telephone lines.

**Mouse** A device that rolls on a flat surface and has one or more buttons on it used to interact with a computer.

**Multiple Selection Filter** A database operation that displays records that meet several criteria simultaneously.

**My Computer** A program to help you organize and manage your files.

## N

**Navigation Buttons** Buttons in the Form view window that allow you to move among records.

**Next Record Search** A database operation that finds the first record after the highlight in which the specified data is present.

## O

**On-Line Services** Larger, commercial versions of BBSs that charge for access.

**Open** The process of loading a file from a disk onto the screen.

**Operand** A number, cell reference, or field name used in a calculation in the formulas of spreadsheets or databases; in a database the operands are field names.

**Operator** Tells Works what to do with the operands in a formula.

**Order of Evaluation** The sequence used to calculate the value of a formula.

**Overtype** Replaces the characters on the screen with new characters as you enter them.

## P

**Page Break** The place where one page ends and another begins.

**Pagination** Works' process of automatically breaking long documents into pages by inserting page breaks.

**Pane** An area of the document that contains separate scroll bars to allow you to move through that part of the document.

**Paragraph Indent** A first-line indent at the beginning of each paragraph.

**Parity Bit** Allows the modem software to verify that the character was transferred without error.

**Path** The location of a file on a disk.

**Pathname** See *path.*

**Pie Chart** A chart that shows the relationship of a part to a whole.

**Placeholders** Help you key in the right place and help you to write appropriate text by giving you hints about the kind of information to include in each section.

**Pointer** Indicates the position of the mouse.

## R

**Range** A selected group of cells in a spreadsheet and entries in a database; a range is identified by the cell in the upper left corner and the cell in the lower right corner, separated by a colon (for example, A3:C5).

**Record** A complete set of field entries.

**Record Number** The number on the left side of a screen that identifies the sequence of a record in a database.

**Recycle Bin** Place to get rid of files or folders that are no longer needed.

**Relative Cell Reference** A cell reference that adjusts to a new location when copied or moved.

**Report View** Screen appearance for the database in which a database report is created and changed.

**Restore Button** A button at the right side of the title bar that returns a maximized window to its regular size.

**Resume** A professional document which gives an employer concise information about you.

**Row Labels** Columns on the left side of the Report view of the database that determine the appearance of the database report.

**Rows** Appear horizontally in the spreadsheet and are identified by numbers on the left side of the spreadsheet window.

**Ruler** Lets you quickly change indentions, tabs, and margins.

## S

**Sans Serif Font** A font without serifs.

**Save** The process of storing a file on disk.

**Scale** Resizing a graphic so that its proportions are correct.

**Scatter Chart** A chart that shows the relationship of two categories of data.

**Scroll Bar** Appears at the bottom and/or right side of a window to allow the user to view another part of the window's contents.

**Scroll Box** Small box in the scroll bar that indicates your position within the contents of the window.

**Searching** The process of locating specific data in a database.

**Selecting** Highlighting a block of text.

**Serial** A device that deals with one bit at a time.

**Serial Port** The port to which the modem is attached.

**Serif Font** A font with serifs.

**Serifs** Small lines at the ends of characters.

**Shift-Clicking** One way to select objects: hold down the Shift key and click each of the objects you want to select.

**Software** Lists of instructions that computers follow to perform specific tasks; a program.

**Sorting** A database operation that arranges records in the database in a specific order (such as alphabetically or largest to smallest).

**Spacing** The distance between lines of text or paragraphs.

**Splitting** An operation that permits you to view several parts of a file on the screen simultaneously.

**Spreadsheet** A grid of rows and columns containing numbers, text, and formulas. The purpose of a spreadsheet is to solve problems that involve numbers.

**Start** A button on the taskbar that brings up menus with a variety of options.

**Status Bar** Gives you directions on how to access menus and briefly summarizes the actions of commands that you choose.

**Stop Bits** Bits necessary to signal the end of the character's transfer.

**Subdirectory** A directory within a directory.

**T**

**Tabs** Mark the place the insertion point will stop when the tab key is pressed.

**Taskbar** Shows the names of all open programs.

**TaskWizards** Programs within Works that create documents based on your specifications.

**Telecommunication** Transferring information from one place to another electronically.

**Terminal** The computer that calls a bulletin board system or an on-line service.

**Terminal Emulation** The way text coming over the modem is presented on the screen.

**Text File** A document that does not contain any of the codes that control fonts, font size, and type style.

**Thesaurus** A useful feature for finding a synonym for a word in your document.

**Title Bar** Contains the name of the program or document in the window.

**Toolbar** Contains common word processing commands you can use by simply clicking the correct button.

**Trackball** Alternative form of a mouse which has an embedded ball that the user rotates.

**Type Size** Determined by measuring the height of characters in units called points.

**Type Style** Certain standard changes in the appearance of a font.

**Typeface** Another term for a font.

**U**

**Undo** Will reverse a previous command to delete text or change the format of text.

**Uploading** Sending a file to a host computer.

**W**

**Wildcard** A character in a search that permits any character to be specified. For example, the search criteria *al\** will find *Alabama, already,* or *Albert.* In a database search, the asterisk (*) is the wildcard character to replace one or more letters; the question mark (?) is the wildcard character to replace only one letter.

**Word Processing** The use of computer software to enter and edit text.

**Wordwrap** Text automatically wraps to the next line.

# INDEX

# UPDATE FOR MICROSOFT WORKS 4.0: MICROSOFT WORKS 4.5 AND THE INTERNET

## LEARNING OBJECTIVES
### In this update, you will learn to:

1. Access the Internet and use Microsoft's Internet Explorer.

2. Compose and send e-mail.

# Accessing the Internet

The *Internet* is a vast network of computers linked to one another. The Internet (sometimes referred to as "the Net") allows people around the world to share information and ideas.

The Internet is also called the information superhighway, a virtual community, or cyberspace. Regardless of the terminology used, the Internet holds the promise of being an important information and communication resource. Connecting to the Internet requires special hardware and software and an *Internet Service Provider (ISP)*. Before you can use the Internet, someone will actually connect your school's computers to the Internet and inform your instructor about how to access the Internet.

The *World Wide Web* is a system of computers that share information by means of hypertext links on "pages." The Internet is its carrier. You can click on a *hypertext* link to jump to another part of a document or another Web site. To identify hypertext documents, the Web uses addresses called *Uniform Resource Locators (URLs)*. Here are some examples of URLs:

http://www.whitehouse.gov

http://www.microsoft.com

http://www.thomson.com/swpco

The first part of the URL (*http*) stands for **hypertext transfer protocol** and indicates that this is a Web page. The remainder of the URL indicates which computer on the Internet holds the file, the location of the file on that computer, and the file's name.

Just as cities have different ZIP codes, Internet addresses have different codes depending on the domain you want to access. Addresses on the Internet follow the **Domain Name System (DNS).** Table 1 shows a list of various domain extensions.

**TABLE 1**

## DOMAIN NAMES

| | |
|---|---|
| .mil = military | .edu = education |
| .com = commercial | .org = organization |
| .gov = government | .net = network provider |
| .uk = United Kingdom | .ca = Canada |
| .hk = Hong Kong | .fi = Finland |
| .ut = Utah | .tn = Tennessee |
| .us = United States | .mo = Missouri |
| .sa = Saudia Arabia | .au = Australia |

Most of the addresses you will use on the Internet to locate files will follow these conventions or rules. However, not all WWW addresses use the letters *www* or end with an extension listed in Table 1, so be sure to key in addresses exactly as given.

# Viewing Web Pages

To view hypertext documents on the Web, you need special software. A **Web browser** is software used to display Web pages on your computer monitor. Microsoft's **Internet Explorer** is a browser for navigating the Web that came with the Works 4.5 software. You can launch Internet Explorer by clicking the icon on the desktop or by clicking the Start button and choosing it from the Programs menu. Depending on your type of Internet connection, you may have to connect to your ISP first. As shown in Figure 1, Internet Explorer contains a toolbar with buttons to help you navigate the Web.

**FIGURE 1**
Internet Explorer is a browser that allows you to display Web pages on your computer.

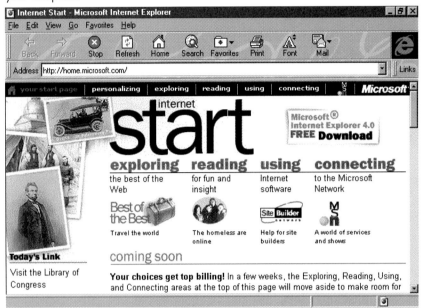

The functions of the buttons on the Internet Explorer toolbar are explained in Table 2.

**TABLE 2**

| BUTTON | FUNCTION |
|---|---|
| Back | takes you to the previous page |
| Forward | takes you to the next page |
| Stop | stops loading the current page |
| Refresh | reloads the current page |
| Home | loads the home page that appears when you first open the browser |
| Search | opens a page where you can key words and search the Internet |
| Favorites | lists favorite sites so you can return to them easily |
| Print | prints the current page |
| Font | increases or decreases the point size of the text of the current page |
| Mail | use to send and read e-mail or read newsgroups |

**HOT TIPS**

Since Microsoft updates this page every day, your page may not look exactly like the one shown in Figure 1.

**CONCEPT BUILDER**

There are two basic types of Internet connections. *Dial-up access* is using a telephone line to communicate between your computer and the Internet using a modem. Most individual users and small businesses have dial-up access. *Direct access* is using a special high-speed connection between a computer network and the Internet. This access is faster but more expensive than dial-up access. Many businesses and institutions have direct access.

## Accessing a Web Site

1. Connect to your ISP if you're not connected already.

2. Launch the Microsoft Internet Explorer browser by clicking **Start, Programs,** and then **Internet Explorer.**

3. Microsoft Internet Explorer opens and the start page begins loading, as shown in Figure 1. Wait a few moments for the page to load. Your start page may be different from the one shown, since this page can be changed easily by choosing Options from the View menu.

4. Click the **Search** button. A new page loads where you can search for a topic on the Web.

5. Click the **Back** button to return to the start page.

6. In the address box, key **www.yahoo.com** and press **Enter** to access the Yahoo search site.

7. Choose **Web Tutorial** from the Help menu. The Internet Tutorial page loads in Internet Explorer.

8. Click the **Introduction** icon. Complete the tutorial.

9. When you're finished with the tutorial, choose **Close** from the **File** menu to close Internet Explorer and then disconnect from your ISP.

### CONCEPT BUILDER

To search for topics on the Web using Microsoft's Search page, key your topic in the Search box, choose a search engine, and click Search.

# Sending and Receiving E-mail

One of the most common and most useful services of the Internet is *electronic mail (e-mail),* the use of a computer network to send and receive messages. The value of e-mail is that it is faster than *snail mail* (the United States Postal Service method of delivering letters), less expensive, and more efficient, since it allows you to send a message to more than one person at the same time. E-mail is global and it is environment-friendly, since it does not require paper or fuel. Check with your teacher to find out your unique e-mail address and what software program is being used to send and receive e-mail.

A few of the more common e-mail software packages are Eudora, Kermit, Microsoft Exchange Inbox, Pegasus Mail, and Pine. You can download a free or demo version of many of these programs from the Internet. For these activities, we assume you are using Microsoft Internet Mail, but you can designate any e-mail program you want by choosing Options from the View menu and clicking the Programs tab.

To use electronic mail, you need to learn the correct way to key an address and to share your e-mail address with others. The division of an e-mail address looks like this:

_____ @ _____ . _____
Your name           Host/server and domain            Type of organization

In the above illustration, the address includes your name as the network user, your host/server/domain name (might be your school's mascot), and a domain extension that tells other users whether the e-mail account is at a school, business, government location, or another country. No one has your unique e-mail address. Some typical e-mail addresses look like this:

d.everet@morehead-st.edu (an education e-mail address)

brendas@auvix.org (an organization e-mail address)

dateline@abc.com (a commercial enterprise e-mail address)

president@whitehouse.gov (a government address)

You key the entire address without any spaces. Most mailing systems are flexible enough to permit either lowercase or uppercase letters. Your teacher, media specialist, or technology specialist will give you instructions for using your e-mail package.

Using Microsoft Internet Mail (or another e-mail program), you can send e-mail messages to anyone around the world who has an Internet connection. E-mail has transformed business and personal communication to become an efficient and often preferred way to communicate with clients, co-workers, friends, and family. Your software will need to be configured with the appropriate profile and service settings to send and receive e-mail.

When Internet Explorer is open, click the Mail button and choose Read Mail to read your e-mail. An Internet Mail window opens as shown in Figure 2. Double-click a message in the Inbox to open it. After reading a message, you can send a reply to the author of the message by clicking the Reply button on the toolbar. You can forward or delete the message using the buttons on the toolbar. You can also print the message or click the Next button to read your next message.

**HOT TIPS**

It is important to manage your e-mail. You should save and delete messages as necessary, since everyone who has an e-mail account has a limited amount of space available for messages.

**FIGURE 2**

You can read your e-mail in the Internet Mail window.

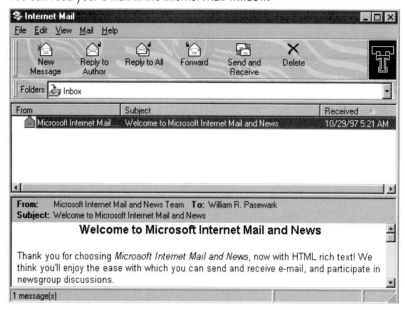

There is a pull-down Folders menu right below the toolbar that lists your options. The Inbox folder is where incoming mail is stored, the Outbox stores outgoing mail, Sent Items stores the e-mail messages you've sent, and Deleted Items are the messages you've deleted.

To send e-mail, click the Mail button on the toolbar in the Internet Explorer browser window and choose New Message. Or, click the New Message button on the toolbar in the Internet Mail window. A blank e-mail message appears, like that shown in Figure 3. In the To box, key the e-mail address of the person to whom you are sending the message. You can send a copy of the message to someone by keying his or her e-mail address in the Cc box. Key the subject of your message in the Subject box and key your message in the message window.

You can change the font, size, color, style, and alignment of text in your message by choosing HTML from the Format menu and then using the buttons on the toolbar that appears. (If it does not appear, choose Formatting Toolbar from the View menu.) You can also attach a file to an e-mail message by choosing File Attachment from the Insert menu, locating the file you want to attach, and clicking Attach. When you're finished writing your message, you can send it by clicking the Send button on the toolbar. The Message will be stored in the Outbox until you click the Send and Receive button in the Internet Mail window while connected to your ISP.

**FIGURE 3**
A blank e-mail message appears when you click the New Message button.

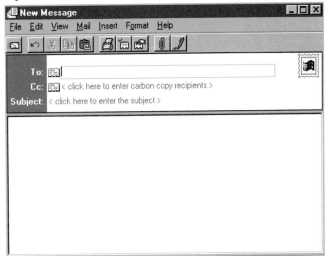

---

## ACTIVITY

# Sending and Receiving E-mail

1. Open Microsoft Internet Explorer.

2. Click the **Mail** button on the toolbar. A pull-down menu appears.

3. Choose **Read Mail.** Your screen should look similar to Figure 2, with the Inbox contents displayed.

4. Double-click the message from Microsoft or another message in your Inbox.

5. Scroll through and read the message from Microsoft. Notice all the formatting features used in the message.

6. Choose **Close** from the **File** menu. The message closes.

7. Click the **New Message** button. A blank e-mail message form appears, as shown in Figure 3.

8. Key your e-mail address in the *To* box.

9. Key **test** in the *Subject* box.

10. In the message window, key **This is a test**.

11. Click the **Send** button. Your mail is placed in the Outbox.

12. To view your outgoing mail, choose **Outbox** from the pull-down Folders menu. The mail in the Outbox can be seen, as shown in Figure 4.

**13.** Connect to your ISP.

**14.** Click the **Send and Receive** button.

**15.** The mail in the Outbox is automatically sent and the Outbox is now empty.

**16.** Any new messages are automatically retrieved and placed in the Inbox. Choose **Inbox** from the Folders pull-down menu. The message you sent yourself should be in here. (It may take a minute for the message you sent yourself to arrive. You might need to click the Send and Receive button again to get the message.)

**17.** Choose **Sent Items** from the Folders pull-down menu. The message you sent should be there.

**18.** Click on the message to select it and then click the **Delete** button.

**19.** Disconnect from your ISP.

**20.** Choose **Close** from the **File** menu.

**FIGURE 4**
Outgoing mail is stored in the Outbox until you connect to your ISP.

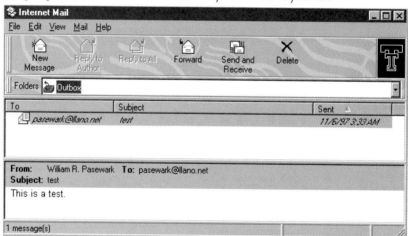

# *Summary*

- ■ The Internet is a vast network of computers linked to one another. The Internet allows people around the world to share information and ideas. The World Wide Web is a system of computers that share information by means of hypertext links. The Internet is its carrier.

- ■ A Web browser is software used to display Web pages on your computer monitor. Microsoft's Internet Explorer is a browser for navigating the Web that comes with Works 4.5.

- The value of e-mail is that it is faster, less expensive, and more efficient than snail mail. E-mail is global and it is environment-friendly, since it does not require paper or fuel.

- Using an e-mail program, you can send e-mail messages to anyone around the world who also has an Internet connection.

● ● ● ● ● ● ● ● ● ● ● ● ●

## APPLICATION 1

1. Connect to your ISP if you're not connected already. Open Microsoft Internet Explorer browser.

2. Choose **Microsoft on the Web** from the **Help** menu, and then choose **Best of the Web** from the submenu.

3. Under Best of the Web, click a topic of your choice to explore.

4. Print one page from the Web. (Scroll down the page to be sure you're printing only one 8½" × 11" page—some Web pages can be very long.)

5. Go back to the Best of the Web topics and choose another to explore.

6. Print one page from this topic.

7. Keep Microsoft Internet Explorer open and stay connected to the Internet for the next application.

## APPLICATION 2

1. With Internet Explorer open, key **http://www.webcrawler.com** as the URL and press **Enter.**

2. In the search form, key **homework help** and click **Search.** Notice the number of matching documents that were found.

3. In the search form, highlight the existing words and key **homework and help** and click **Search**. Notice the number of matching documents is smaller.

4. Key **homework and help and math** in the search form and click **Search.** Notice the number of matching documents is even smaller.

5. Print the page that lists the first 25 results of your search.

6. Click the **summaries** link below the Search Results title. The search engine lists summaries of the first 25 results.

7. Click one of the links to go to that page. A new page loads.

8. Click the **Back** button twice to return to the list of results without summaries.

9. Leave Internet Explorer open for the next application.

## APPLICATION 3

1. Key **http://www.usatoday.com/weather/wfront.htm** as the URL and press **Enter.**

2. Click the U.S. map.

3. Click **Regional Forecasts**.

4. Click 5-**day city forecasts** under *Eastern regional forecast.*

5. Scroll to Connecticut and choose the city of **Hartford**.

6. Print the 5-day forecast for Hartford, Conn.

7. Use the **Back** button to return to the *Regional Forecasts* page and then find the temperatures for Mesa, Arizona.

8. Print the 5-day forecast for Mesa, Ariz.

9. Use the same steps to find and print the temperatures for your city or the city nearest you.

10. Leave Internet Explorer open for the next application.

## APPLICATION 4

1. Enter **http://www.wordsrus.com** as the URL.

2. Click the link for the weekly theme.

3. Read the words for the week.

4. Write the words and their definitions on a sheet of paper or in a word processing document. Also, write a sentence using each word.

5. With your teacher's permission, fill in the online form and subscribe to the mailing list. You will receive a new word each day by e-mail. You can also subscribe by sending e-mail to **dailypower-request@wordsrus.com**.

6. Leave Internet Explorer open for the next application.

## APPLICATION 5

1. Open your mail program and check your e-mail.

2. Open a new message form.

3. Key **president@whitehouse.gov** as the e-mail address.

4. Decide on a topic for your message. You might address a problem with an administration policy or send a word of praise or criticism. You also might ask the President a question about a particular issue. Be sure the message has some meaning. Key the topic of your message on the Subject line of the form.

5. Key your message in the message window. Use concise and grammatically correct English.

6. Send a copy of the message to your teacher, if possible, by keying his or her e-mail address beside Cc.

7. Print your message.

8. Send your message. Check your e-mail daily and look for a reply from the President. Print the President's message to you and attach it to the message you wrote.

9. Close your mail program, close Internet Explorer, and disconnect from the Internet.

## APPLICATION 6

1. Open Microsoft Works 4.5.

2. In the Works Task Launcher, choose the TaskWizards tab.

3. Under Envelopes and Labels, choose the *Return Address Labels* wizard.

4. Run the TaskWizard to create return address labels.

5. Print a sheet of return labels.

6. Close the document without saving it.

## APPLICATION 7

1. Under User Defined Templates, open the *Certificate of Membership* wizard.

2. Replace Continental Museum of Science with some group that you belong to (school, church, civic).

3. Replace the clip art of leaves with something appropriate to your group. (Double-click on the clip art to open the Microsoft Clip Gallery.)

4. Save the certificate and print it.

5. Close the document.

## APPLICATION 8

1. Under User Defined Templates, open the *Conversion Table, Temperature* wizard and answer these questions:

   a. At 125 degrees Celsius, what is the temperature in Kelvin?
   b. At 90 degrees Fahrenheit, what is the temperature in Celsius?
   c. At 279 degrees Kelvin, what is the temperature in Fahrenheit?
   d. At 20 degrees Celsius, what is the temperature in Fahrenheit?
   e. At 313 degrees Kelvin, what is the temperature in Celsius?
   f. At 32 degrees Fahrenheit, what is the temperature in Kelvin?

## Problem-Solving Applications

The remaining applications are problem-solving applications that will give you an opportunity to practice the computer concepts and skills you have acquired throughout the book. These applications simulate real life since they have few specific instructions and you will have to make decisions on your own, including what type of program should be used, where to locate the information that is needed, and how to complete the application with an acceptable solution. Many times there is an appropriate TaskWizard available to help you get started. Some of the applications list Web sites as a possible source of information.

## APPLICATION 9—ADDRESS LIST

A. You decide to make an address list to keep track of your friends and relatives. Include information for at least 15 people such as: First Name, Last Name, Address, Phone Number, Birthday, and E-mail Address.

B. Print out a Birthday List that contains each person's name and birthday. Separate the list into months, put the birthdays in order, and add clip art.

C. Create a holiday newsletter you will send to all your friends and relatives this year.

D. Create a way to keep track of who you send holiday newsletters to and who you receive them from.

E. Create mailing labels to use when sending the newsletters.

## APPLICATION 10—COLLEGE CHOICE

A. Decide what criteria (cost, size, location) you would use to choose a college. Select three colleges that meet your criteria and gather pertinent information about each college. Some Web sites to check are:

- Christine DeMello's College and University Home Pages Listing at
  **http://www.mit. edu:8001/people/cdemello/univ.html**
- Mike Conlon's American Universities Home Pages Listing at
  **http://www.clas.ufl.edu/ CLAS/american-universities.html**

B. Write a form letter to send to each school asking for an application form.

C. Prepare a chart comparing the cost of attending each school for four years.

D. Search the Internet for scholarships for which you might be eligible at Web pages such as these:

- The Financial Aid Information Page at **http://www.finaid.org/**
- FastWeb at **http://www.fastweb.com/**
- SRN Express at **http://www.finaid.org/finaid/srn.html**

## APPLICATION 11—DRAMA PRODUCTION

**A.** The school drama team is doing a production of *Hamlet* (or any play you choose). Create a flyer to be distributed in each homeroom.

**B.** You are having a party for the drama team at your house after the production. Provide exact written directions from the school to your house.

**C.** Create a map to include with the directions. Label significant streets and landmarks to help students find their way from school to your house.

**D.** Create tickets that will be sold for the production. Make 10 tickets fit on one page or make 5 tickets fit on a page with a tear-off receipt on each ticket.

**E.** Create a program for the production that will be handed out the night of the production (including information such as cast members and scene summaries).

## APPLICATION 12—FUN & FITNESS HEALTH CENTER

**A.** You are an employee for the Fun & Fitness Health Center that started business a year ago. The owner, Oliver Castellano, asks you to prepare a membership list. The 30-member list should contain the Last Name, First Name, Address, Phone Number, and Type of Membership, either a year membership for $300 or a six-month membership for $225. Each type of membership pays dues monthly: year membership = $30 a month and six-month membership = $42.50 a month.

**B.** Prepare an accounts receivable record so Mr. Castellano can see the payment status of each member. The record should contain the following information: Name, Date of Payment, and Payment Amount for each month of the year. Three members with a six-month membership are 60 days behind in payments and two members with a year membership are 90 days behind in payments.

**C.** Mr. Castellano asks you to write a collection form letter to send to members who are more than 30 days behind in payments.

**D.** In an effort to increase health club memberships, one month of free membership will be given to each member who recruits a new member. Create a flyer to advertise the upcoming promotion.

**E.** Mr. Castellano asks you to create an attractive one-page newsletter that will be sent to members. The newsletter will announce new programs and equipment at the club, as well as fitness tips for leading a healthy lifestyle.

**F.** Create mailing labels you can use to send the newsletter to all members.

## APPLICATION 13—HOME BUSINESS

**A.** You are starting a home desktop publishing business. Decide what kind of equipment (e.g., computer, printer, scanner) and supplies (e.g., paper, disks, envelopes) you will need. List at least 10 items. Then record three businesses that sell these items. Call the stores or look up the prices in a catalog and determine the best buy for each item.

**B.** Design a letterhead for your new business.

**C.** Create a promotional brochure that advertises your new business and the services you provide.

**D.** Prepare a sheet of labels with your return mailing address to use for business correspondence.

**E.** Get information about developing a small business from online sources such as:

- Small Business Administration at **http://www.sbaonline.sba.gov/**
- Home Business Center at **http://www.homebusiness.com**
- Idea Cafe at **http://www.IdeaCafe.com/**

## APPLICATION 14—PLANNING A TRIP

**A.** You are planning a trip with a family member or friend. You have $2,000 to spend and will be gone no longer than one week. Choose any destination and any mode of transportation. You can use the Internet to get travel, lodging, and entertainment information at sites such as:

- The Internet Vacation Guide at **http://www.whitehawk.com/vacation/**
- The Travel Channel Online Network at **http://www.travelchannel.com/vacation/vacation.htm**

**B.** Prepare a budget showing how much you will spend on each expense, such as transportation, lodging, meals, and entertainment.

**C.** Prepare an itinerary for each day you will be gone.

## APPLICATION 15—PURCHASING AND MAINTAINING A CAR

**A.** You plan to buy a used car. Decide what make and model cars you will consider, the features you are looking for, and the amount you want to spend. Look in the classified section of a local newspaper and find five used cars that you would consider buying. Compare the features of these cars including such things as the year, make, model, mileage, color, and price.

**B.** Research the wholesale and retail values of the cars you are considering in *Edmund's Automobile Buyer's Guide*. You can find it at your local newsstand, bookstore, or online at **http://www.edmunds.com/edweb/used/usedcars.html**. Narrow your choices down to two cars and use *Edmund's* to get rating and review information.

C. Select the car you believe would be the best purchase. Present your decision to the class. Support your choice based on the research you have done.

D. You have to take out a loan for 80% of the car's price. Find out the interest rate and terms of a car loan at three different financial institutions and compare them. Choose the best loan and chart the payments you will make during the life of the loan.

E. Prepare a maintenance record you will use to track repairs and maintenance on the car. Include the problem or service, the date, cost, and place of the repair/maintenance.

F. Get quotes from three different insurance companies for the car you chose. Compare the insurance rates and decide on the best policy for you.

G. Prepare a yearly budget to estimate the expense of owning and maintaining the car you chose. Include your loan payment, insurance payment, estimated maintenance/repair costs, and estimated gas costs.

## APPLICATION 16—SAFE RIDES

Your school is starting a Safe Rides program to cut down on students driving under the influence of alcohol or drugs. On weekend nights, volunteers will be available to give free rides to students in need of safe transportation home.

A. Create a schedule for the current month that includes at least 12 volunteers, their phone numbers, and the days they will be "on call" to give safe rides.

B. Design a flyer that reminds students not to drive under the influence of alcohol or drugs.

C. Research the adverse effects of alcohol and drugs and create a pamphlet that educates students on the hazards of using them.

## APPLICATION 17—THOUGHT FOR THE DAY

The principal of your school concludes the morning announcements with a "Thought for the Day," which is a quote or proverb that provides an inspirational, humorous, or thought-provoking idea. As a Gold Key member, it is your turn next week to provide each day's "Thought for the Day." Submit a list of five quotes or proverbs that would be appropriate and document your sources. Some Internet sources include:

- Bartlett's Familiar Quotations at **http://www.columbia.edu/acis/bartleby/bartlett/**
- The Quotations Site at **http://www.smackem.com/quotes**

# TaskWizards New to Works 4.5

Gift Tags (4 styles)
Home Budget, Monthly
Home Budget, Personal
Graph Paper, 10×10
Graph Paper, plain sm
Graph Paper, plain lg
Graph Paper, plain
Graph Paper 5×5, sm
Graph Paper 5×5
Sizes & Favorites
Gift List
Greeting Card Register
Travel Planner, Budget
Travel Planner, Checklist
Travel Planner, Packing List
Conversion Table, Troy Weight
Conversion Table, Liquid & Dry Measure
Conversion Table, Temperature
Conversion Table, Circular Measure
Conversion Table, Nautical
Conversion Table, Area
Conversion Table, Linear
Lawn & Garden, Project Worksheet
Lawn & Garden, Almanac
Lawn & Garden, Plant Description
Fitness Tracker, Strength Training Log
Fitness Tracker, Daily Food Diary
Fitness Tracker, Aerobic Activity Log
Dontation Pledge Form
Pledge Form
Donation Receipt
Volunteer Pledge Form
Phone Cards, 3×5
Phone Cards, Small
Move Planner, Cost Calculator
Move Planner, Packing List
Moving, Postcard
Move Planner, Checklist
Place Card, jazzy
Place Card, festive
Place Card, informal
Place Card, formal
Menu Card, informal

Menu Card, formal
Grocery List
Meal Planner
Recipe, full page
Recipe Cards, 4×6
Chore List, Daily Personal
Chore List, Daily Household
Chore List, Child's
Chore List, Weekly Housekeeping
Certificate of Membership
Certificate of Merit
Certificate of Achievement
Party Planner
Sports, Game Schedule
Sports, Team Standings
Sports, Training Record
Sports, Team Roster
Sports, Coach Letter
Sports, Performance Letter
Gift Certificate, Housework
Gift Certificate, Yardwork
Gift Certificate, Personal
Credit Card Log
Insurance Policy Log
Babysitter Notes
Eldercare Notes
Daily Instruction Sheet
Home Improvement, Work Record
Home Maintenance Checklist
Fundraising, Budget Worksheet
Fundraising, Project Task List
Fundraising, Donations Log
Fundraising, Pledge Log
Fundraising, Volunteer Log
Recital Flyer
Garage Sale Flyer
Vehicle Details
Vehicle Repair Log
Vehicle Road Trip Log
Vehicle Maintenance Checklist
Medication Record
Hospital & Illness Record
Family Medical History
Dental Record
Personal Medical History
Stationery, Floral
Stationery, Simple

Stationery, Casual
Events Program, Sports
Events Program, Theater
Events Program, Club
Events Program, School Fair
Envelope, Floral
Envelope, Simple
Envelope, Casual
Labels, Shipping
Labels, Return Address